EXCEL 3 FOR THE MACINTOSH
MADE EASY

EXCEL 3
FOR THE MACINTOSH
MADE EASY

Edward Jones

Osborne **McGraw-Hill**
Berkeley New York St. Louis San Francisco
Auckland Bogotá Hamburg London Madrid
Mexico City Milan Montreal New Delhi Panama City
Paris São Paulo Singapore Sydney
Tokyo Toronto

Osborne **McGraw-Hill**
2600 Tenth Street
Berkeley, California 94710
U.S.A.

Osborne **McGraw-Hill** offers software for sale. For information on software, translations, or book distributors outside of the U.S.A., please write to Osborne **McGraw-Hill** at the above address.

Excel 3 for the Macintosh Made Easy

234567890 DOC 9987654321

ISBN 0-07-881724-2

CONTENTS AT A GLANCE

CONTENTS

How the Macro Works   358

ACKNOWLEDGMENTS

Like most books, this one was helped to press through the combined efforts of many. I'd like to thank Liz Fisher of Osborne/McGraw-Hill, whose original encouragement of this idea resulted in my becoming firmly committed to the Macintosh market. Thanks to Roger Stewart for spearheading the revision of this book to include version 3. Many thanks to Paul Hoffman for a thorough job of technical editing. Thanks also go to Jill Pisoni for providing the all-important manuscript preparation and managing to squeeze this project into a quarter heavily crowded with the demands of new software releases. And a note of continuing thanks to Microsoft Corporation, for keeping us supplied with beta software, documentation, and answers to questions. If all software companies were so cooperative, authors' lives would be made easier.

ACKNOWLEDGMENTS

INTRODUCTION

Welcome to Excel for the Macintosh, the leading spreadsheet in the Macintosh environment. Excel is an integrated program, offering spreadsheet capabilities, business graphics, and database management in a single package. This brief description makes Excel sound like a number of competing products. But if you've worked with some of those products, you'll soon find that Excel offers a depth of features unmatched by most of its competition. The spreadsheet offers all of the financial, statistical, and scientific features that "power users" are accustomed to finding in a first-rate spreadsheet package. The business graphics are presentation-level quality. The database is capable of storing large files, with room for over 16,000 records. The macro features let you automate common tasks easily and quickly.

If you have never used Excel or are just getting started, the quick and easy example format used in this book will help you get the most out of Excel. You will get the best results when using this book if you already have Excel installed on your system and you follow the exercises; you can even build your own applications with Excel. If you do not have a system, this book has ample illustrations and is, therefore, an effective way to become familiar with Excel.

Even though this book is written for the new user, all features of Excel, including its powerful macro capabilities, are covered. By the time you finish *Excel 3 for the Macintosh Made Easy,* you will be fully acquainted with the wide range of features Excel offers. If you're like most spreadsheet users, you will find Excel to be everything you've expected, and more.

WHAT YOU'LL FIND IN THIS BOOK

After beginning with a short description of the program's capabilities, Chapter 1 explains how to start the program and how to use windows, menus, dialog boxes, how to obtain help, and how to access Excel commands through its menu system. Chapter 2 covers the design and construction of a worksheet, with an emphasis on the basics behind entering formulas, values, and text. Also included in this chapter are methods of navigating around the worksheet, data entry, and methods of selecting cell ranges. In the latter half of the chapter the reader creates a worksheet that is then used as an example through much of the text.

Chapter 3 explains how to edit existing worksheets, including ways to insert and delete rows and columns, ways to copy and move data, and ways to format cells so the data is displayed to your liking. Excel offers options for customized formatting of cells, and Chapter 4 shows you how to use these features to add visual pizzazz to your worksheets.

Chapter 5 provides a comprehensive examination of Excel's graphics capabilities. The chapter describes how to make simple charts in seconds, how to save and print charts, and how to select different styles of charts from the "galleries" within Excel. The second half of the chapter covers optional chart features in detail, including how you can edit the formulas that are used to construct the charts; how you can change the assumptions Excel uses to draw a chart; how to add arrows, borders, legends, and text to a chart; how to change the patterns and colors used in the chart; and how to insert charts directly into worksheets. Chapter 5 also provides details on how you can use the freehand graphics features in Excel version 3.0 and above.

Chapter 6 offers tips on printing. The chapter covers printer settings for the ImageWriter II and Apple LaserWriter printers, and information is also provided on the use of non-Apple printers. Sections of the chapter explore the use of page breaks and print titles, the Page Preview option, and the printing of charts.

Chapter 7 highlights database management. Explanations are provided for creating databases, finding and retrieving (or "extracting") selected data, sorting a database, and using Excel's Form command to display on-screen forms for editing and adding records. The end of the chapter contains general discussion for those new to the concept of databases, detailing the steps behind the proper design of a database.

Chapter 8 covers the subject of multiple windows. The chapter shows how you can divide a worksheet into two or more views in separate windows or in the same window, and how you can view multiple documents at the same time. Also covered in this chapter is Excel's versatile three-dimensional capability, which lets you link cells in one worksheet to cells in another.

Chapter 9 provides a detailed introduction to Excel macros. Examples in this chapter show how you can automate your common business tasks with macros. The chapter also provides helpful tips for finding the problem when a macro does not operate as it should.

Chapter 10 provides an introduction to Excel's most commonly used functions—built-in shortcuts for performing unique tasks. Most functions are provided with examples that clearly illustrate their use.

Chapter 11 covers Excel's more advanced features, including working with dates and times, controlling calculation, using arrays and tables, protecting cells and documents, and making use of Excel's Find capability.

Chapter 12 shows how you can exchange data between Excel and other programs. Topics covered include how to use the Mac Clipboard, Switcher, or MultiFinder to transfer data between programs; how to open and save files in other file formats including dBASE and Lotus 1-2-3; how to export Excel data to word processors; and tips on importing data from mainframe computers. A special section of this chapter provides tips for conversions between Excel and Lotus 1-2-3.

Chapter 13 contains a number of sample worksheets that you can use for your own applications. Included are models for income tax forms, loan amortization, managing cash flow, performing a break-even analysis, and managing personnel.

Appendix A lists worksheet and chart commands in a handy reference format.

The tutorial and sample worksheets described in this text are also available on diskette. (The IRS tax worksheets in Chapter 13 are updated yearly to keep up with currently available IRS forms, and the diskette includes worksheets for additional IRS forms.) The complete cost of the diskette package is $20.00, which covers the costs of duplication, postage, and handling. (Add $3.00 for Canadian or $5.00 for other foreign orders; foreign orders must be payable in U.S. funds.)

Please send me the diskette package that accompanies *Excel 3 for the Macintosh Made Easy*. My payment of $20.00 ($23.00 Canadian or $25.00 foreign) is enclosed.

Name_____

Address_____

City_____ State_____ ZIP_____

Send payment to:

J.E.J.A. Software, Inc.
P.O. Box 323
Falls Church, VA 22046-323

This offer is solely the responsibility of J.E.J.A. Software, Inc. Osborne/McGraw-Hill takes NO responsibility for the fulfillment of this offer.
Please allow 4 to 6 weeks for delivery.

chapter 1

GETTING STARTED WITH EXCEL

Excel is an integrated spreadsheet program for the Apple Macintosh. It combines the capabilities of a spreadsheet, a database manager, and a graphics program within a single package. Although you can perform rudimentary word processing within an Excel spreadsheet, the program is not designed for word processing, nor does it provide communications features. However, Excel's capabilities are so rich that it is unmatched by any other program in its class.

Because Excel has so many features, learning all of them would take a major investment of time. You can, however, master the basic features of Excel quickly, and this book is designed to help you do precisely that. Follow the numerous exercises and examples in this book on your system.

WHY A SPREADSHEET?

Spreadsheets have been designed to answer "what if" questions. Using a spreadsheet, you can change variables and create different numeric models to determine the effects of particular scenarios. What if your sales increase by 22%? What if your market share drops by 8%, and your employees threaten a strike unless they are granted a 4% cost-of-living increase? A spreadsheet can immediately answer these kinds of questions.

EXCEL'S CAPABILITIES

To say that Excel is a spreadsheet with graphics and database management features is an understatement. The program makes full use of the Macintosh operating environment and is designed to offer multitasking capabilities when used with MultiFinder and sufficient amounts of memory, or under Apple's new System 7.0.

The Spreadsheet

A spreadsheet is an electronic version of old bookkeeping tools: the ledger pad, pencil, and calculator. Excel's spreadsheet, called a *worksheet* in Microsoft terminology, can be likened to a huge sheet of ledger paper. The worksheet measures 16,384 rows by 256 columns, for a total of 4,194,304 cells. By moving the cursor, you can reach any of the available cells. A sample Excel worksheet is shown in Figure 1-1. Your Excel worksheet may differ in size because of its setup or the hardware you are using.

Every cell or location in a worksheet has its own address, called the *cell address*. Cell addresses within an Excel worksheet can be referred to with either of two methods. The first, displayed in the worksheet in Figure 1-1, is the popular *A1 style* of referencing. Columns are referred to by letters and combinations of letters from A through IV, and rows are designated by numbers from 1 to 16,384. This is the cell-referencing method used by Lotus 1-2-3, Symphony, and most other spreadsheets. The second style of referencing, known as the *R1C1 style,* is shown in Figure 1-2. It uses numbers for both rows and columns. The letters R and C refer to the row number and column number, respectively. Thus, row 1, column 1 is referenced as R1C1. Microsoft's Multiplan is one program that uses the R1C1 style of referencing.

Data that you enter in a worksheet can take the form of *constant values* or of *variables* that are based on formulas. Constant values, such as a number (9.5) or a name (John Jones), do not change. Values derived from formulas often refer to other

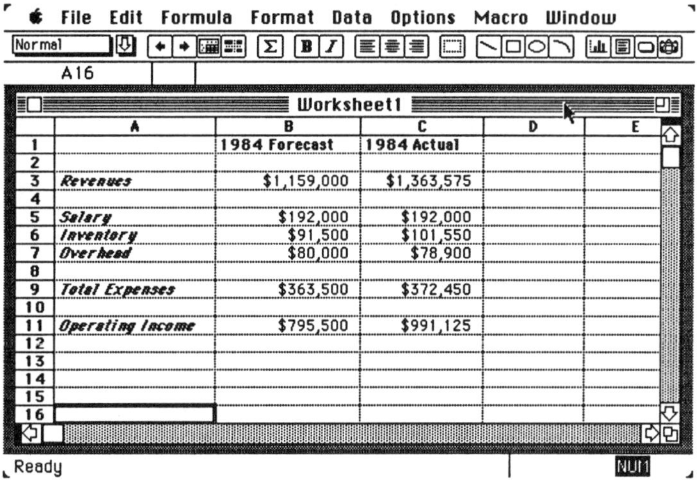

FIGURE 1-1.   Sample Excel worksheet

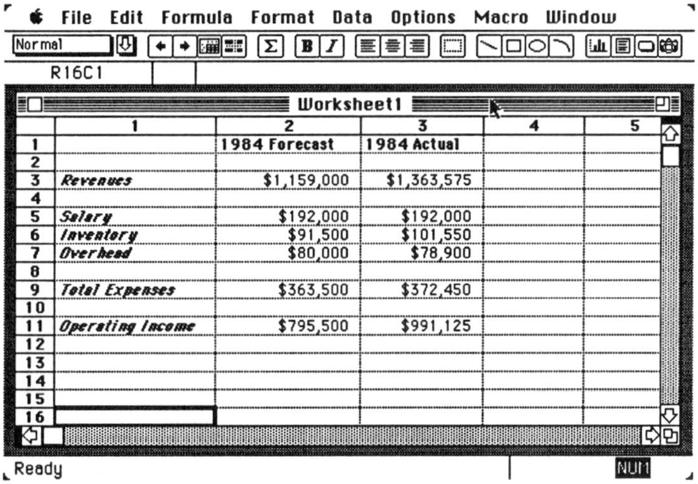

FIGURE 1-2.   R1C1 style of referencing

cells in the worksheet. For example, a cell might contain the formula C5 + C6, which adds the contents of two other cells in the worksheet, C5 and C6.

Excel's worksheet can display data in a wide variety of formats. It can display numeric values with or without decimals, as dollar amounts, or as exponential values. You can enter numbers in scientific format, as in 1.59–E17, or with decimal places, as in 23.4789001. Excel maintains accuracy to 14 decimal places. You can also enter text constants, such as the name of a month or a product model name.

You can store and display date and time-of-day data in the worksheet cells. During the data entry process, you can enter dates in common formats (such as 12/05/85) and Excel will recognize the format and store the information as a date in the format indicated. You can also design and implement custom display formats. Using a custom format, you might want to display a dollar amount with four decimal places, or a date accompanied by the day of the week.

Excel allows more than one worksheet to be open at a time. Each open worksheet is contained within a *window,* a discrete rectangular area on your screen. Windows can overlap each other, and you can adjust the size of each window to make portions of different worksheets visible.

A major feature of Excel is its ability to *link* worksheets, so that the data within one worksheet can be used as a reference within another worksheet. By comparison, many older spreadsheet programs cannot link worksheets. Without this feature you are forced either to store all of the data in one large worksheet or to update data between multiple worksheets manually, an extremely time-consuming process.

Excel offers a rich assortment of *functions,* which are special formulas built into a program to provide a variety of calculations (the average of a series of values, for example, or the square root of a number). Excel provides functions for mathematical, statistical, financial, logical, date, text, and special-purpose operations.

The Database

Excel allows all or a portion of any worksheet to be defined as a *database.* A database is a collection of related information grouped as a single item. (Even a filing cabinet can be considered to be a database, because it contains records or card files with names and phone numbers—a collection of related information.) The information contained in a computer database can usually be stored and organized in the form of a table, by rows and columns, and the design of an Excel worksheet makes it ideal for storing data in this form.

In the sample Excel database shown in Figure 1-3, each row in the worksheet is a *record* in the database. Each record is made up of areas of information called *fields,*

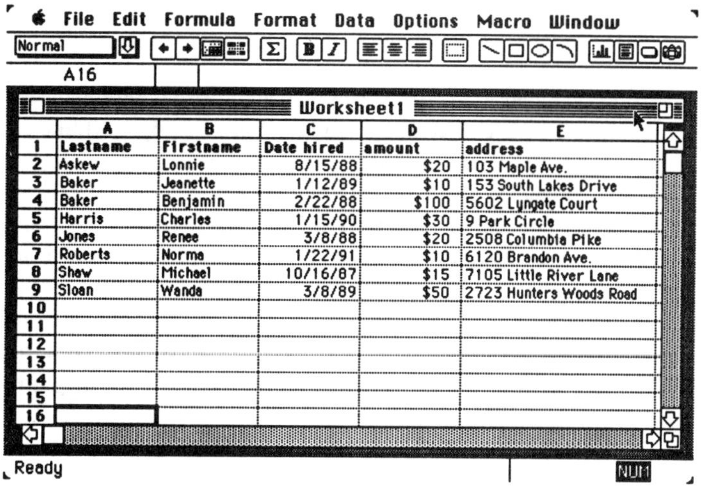

	A	B	C	D	E
1	Lastname	Firstname	Date hired	amount	address
2	Askew	Lonnie	8/15/88	$20	103 Maple Ave.
3	Baker	Jeanette	1/12/89	$10	153 South Lakes Drive
4	Baker	Benjamin	2/22/88	$100	5602 Lyngate Court
5	Harris	Charles	1/15/90	$30	9 Park Circle
6	Jones	Renee	3/8/88	$20	2508 Columbia Pike
7	Roberts	Norma	1/22/91	$10	6120 Brandon Ave.
8	Shaw	Michael	10/16/87	$15	7105 Little River Lane
9	Sloan	Wanda	3/8/89	$50	2723 Hunters Woods Road
10					
11					
12					
13					
14					
15					
16					

FIGURE 1-3. Sample database

containing such information as last name, first name, address, and dollar amounts. An Excel database can contain up to 256 fields, with each field having a maximum length of 255 characters. More than 16,300 records can be stored within an Excel database.

Once you have defined a range for a database, you can identify criteria to be used to qualify the desired data. You can select all records that meet a specific criterion, such as all addresses having a ZIP code that begins with 94. You can tell Excel to provide data on only those persons whose last name is Smith and whose account balances are greater than $500. Based on your qualifiers, you can immediately extract all records meeting the criteria for a report, or you can store the extracted data in another part of the worksheet.

Records in a database can be sorted in a particular order based on any field you choose. As an example, you might want to sort a database of last names in alphabetical order or in chronological order by the date hired. Excel also lets you create on-screen forms, which makes data entry easier than it is with other spreadsheets.

Although Excel's database capabilities match or exceed those of other spreadsheets, Excel is not designed to match a full-scale database manager like 4th Dimension or FileMaker Pro. If you need the more powerful capabilities of a database management package, Excel can export data to many database managers by means of common dBASE III/III PLUS and DIF file formats, such as tab-delimited files.

Graphics

Data contained in an Excel worksheet can be represented visually in the form of a graph, which is called a *chart* in Excel terminology. Unlike some other spreadsheet programs, Excel offers a wide range of presentation-quality charts—68 types to be exact—including bar, pie, line, scatter, high-low-close (for investments), area charts, and three-dimensional charts. You can also customize the available types to create an unlimited number of chart styles. Some examples of Excel charts are shown in Figure 1-4.

As with worksheets, you can display more than one chart on the screen at a time. Excel normally stores charts as individual files rather than as a part of the worksheet. This makes it easier to display and print charts when they are needed, because you don't have to load a worksheet and redefine all the chart settings each time; however, if you want to associate a chart with a particular worksheet, Excel also lets you store a chart as a portion of a worksheet. Charts can be displayed simultaneously with data or printed directly from Excel. Unlike some popular spreadsheets, Excel does not require that you exit the spreadsheet and load a different program to print a graph.

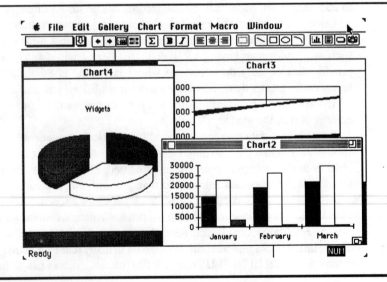

FIGURE 1-4. Sample charts

The User Interface

Excel's user interface—its method of communicating with you—consists of a series of menus that present various commands in the form of options. Figure 1-5 shows an example of a menu. Excel's menus pull down from a *menu bar,* which is always displayed at the top of the screen. You select items from a menu by using the mouse or by using the slash (/) key followed by various letter keys. Thus, Lotus 1-2-3 users who are accustomed to entering a slash followed by a letter-key sequence can use the same technique with Excel. (Note that early versions of Excel do not support the use of the slash key for menus.)

Excel's menus arc laycrcd, and they often provide additional, detailed options once you make an initial selection. Many menu selections cause a dialog box to appear (see Figure 1-6). Appropriate selections can then be made from within the dialog box. You will find that some menu options appear dimmer than others. This is Excel's way of indicating that a particular menu option is not presently available.

Experienced users can select commands quickly with *hot keys,* which are COM-MAND-key sequences that can access most menu commands. For example, pressing

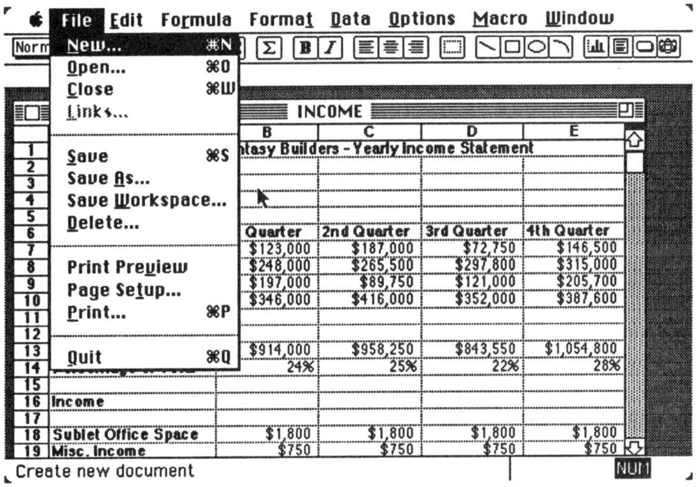

FIGURE 1-5.   Sample Excel menu

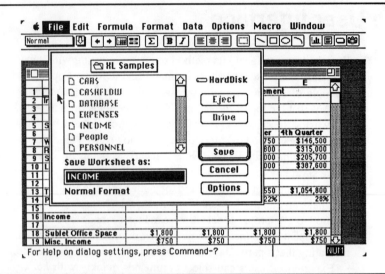

FIGURE 1-6.   Sample dialog box

COMMAND-P is equivalent to opening the File menu and selecting the Print command. Once committed to memory, these key sequences can save you considerable time.

Macros

Excel offers *macros,* which are stored sequences of keystrokes that can be played back at any time. You can store a macro on disk for future use, and when you play the macro back, Excel will perform as if you had manually typed the characters in the macro. Macros are useful for reducing to a few keys long sequences of keystrokes that are used repeatedly.

You can create macros by entering commands into a special kind of worksheet or by turning on Excel's Macro Recorder. This powerful feature monitors the keyboard, records your entries in a worksheet, and builds the desired macro.

Macros can range from simple to extremely complex. A simple one might enter headings for months of the year across the top of a worksheet. A more complex macro might automate a lengthy sequence of menu selections. Excel's macros are considerably easier to use than are similar features in many other spreadsheets.

Unlimited Windows

Each Excel worksheet or chart occupies a window. There is no limit to the number of windows that can be open at once, which means you can work on one worksheet while another worksheet is visible on the screen. You can also move quickly between windows, or move and adjust the size of individual windows. If you use Excel along with MultiFinder, you can run Excel simultaneously with other Macintosh applications software.

Presentation-Quality Output

Excel's wide range of worksheet and chart formats lets you create presentation-quality reports. It is no longer necessary to purchase third-party "add-on" programs or vendor "options" to print top-notch worksheets, reports, or charts. Excel provides full support for the Apple LaserWriter, along with a variety of fonts.

Full 1-2-3 Compatibility

Excel can read and write files using the file structure of Lotus 1-2-3. Though many competing spreadsheets claim to offer this feature, few can handle the task with the simplicity of Excel. Excel can analyze the structure of a file produced by other software (such as Lotus 1-2-3) and automatically translate the file into Excel's own file format. Therefore, you can use the same Save and Open commands in the File menu for loading 1-2-3 or Symphony files that you use to load Excel files. It is not necessary to exit a worksheet and run a translation program to load or save a file in 1-2-3 format.

Data Interchange

Excel can share data with the more popular personal computer software by reading and writing data in tab-delimited, Lotus 1-2-3, dBASE III/III PLUS, or DIF file formats. No translation utility is necessary for this. You can save files in any of these formats simply by choosing options from the dialog box that appears when you select the Save As command. When you load a file, Excel automatically determines the type of file by examining the file's structure. Excel for the Macintosh is also completely compatible with files created by the IBM PC version of Excel.

Arrays

Excel supports the use of *arrays*, which are groups of two or more adjacent cells that are arranged in the shape of a rectangle and behave like a single cell. Using an array, you can apply a single value or formula to a block of cells without having to duplicate the formula for each cell within the block.

Background Recalculation

If you are using Excel with MultiFinder and two or more megabytes of memory or are running System 7.0, you can turn on *background recalculation* while you are using another application. This can be a particularly useful feature with large worksheets that may be time-consuming to recalculate. Using background recalculation, you can switch to another application (such as word processing) while Excel continues to recalculate a worksheet.

Context-Sensitive Help Screens

Excel provides context-sensitive help screens that provide information concerning the area you are working in at a particular time. If you choose, you can also browse through these screens. You do not need to exit the program to use the Help feature; you can call up a help screen on any topic while you are working on a worksheet, and then return to the worksheet when you are done using the Help system.

HOW EXCEL MEASURES UP

Spreadsheet programs for personal computers fall into two main categories: *stand-alone* and *integrated* spreadsheets. Stand-alone spreadsheets offer only spreadsheet capabilities, while integrated spreadsheets offer features such as graphics and database management. Excel falls into the integrated category. Other products in this category include WingZ and Full Impact. The stand-alone category of spreadsheets includes such products as Multiplan and Crunch.

As a product, Excel appeals to numbers-oriented PC users who must manage numbers on a day-to-day basis. It also works well for those who need to highlight numeric data with presentation graphics. Because Excel was developed "from the ground up" for the Apple Macintosh, it is an extremely visual package. This design, with its heavy reliance on pull-down menus, makes Excel easier to learn than some other programs. Built-in help screens, feature guides, and a tutorial also make Excel easier to master than other programs.

HARDWARE REQUIREMENTS

Version 3.0 of Excel for the Macintosh requires a Macintosh Plus, Macintosh SE, Macintosh II, or Macintosh IIX, with one floppy-disk drive and a hard disk. A minimum of 1 megabyte of memory is required to use all versions from 2.2 on.

STARTING EXCEL

The Excel package includes assorted manuals, a container that holds the Excel disks, a registration card and license agreement, and a "Read Me First" card that provides tips for learning Excel. You should immediately make working copies of each of the disks supplied in your package so that you have a replacement if a disk is damaged or erased.

After you have made backup copies of your disks, put the original disks away for safekeeping and use the backup copies. If you have not yet installed Excel on your hard disk, refer to your manual and perform the steps described there before proceeding.

To load Excel, double-click on the Excel icon. As the program loads, a copyright message will appear. Then Excel will display a blank worksheet titled "Worksheet1," as shown in Figure 1-7.

WINDOWS

Like most Macintosh software, Excel makes extensive use of windows as work areas. Most windows have certain elements in common. Among these are a menu bar and several *icons,* or small graphics symbols that represent a particular function. These common elements are illustrated in Figure 1-8.

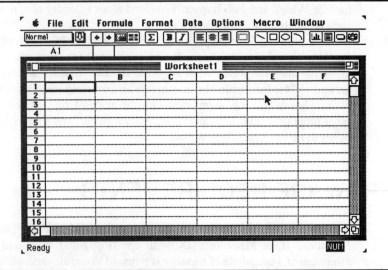

FIGURE 1-7. Blank worksheet

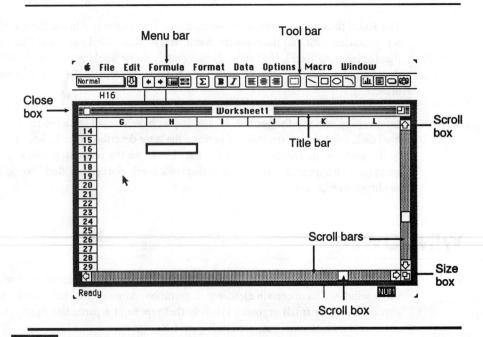

FIGURE 1-8. Parts of a window

The worksheet appears in a window, as do all documents within Excel. You can create three types of windows while in Excel: worksheet windows, chart windows, and macro windows. You perform different tasks with the different types of windows, but the ways you navigate within and work with the windows are similar.

The Scroll Bars

You can use the *scroll bars* at the bottom and right edges of the worksheet to move to other areas of the worksheet. The arrows located within the scroll bars can be used to move a row or a column at a time. Clicking the mouse button on the up or down arrow in the right scroll bar moves you up or down a row at a time. In a similar fashion, clicking on the left or right arrow in the scroll bar at the bottom of the window moves the worksheet left or right a column at a time.

You can also click in the shaded area of the scroll bar to move by a complete screenful. Click in the shaded area to the right of the scroll box (at the bottom) to move to the right by one screen, or click in the shaded area to the left of the scroll box to move to the left by one screen. Using the scroll bar at the right edge of the window, you can click in the shaded area above the scroll box to move up by a screen, or click below the scroll box to move down by a screen.

The Title Bar and Close Box

At the top of the window appear the *title bar* and *close box*. The title bar contains the title of the worksheet. Although the first worksheet to appear when you load Excel is automatically called Worksheet1, you can save worksheets under any name you wish.

At the left corner of the title bar is the close box. Clicking this box will close any open window that you no longer need. If you have not yet saved the contents of the window, Excel will display a dialog box asking if you want to save the document.

The title bar can also be used to drag a window to a new screen location. To reposition any window, click the title bar and drag the window to its desired location. (See "The Mouse" later in this chapter for a description of clicking and dragging).

The Size Box

The size box, located at the lower-right corner of the window, is used to change the size of a window. To change a window's size, click the size box and drag it until the window assumes the desired size. Changing the size and location of a window allows the use of multiple windows simultaneously, a topic that is covered in more detail in Chapter 8.

The Menu Bar

Above the worksheet window, at the top of the screen, is the menu bar. It always displays a series of choices appropriate to the window you are currently using. The actual choices shown in the menu bar depend on whether you are using worksheets or charts, but you always select menu options by using the mouse or by pressing the slash key followed by the underlined letter of the desired menu choice. Figure 1-5 shows an example of the File menu. Open this menu now by pointing to File and clicking the mouse, or by pressing the slash key followed by the F key.

If you don't see the same choices on your File menu as are shown in the figure, don't worry. Excel offers two systems of menus, one for new users and another for seasoned users. Open the Options menu, and choose the last menu choice, Full Menus.

The available menus, and the options for each menu, are covered extensively in Chapter 2. Use the menus to access any desired command within Excel.

DIALOG BOXES

Notice that some menu commands are followed by an ellipsis (...). This indicates that a command, when chosen, requires additional information. The information is supplied through a dialog box that Excel displays when the command is selected. As an example, the dialog box displayed when the Apply Names command is selected from the Formula menu looks like this:

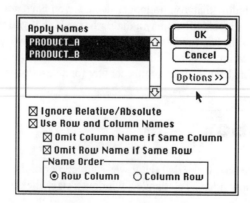

Other dialog boxes contain some or all of the options shown in this example. A dialog box may contain a number of different options, such as check boxes, list boxes, command buttons, option buttons, and text boxes. Here is a description of these items:

- A *check box* is a small square box that you use to turn an option on or off.

- A *list box* is a larger rectangular area used to display a list of available names, such as file names.

- A *command button* is a rectangular block with rounded edges used to implement a command or some other action. Nearly all dialog boxes contain at least two command buttons: an OK button and a Cancel button. The OK button is used to accept the options chosen within the dialog box, and the Cancel button is used to cancel the operation and remove the dialog box from the screen. Some dialog boxes may contain other command buttons (such as Edit or Save) for performing various operations.

- An *option button* is a small circle used to choose from a list of available options.

- A *text box* is a rectangular area in which text that is needed for the command can be entered.

Each dialog box is covered in detail in later chapters, but these basics apply to all dialog boxes:

- You can select any option in a dialog box by pointing to the option and clicking the mouse.

- Clicking within a check box alternately turns an option on and off.

- To enter text in a text box, you first click anywhere within the box and then start typing.

- Once you've made all the desired choices, you click the OK button to implement the settings.

- Clicking the Cancel button cancels the settings and removes the dialog box from the screen.

 You can simultaneously select an option and select the OK button by double-clicking on the desired option.

THE TOOL BAR

Assuming you are using Excel version 3.0 or higher, the tool bar appears directly below the menu bar. If you are using version 3.0 or higher and the tool bar is not visible below the menu bar, it has been turned off by someone. You can turn the tool bar back on by choosing Workspace from the Options menu, and then turning on the tool bar check box that appears. Figure 1-9 shows the parts of the tool bar.

The tool bar can be used to quickly add graphic elements to worksheets, and to change the style or alignment of worksheet entries. Because the various options of the tool bar perform many functions in Excel, they will be covered in different chapters of this text. For now, a brief overview of the tools provided by the tool bar will suffice.

The Style List Box

The Style List box can be used to apply various styles to selected cells. Clicking on the arrow in the Style List box causes a pull-down menu with a list of available styles to appear. The desired styles can be chosen from this list.

The Promote and Demote Buttons

The Promote and Demote buttons are used to promote (raise the order of) and demote (lower the order of) sections of a worksheet that make up an outline. (Creating outlines in Excel is covered in Chapter 11.)

The Display Outline Symbols Button

The Display Outline Symbols button turns on (or off) the display of outline symbols within an outline (see Chapter 11).

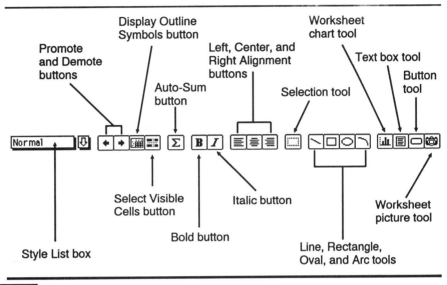

FIGURE 1-9. Parts of the tool bar

The Select Visible Cells Button

The Select Visible Cells button is used when you create outlines to determine whether all cells or only visible (nonhidden) cells should be used when copying ranges, formatting ranges, or adding charts.

The Auto-Sum Button

The Auto-Sum button is used to automatically enter a SUM formula in the active cell, based on a range of values above or to the left of the active cell.

The Bold and Italic Buttons

The Bold and Italic buttons can be used to apply a bold format or an italic format to the entries in selected cells.

The Alignment Buttons

The Alignment buttons are used to left-align, center-align, or right-align entries in selected cells.

The Selection Tool

The selection tool is used to select multiple objects so that they can be moved, sized, or formatted as a group.

The Line, Rectangle, Oval, and Arc Tools

These tools are used to draw graphic objects in a worksheet.

The Worksheet Chart Tool

The worksheet chart tool creates a chart directly on the worksheet. The selected range is used as the basis for the chart.

The Text Box Tool

The text box tool is used to create a text box. Text can be typed into the text box, and you can apply a variety of text styles, alignments, and formatting to the text in the text box.

The Button Tool

The button tool is used to create buttons. You can use buttons to run macros easily from within a worksheet.

The Worksheet Picture Tool

The worksheet picture tool is used to take a "snapshot" of a selected area of a worksheet.

GETTING HELP

Excel offers a detailed help system that provides you with information on Excel commands, procedures, worksheet functions, and error messages. You can use the help system in two ways. First, you can obtain context-sensitive help (concerning the area within which you are currently working) by pressing COMMAND- ?. The pointer will become a question mark. Then, choose menu command, or click in the document or the dialog box for which you desire help. Second, you can browse through the help screens, using them as a reference. Help screens are displayed within a Help window that appears on the screen when you choose Help from the Window menu. The help screen that appears when you select the Help command is shown here:

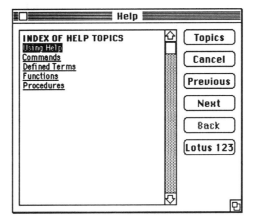

The Help window contains scroll bars, which you can use to examine and select the names of all of the topics in the Help Index. You can click on and drag the boxes within the scroll bars to move among the list of topics. To select any topic, point to the topic's name and click the mouse. The Help window then displays a help menu for that topic. You will often see additional topics listed; you can continue to click the desired topic for additional help. You can also use the Next and Previous buttons to move forward or backward within the help system. Lotus 1-2-3 users can click the Lotus 1-2-3 button for access to a listing of Lotus 1-2-3 commands and their equivalent

Excel commands. Clicking the Topics button at any point returns you to the main list of topics.

You may want to take some time now to browse through the help system. When you are done, click Cancel to exit from the system.

THE KEYBOARD

Excel uses a number of special-purpose keys for various operations. (If you are already familiar with the use of the Macintosh, you may want to skip ahead to the start of the next chapter.) In addition to the letter and number keys, you'll often use certain COMMAND-key combinations. Grouped on the left side of the keyboard are three frequently used keys: the TAB key, the COMMAND key, and the SHIFT key. The COMMAND key is located directly to the left of the spacebar and contains a cloverleaf-shaped symbol. Before going further, find these keys; they will prove helpful for several operations.

Above the left SHIFT key is the CAPS LOCK key, which is used to type all letters in uppercase. (The CAPS LOCK key does not change the format of the numbers on the top row of the keyboard.) Another SHIFT key is located on the right side of the keyboard. Just above it is the RETURN key, which performs similarly to the return key on a typewriter. Above the RETURN key is the BACKSPACE key.

On newer models of the Macintosh, the far-right side of the keyboard also contains a numeric keypad. This area serves a dual purpose. By pressing the SHIFT-CLEAR key on the numeric keypad, you can shift in and out of numeric keypad mode. You are in numeric keypad mode when NUM appears at the right side of the bottom scroll bar. When you are in the numeric keypad mode, the keys in this area produce numbers; when you are not in numeric keypad mode, these keys move the cursor.

THE MOUSE

Excel is designed to make extensive use of the mouse. You can perform three basic operations with the mouse: pointing, clicking, and selecting (also called dragging). The mouse controls the location of a special cursor called the *mouse pointer*. Depending on where the mouse pointer is located, it assumes a different shape. At most locations within Excel, the mouse pointer is an arrow with a single head, but at certain locations and during certain operations, the mouse pointer may become a cross, an arrow with heads on both ends, a magnifying glass, or a wristwatch. The wristwatch indicates that Excel is performing an operation, and you must wait for that operation to be completed before you continue.

To point at an object with the mouse, simply move the mouse in the direction of the object. As you do so, the mouse pointer on the screen will move in the same direction. The term *clicking* means pointing to an object and pressing the mouse button to select it. For example, the expression "click the close box" means to point to the close box on the screen with the mouse pointer and then press the mouse button. To *double-click* means to press the mouse button twice in succession.

The term *dragging* refers to pressing and holding down the mouse button while moving the mouse. This is commonly done to select multiple objects within Excel. For example, you can select a group of cells by pointing at the first cell in the group, pressing and holding down the mouse button, and moving the mouse pointer to the last cell in the group.

If you are new to the Macintosh, a few hints are in order. Obviously, you'll need enough space on your desk to manipulate the mouse. What is less obvious is the fact that some desk surfaces work better than others. A surface with a small amount of friction seems to work better than a very smooth desk; commercial pads are available if your desktop is too smooth to obtain good results. Also, the mouse requires cleaning from time to time. Refer to your Macintosh owner's manual for cleaning instructions.

At this point, you're ready to proceed to the next chapter. Remember, whenever you want to get started with Excel, double-click on the Excel icon.

chapter **2**

BUILDING A
WORKSHEET

In this chapter you will learn how to enter text, numbers, and formulas; how to "navigate" through a worksheet; and how to print and save a worksheet. If you haven't already started Excel, do so now by following the instructions in Chapter 1.

The blank worksheet you will see on your screen—Worksheet1—is divided into rows numbered from 1 through 16 and columns headed A through F (see Figure 1-7). If you are using a large monitor or if the tool bar is turned off, you may see additional rows or columns. The precise number of visible rows and columns varies, depending on your graphics hardware and on whether you have changed the size of the window. Each intersection of a row and column—referred to as a cell—contains numbers, descriptive words or labels, or formulas. Each cell coordinate is referred to by a column and row designation. The cell in the extreme upper-left corner is referred to as cell A1 (column A, row 1), and to its right is B1; below cell A1 is A2, and at the extreme lower-right corner of the worksheet (which you cannot currently see on the screen) is cell IV16384 (column IV, row 16,384). Excel displays the location of the cursor near the top-left corner of the screen. This area is called the *active cell reference*.

Excel's worksheet contains 256 columns and 16,384 rows. The columns are labeled A through Z and continue with AA through AZ, BA through BZ, CA through CZ, and so on until the final column, IV. Only a portion of the worksheet is visible at any one time. On a Macintosh Classic, Plus, or SE, using standard column widths, Excel normally displays about 6 columns and 16 rows. An actual worksheet may show more or fewer cells than you see here. You'll learn how to change the width of a column later in this chapter.

If you haven't moved the cursor, it should be highlighting cell A1. The cell highlighted by the cursor is the *active cell.* Any text or number that you enter usually appears in the active cell.

EXCEL MENUS

Above the worksheet is a highlighted bar that displays Excel's menu commands. Excel's system of pull-down menus lets you choose various functions, such as changing the width of a column or printing a worksheet. These menu commands can be chosen by using either the keyboard or the mouse. From the keyboard, the menus are accessed by pressing the slash key followed by the underlined letter of the menu name. (Note that the underlined letter is usually, but not always, the first letter of the menu name. Also, the underlines appear only when you select menu commands with the keyboard, not with the mouse.) When selecting commands with some keyboards, be careful to press the slash (/) key and not the reverse-slash key (\) located just to the right of the spacebar.

As an exercise, press the slash key and then the F key. The File menu will open, as shown in Figure 1-5. If you prefer to use the mouse, select the desired menu name by clicking, and drag down until the desired menu option is highlighted.

══ *note* ══ Compare the appearance of your File menu with the one shown in Figure 1-5. If the menu does not contain all of the options shown, your copy of Excel is set to Short Menus. Excel has two sets of menus, one for novice users and another for veterans. Open the Options menu and then select Full Menus. You will then be able to see all of the choices described in this chapter.

If you opened the menus with the slash key rather than the mouse, you can use the UP and DOWN ARROW keys on the main part of the keyboard (but not those on the numeric keypad) to highlight any command. You can then select the various commands by pressing RETURN while the command is highlighted, or by pressing the underlined letter in the command name once the menu is open. To get out of a menu without selecting any commands, click anywhere outside the menu with the mouse.

While you are examining the menus, note that some of the menu commands are dimmed. If you open the Edit menu, for example, you will see that the Paste Special and Paste Link commands are dimmed. These commands are not available to you now but can be made available when necessary. The availability of a command depends on your prior actions within Excel. For example, the Undo command within the Edit menu normally lets you undo the previous command. Since you haven't yet given Excel a command, this command is not valid at this time, so it is dimmed on the menu.

Some of the menu commands also have a COMMAND-key alternative shown next to the command. For example, in the File menu, you will see ⌘-P next to the command for Print and   -S next to the command for Save. These designations indicate COMMAND-key shortcuts that can be used to select many commands in Excel. For example, pressing COMMAND-P is equivalent to opening the File menu and choosing Print.

All of Excel's menu commands will be covered in greater detail at the end of this chapter. For future reference, note that opening the menus with the slash key does not work when you are in the process of building a formula. Building formulas will be covered shortly.

NAVIGATING WITHIN A WORKSHEET

When no menu is open, you can use the arrow keys to move the cursor around the worksheet. For this reason, the arrow keys are often referred to informally as *cursor keys*. Try pressing each of the cursor keys, and note the movement of the cursor. As you reach the right side or the bottom row of the worksheet, pressing the same cursor key once more causes the worksheet to scroll, bringing an additional row or column into view.

The TAB and RETURN keys, used alone or in combination with the SHIFT key, will also move the cursor. Pressing TAB moves the cursor to the right, while SHIFT-TAB moves the cursor to the left. Pressing RETURN moves the cursor down and pressing SHIFT-RETURN moves it up.

The Go To Key

One often-used key is the Go To (COMMAND-G) key. Press COMMAND-G, and a dialog box appears, asking you for a cell reference to go to. Enter **AZ400** and press RETURN, and the cursor will move to cell AZ400. You can choose the same Go To command by selecting Goto from the Formula menu. Use this method now to return to cell A1.

The mouse is your primary means of navigation within the worksheet. At the far right and bottom of the worksheet are bars that contain arrows (see Figure 2-1). These are scroll bars. The mouse pointer, which moves whenever you move your mouse, changes shape depending on its location. Within most areas of the worksheet, the pointer resembles a cross. In most areas outside of the worksheet or over the scroll bars, the pointer changes shape to resemble an arrow.

You can scroll the worksheet one row or one column at a time by pointing to the arrows at the ends of the scroll bars and clicking the mouse button. You can also point to one of the two solid white blocks within the scroll bars, press and hold down the mouse button, and move (drag) the block with the mouse. The box is referred to as a scroll box, and dragging it will cause the worksheet to scroll numerous rows or columns when you release the mouse button. As you use this technique, note that the row or column reference at the upper-left corner of the screen changes to indicate your position within the worksheet. If you click to the right of the scroll box at the bottom of the screen, Excel scrolls the worksheet to the right by one full screen; if you click to the left of the scroll box, Excel scrolls the worksheet left by one full screen. Similarly, clicking in the area below the scroll box at the right side of the worksheet causes Excel to scroll down by one full screen; clicking in the area above the scroll box causes Excel to scroll up by one full screen.

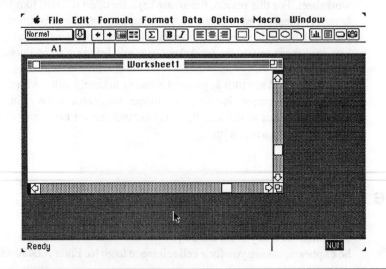

═══ **FIGURE 2-1.**   Scroll bars

ENTERING INFORMATION

If your cursor is not at cell A1, move it there now by pressing COMMAND-G and entering **A1** as a cell reference. With A1 as the active cell, type **23456**. Note that as you begin to type the entry, it appears in two places: in the active cell, and in an area at the top of the screen, beside the cell reference. This area, called the *formula bar,* displays the current contents of a cell. Once you have finished typing the numbers, press RETURN. The cursor moves down to cell A2. (If your cursor does not move after you press RETURN, someone may have changed an option with the Workspace command of the Options menu. Select Workspace from the Options menu now, and double-click the Move Selection After Return button that appears.)

Next, enter **10000** and press RETURN. Use the DOWN ARROW key or the mouse to move the cursor down to cell A5. Enter **total** and press RETURN to move to cell A6. You can use both uppercase and lowercase letters if you wish.

Now type an equal sign (=). Whenever you begin a cell entry with this symbol, you are telling Excel that you want to place a formula in that cell. For example, to add the values in cells A1 and A2, enter **A1+A2** and press RETURN. In this case, the formula =A1+A2 tells Excel to add the contents of cells A1 and A2 and to display the results in cell A6.

  Do not assume that the plus symbol on the numeric keyboard of newer Macintosh computers can always be used to enter a plus symbol. This key will produce different results, depending on whether you are in numeric keypad mode or not. To move in and out of this mode, press SHIFT-CLEAR on the numeric keypad. To be safe, use the plus symbol at the top row of the keyboard when entering formulas.

You may have noticed that when you press RETURN after making an entry, Excel moves the cursor to the cell below the entry. You can also complete an entry by pressing TAB, in which case Excel moves the cursor to the right. Other ways to complete an entry are with SHIFT-TAB (the cursor moves left) and SHIFT-RETURN (the cursor moves up). If your Macintosh keyboard has an ENTER key, it can also be used to complete an entry, but the cursor does not move when the ENTER key is used.

TEXT, VALUES,
AND FORMULAS

Your worksheet now contains all three types of data used within a worksheet: values, text, and formulas. In cells A1 and A2, you entered actual numbers or values. In cell

A5, you entered a name, which is text; anytime you begin a cell entry with a letter, Excel assumes the entry is text. In cell A6, you entered a formula; the contents of that formula are used to obtain a result based on values within the worksheet.

For text entries, you are limited to a maximum of 255 characters within any single cell. Text is any entry that Excel is unable to interpret as a formula or a numeric value. In some cases, you may want to enter text composed of a series of numbers but want Excel to interpret the numbers as text and not as a value. In such cases, you can enclose the numbers in quotation marks. For example, Excel would interpret the entry "1988" as a text string and not as the value 1988.

Numbers entered into an Excel worksheet can consist of any digit and some symbols. Acceptable symbols are the plus and minus symbols (+ and -), denoting positive and negative values; the period, denoting a decimal point; and the letter E, denoting scientific (exponential) notation. As an example, if you enter **2E7** in a cell, Excel will evaluate the entry as 20,000,000 (or 2 times 10 to the power of 7). If a number is entered as a constant value and not as a part of a formula, you can also include a dollar sign, a percent symbol, commas, and parentheses. If you add a dollar sign, Excel automatically displays that cell's contents with the dollar sign included in the format of the cell. If you enter a number followed by a percent symbol, Excel automatically displays the value as a percentage.

You can also enter a number surrounded by parentheses to indicate a negative value, a standard accounting practice. For example, if you enter **(355.45)** in a cell, Excel will store a value of -355.45 in the cell, and it will display the value as (355.45). If you prefer, you can use the minus sign instead, and Excel will display the value preceded by the minus sign.

If you enter information containing both numbers and text, Excel assumes that the entry is text and not a value. For example, the entry

123 Main Street

would be stored by Excel as text, even though the entry begins with numbers. If you are in doubt as to whether an entry has been stored as text or as a value, one quick way to tell is to examine how Excel displays the entry. Values are normally displayed flush right (at the right side of the cell), and text is displayed flush left (at the left side of the cell). Note that this is the default method Excel uses to display text and values; if the formatting of the cells has been changed with the Alignment option of the Format menu, the alignment may be different.

As long as a formula within a worksheet remains intact, you can change the values, and Excel will recalculate the result based on the new values. To see how this works, use the arrow keys to move the cursor to cell A2; then enter **25,000** as a new value. Once you've pressed RETURN to enter the value, Excel will display a corrected total in cell A6.

DISPLAYED VALUES
AND UNDERLYING VALUES

Excel displays values according to some precise rules; what these rules are depends on what formats you have applied to the cells in a worksheet. Consider an example. In a blank worksheet, with no formatting applied, try entering the following data exactly as shown:

Cell	Entry
A1	1234567890.1234
A2	$100.5575
A3	75%
A4	2E12

The results will appear as shown here:

If you move the cursor between the cells containing the data and note the contents of each cell in the formula bar, one fact quickly becomes apparent: Excel's display of data can be different from the data that is actually stored.

Excel stores the data as you enter it, but it displays the data according to any formatting rules you have established (or according to the rules of the general format if no formatting has been applied). Because the entries in cells A2, A3, and A4 included symbols, Excel automatically formatted these cells and displayed the contents according to those formats. (You can also select formats by means of menu commands; Chapter 3 covers this topic in detail.) Also, because the value in cell A1 is too large to fit in a cell of standard ten-column width, Excel displays only the whole numbers.

In each case, what appears in the cell is the *displayed value.* What appears in the formula bar is the *underlying value.* When calculating your formulas, Excel always uses the underlying value unless you tell it otherwise. Chapter 11 will discuss how you can tell Excel to use the displayed values as the basis for further calculations. For

now, you should just be aware of the possible differences between underlying values
and displayed values.

ENTERING DATES AND TIMES

You can also store dates and times within an Excel worksheet. This capability can be
useful for recording chronological data, such as employees' dates of hire or the time
spent on billable tasks. When you enter a date or a time in an acceptable format, Excel
automatically stores and displays the data using that format. The standard formats for
dates and times are as shown in the following table.

Date Formats	Time Formats
6/22/54	3:15 PM
22-Jun-54	3:15:17 PM
22-Jun	15:15:17
Jun-54	11:12

Excel displays dates and times in a standard format but stores them as whole or
fractional numbers, from 0 to 49,710. The number 0 represents January 1, 1904, and
the number 49,710 represents February 6, 2040. Times are stored as fractional
numbers; for example, if a time value of 12:35 PM is entered into a cell, Excel stores
the data internally as 0.524305556.

Dates and times can be stored within the same cell. For example, you can enter
6/22/54 09:16 PM into a cell as a valid value. If you choose to store dates and times
within the same cell, the dates and times should be separated by a space.

Excel's ability to handle dates and times as real values is a significant benefit in
some applications, because you can use Excel's computational abilities to perform
math on dates and times. For example, Excel can subtract one date from another to
provide the number of days between the two dates.

SELECTING A GROUP OF CELLS

Now that you are familiar with navigation and data entry, you can build a more
complex worksheet and use it along with this text. First, however, you must erase the
existing information. Move the cursor to A1, and while holding down the mouse
button, drag down to cell A6. As you do so, cells A1 through A6 are selected. (Note
that the first cell does not appear in reverse video as the others do; nevertheless, it is

one of the selected cells.) By placing the cursor at any cell and clicking and dragging the mouse, you can select any block of cells.

With cells A1 through A6 selected, open the Edit menu and select the Clear command from it. A dialog box will appear, containing four options: All, Formats, Formulas, and Notes. Choosing Formulas would clear only the formulas or any number or text entries in the selected area; choosing Formats would clear various format settings. For now, click the OK button. The cells reappear with no entries in them. The next action you perform in Excel will "unhighlight" the cells.

You should know about the other ways to select a group of cells. You can select an entire row by clicking the row number at the left edge of the worksheet. A column can be selected by clicking the column heading at the top of the worksheet. To select more than one complete row or column of a worksheet, click and drag across a series of column headings or down a series of row headings. For example, if you want to select all of rows 4, 5, and 6, first place the cursor over the row 4 heading, and then click and drag across rows 5 and 6.

Using Selected Cells
To Make Data Entry Easier

If you select a group of cells, Excel will move the cursor within the selection each time you press the RETURN or ENTER key after an entry. This can greatly simplify the repetitive task of data entry. If you haven't selected a group of cells, when you enter a formula or value and press RETURN, Excel usually moves the cursor down in response to the RETURN key. If you use the ENTER key, the cursor usually stays in the same location. However, if you have selected a group of cells, after each entry is completed, the cursor moves within the selected cells.

Consider the common task of entering data in multiple columns, with a set number of entries in each column. If you select a group of cells by placing the cursor in cell C3 and dragging down to cell D9, the selected cells would be in the pattern illustrated in Figure 2-2. If you then enter data into the worksheet and press RETURN at the end of each entry, the cursor moves down to the next cell each time RETURN is pressed until the bottom of the selection is reached; then the cursor moves over to the next column and continues its downward movement, starting from the top. In this example, the cells in the left column fill with data first, followed by the cells in the right column (see Figure 2-3). However, if you use the ENTER key instead of the RETURN key, the cursor will move in an altogether different pattern: left to right, then down one line, then left to right, then down one line, and so on.

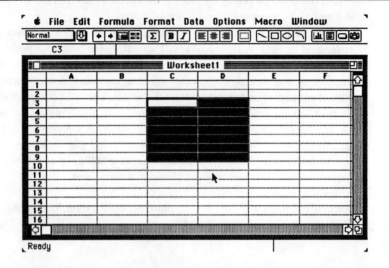

FIGURE 2-2.   Pattern of selected cells

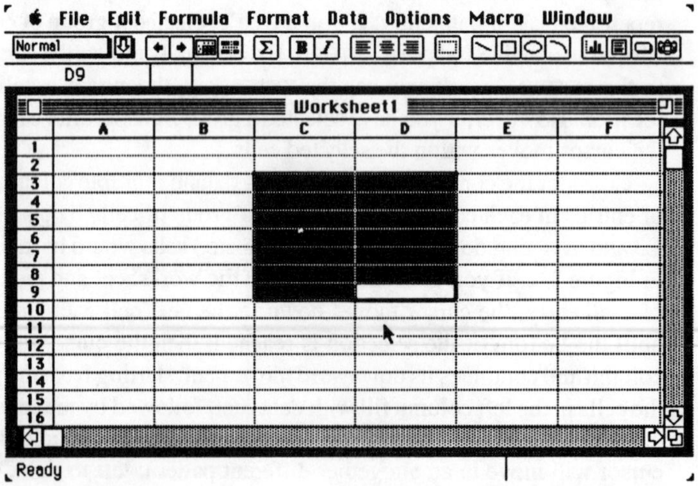

FIGURE 2-3.   Pattern of data entry

Whenever you select cells and enter data, Excel moves the cursor in one of these two ways, depending on whether you use RETURN or ENTER. To override this pattern of data entry, simply select any individual cell.

Extending Selections with the SHIFT Key

Another method of selecting a large range of cells is with the mouse and the SHIFT key. You can do this by clicking in a cell in any corner of the desired range, holding down the SHIFT key, and clicking at the opposite corner of the range. The entire range is then selected, and the active cell is the first cell you selected. For example, if you click in cell B2, hold down the SHIFT key, and click in cell E15, the entire range from B2 to E15 is selected, and the active cell becomes cell B2, as shown in Figure 2-4.

Selecting Discontinuous Ranges

With Excel, you can also select different areas. Say you want to select a range from B2 to C10, and another range from D12 to E16. To do this, just select the first range in the usual manner. Then hold down the COMMAND key and select the second range

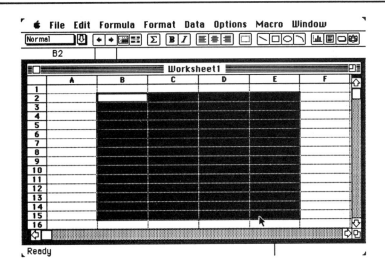

FIGURE 2-4.   Extended selection made with SHIFT key

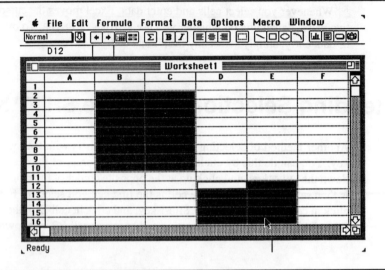

FIGURE 2-5. Selection of discontinuous ranges

by clicking and dragging. Excel selects the second area without deselecting the first. Figure 2-5 shows the result of clicking and dragging from B2 to C10, holding down the COMMAND key, and then clicking and dragging from D12 to E16.

When do you need to select multiple ranges in this manner? This technique is commonly used when you are applying a specific formatting style, such as bold or italic font, to different areas of the worksheet. Chapter 4 will discuss the ways in which you can change the appearance of your worksheets.

BUILDING THE INCOME WORKSHEET

To demonstrate how you can use Excel in your business, this book will present worksheets that you can quickly duplicate. The first one, an income worksheet, shows the sales of a building company's housing developments and its other sources of income. The company requires that income be broken down by calendar quarter, and that a figure be provided for a yearly total. When completed, the worksheet will resemble the one in Figure 2-6.

Before you design any worksheet, you may find it helpful to draw a representation of it similar to the one shown in the figure. If you are converting an existing

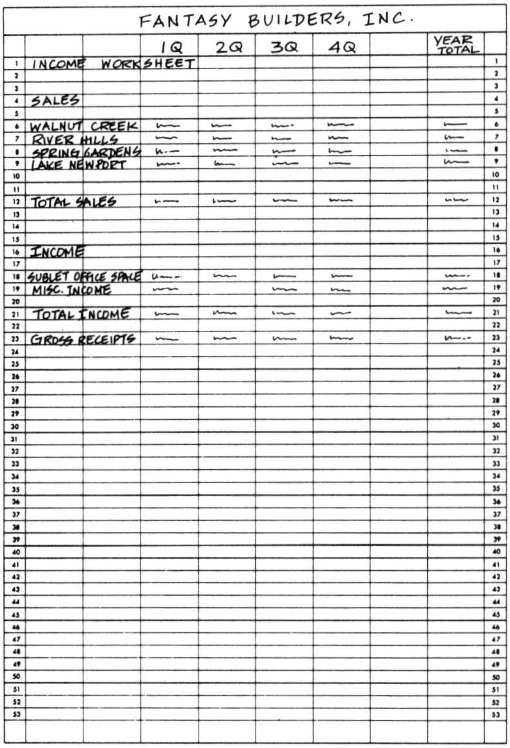

FIGURE 2-6.   Income worksheet design

paper-based system to Excel files, you can work from the actual accounting or ledger sheets.

The first task in building a worksheet is to type the headings. With a blank worksheet open, enter the text shown here in the respective cell locations:

Cell	Entry
A1	Income Worksheet
A4	Sales
A6	Walnut Creek

A7	River Hills
A8	Spring Gardens
A9	Lake Newport
A12	Total Sales
A16	Income
A18	Sublet Office Space
A19	Misc. Income
A21	Total Income
A23	Gross Receipts

As you make each cell entry, you may notice two boxes that appear in the formula bar above the worksheet. You can click these boxes during data entry. Clicking the box with the X (the Cancel box) cancels an entry, and clicking the box with the check mark (the Enter box) is equivalent to pressing RETURN.

CHANGING A COLUMN WIDTH

After you have entered the text just shown, ·click once above the right scroll box to get back to cell A1. Notice that many of the labels are wider than their columns. If additional data is entered in the adjacent cells in column B, some of the labels in column A will be cut off. You can solve this problem by increasing the column width.

With the cursor now in column A, open the Format menu and choose the Column Width command. Excel displays a dialog box that asks for a column width, as shown here:

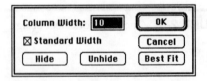

To provide sufficient room to display the names, enter **20** in this box, and the column will assume the new width. You can also widen a column by moving the pointer within the column heading area until it changes to a horizontal double arrow with a vertical cross, and then clicking and dragging the column to the new width.

Place the cursor at cell B6, and enter **123000**. In cell B7, enter **248000**. In cell B8, enter **97000**. In cell B9, enter **346000**. These values represent the first-quarter sales for each housing development.

Move to cell B18, and enter **1800**. In cell B19, enter **750**. For now, only these values are needed. Excel will calculate the totals after you enter the necessary formulas.

BUILDING FORMULAS

What's needed now are calculations of the company's total sales and total income for the first quarter; the resulting values can then be combined to provide a gross receipts value. With Excel, you build a formula by indicating which values should be used and which calculations should apply to these values. Don't forget, Excel formulas always begin with an equal sign.

Cell B12 needs a formula to calculate total sales. Place the cursor at B12 and type an equal sign (=) to start the formula. The equal symbol and a flashing cursor appear in the formula bar at the top of the screen. Now enter the following. (You do not need to include spaces between the entries.)

B6 + B7 + B8 + B9

As you enter the formula, it appears within the formula bar. Once you press RETURN, Excel performs the calculation based on the formula and displays the total in cell B12, as shown in Figure 2-7.

Formulas are used to calculate a value based on a combination of other values. These other values can be numbers, cell references, operators (+, -, *, and /), or other formulas. Formulas can also include the names of other areas in the worksheet, as well as cell references in other worksheets; these topics will be covered in a later chapter.

Math operators are used to produce numeric results. Besides addition (+), subtraction (-), multiplication (*), and division (/) symbols, Excel also accepts the exponentiation (^) and percentage (%) symbols as math operators. It accepts an ampersand (&) as a text operator for strings of text, as well as comparison operators (=, >, <, >=, <=, and < >) for comparing one value to another. The ampersand is used to combine text strings, which is known as *concatenation*. For example, if cell B12 contains "John" and cell B13 contains "Smith," the formula B12 & B13 would yield the result "John Smith."

The following comparison operators are used to compare values and to provide a logical value (TRUE or FALSE) based on the comparison.

<	Less than
>	Greater than
=	Equal to
< >	Not equal to
<=	Less than or equal to
>=	Greater than or equal to

In a cell, the simple comparison = 6 < 7 would result in a value of TRUE because 6 is less than 7. The result of = 6 < Number depends on the value of Number.

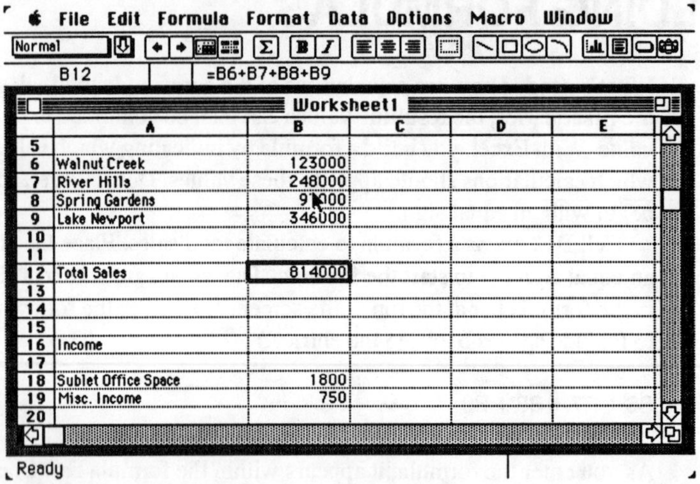

FIGURE 2-7. Total of sales

You use comparison operators with cell references to determine whether a desired result is true or false. For example, consider the worksheet shown here:

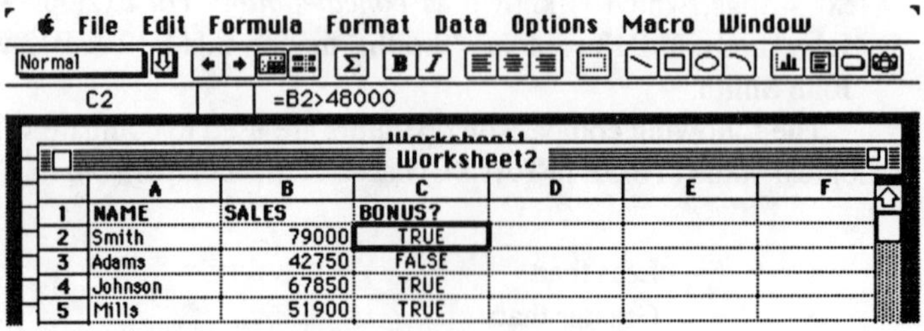

In this example, the formulas in cells C2 through C5 are based on a comparison. Cell C2 contains the formula =B2 >48000. Cells C3, C4, and C5 contain similar formulas. The comparison translates to this: "If the value in B2 is greater than 48,000, display a value of TRUE in C2; otherwise, display a value of FALSE in C2."

Excel has the following precise order of precedence in building formulas:

–	Unary minus or negation
%	Percent
^	Exponentiation
* or /	Multiplication or division
+ or –	Addition or subtraction
&	Text operator
<> or =	Comparison operators

Depending on how you structure your formulas, you may wish to alter this order of precedence. For example, if you want to add the contents of cells B2 and B3 and divide the resulting total by 5, you could not use the simple formula

=B2 + B3 / 5

because Excel performs division before addition in its order of precedence. If you used this formula, the value in B3 would be divided by 5, and that value would be added to the value of B2, producing an erroneous result.

To change the order of precedence, insert parentheses around calculations that are to be performed first. Calculations surrounded by parentheses are always performed first, no matter where they fall in the order of precedence. The formula

=(B2 + B3) / 5

would obtain the desired result. Excel would calculate the expression within the parentheses first, and then divide that figure by the constant (in this example, 5).

USING FUNCTIONS TO BUILD FORMULAS

Typing each cell reference is fine when you are adding a short column of numbers, but larger columns can be time-consuming. Fortunately, Excel offers *functions,* which can be thought of as built-in shortcuts for performing specialized operations. Excel has many different functions for tasks that range from calculating the square root of a number to finding the future value of an investment. You'll learn more about many of Excel's functions in a later chapter. However, you should now know about statistical functions that are commonly used in spreadsheet work: the AVERAGE, MAX, MIN, and SUM functions.

The AVERAGE function calculates the average of a series of values. This function can be expressed as

=AVERAGE(*1st value, 2nd value, 3rd value...last value*)

For example, the expression =AVERAGE(6,12,15,18) would yield the value 12.75. Similarly, the expression =AVERAGE(B10:B15) would provide the average of the values from cells B10 through B15.

The MAX and MIN functions provide the maximum and minimum values, respectively, of all values in the specified range or list of numbers. These functions can be expressed as

=MAX(*1st value, 2nd value, 3rd value...last value*)
=MIN(*1st value, 2nd value, 3rd value...last value*)

For example, consider the worksheet shown in Figure 2-8. The formula in cell B11 is =MIN(B1:B4). The value that results from this formula is the smallest value in the range of cells from B1 through B4. The formula in cell B12, which is =MAX(B1:B4), has precisely the opposite effect; the largest value of those found in the specified range of cells is displayed.

The SUM function is used to provide the sum of a list of values, commonly indicated by referencing a range of cells. For example, the expression =SUM(5,10,12) would provide a value of 27. The formula =SUM(B5:B60) would provide the sum of all numeric values contained in the range of cells from B5 to B60.

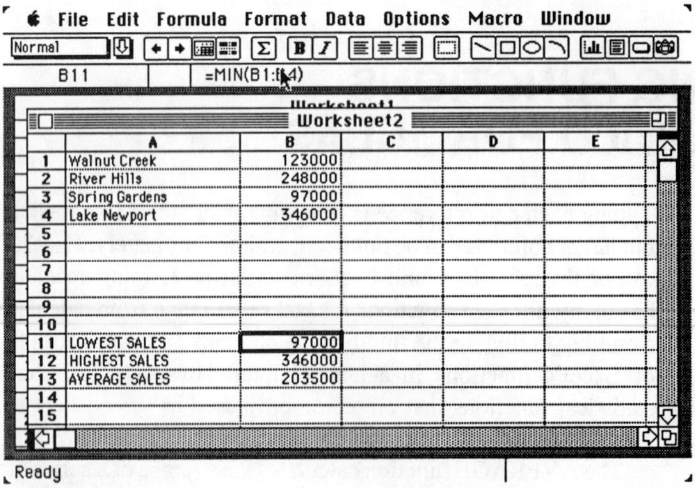

FIGURE 2-8.   Use of MAX and MIN functions

The SUM function offers an easy way to add a column of numbers. As an exercise, place the cursor at B12 and type an equal sign to begin another formula. You can type functions, or you can access them through the Paste Function command of the Formula menu. Open the Formula menu and select the Paste Function command. A dialog box containing a list of Excel's functions appears (see Figure 2-9). To choose a function, simply double-click the desired function name, or click the desired function once and press RETURN. You could reach the SUM function by dragging the scroll box until the SUM function scrolled into view, but a faster way is to press the first letter of the function; the functions that begin with that letter will scroll into view.

Since the SUM function is needed in this case, press s. Then drag the scroll box down and highlight the SUM function; click the function name "SUM" and then click the OK button. The function appears within the formula bar at the top of the worksheet.

To use the SUM function, delete any example that appears between the parentheses and enter the starting and ending cell references, separated by a colon. The SUM function will add all cells between the starting and ending cells and provide a total. For this example, enter

B6:B9

Once you press RETURN or click OK, the total will appear in cell B12.

Use the mouse or the Go To (COMMAND-G) key to go to cell B21, and start a formula with an equal symbol. Open the Formula menu, and choose the Paste Function command. Press s and double-click the SUM function. Delete any example that appears between the parentheses and enter

B18:B19

for the beginning and ending cell references. To obtain a value for gross receipts, one more formula is needed for adding total sales and total income. Move to cell B23 and enter the formula

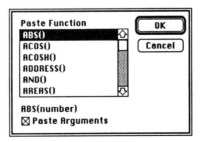

FIGURE 2-9.   Functions dialog box

=B12 + B21

Excel will calculate gross receipts. Your worksheet should resemble the one shown in Figure 2-10.

USING THE AUTOSUM FEATURE

Excel provides a very useful feature called Autosum. The Autosum feature automatically provides a sum formula for an adjacent row or column of numbers. Since much of your work in Excel will involve rows or columns of numbers, Autosum will probably prove quite useful.

The Autosum feature is accessed with the Autosum button of the tool bar. It is easy to find, because the symbol on the button resembles a capital E, as shown here:

To use Autosum, you simply place the cursor in the cell where the sum formula is to appear, then click on the Autosum button. Excel will make its best guess about what

	A	B	C	D	E	
7	River Hills	248000				
8	Spring Gardens	97000				
9	Lake Newport	346000				
10						
11						
12	Total Sales	814000				
13						
14						
15						
16	Income					
17						
18	Sublet Office Space	1800				
19	Misc. Income	750				
20						
21	Total Income	2550				
22						
23	Gross Receipts	816550				

Cell reference: B23 =B12+B21

Menu bar: ‏‎File Edit Formula Format Data Options Macro Window

Ready

═══ **FIGURE 2-10.** Completed Income Worksheet

data you want to sum, and will place a formula in the formula bar. You can then press RETURN to store the formula. Note that Excel makes its guess by looking for a continuous range of numbers above the current cell, or to the left of the current cell.

As an example, place the cursor in cell B12, and press COMMAND-B to clear the existing sum formula. Then, click on the Autosum button. In a moment, the formula bar will display the formula

=SUM(B6:B11)

Press the RETURN key now, and the formula will be stored, displaying the total in cell B12. Note that when Excel guessed at the desired range to sum, it included all cells from the first numeric value in the column of numbers immediately above the current cell (cell B6), and included all cells down to the cell immediately above the current cell (cell B11). If you do not agree with the assumption made by Excel, you can edit the formula as desired before you press RETURN to store it.

PRINTING THE WORKSHEET

To print an Excel worksheet, open the File menu and select the Print command. A Printer dialog box appears, as shown here:

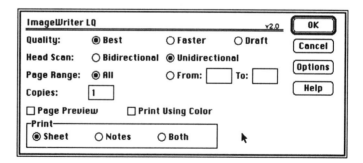

Your dialog box may differ slightly, depending on the type of printer you are using. You can press RETURN or click OK to begin printing; doing so will select the default values for the options shown. If you desire, any of the default options can be changed by clicking the desired option and then clicking OK to start the printing. The available printing options are covered in Chapter 6.

Click the OK button now if you haven't already done so. Your printer should start printing the worksheet. If you don't get satisfactory results, you may need to select the proper printer port using the Chooser option of the Apple menu. See the documentation that came with your Macintosh and your printer for details.

SAVING THE WORKSHEET

It's good practice to save your worksheet on disk periodically, even if you plan to continue working on the worksheet later. Doing so avoids the possibility of losing information because of a power failure or some other accident. The commands used for saving worksheets—Save, Save As, and Save Workspace—are found in the File menu.

The Save and Save As commands are used to save worksheets on disk. The Save As command will prompt you for a new file name, while the Save command will save the worksheet under the existing name (once it has been saved for the first time). The Save As command is also used to save files in formats different from Excel's normal file format. Worksheet data can be saved as ASCII text (a format that most word processors can read); in Excel version 2.2 format; in various Lotus 1-2-3 file formats (saved with a WKS, WK1, or WK3 extension); in dBASE II, dBASE III, and dBASE IV formats; in TEXT (Windows or DOS) formats; and in other Microsoft products' file formats.

The Save Workspace command lets you save to a file a record of all your open documents, including worksheets and any charts. Later, when you double-click that file to open it from the Finder, all of the documents that were saved will be reopened in the same screen positions.

To save your worksheet, open the File menu now and choose the Save command. When you do this, the dialog box shown here appears.

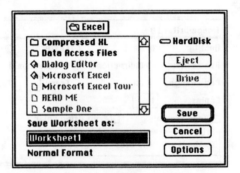

Clicking the Drive button changes the default drive used to store your worksheet, assuming you have a floppy disk inserted in a drive. Clicking the Eject button ejects the current disk, and clicking Cancel closes the dialog box without saving the worksheet. (The Options button is used to save files in other file formats; see Chapter 11 for details.)

You can enter a title for the worksheet in the Save Worksheet As text box. For this worksheet, enter **Income** as a file name and press RETURN to confirm the entry. Once you press RETURN, the worksheet is saved on disk.

MORE ABOUT EXCEL'S MENUS

Menu commands provide access to all of the functions of Excel. You have just seen the commands used to save worksheets. It's a good idea to become familiar with all of the menu commands and their uses.

The File Menu

The File menu (Figure 1-5) contains commands for retrieving (opening) and saving worksheets to and from disk, for opening and closing worksheets, for printing worksheets, and for deleting worksheets from disk.

New worksheets are created with the New command, and existing worksheets can be loaded with the Open command. Users of Lotus 1-2-3 or Microsoft Multiplan should note that the Open command can also be used to convert a Lotus 1-2-3 or Multiplan worksheet to an Excel format; Excel handles the conversion while loading the file. The Close command is used to close a worksheet. (You can also close a worksheet by clicking the close box.) You saw the Save, Save As, and Save Workspace commands in the previous section.

 While there is no theoretical limit to the number of files you can open, available memory will limit the practical number of open files. Since each open worksheet consumes memory, try to limit the number of worksheets you open at any one time.

The Print Preview command is used to display a visual representation of what a printed worksheet will look like. Using Print Preview can help you avoid wasting paper, by giving you an idea of what the printed worksheet's appearance will be before you begin printing.

The Page Setup command lets you change various settings for headers, footers, margins, and paper orientation, and the Printer Setup command lets you select various printers for use with Excel. The Quit command is used to exit Excel and return to the Macintosh desktop (Finder).

The Print command is used to tell Excel to begin printing the worksheet. When you select this command, a dialog box lets you select additional options, such as the desired print quality, the range of pages to print, and the number of copies to be printed (the default is 1).

If they appear, the Open Mail and Send Mail commands apply to earlier versions of Excel, and then only to machines connected to a network that uses Microsoft Mail. The Send Mail command allows users to send Excel documents to other network users.

Documents sent from other users can be retrieved with the Open Mail command. (The use of the Mail feature and of local-area networks is beyond the scope of this book; see your network administrator or your Microsoft Mail documentation for details.)

The Quit command is used to exit from Microsoft Excel.

The Edit Menu

The Edit menu, shown here,

```
Edit
Can't Undo        ⌘Z
Repeat Close      ⌘Y

Cut               ⌘X
Copy              ⌘C
Paste             ⌘V
Clear...          ⌘B
Paste Special...
Paste Link

Delete...         ⌘K
Insert...         ⌘I

Fill Right        ⌘R
Fill Down         ⌘D
Fill Workgroup...
```

provides a number of commands for editing the contents of a worksheet. The Undo command reverses the action of the last command. Note that the Undo command cannot be used to "undelete" a file once that file has been deleted. Nor can it cancel the sorting of an Excel database undertaken with the Sort command of the Data menu. However, the Undo command does work on itself; that is, Undo can be used to undo the effects of the last Undo command.

The Undo command only appears on the Edit menu when it is appropriate. If there is no last action to undo, a dimmed "Can't Undo" designation appears in its place. What appears in your menu directly underneath the Undo command also varies, depending on what your last action with Excel was. For example, if your last action could not be repeated, the menu choice under Undo would be Can't Repeat.

The Cut, Copy, and Paste commands are used to move information within a worksheet and between worksheets. You can mark a section of data within a worksheet, cut that portion of data out of the worksheet, and then paste it into another section of the same worksheet or into another worksheet. You can also copy data from one area of a worksheet into another area or into a different worksheet.

You use the Clear command to clear a cell or group of cells of its contents. The Clear command can be used selectively to clear formulas only, formats only (such as style of appearance and column widths), notes only, or all contents of a worksheet. The Paste Special and Paste Link commands are special-purpose commands for performing special kinds of "data pasting" into selected cells. These commands are described in later chapters.

The Delete command deletes a portion of a worksheet, and the Insert command inserts space into a worksheet. The Insert command offers the flexibility of inserting a block of cells or entire rows or columns into the worksheet. When you insert cells, you can shift existing cells downward or to the right as you desire. You use the Fill Right command to copy data from a cell or group of cells into cells that are located to the right of the original group. The Fill Down command copies data from a cell or group of cells into selected cells that are located below the original group of cells. The Fill Workgroup command is a special-purpose command that applies the changes you make on one worksheet to other worksheets in a group. Chapter 11 contains additional details on using groups of worksheets, or "workgroups."

The Formula Menu

The Formula menu, shown here,

Formula	
Paste Name...	
Pas**t**e Function...	
Reference	⌘T
Define Name...	⌘L
Create Names...	
Apply Names...	
Note...	
Goto...	⌘G
Find...	⌘H
Replace...	
Select Special...	
Show Active Cell	
Outline...	
Goal Seek...	

allows you to build formulas, locate a specific portion of a worksheet, assign a name to a portion of a worksheet, and add notes to individual cells. The Paste Name command in this menu is used to insert (paste) a name into a formula. These names have been previously assigned to portions of a worksheet by the user. If you haven't defined any names within a worksheet, you cannot use the Paste Name command.

The Paste Function command lets you paste an Excel function into a formula. Functions are special built-in formulas that perform complex calculations, such as the average of a column of values or the square root of a given value. When you use the Paste Function command, Excel displays the list of available functions you saw in Figure 2-9. You can then select the appropriate function for your task from this list. The details of these functions can be found in Chapter 10.

The Reference command of the Formula menu is used to change cell references within a formula from relative to absolute references, and vice versa. (Relative and absolute references are covered in Chapter 3.) The Define Name command lets you assign a name to a cell or a group of cells, a value, or a formula. (You can also use this command to change or remove a name from a cell or group of cells, a value, or a formula.) The Create Names command offers you a shortcut for naming several areas in a worksheet at one time. The Apply Names command lets you quickly apply names to various references throughout a worksheet.

The Note command lets you assign a descriptive note to any cell within a worksheet. Such notes can be helpful for remembering the rationale behind a particular formula. The Goto command is used to move the cursor to a specific cell or cell reference. The Find command searches the worksheet for a cell containing specific text or a specific value, and then makes that cell the active cell. The Replace command is used to replace specific text in cells with other text. The Select Special command lets you select cells of a specified type, such as cells that contain formulas. The Show Active Cell command brings the active cell into view, no matter where you are on the spreadsheet. The Outline and Goal Seek commands are advanced commands used in outlining and in seeking goals. These topics are covered in Chapter 11.

The Format Menu

The Format Menu, shown here,

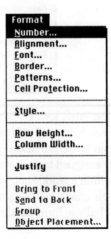

provides commands that affect the way worksheet data is displayed. The Number command sets the display format of numeric values, including dates and times. You can display numbers with or without decimal places or dollar signs, as percentages, or as scientific (exponential) numbers. Excel also lets you create customized number formats if none of the standard formats appeals to you.

The Alignment command is used to change the alignment of text or values that are stored in a selected cell or group of cells. Excel usually aligns text on the left side of the cell and aligns values on the right side of the cell. These automatic settings (called *default values*), can be changed with the Alignment command. The Font command provides various choices of fonts (character styles) and colors for text and numbers.

With the Border command, you can change the borders of a group of cells. Excel lets you place solid borders on any side of a group of cells or completely around a group of cells. You can also shade an area of the worksheet with the Border command. The Patterns command is used to change patterns and colors for a selected part of a worksheet. The Cell Protection command lets you prevent a cell or group of cells from being edited accidentally. The Style command is used to apply or define a style to a worksheet cell. The Row Height and Column Width commands let you change the height of rows and the width of columns. With the Justify command you can shape text so that it fills a selected group of cells. In version 3.0, the Bring To Front, Send To Back, Group, and Object Placement commands are used to control the placement of graphic objects drawn on worksheets. These commands are detailed in Chapter 5.

The Data Menu

The Data menu, shown here,

is used for Excel's database management tasks. The commands in this menu are discussed in Chapter 7.

The Options Menu

The Options menu, shown here,

contains commands that affect the printing and display of worksheets. The Options menu can also be used to password-protect a worksheet, and to determine whether Excel recalculates a worksheet after each edit or only when you tell it to do so. The Set Print Area command lets you select a specific area of a worksheet for printing. The Set Print Titles command determines what text should be printed as a title at the top of each printed page. The Set Page Break command is used to insert a manual page break.

The Display command of the Options menu controls the appearance of formulas, gridlines (the fine lines that divide the rows and columns), and the row and column headings. With this command you can also change the colors used for headings and gridlines. The Freeze Panes command lets you freeze the display of cells above and to the left of a given cell while you scroll the rest of a worksheet. Titles and headings can thus be held in place while you review a large worksheet.

The Color Palette command is used to change the default colors Excel uses.

The Protect Document command offers password protection for a worksheet. If you use this command, write the password on a piece of paper and keep it in a safe place; you cannot access the password of a protected document from the computer if you forget it.

The Calculation and Calculate Now commands let you determine whether Excel recalculates the entire worksheet each time you change a value or formula. Normally, calculation is automatic, meaning Excel recalculates the worksheet each time you change a value or formula. With large worksheets, this recalculation can be time-consuming, so you are given the option of turning recalculation off by setting the Calculation option on the menu to Manual. If Calculation is set to Manual, you must use the Calculate Now option of the menu to tell Excel when to recalculate the entire worksheet.

You use the Workspace command to change the default settings for the way things appear on the screen: the number of decimal places, the style of display for rows and columns, and whether the status bar, tool bar, scroll bars, and formula bars are revealed or hidden. The style of display for the rows and columns can be either A1 style (Lotus 1-2-3) or R1C1 style (Microsoft Multiplan). Excel's default setting is the A1 style of cell references. The Workspace command can also be used to change the key used to bring up the menus; the default is the slash key (/), which is also used in Lotus 1-2-3.

The final choice on the Options menu is either Short Menus or Full Menus. The Short Menus command is used to display shorter menus containing only the commands that are used most often; the Full Menus command displays longer menus that list all available commands.

The Macro Menu

The Macro menu, shown here,

lets you create and change macros—automated sequences of keystrokes that perform specific tasks. Macros, and the commands within the Macro menu, are discussed in Chapter 9.

The Window Menu

The Window menu, shown here,

is used to open and close multiple windows that can each contain different worksheets. The help command lets you access the on-line help system. The New Window command opens a new worksheet window, which overlays the current window. The Show Clipboard command displays the contents of the Macintosh Clipboard. The Show Info command displays the contents of a cell, as well as any notes that have been entered for that cell. The Arrange All command lets you arrange the layout of multiple worksheets. The Workgroup command lets you define a group of worksheets as a workgroup. Once this is done, group editing can be done on multiple sheets in the group. The Hide and Unhide commands are used to hide or display windows.

In addition to the available commands, the names of any open worksheets are displayed in the Window menu. You can bring any worksheet that is hidden by another worksheet to the front of the screen by selecting that worksheet by name from the Window menu.

When chosen, the Help command of the Window menu displays an index of topics; you can select the appropriate topic from the index by double-clicking on it. When you are done with the help screens, you can close the Help window by clicking the close box.

chapter **3**

EDITING THE
WORKSHEET

Data entry represents only a part of the work involved in creating any worksheet. Editing and formatting the entries for proper appearance are also crucial, and this chapter covers these subjects in detail. Excel lets you add rows and columns, remove the contents of a cell or group of cells, and move or copy information from one area of the worksheet to another. You can also change the style of the labels and values, as well as adding borders to areas of the worksheet.

EDITING AN EXISTING CELL

The most straightforward way to change the data in an existing cell is to go to that cell and type the new information; the new data will be written over the existing data. For example, you may find that a drastic error has been made in the sales reported for the Spring Gardens development on the Income worksheet; the amount entered as $97,000 should really be $197,000. Using the mouse or the Go To (COMMAND-G) key, go to cell B8 and enter **197,000**. Note that as you do so, the new entry overwrites the existing entry.

Occasionally, you may enter information in the wrong cell. Once you have moved to the offending cell, there are a number of ways to clear the cell. One quick way is to press the spacebar once, followed by the RETURN key. Another way to clear a cell is to press COMMAND-B. (Recall that COMMAND-B is the hot key for the Clear command.) Still another way to clear a cell is to choose the Clear command from the Edit menu and click the OK button.

===== *note* ===== You will find an appendix listing all command functions and corresponding command keys at the back of this book.

To clear information from a group of cells, you must first select the cells and then choose the Clear command or use the COMMAND-B hot key. To see how this works, place the cursor in a blank area of the worksheet and enter values in a small group of cells. Select this group of cells by dragging with the mouse to the last cell. Then press COMMAND-B. The group of cells will be cleared of any values, text, or formulas. The highlight vanishes once you select another cell.

You can edit existing values, formulas, or labels without retyping the entire entry by moving the cursor to the formula bar during editing operations. To see how this is done, go to cell A7. The entry "River Hills" should actually be "River Hollow," so place the pointer in the formula bar. Note that it changes shape while it is in this bar. You can place the insertion pointer at the desired location for editing and click the mouse button to begin editing. When you do so, the pointer changes to a single-line cursor within the formula bar, as shown in Figure 3-1.

Also, by clicking the Cancel box (the one containing the X), you can exit Edit mode without saving any changes (edits). Clicking the Enter box (the one containing a check mark) is equivalent to pressing RETURN; this saves your edits as a part of the cell contents. While you are in Edit mode, the BACKSPACE key removes characters to the left of the cursor. Any new characters that you type are inserted at the cursor position, and any existing characters to the right of the cursor are pushed to the right to make room for the new characters.

For example, move the cursor to the end of the word "Hills," click the mouse to begin editing, and use the BACKSPACE key to delete the word. Then enter **Hollow** and press RETURN (or click the Enter box) to complete the change. Note that if you wish to cancel an edit during the editing process, you can click the Cancel box with the mouse. Doing so restores the previous entry within the cell. You can only do this, however, before you have completed an edit; once you complete the editing of a cell (by pressing RETURN or ENTER, or by clicking the Enter box), the changes are stored in the cell. If you then change your mind, you must use the Undo command of the Edit menu.

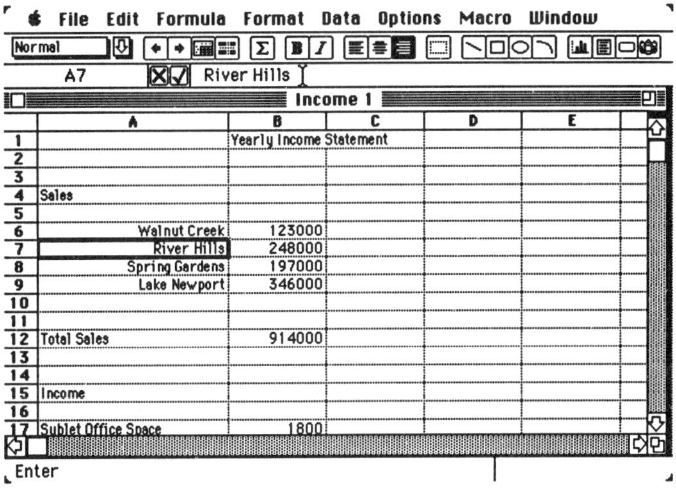

FIGURE 3-1.   Single-line cursor in formula bar

UNDOING AN EDIT

Excel contains a very useful "undo" feature that cancels the effect of your last edit. If you delete the contents of a cell, a group of cells, a row, or a column and you then change your mind, open the Edit menu and choose the Undo command. In most cases, the Undo command can correct the damage. However, you cannot undo a command once you have selected another command.

Once you use the Undo command to undo an entry, the name of the command changes to Redo Entry. You can reenter the adjusted entry by choosing the Redo Entry command.

tip   For the most part, Undo is specific to the Edit menu and to the editing of cells. You cannot undo most of the commands that are located on other menus.

WORKING WITH NAMED RANGES

You can refer to a cell or a group of cells by a name instead of by a cell reference and then use the name within your formulas. Many spreadsheet users find it easier to remember the logic of a formula if it is composed of names that relate to the type of information stored. For example, you could give row 1 of a worksheet the name Income and give row 3 the name Expenses. A formula in row 5 that computes net profits could then read =Income – Expenses rather than =B1-B3.

To assign a name to a cell or a group of cells, you must select the desired cell or cells and then choose the Define Name command in the Formula menu. In the dialog box that appears, you can enter the name that is to be assigned to the range.

To try this, select row 6 by clicking the row 6 heading at the far-left side of the worksheet. An appropriate name for this row would be Walnut Creek, since all values in this row refer to the Walnut Creek subdivision. Open the Formula menu and choose the Define Name command. The Define Name dialog box then appears, as shown here:

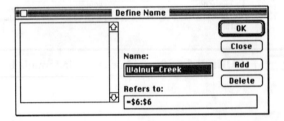

Examine the entries that already appear within the dialog box, and note an important feature. When you ask Excel to define a name for a range of cells, the program looks for text in the selected cells. If it finds text, Excel suggests that text as a name for the range, with the spaces in the name converted to underlines. Excel also enters a suggested reference for the range of cells. In this case, the reference is an *absolute reference* to row 6, meaning that the name will always refer to row 6. The dollar signs in the reference indicate an absolute reference. (Absolute references are covered later in this chapter.)

Press RETURN now or click the OK button with the mouse to accept the suggested name for the range. Next, select row 7 by clicking the Row 7 heading. Open the Formula menu, and again choose the Define Name command. In the dialog box that appears, Excel will suggest River_Hollow as the name of the range. Press RETURN or click the OK button with the mouse to accept this name.

You may now use the names Walnut_Creek and River_Hollow instead of cell references within a formula. To see how this works, place the cursor at cell B14. Type the equal sign to start a formula, and enter the following. (Note that spaces around the operators in a formula are optional. Excel ignores spaces, but you may want to use them for readability.)

Walnut_Creek + River_Hollow

Once you enter the formula, the correct total is displayed within the cell. In this case, Excel has calculated the value based on the names given to the ranges of cells.

This entry isn't needed in our worksheet, so clear the entry by moving to the cell and pressing COMMAND-B.

Using Create Names To Name a Range of Cells

If your worksheet contains multiple rows or columns and they contain text that is acceptable to you as range names, you can tell Excel to define names for all of the rows or columns at once. For example, you might decide that each of the names in rows 6 through 9 are acceptable as names for the cells in those rows. Select rows 6 through 9 now by placing the pointer at the heading for row 6 and dragging down to row 9. Open the Formula menu and select the Create Names command. A dialog box asks you if you want to create names in the top row, the left column, the bottom row, or the right column of the selection. Choose the left column by clicking the Left Column box with the mouse and then clicking OK.

Because you previously defined a portion of the selection as the named ranges Walnut_Creek and River_Hollow, Excel displays a dialog box asking if you want to change the existing definition for those names. Select Yes each time you are asked if you wish to replace the definitions. You can now use a formula in B12 for Total Sales, and the formula can include the named ranges.

Range names can be used within a function, just as they can be used in other parts of a formula. Place the cursor at cell B12 and start a new formula with the equal sign. Enter

SUM(Walnut_Creek:Lake_Newport)

You can use uppercase or lowercase letters; Excel ignores the case that you use. However, the underlines between the words are important. If spaces are used between the words of a name for a range, Excel will not interpret the formula correctly and will display an error message.

Once you press RETURN to complete the entry of the formula, the correct total appears. You may prefer to use either actual cell references or named ranges in your formulas. Keep in mind, however, that other people who must edit a worksheet you have designed might find it easier to understand if you use named ranges.

Because the named range may create a problem later when you copy the values to other cells in the worksheet, change the formula in B12 back to the original formula now. With the cursor in B12, edit the formula so it reads =SUM(B6:B9), and then press RETURN.

ADDING NOTES

You can add notes to any cell in an Excel worksheet by using the Note command of the Formula menu. Notes are normally not visible but can be displayed or edited at any time. They store information that others may find helpful when working with a particular worksheet. To enter a note, place the cursor at the desired cell. Then select the Note command from the Formula menu and enter the text of the note. You complete the note by pressing RETURN or clicking the OK button with the mouse.

As an exercise, place the cursor at cell B12. Open the Formula menu and select the Note command. The Cell Note window appears, as shown here:

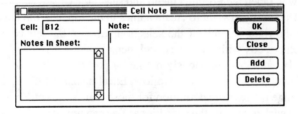

Type

all new subdivisions must be added between rows 8 and 9

and then press RETURN or click OK. The note is stored, and the worksheet underneath reappears.

Open the Formula menu again and choose the Note command. This time, because a note exists in the worksheet, the cell location and starting text for the note appears in the list box at the left side of the Cell Note window. This list box displays all notes stored in a worksheet. You can use the scroll bars along with the mouse to find any note you wish to read or edit.

Notice the additional buttons labeled Add and Delete within the Cell Note window. You can delete a note from the worksheet by highlighting that note within the scroll box and clicking the Delete button. The Add button can be used to add an existing note to another cell. Select the Add button, and then enter a cell reference for the desired cell. The note currently displayed is added to that cell. For now, click Close to close the Note dialog box.

INSERTING ROWS AND COLUMNS

You'll often need to insert rows or columns into a worksheet to provide space for additional sets of figures or for headings. Sometimes, you'll simply want blank rows or columns to break up large portions of figures; adding such "white space" can make a worksheet more appealing visually.

To insert a row or column, you must first select an existing row or column within the spreadsheet. (Remember, you can select a row or column by clicking in the row or column border.) Once you have selected a row or a column, choose Insert from the Edit menu or use the Insert hot key, COMMAND-I. When you add the new row or column, Excel inserts the new rows or columns over the existing ones. If the insertion is a column, the existing data is pushed to the right. If it is a row, the existing data is moved down.

As an example, a title for the Income worksheet would be visually appealing, but the worksheet currently has no space to add one. Select row 1 by clicking the number 1 in the row border with the mouse. When you select a row or column, the entire row or column is highlighted, as shown in Figure 3-2.

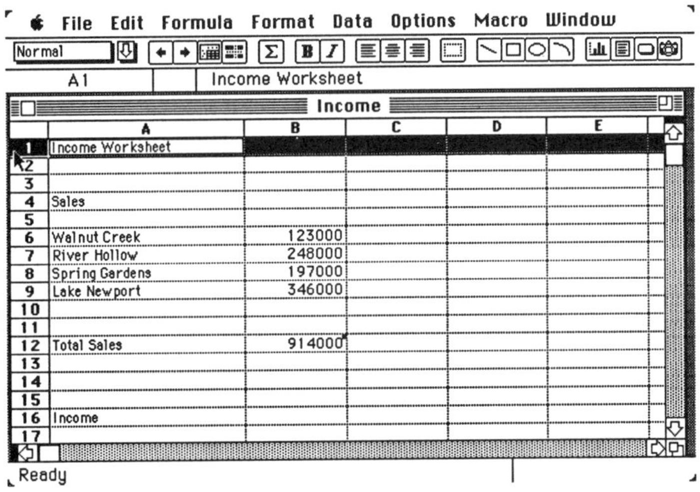

FIGURE 3-2.   Selected row

After you select row 1, open the Edit menu and choose the Insert command. A new row is automatically inserted above the existing row. Go to cell B1, and enter the following label:

Yearly Income Statement

If you wish to insert more than one row or column at a time, select the number of columns or rows you wish to insert. For example, if you want to add five blank rows, first select five rows in the border; then use the Insert command of the Edit menu, and five new rows will be added.

INSERTING SPACE

Excel also lets you insert space or cells within a row or column, as opposed to inserting an entire row or column. The method of doing this is similar to the one used to insert a row or column, but only a portion of the worksheet (instead of the entire worksheet) is affected by the insertion.

Assume, for example, that you want to insert two blank cells below A6. First select the two cells that occupy two successive rows (A7 and A8). Then open the Edit menu and choose the Insert command. The following dialog box appears:

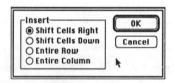

Now you must tell Excel where to move the information in cells A7 and A8. The dialog box presents four options: Shift Cells Right, Shift Cells Down, Entire Row, and Entire Column. In this case, select Shift Cells Down and click the OK button to complete the entry. The new space is inserted in the column. The rest of the worksheet remains unaffected by the insertion, as you can see in Figure 3-3.

The names are no longer aligned with the values, so you should now cancel the effects of this insertion. The easiest way is to open the Edit menu and choose the Undo command (which will now appear as Undo Insert because the last command you performed was an Insert command). Once you select the Undo command, the worksheet returns to its prior state.

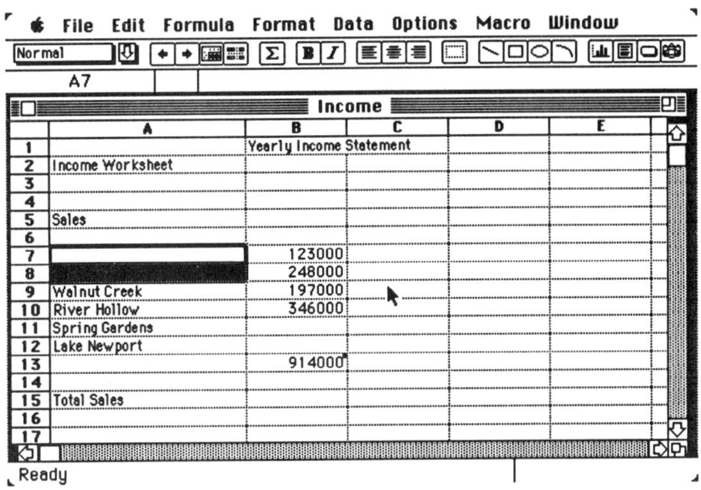

FIGURE 3-3.   Worksheet with space inserted

DELETING ROWS AND COLUMNS

In a fashion similar to inserting, you can delete entire rows and columns by selecting the desired rows or columns and choosing the Delete command from the Edit menu. As an exercise, select row 15 by clicking the number 15 in the row border. Then open the Edit menu and select the Delete command. The row will be deleted, and the existing data below the deleted row will be shifted upward automatically.

Delete with Care

Any deletion should be performed with care. This is particularly true of massive deletions, such as entire rows or columns. With large worksheets, there may be other data, formulas, or comments that are not in sight, so you should scroll through your worksheet before deleting a large area. The Undo command can be used to recover from a deletion, but missing data often isn't noticed until many steps later, when it is too late for Undo to help.

If you delete a cell or cells referenced by other cells in the worksheet, Excel can no longer complete the calculation. The #REF! error message appears in the affected cells. Consider the example shown in Figures 3-4 and 3-5. In Figure 3-4, cell C6 contains the formula =C2+C3+C4. In Figure 3-5, row 4 has been deleted, and the contents of row 5 shift up to fill row 4. The formula that was in C6 still depends on a value in C4, which is no longer available. As a result, Excel returns an error message.

One way to avoid such problems is to use functions whenever possible, because functions make automatic adjustments when such deletions are made. In the original example, cell C6 contained the formula =C2+C3+C4. If the SUM function had been used instead, the formula would have contained =SUM(C2:C4). Then, when row 4 was deleted, Excel would have automatically changed the formula to =SUM(C2:C3), thus ensuring a correct result.

COPYING AND MOVING DATA

In many cases you can save time by copying data from one place on the worksheet to another, or by moving data within the worksheet. As an example, perhaps you need a

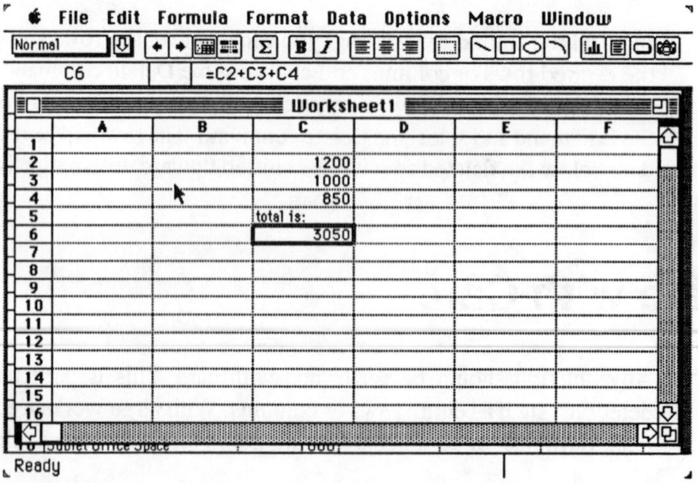

FIGURE 3-4. Worksheet before deletion

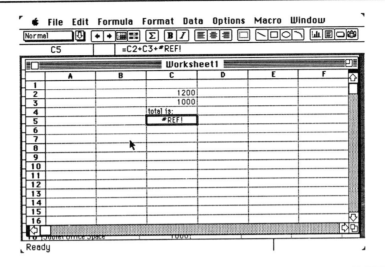

FIGURE 3-5.   Worksheet after deletion

projection for the entire year based on the sales in the first quarter (shown in column B of the worksheet). Projecting that the company will have the same sales in the second, third, and fourth quarters that they had in the first quarter, you could type the same figures and formulas into the appropriate locations in columns C, D, and E. This procedure would be time-consuming, however, compared to copying the data from one area to another.

There are two ways to copy data. You can use the Copy and Paste commands to copy the desired data from one area and paste it into another area, or you can use the Fill Right and Fill Down commands. The Fill Right and Fill Down commands assume that you want to fill the empty cells to the right or below a selected group of cells with whatever data is in the selected group of cells.

In this example, all of the numbers and formulas in cells B7 through B23 must be copied into the corresponding locations in columns C, D, and E. The value in B7 must be copied into C7, D7, and E7; the value in B9 must be copied into C9, D9, and E9; the formula in B13 must be copied into C13, D13, and E13; and so on.

First try the copy and paste method. The general procedure for doing this is

1. Select the desired cells to copy.

2. Use the Copy command of the Edit menu to copy the contents into memory.

3. Place the cursor at the insertion point.

4. Use the Paste command of the Edit menu to paste the cells into the new location.

As an exercise, select cells B7 to B23 by clicking and dragging from B7 to B23. With these cells selected, open the Edit menu and choose the Copy command. When you do this, a dotted border appears around the selected cells, as shown in Figure 3-6.

When identifying the destination for the copied data, you can either select the cell in the upper-left corner of the area or you can select an area equal in size to the area you are copying. Since you started copying from cell B7, you want the copy of the cells to appear in C7 so the figures will be aligned. Move the cursor to cell C7, and open the Edit menu. Note that the Paste command, which was not available before, is now available as a command; once data has been copied into memory, the Paste command can be used to paste that data to any location. With the cursor on cell C7, choose the Paste command. An identical copy of the data appears in column C, as shown in Figure 3-7. The dotted border will vanish when you perform another operation.

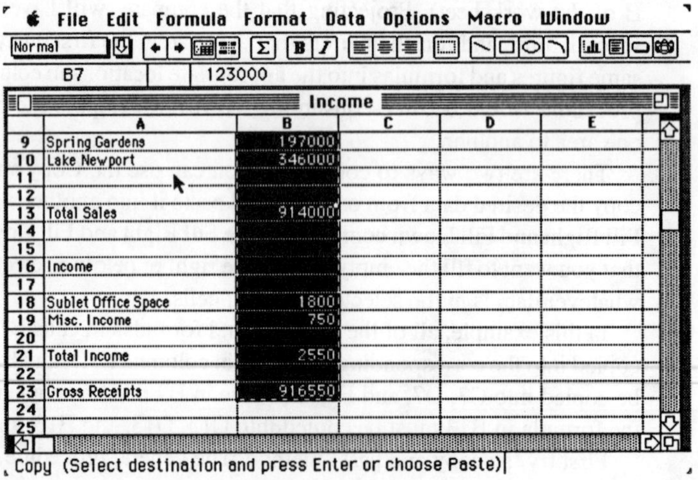

	File	**Edit**	**Formula**	**Format**	**Data**	**Options**	**Macro**	**Window**	

Normal [U] [◆][◆][▦][▦] Σ [B][I] [≡][≡][≡] [▢] [◥◻◻◠] [山][▤][◻][✿]

B7		123000				

Income

	A	B	C	D	E	
9	Spring Gardens	197000				
10	Lake Newport	346000				
11						
12						
13	Total Sales	914000				
14						
15						
16	Income					
17						
18	Sublet Office Space	1800				
19	Misc. Income	750				
20						
21	Total Income	2550				
22						
23	Gross Receipts	916550				
24						
25						

Copy (Select destination and press Enter or choose Paste)

FIGURE 3-6. Border resulting from Copy command

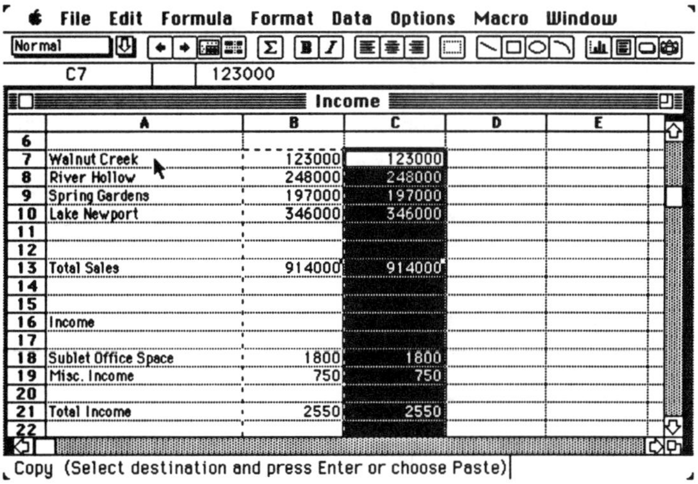

FIGURE 3-7. Worksheet with data pasted into column C

Copying Data with The Fill Commands

Another way of copying data is to use the Edit menu's Fill Right and Fill Down commands. These commands are designed to work with a selected group of cells. The Fill Right command copies formulas and values from the original column into all other columns in the selection. The Fill Down command copies formulas and values from the original row into all other rows in the selection. The following illustration shows how Fill Right and Fill Down work.

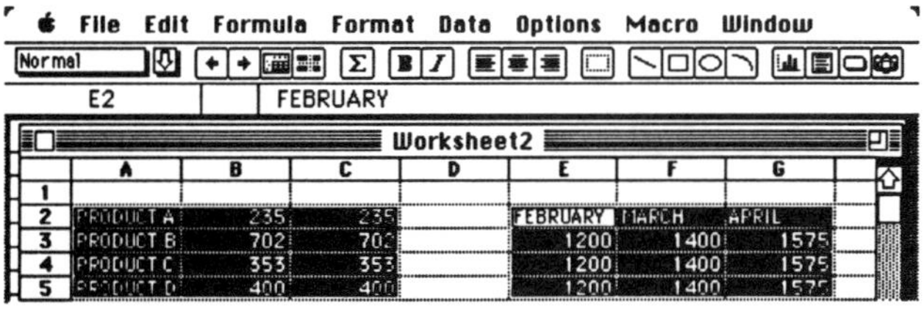

To use the Fill Right or Fill Down command, simply select the cells to be copied, along with the successive rows or columns on which the data is to be copied. Then open the Edit menu and choose the Fill Right command to copy the contents of a column to the right or the Fill Down command to copy the contents of a row downward.

Select cells C7 through E23 now. Open the Edit menu and choose the Fill Right command. The contents of cells C7 through C23 are copied, or "filled in," at columns D and E. All you need to make your projections complete is a column for a yearly total, along with headings for each quarter. Enter the following headings in the cells listed:

Cell	Heading
B6	1st Quarter
C6	2nd Quarter
D6	3rd Quarter
E6	4th Quarter
F6	Yearly Total

The next step is to provide formulas for the totals of the quarterly figures. As an example, the total figure for the Walnut Creek subdivision could be calculated in cell F7 with the formula =SUM(B7:E7). In cell F7, start a formula with an equal sign. Open the Formula menu, and choose the Paste Function command. When the Paste Function dialog box appears, press s to quickly access the functions that start with the letter S, and then select the SUM function. (Also, if you click on the Paste Arguments box to turn off the check box, you will not need to delete any examples when the function is entered.) Enter **B7:E7** to complete the formula.

Because you need the same type of formula for the other rows, you can use the Copy and Fill Down commands to copy the formula to the successive rows within column F. Select cells F7 through F10, open the Edit menu, and choose the Fill Down command to copy the formula into cells F8, F9, and F10.

Next, highlight cell F10, open the Edit menu, and choose the Copy command to copy the formula into memory. Then move to cells F13, F18, F19, F21, and F23, and use the Paste command from the Edit menu to paste the formula from memory into those cells.

MOVING DATA

You can use the Edit menu's Cut and Paste commands to move data from one location to another. In our example, the income worksheet might be more attractive if a blank column appeared between the fourth-quarter figures and the projected annual figures.

You could simply insert a column, but for demonstration purposes let's move the data instead, which has the same result.

First select cells F6 through F23. With the block of cells selected, open the Edit menu and choose the Cut command. Go to cell G6, open the Edit menu, and choose the Paste command. The data is removed (cut) from column F and reappears in the new locations in column G.

You can replace projected figures for the Income worksheet with actual sales figures. Enter the following information:

Cell	Entry
C7	187,000
C8	265,500
C9	89,750
C10	416,000
D7	72,750
D8	297,800
D9	121,000
D10	352,000
E7	146,500
E8	315,000
E9	205,700
E10	387,600

As you enter these values, Excel updates the total sales and the yearly totals in the worksheet to reflect the changed values.

A percentage figure that shows each quarter's percentage in relation to total sales might be another desirable addition. This percentage can be derived from the simple formula

% TOTAL, 1st quarter = Total Sales, 1st Quarter / Yearly Total

In cell A14, enter **Percentage of Total** as the label. Move to cell B14, start the formula with an equal sign, and move the cursor up to B13. Type a slash, and then move the cursor to cell G13. The formula bar should now display the formula =B13/G13, which is the correct formula for the percentage, so press RETURN. The percentage appears in cell B14 as 0.24240174 (roughly 24%). You'll learn shortly how to display the data with a percent sign.

You now want to copy the percentage formula into adjacent cells. Select cells B14 through E14, open the Edit menu, and choose Fill Right. Don't be surprised by the results. If you have followed directions, Excel is displaying the error message #DIV/0!, which means you are attempting to divide by zero in each of the adjacent cells. This has occurred because of two important Excel concepts—relative and absolute cell references.

Excel, unless told otherwise, deals with formulas on a relative basis. When you copy formulas from one area of the worksheet to another area, Excel assumes that the formulas should be adjusted for each new row. Recall when you first used the Copy command to copy the existing data in column B into column C. When the formulas in cells B13, B21, and B23 were copied to cells C13, C21, and C23, Excel did not copy the formulas precisely. (If it had, the totals in column C would have reflected the values in column B.) Instead, Excel assumed that the cell references contained in the formulas would need to be adjusted for the new columns. As a result, the copied formulas reflected the values in column C, rather than those in column B. Cell references that are adjusted in this way when data is copied are known as *relative references.*

On the other hand, the last copy operation makes it clear that sometimes you don't want Excel to make assumptions when you are copying data. Instead, you want Excel to leave a cell reference alone, regardless of the operation. You can change a cell reference from a relative reference to an *absolute reference,* which is simply a cell reference that does not change. To specify a reference as absolute, you must place a dollar sign before the characters indicating the row or column. Either the row or the column, or both, can be specified as an absolute reference. The examples that follow show how a cell reference can be defined as absolute.

B14	Relative reference
$B14	Column reference is absolute, row is relative
B$14	Column is relative, row reference is absolute
$B$14	Entire reference is absolute

Returning to our problem, because Excel adjusted the formulas that were copied into cells C14, C15, and C16, these formulas are incorrect. The formula in C14 is attempting to divide the contents of C13 by the contents of H13, which is an empty cell. Cells C15 and C16 contain similar erroneous formulas. What's needed in this case is an absolute reference in the formula contained in cell B14. The formula that currently reads

=B13/G13

must be changed to read

=B13/$G13

so that any copying of data does not affect the reference to column G, which contains the yearly total figure.

Place the cursor at cell B14 and begin editing the existing formula. Move the insertion pointer in the formula bar until it is between the slash and the letter G, and click the mouse to begin editing. Enter a dollar sign and press RETURN to store the edited formula.

The new formula must still be copied to the adjacent cells to obtain the proper result. Select cells B14 through E14 again. Open the Edit menu and choose Fill Right. The correct percentage values will appear in the cells.

Note that there is an important difference between copying data from cells with the Edit menu's Copy command and moving (or cutting and pasting) data. When you copy data to another portion of a worksheet, Excel automatically adjusts any relative references within the cells. When you move data by cutting and pasting, Excel leaves the references alone; any relative references still refer to the same cells that they referred to before the cut and paste operation. For example, consider the worksheet in Figure 3-8. When the contents of cell B5 (representing the total of cells B2 and B3) are copied to cell B11, the formula stored in cell B11 is a relative copy of the formula in cell B5; the formula now refers to the total of cells B8 and B9. In contrast, consider the example shown in Figure 3-9. The contents of cell B5, representing the first total, are cut and pasted into cell B11. The contents of the formula are unchanged by the cut and paste; the cell still refers to cells B2 and B3 to obtain the total (erroneous) value.

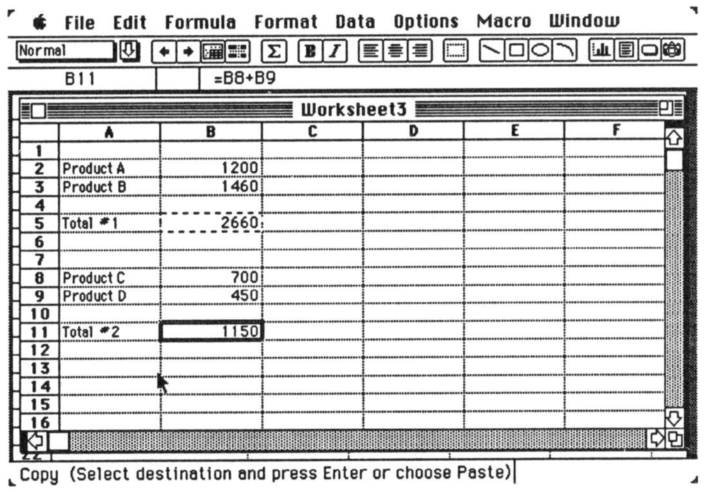

FIGURE 3-8.   Results of sample copy

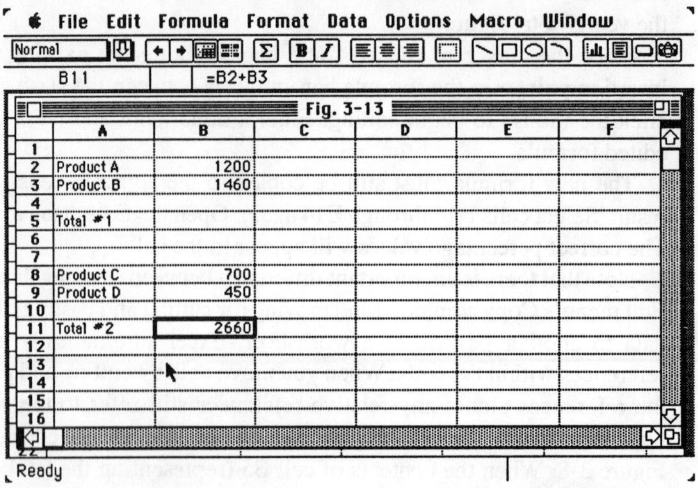

FIGURE 3-9. Results of sample cut and paste

FORMATTING VALUES

You can control how Excel displays values in the worksheet by changing the format of the cells. For example, you may want dollar amounts to be displayed with a dollar sign and cents. You may or may not desire commas in thousand amounts. Percentages might look better with a percent sign (24%) instead of a decimal (0.24240174). These and similar options can be changed. The commands used for changing cell formats are accessed through the Format menu.

In our sample Income worksheet, the numbers represent dollar amounts, so you might want to set the format to show dollar signs. First you need to select the desired cells for formatting. You could use the mouse to select all of the cells containing numbers in the worksheet, but there is a faster way. Nearly all of the values in this worksheet use the same format, so it would be faster to select the entire worksheet and then apply the desired format.

To select the entire worksheet, click the corner box between A and 1. (This is the upper-left corner of the worksheet, above the topmost row number and to the left of the leftmost column letter.) With the entire worksheet selected, open the Format menu and select the Number command. The following dialog box appears:

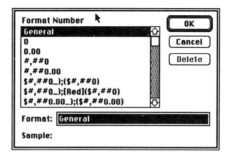

In this case, the desired format is $#,##0_);($#,##0). Select this format now to apply it to all of the values within the worksheet. Click the OK button to implement the change.

One more change is still needed: The percentages are displayed as if they were dollar amounts, because the entire worksheet was formatted with that command. Select cells B14 through E14. Open the Format menu again, select the Number command, and choose the Percent format (0%) from within the dialog box. (Be sure to use the scroll bar in the border of the dialog box to display all the options.) Then select the OK button to implement the format. Your worksheet should now resemble the one shown in Figure 3-10.

Excel lets you display values in General, Scientific, and various Currency formats. Figure 3-11 shows a worksheet with numeric formats and date formats displayed. Excel normally defaults to General format, which displays values with as much precision as possible. Decimals are displayed if needed, and if a number is too large to fit in a cell, scientific notation is used.

Note that you can access some commonly used formats (including Currency and Percent) by clicking on the down arrow of the tool bar. When you select a cell or range of cells and click on the down arrow of the tool bar, a list box of common formats appears. Select the desired format from the list, and it will be applied to the selected cells.

Each format symbol has a particular meaning. The zero is used as a digit placeholder. If the value to be displayed contains fewer digits than there are zeros in the format, Excel displays the extra digits as zeros. If the value contains more digits on the right side of the decimal point than format zeros, Excel rounds off the value to match the number of zeros in the format. If the value contains more digits on the left side of the decimal point than there are zeros in the format, Excel shows the extra places as zeros.

The number sign (#) is also used as a placeholder, but with an important difference. If the value has fewer digits on either side of the decimal point than # signs in the format, Excel drops the extra zeros from the value that is displayed. The decimal point is used in the format to indicate where the decimal point should occur in the value (if

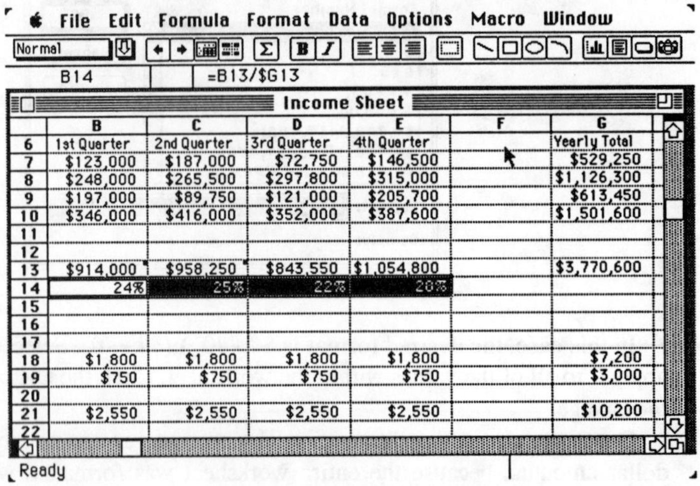

É File Edit Formula Format Data Options Macro Window

| Normal | | | Σ | B | I | | | | | | | | | | |

B14   =B13/$G13

Income Sheet

	B	C	D	E	F	G
	1st Quarter	2nd Quarter	3rd Quarter	4th Quarter		Yearly Total
6						
7	$123,000	$187,000	$72,750	$146,500		$529,250
8	$248,000	$265,500	$297,800	$315,000		$1,126,300
9	$197,000	$89,750	$121,000	$205,700		$613,450
10	$346,000	$416,000	$352,000	$387,600		$1,501,600
11						
12						
13	$914,000	$958,250	$843,550	$1,054,800		$3,770,600
14	24%	25%	22%	28%		
15						
16						
17						
18	$1,800	$1,800	$1,800	$1,800		$7,200
19	$750	$750	$750	$750		$3,000
20						
21	$2,550	$2,550	$2,550	$2,550		$10,200
22						

Ready

FIGURE 3-10.   Worksheet with formatted values

at all). The percent symbol indicates a percentage format; when this symbol is used, Excel automatically multiplies the value of the cell by 100 and inserts the % sign. The comma is used as a thousands separator to indicate where commas should appear when a value is 1,000 or higher. The letter E is used to indicate Scientific, or Exponential, formats. The symbols

$: + ( )

are displayed in the same position in which they appear in a custom format, as are spaces.

Designing Custom Formats

Understanding the symbols used in formatting is important because Excel lets you design custom formats with them. For example, you might want to display a dollar amount, but with the cents value carried to four decimal places. The available format choices for dollar amounts shown in Figure 3-11 do not suffice, because the only

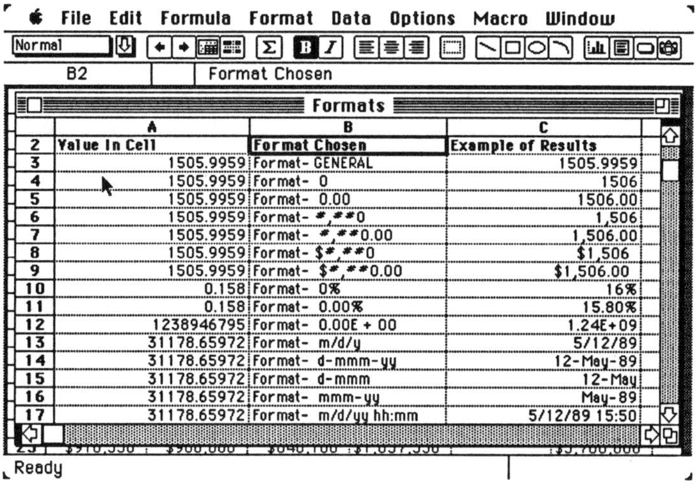

FIGURE 3-11.   Available standard formats

option that displays dollars and cents uses only two decimal places, not four. For such a task, you need a custom format.

You create custom formats by selecting the cells to which the format will apply, choosing the Number command from the Format menu, and entering the desired symbols in the Format box. To create the custom format for showing dollars and cents to four decimal places, you would use a format like this one to display the value:

$#,##0.0000

You may want to try building a custom format now. If so, use the scroll bars to move to a blank area of the worksheet, and enter a value with four decimal places (such as 5101.0357) in a cell. With the cursor in that cell, open the Format menu and select Number. Instead of choosing a standard format, enter the following:

$#,##0.0000

As you enter the symbols, note that they appear in the text box at the bottom of the dialog box. When you press RETURN, the value will be displayed in the chosen format. Note also that Excel adds your custom format to the list of available formats in the dialog box. Once you create a custom format to use in a particular worksheet, it will be available whenever that worksheet is open.

The symbols that can be used in a custom format offer much flexibility. If, for example, you want to store a list of phone numbers and have the area code surrounded by parentheses and the prefix and suffix separated by a hyphen, you would use the format

(000) 000-0000

The value 2128765555 would be displayed as (212) 876-5555. You can also enter text by enclosing the text within quotes as a part of the format. If you want to add the prefix, Part No., to a series of numbers, you might create a format like

"Part No. " ###-####

A number entered as 1014052 would then be displayed as Part No. 101- 4052.

 If you need a format that is similar to an existing format, select the existing format. Once you select the format, it appears below in the text box. Move the pointer to the Format box, and edit the existing format. The edited version will be added to the list of available formats.

Deleting Custom Formats

You can delete a custom format by selecting the format from the list of available formats and then clicking the Delete button. As a safeguard, Excel only lets you delete custom formats; you cannot delete the standard formats.

If you created some examples of custom formats in a remote area of the worksheet, you may want to clear this area before going on (so that it does not print in later printing operations). Select the area, press COMMAND-B, and then press RETURN to clear the cells.

Aligning the Contents of a Cell

Excel usually aligns labels or text at the left side of a cell. Values are normally placed flush right, or aligned at the right side of the cell. This type of alignment is referred to as General alignment. It is just one of five options for aligning the contents of cells. The other options are Left, Center, Right, and Fill.

Alignment commands are reached from the Format menu. If you want to align the contents of a single cell, place the cursor at that cell, choose the Alignment command of the Format menu, and select the desired alignment option. If you want to align a group of cells, first select the group and then make the appropriate choices from the menus.

In the Income worksheet example, the names of the housing developments could be right-aligned to stand out from the other headings. To do this, select cells A7 through A10, open the Format menu, and choose the Alignment command. The dialog box shown here will appear:

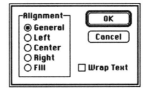

In this example, right-alignment is desired, so select the Right option from the menu and click OK. The labels within the cells become aligned with the right side of the cells. Select cells A18 and A19, and perform the same steps to right-align the contents of those cells.

You can also align the contents of cells by selecting the desired cells, and then clicking on one of the alignment symbols in the tool bar. (This is often faster than making a menu selection.) Just select the desired cells, and then click on the desired alignment button to left-align, center, or right-align the entries in the cells.

At this point, you have the complete Income worksheet, which should resemble the one shown in Figure 3-12. Before continuing, save the latest changes to your worksheet by opening the File menu and selecting the Save command. You will use this worksheet, in its present form, in later chapters.

COMMAND KEYS USED WITH EDIT

You'll save numerous keystrokes if you utilize the COMMAND-key sequences in place of the Edit menu's commands. Most commands on the Edit menu can be chosen by means of a COMMAND key; simply select the desired cells, and then press the appropriate COMMAND key. As a reminder, the COMMAND keys representing the Edit menu commands appear in Table 3-1; they are also listed in Appendix A.

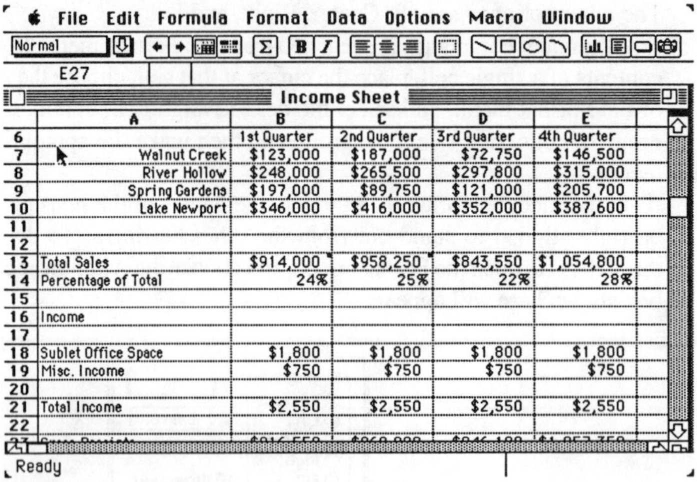

FIGURE 3-12. Completed Income worksheet

ERROR MESSAGES

No program is perfect, and at times we all ask our software to accomplish tasks that simply are beyond its limits. When this happens in an Excel worksheet, the program

Clear	COMMAND-B
Copy	COMMAND-C
Cut	COMMAND-X
Delete	COMMAND-K
Insert	COMMAND-I
Fill Down	COMMAND-D
Fill Right	COMMAND-R
Paste	COMMAND-V
Undo	COMMAND-Z

TABLE 3-1. COMMAND Keys Used with Edit

Message	Problem
#DIV/0!	An attempt was made to divide by 0, a mathematical impossibility.
#N/A!	A value is not available at this cell, so the cell contains no value.
#NAME?	You have included text within a formula. (Excel assumes that the text refers to a named range on a worksheet, and it is unable to find the named range. This error commonly results from misspelled functions or range references with colons accidentally left out.)
#NULL!	You have specified the intersection of two areas that do not intersect.
#NUM!	You have used a math function incorrectly or in a way that has produced a number so large or so small that Excel cannot handle the value.
#REF!	A named area that was part of a formula has been deleted, or a reference has been made to a cell that does not exist on the worksheet
#VALUE!	Either you tried to use text where Excel requires a number, or an incorrect operator has been entered.

TABLE 3-2.   Excel Error Messages and Their Meanings

tells you about it by displaying an error message in the offending cell. Note that a cell that contains such a message isn't always the source of the problem. If that cell refers to another cell, both cells may contain the error.

Unlike some competing products, Excel provides strong hints about the source of the problem by offering a number of different error messages. Excel's error messages and their meanings are shown in Table 3-2 and are also included in Appendix A.

Like any spreadsheet, Excel only complains about errors that make proper calculations impossible. Worksheets may contain design or logic errors, and these go unnoticed by Excel or by any other spreadsheet. Until mind-reading personal computers are developed, the responsibility for double-checking assumptions will rest with the user.

THE CIRCULAR
REFERENCE ERROR

One type of error that you may encounter is a *circular reference error,* which occurs when two cells in a worksheet refer to each other in the process of calculating a formula. For example, if you store the formula

=B1 + 5

in cell A1, and then store the formula

=A1 * 3

in cell B1, Excel will display the error message "Can't resolve circular references." You can get around this error by pressing RETURN or clicking the OK button in the message box. Excel then stores a value of 0 in the offending cell. Because cell A1 depends on B1 for its result, and cell B1 depends on A1 for its result, a spreadsheet attempting to calculate a formula normally would get locked into an endless loop, with the computer, in effect, chasing its own tail. Most spreadsheets, including Excel, provide an error message if you create a formula that results in a circular reference so that you can track down the offending formula and correct the error. However, there are ways to use intentional circular references. These are discussed in Chapter 11, "Assorted Features."

chapter **4**

CHANGING A WORKSHEET'S APPEARANCE

The previous chapter touched on the formatting of cells as one way to affect the appearance of a worksheet. This chapter will show you the other methods you can use to change the style and appearance of your worksheets.

An example of the flexibility offered by Excel in changing a worksheet's appearance can be seen in the difference between Figure 4-1 and Figure 4-2. In Figure 4-1, the absence of any formatting makes for a worksheet that appears busy or visually crowded. Figure 4-2 shows the same worksheet, but its appearance has been improved with various formatting options offered by Excel.

You'll find the commands you need to perform such changes under the Format and Options menus. The Format menu offers the Number, Alignment, Font, Border, Cell Protection, Row Height, Column Width, and Justify commands. These commands affect the formatting of data in different ways. From the Options menu, the Display command affects some overall characteristics of a worksheet's display, such as

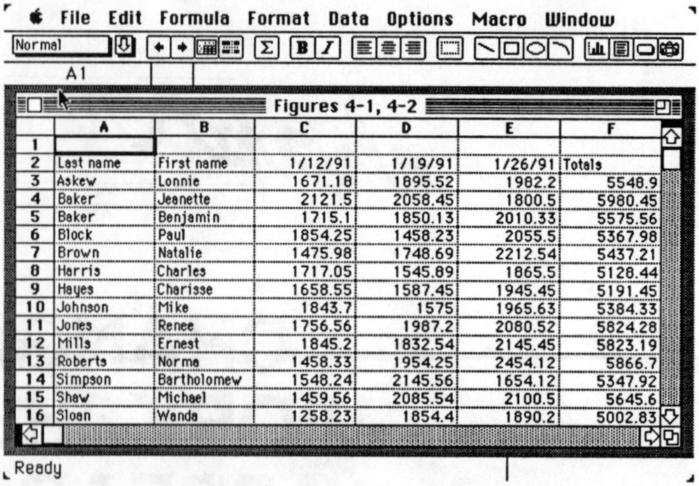

FIGURE 4-1. Sample worksheet without formatting

whether gridlines or row and column headings appear, and what colors are used (by hardware that supports the display or printing of color).

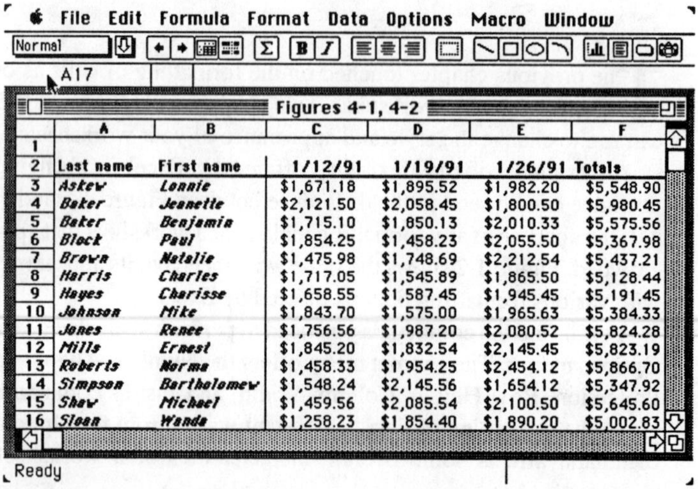

FIGURE 4-2. Sample worksheet with formatting

As you learned earlier, you can apply a number format to a selection by making the selection and choosing Number from the Format menu, and then selecting the desired format from the list box that appears. The entire selection then takes on the characteristics of the chosen format, and any values or results of formulas in cells within that selection will be displayed according to your chosen format. If you decide you no longer want a group of cells formatted, select the cells, choose Clear from the Edit menu, and double-click the Formats button when the dialog box appears. This action will clear all formats from the selected cells, and the cells will revert to the General format.

 Remember, you can select common formats, such as Currency and Percent, by highlighting a selection, clicking on the down arrow in the tool bar, and selecting from the list that appears.

FORMATTING TEXT

Excel applies any formatting you have chosen with the Number command to numbers only. For formatting text, you use the Alignment command. Any text entered into a cell will be left-aligned unless you use the Alignment command to tell Excel otherwise. The sample worksheet in Figure 4-3 clearly demonstrates the effects of the Alignment command on text entries. Cells B4, B6, and B8 all contain the same text, entered in an identical manner. Choosing Alignment from the Format menu provides a dialog box with five options: General, Left, Center, Right, and Fill. In this example, cell B4 was formatted with the Left option, cell B6 with the Center option, and cell B8 with the Right option.

Keep in mind that if you need to left-align, center, or right-align entries in cells, you can also use the alignment buttons on the tool bar. The left-alignment, center, and right-alignment buttons are located near the center of the tool bar. Select the desired cell or cells, click on the alignment button of your choice, and the entry will be aligned.

One pleasant trait of Excel is its ability to align text that overruns a cell. If you enter a label that is too long for a particular cell and the adjacent cells are blank, Excel will use the adjacent cells automatically and align the text properly, as shown in Figure 4-4. This is helpful when you are creating descriptive titles within your worksheet.

Using the Fill Option

Use the Fill option of the Alignment command to fill a cell (or a selection of cells) with a single character. You can use this option with any character, but it is usually

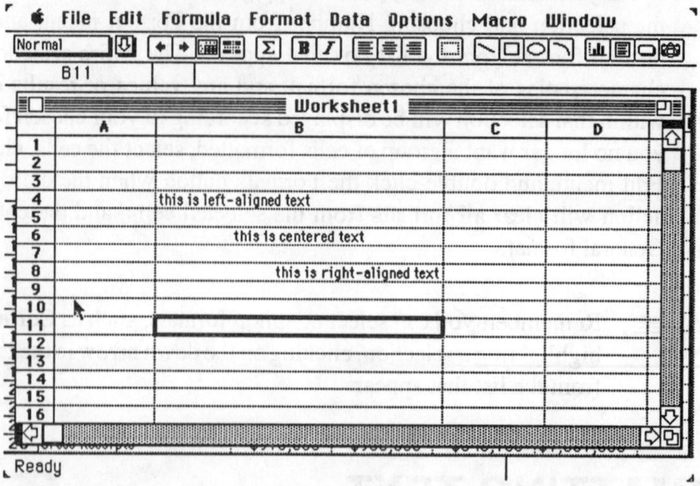

FIGURE 4-3. Sample worksheet containing text

used with punctuation marks (such as hyphens, asterisks, or equal signs) to quickly
fill a row of cells with a desired border or separation marker.

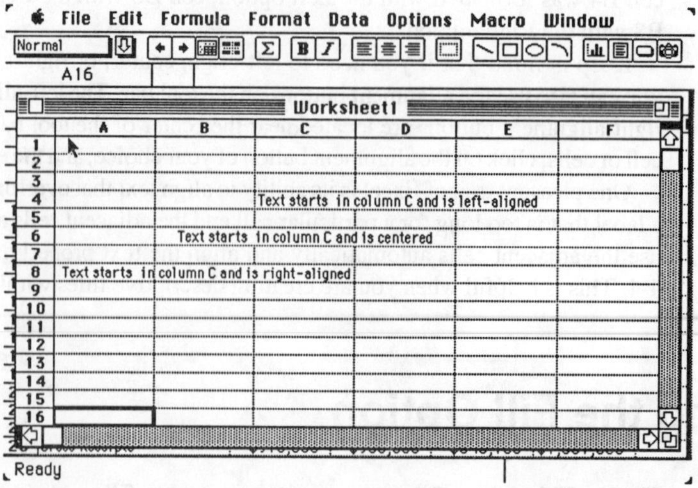

FIGURE 4-4. Effects of alignment in adjacent cells

As an example, say you have three columns of figures in columns B, C, and D, and you want a row of equal signs underneath these figures in row 10, as shown in Figure 4-5. Place the cursor in cell B10, and enter a single equal sign. Next, select the desired cells; in Figure 4-5, cells B10, C10, and D10 were selected. Then open the Format menu, choose Alignment, and double-click the Fill button. The selected cells fill with equal signs as a result.

Veteran spreadsheet users are accustomed to creating such borders by filling a cell with the desired character and duplicating the cell across a row. However, the Fill option offers a decided advantage over that method. With Fill, if you later widen a column width, you won't need to go back and add more symbols to fill the cell.

Using the Justify Command

The last command in the Format menu, Justify, also affects text. This very useful command can reshape your text to fill a group of cells. Consider the sample worksheet in Figure 4-6. A descriptive sentence of text has been entered in cells A1 and A2, just above the sales figures. The text would look better, however, if the margins of the sentence were aligned visually with the borders of the sales figures. To do this with most programs, you would have to retype the text. With Excel, however, you just select the area in which the sentence should fit. For example, you could select A1 to

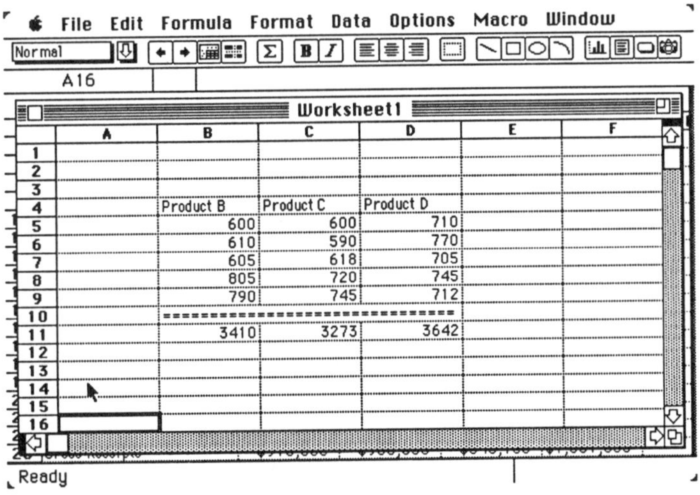

FIGURE 4-5.   Use of Fill option

```
 ╭  ● File  Edit  Formula  Format  Data  Options  Macro  Window        ╮
 │Normal  │⬇️│←│→│▦▥│Σ│B│I│▤▥▦│□│⟍□○⟋│▦▤◻◉│
 │  A16   │
```

	A	B	C	D	E	F	
1	The sales for our new product lines show seasonal variations. However, we are						
2	pleased on an overall basis with the results of our sales promotions.						
3							
4	Product A	Product B	Product C	Product D			
5	550	600	600	710			
6	580	610	590	770			
7	610	605	618	705			
8	490	805	720	745			
9	575	790	745	712			
10	=========	=========	=========	=========			
11	2805	3410	3273	3642			
12							
13							
14							
15							
16							

Ready

FIGURE 4-6.   Descriptive text before Justify

D3 in Figure 4-6's sample worksheet and then choose Justify from the Format menu. The results, shown in Figure 4-7, demonstrate the Justify command's ability to rearrange your text without the need for editing or retyping.

CHANGING FONTS

Probably the most noticeable change you can make in a worksheet is to vary your *fonts* (the style of character used). Any changes you make with the Font command will have an immediate effect on your worksheet's appearance. When you select a cell or a group of cells and choose Font from the Format menu, you see the dialog box shown here:

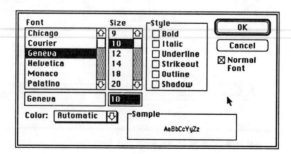

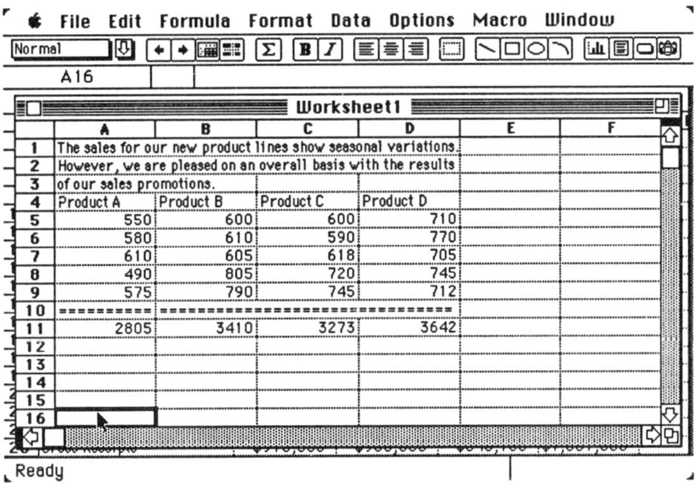

```
  ✦  File  Edit  Formula  Format  Data  Options  Macro  Window
Normal      🔲 ← → 🔳🔳 Σ B I ▤▤▤ ▢ ◥◻◻◻ ⊞▤◻🔳
     A16
```

	A	B	C	D	E	F
1	The sales for our new product lines show seasonal variations.					
2	However, we are pleased on an overall basis with the results					
3	of our sales promotions.					
4	Product A	Product B	Product C	Product D		
5	550	600	600	710		
6	580	610	590	770		
7	610	605	618	705		
8	490	805	720	745		
9	575	790	745	712		
10	=========	=========	=========	=========		
11	2805	3410	3273	3642		
12						
13						
14						
15						
16						

Ready

FIGURE 4-7. Descriptive text after Justify

Be sure to scroll up and down the dialog box to review all of the available options.

Among the choices in the Fonts dialog box are the character fonts, their sizes, possible styles (bold, italic, and so on), and a choice of colors. If your Macintosh does not have a color screen, you can still select colors for the printed output, assuming your printer supports colors. (The Apple ImageWriter II dot-matrix printer can provide color printing if a multicolor ribbon has been installed in the printer.)

Choose the font you desire by clicking its name in the list box. (Note that your available fonts may be different from those shown if you are using a printer other than the ImageWriter.) The fonts that appear in the list box depend on the fonts installed in the System File located on your startup disk. You can add new fonts by using the Font/DA Mover utility to add fonts; see your Macintosh utilities user's guide for details.

In the Size box, you can select the desired point size for the characters by clicking. Any of the desired Style options can also be selected by clicking. Once you have selected a Style option, you can deselect it if you wish by clicking the option box again. Figure 4-8 shows a sample of text using various fonts and styles.

You can change any selection you make into the standard font by choosing the desired font and clicking the Standard Font box. Once you do so, it will become the default font for all new worksheets. Use the Color options to choose a color, or click Automatic to tell Excel to use the default (system) font color.

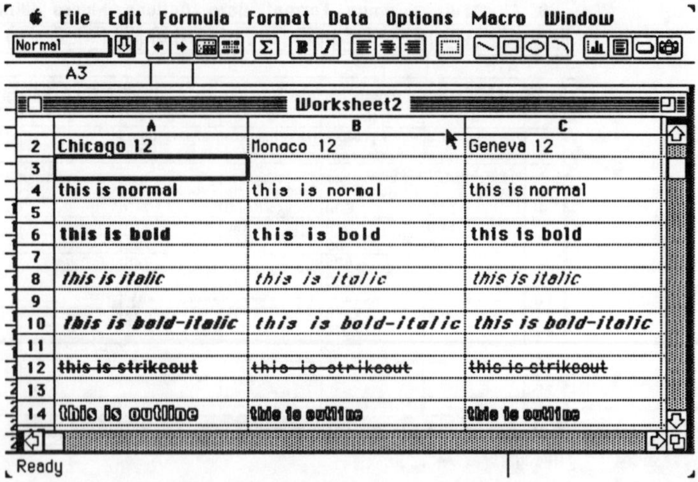

FIGURE 4-8. Sample typestyles

Remember, your choices in the Font dialog box apply only to the selected cells. This gives you great flexibility. By selecting different areas and using the Font command, you can apply different styles to different parts of a worksheet, as the example in Figure 4-8 shows.

tip If you do not need to change a font's size or type, but just want to apply bold or italic to the existing font, use the bold or italic button of the tool bar. Select the desired cells, and then click on the bold button or the italic button to apply the desired style. (The bold button is the button that contains the letter *B*, and the italic button is the button that contains the letter *I*.)

Figures 4-9 and 4-10 show how changing the Font options can affect a worksheet. Both figures show the Income worksheet you created in previous chapters. In Figure 4-9, 9-point Geneva was used as the font, and in Figure 4-10, 12-point Chicago was used as the font.

tip Users of the Apple LaserWriter printer should be aware that with fonts, what you see may not be precisely what you get. The ROM built into the LaserWriter does not support the default Macintosh fonts of Geneva and Monaco, but it does

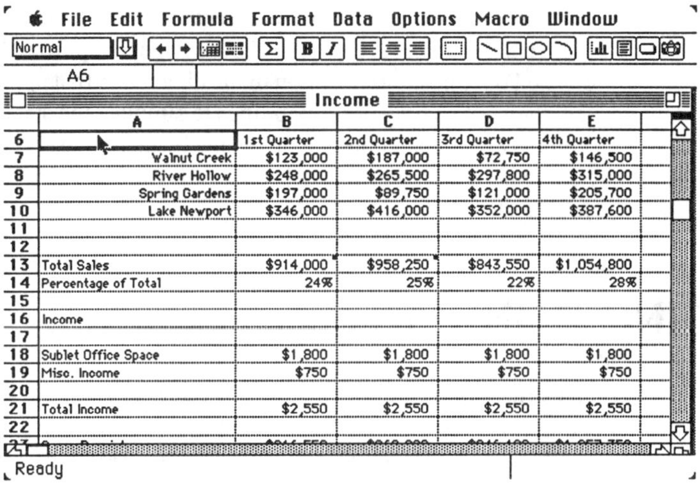

File Edit Formula Format Data Options Macro Window

	A	B	C	D	E
6		1st Quarter	2nd Quarter	3rd Quarter	4th Quarter
7	Walnut Creek	$123,000	$187,000	$72,750	$146,500
8	River Hollow	$248,000	$265,500	$297,800	$315,000
9	Spring Gardens	$197,000	$89,750	$121,000	$205,700
10	Lake Newport	$346,000	$416,000	$352,000	$387,600
11					
12					
13	Total Sales	$914,000	$958,250	$843,550	$1,054,800
14	Percentage of Total	24%	25%	22%	28%
15					
16	Income				
17					
18	Sublet Office Space	$1,800	$1,800	$1,800	$1,800
19	Misc. Income	$750	$750	$750	$750
20					
21	Total Income	$2,550	$2,550	$2,550	$2,550
22					

Ready

FIGURE 4-9.   Income worksheet in 9-point Geneva

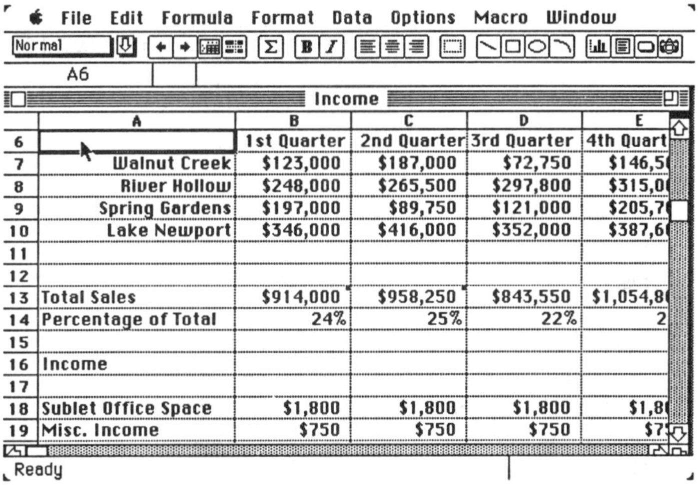

File Edit Formula Format Data Options Macro Window

	A	B	C	D	E
6		1st Quarter	2nd Quarter	3rd Quarter	4th Quart
7	Walnut Creek	$123,000	$187,000	$72,750	$146,5(
8	River Hollow	$248,000	$265,500	$297,800	$315,0(
9	Spring Gardens	$197,000	$89,750	$121,000	$205,7(
10	Lake Newport	$346,000	$416,000	$352,000	$387,6(
11					
12					
13	Total Sales	$914,000	$958,250	$843,550	$1,054,8(
14	Percentage of Total	24%	25%	22%	2
15					
16	Income				
17					
18	Sublet Office Space	$1,800	$1,800	$1,800	$1,8(
19	Misc. Income	$750	$750	$750	$7!

Ready

FIGURE 4-10.   Income worksheet in 12-point Chicago

support Helvetica and Courier. In its default mode in Excel, the LaserWriter will substitute Helvetica for the Geneva font and Courier for the Monaco font. If the results are not acceptable, choose Page Setup from the File menu and turn off the Font Substitution option in the dialog box that appears. The LaserWriter will then use its graphics capabilities to simulate the standard Macintosh fonts. You may also obtain preferable results by using LaserWriter fonts with Excel. See your LaserWriter manual for details on how to add LaserWriter fonts to your System Folder.

ADDING BORDERS

You can use the Format menu's Border command to add shaded borders or solid lines around any cell or group of cells. Borders can be placed on any side or on all four sides of a rectangular selection, and you can also shade a selection.

When you make a selection and choose Border from the Format menu, the following dialog box appears:

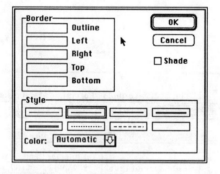

The Outline option places a solid line around the selection. The Left, Right, Top, and Bottom options place a line to the left, to the right, above, or below a selection, respectively. The Style option governs the type of lines used to construct the border, and the Color option defines the colors used (on systems with color capabilities). Checking the Shade box causes the selection to be shaded. The worksheet shown in Figure 4-11 makes use of various border options.

If you no longer want an existing border, simply select the cells that contain the border. Then choose the Border command and turn off the previously selected options. When you click OK, Excel will remove the existing border.

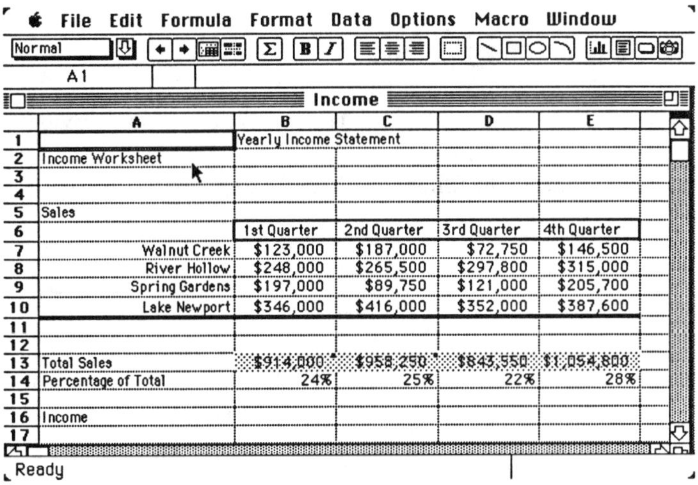

 File Edit Formula Format Data Options Macro Window

		Income			
	A	**B**	**C**	**D**	**E**
1		Yearly Income Statement			
2	Income Worksheet				
3					
4					
5	Sales				
6		1st Quarter	2nd Quarter	3rd Quarter	4th Quarter
7	Walnut Creek	$123,000	$187,000	$72,750	$146,500
8	River Hollow	$248,000	$265,500	$297,800	$315,000
9	Spring Gardens	$197,000	$89,750	$121,000	$205,700
10	Lake Newport	$346,000	$416,000	$352,000	$387,600
11					
12					
13	Total Sales	$914,000	$958,250	$843,550	$1,054,800
14	Percentage of Total	24%	25%	22%	28%
15					
16	Income				
17					

Ready

FIGURE 4-11.   Worksheet formatted with Border options

ADJUSTING ROW HEIGHTS AND COLUMN WIDTHS

The Row Height and Column Width commands can be used to change the height of one or more rows and the width of one or more columns. First, select the desired rows or columns to be changed. With the selection made, choose Row Height or Column Width from the Format menu. When the dialog box appears, enter the desired height or width. If you want the new height or width to become the standard for all new worksheets you create, click the Standard Height or Standard Width box within the dialog box after you've entered the new value.

In the case of Column Width, you can check the Best Fit button in the dialog box, and Excel will size the column to fit the widest entry. This is useful with large worksheets, where you may not be able to identify the widest entry easily.

CHANGING THE DISPLAY OPTIONS

The Display command, located on the Options menu, provides options that affect the entire display of the worksheet. When you choose the Display command from the Options menu, the following dialog box appears:

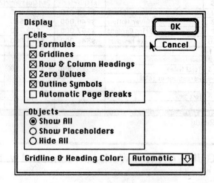

Six options are available: Formulas, Gridlines, Row and Column Headings, Zero Values, Outline Symbols, and Automatic Page Breaks. Once you have selected any desired options, you can click the OK button or press RETURN to implement the changes.

Selecting the Formulas option displays the actual formulas (rather than the resulting values) within the cells that contain formulas. The Gridlines option is used to display or hide the fine lines outlining each cell. Hiding these lines can be very useful for final versions of presentation worksheets. The Row and Column Headings option is used to display or hide the row and column headings. The Zero Values option is used to display or hide zero values; if this option is turned off, cells containing a zero value will appear blank.

The Outline Symbols check box determines whether outline symbols are visible when you use outlines (outlines are covered in Chapter 11). The Automatic Page Breaks check box determines whether page breaks in large worksheets are displayed (if displayed, they appear as dotted lines).

The Show All, Show Placeholders, and Hide All buttons apply to graphic objects added to a worksheet. You can speed up scrolling of a worksheet by choosing Hide All or Show Placeholders. When Show All is chosen, any graphic objects present will appear, but scrolling will be slow.

Note that you can also select various gridline and heading colors by clicking the color options at the bottom of the dialog box.

Figure 4-12 shows the worksheet previously displayed in Figure 4-11, but with the gridlines and row and column headings turned off. Note that the borders are more clearly visible when the gridlines have been removed.

A FORMATTING EXERCISE

The formatting powers of Excel can prove quite useful in today's office, where your coworker may be using desktop publishing software to make her reports outshine yours. Often, worksheets must be integrated into reports, and you may wish to produce a worksheet like the one in Figure 4-13.

With some other spreadsheet programs, you are faced with two options for integrating spreadsheet data into a report. You can print the spreadsheet, trim the edges, and paste it into a word processing document, hoping that the pasted edges won't show in reproduced copies. A better method is to copy the data into the Macintosh Clipboard, exit Excel, load another application, and paste the data from the Clipboard into the other document. You can use either method with Excel, but Excel's advanced formatting options offer yet another alternative: using the Excel worksheet itself as the report.

The report shown in Figure 4-13 was produced entirely within Excel. The following steps show you how to format an Excel worksheet in this manner. If you decide to try

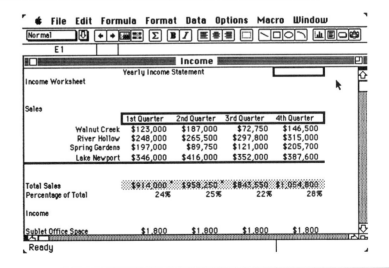

FIGURE 4-12.   Worksheet without gridlines

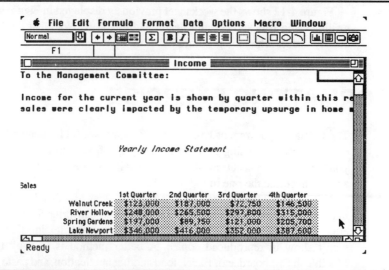

═══════ **FIGURE 4-13.**   Completed Income worksheet

this example, be sure that you have saved the Income worksheet before making these changes; you will want to use the Income worksheet in its current form in later chapters.

The first step in formatting the worksheet to serve as a management report is to add seven new rows at the top of the worksheet. (These rows are used for the text that appears above the worksheet data.) You can do this by clicking and dragging down row headings 1 through 7 with the mouse. After you select the first seven rows, open the Edit menu and select Insert to insert the new rows. Then enter the following text in the appropriate cells:

Cell	Text
A1	To the Management Committee:
A3	Income for the current year is shown by quarter within this report.
A4	Note that 3rd quarter sales were clearly impacted by the temporary upsurge in home mortgage interest rates.
A33	Barring any unforeseen increase in the nation's prime, or a downturn in the economy,
A34	we expect continued strong performance as our new Kingstream subdivision comes on-line.

Select the range from cell A3 to E5. Open the Format menu, and choose Justify to neatly format the text within the selected range.

The text would also appear more dominant in boldface type. Select cells A1 through A5. Open the Format menu and select the Font command. Assuming you are using an Apple Imagewriter printer, the six default fonts that appear in the dialog box are Chicago, Courier, Geneva, Helvetica, Monaco, and Palatino. Since a bold type is desired for the selected text, select Monaco. Then choose 12 as the desired size and click the Bold option's check box. Finally, click OK to accept these selections.

Next, select cells A33 through A34, open the Format menu, and again select the Font command. Choose Monaco 12, click Bold, and click the OK button to implement the change.

The worksheet heading, "Yearly Income Statement," would look attractive in italic, so move the cursor to cell B8. Open the Format menu, select the Font command, and choose Monaco 12. Then click Italic. Press RETURN or click the OK button to implement the change. With the new descriptive text, the title "Income Worksheet" in cell A9 is no longer necessary. Go to cell A9, and press COMMAND-B to clear the cell.

For additional emphasis, the sales figures should be highlighted in this report. Do this with the shading options available through the Options menu. First select the cells from B14 to E17. Open the Format menu, and select the Border command. Click the Shade option to select it, and then click OK.

You can use the same Border command to underline the last row of sales figures. Select cells B17 through E17. Open the Format menu and choose the Border command. Select the Bottom option and then click the OK button. The bottom row of figures is now underlined.

To differentiate the sales figures from the other income figures, add a solid border around the other income figures. Select the area from cell B25 to cell E30, open the Format menu, and choose the Border command. Select the Outline option and then click the OK button. A solid line appears around the selected area.

The dotted lines dividing the cells are no longer needed, nor are the row or column headings. Open the Options menu and select Display. Turn off the Gridline and the Row and Column Heading options by clicking each box. Then click the OK box. The worksheet reappears without the gridlines and headings.

Before printing the results, save this worksheet under a different name. Open the File menu, but *don't* choose Save; instead, select the Save As command. When the Save Worksheet As dialog box appears, enter **INCOME REPORT 1** as the file name and press RETURN. Then open the File menu, select the Print command, and click the OK button from the dialog box that appears. Within a moment, your printer should print the completed report.

The commands and options presented in this chapter affect the appearance of your worksheet both on the screen and when it is printed. Other commands, which are discussed in Chapter 6, change only the printed appearance of a worksheet.

chapter 5

CHARTING A WORKSHEET

Excel offers powerful graphics capabilities for displaying and printing charts. You can prepare charts for data analysis or for presentation-quality reports. Excel provides you with a rich assortment of formatting features and options for enhancing the appearance of your charts.

A TYPICAL CHART

Figure 5-1 shows some typical charts generated with Excel. Charts consist primarily of *markers* representing the data contained within the worksheet. The appearance of the markers varies, depending on the type of chart you select. In a bar or column chart, the markers appear as columns; in a line chart, the markers appear as lines composed of small symbols. The markers in a pie chart appear as wedges of the pie. All charts except for pie charts have two axes: a horizontal axis called the *category axis* and a vertical axis called the *value axis*.

A chart can also contain gridlines, which provide a frame of reference for the values shown on the value axis. You can add descriptive text to a chart, such as a title, and you can place this text in different locations. Your chart can also contain a legend that indicates which data the markers represent.

EMBEDDED CHARTS VERSUS STAND-ALONE CHARTS

All versions of Excel from 3.0 onward can produce both stand-alone charts and embedded charts. Stand-alone charts are separate documents, and are stored as separate files. Embedded charts are charts that appear on the worksheet, and are stored along with the worksheet.

There will be times when you want to use both types of charts. For example, if you want to provide a worksheet for a presentation and you want a graph to be visible simultaneously with the worksheet, you will probably want to embed the graph on the worksheet. On the other hand, if you want to be able to display or print the chart by itself, you'll want to create and store it as a stand-alone chart. The first portion of this

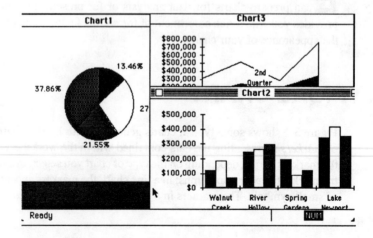

FIGURE 5-1.   Typical charts

chapter deals primarily with stand-alone charts. Embedded charts are covered in the latter portion of the chapter.

MAKING A SIMPLE CHART

Excel's built-in features make it very easy to produce a chart. The basic steps for creating a chart are as follows:

1. Select the area to be charted.

2. Open the File menu and choose the Chart command.

3. Select the OK button in the Chart dialog box that appears.

At first glance, you might think that producing a chart must be more complicated. It can be. Charts can be as simple or as complex as you care to make them. Thanks to Excel's flexible options, you can experiment with different types of charts, customized text and legends, and fancy formatting. If all you need is a basic chart, however, these three steps can produce a complete chart for you.

The Income worksheet described in Chapters 3 and 4 is an ideal candidate for a chart, because it contains categorical data that varies over a period of time. The first step in making the chart is to select the area you want charted. For this example, let's use the numbers for the first and second quarters, which are found in the area from cell B7 through C10. These are the only cells needed for charting the information, but it would be helpful to include the labels in column A in the selected area as well. Excel can automatically assign these names to the chart markers. Select the area from cell A7 through cell C10. The selection should include Walnut Creek, River Hollow, Spring Gardens, Lake Newport, and the sales figures for the first and second quarters for these developments.

Next, open the File menu and choose the New command. The dialog box shown here appears.

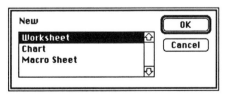

The Worksheet option lets you open another worksheet. The Macro option is covered in Chapter 10. For now, select the Chart option, and then select the OK button. The following chart will appear on your screen.

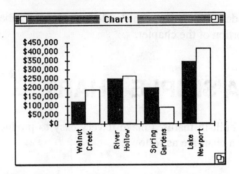

Excel has made a number of assumptions to make the job of drawing the chart less complex. First, Excel assumed that you desired a standard vertical bar chart (a column chart, in Excel terminology). Because your worksheet values are formatted to display dollar signs and commas, Excel displays these numbers on the value axis in the same manner. The names of each development have been taken from cells A7 through A10 and inserted as labels underneath each group of markers. (If you don't see a column chart when you select Chart, the default settings in your Excel package have been changed. Don't be too concerned; you will soon learn how to change the type of chart Excel displays.)

You may also notice that the menu commands have changed. When you open a chart, Excel provides a different set of menu commands than it does for the worksheet. The File, Edit, Macro, and Window menus perform similarly to their worksheet menu equivalents. The Format menu lets you change the type and format settings of the chart.

Two new menus, the Gallery menu and the Chart menu, let you select the type of chart (bar, pie, line, scatter, area, 3-D, or a combination of these types) and add arrows, legends, and gridlines. For example, you might prefer the sales figures to be displayed as a pie chart. Open the Gallery menu and choose the Pie command. A display of six different styles of pie charts should appear, as shown here:

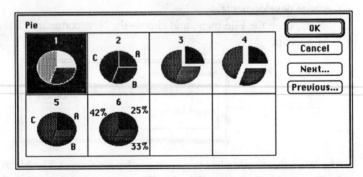

You can select a style by pressing its number or by clicking the desired box. After you have highlighted the selection, press RETURN or click the OK button to display

the chart. In this case, enter **6** to select option number 6 from the available styles. Press
RETURN or click the OK button, and you should see a chart resembling this one:

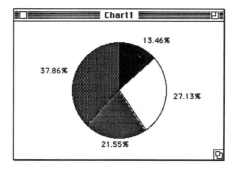

MULTIPLE CHARTS

Excel lets you open more than one chart at a time. You can graph the same data or
different data and display different charts on the screen by resizing and moving the
windows containing the charts. To see an example, click anywhere in the worksheet,
or choose Income from the Window menu. Then open the File menu and choose New.
From the dialog box, select Chart. Press RETURN or click the OK button to draw the chart.

Open the Gallery menu and select Line. When the gallery of line charts appears,
press RETURN or click OK to accept the default selection. The chart should be redrawn
as a line chart. Click anywhere in the title bar, and drag the new chart to the lower-right
corner of the screen. Then choose Chart1 from the Window menu. Portions of both
charts should now be visible. You can make either chart the active chart by clicking
anywhere in the chart or by opening the Window menu and selecting the chart by
name from the list of names that appears in the window.

Excel's ability to display multiple charts at the same time is often helpful for
analyzing data. When you are working with charts, you may want to open several
different types simultaneously to get an idea of the style that works best for your
application.

SAVING CHARTS

Charts can be saved on disk just as worksheets can. In addition, charts that are part of
a worksheet are saved with that worksheet. Some popular spreadsheet programs save
graphics data as a named range in the worksheet. As noted earlier, Excel provides a
more flexible approach by letting you save charts as individual files, or as portions of

a worksheet (but you need not name any range to do so). A major advantage of this choice is familiarity: Users who already know how to save a worksheet file will know how to save a chart file, because the commands are the same.

 As with worksheets, you can use the COMMAND-S hot key to save the active chart.

With either chart active, open the File menu now and choose the Save command. Because you have not saved this chart before, a dialog box asks you for a name for the file. Enter **Income Chart 1** and press RETURN to save the chart. The Save command saves only the active chart. If other new charts are also open, you must save them individually if you want permanent copies of them on disk.

PRINTING A CHART

To print a chart, make sure your printer is turned on, open the File menu, and choose the Print command. Note that the dialog box contains options similar to those available when you print a worksheet. For this example, press RETURN to accept the default options, and the chart will be printed. Additional options for printing charts are detailed in Chapter 6.

If you encounter difficulties in printing your chart, you may want to check your printer selection. Open the Apple menu and select the Chooser option. Make sure your printer is properly identified and that Excel is using the correct printer connection. If your Macintosh is connected to a local area network, you may need to contact your network administrator for assistance in printing charts.

THE PARTS OF A CHART

Before you explore the options Excel offers for creating charts, you should know the parts of a chart and the terminology used to describe these parts. Refer to Figure 5-2 as you read through this section.

CHART   The chart is the entire area contained within the chart window.

PLOT AREA   The plot area contains the chart's essential data: the value axis, the category axis, and all markers that indicate the relative values of your data.

AXES   Axes are the horizontal and vertical frames of reference that appear in all types of charts except pie charts. The horizontal x-axis is called the category axis because categories of data are plotted along this line. The vertical y-axis is called the value axis because values are shown along this line.

TICK MARKS   Tick marks are reference marks that separate the scales of the value axis and the categories of the category axis.

TICK-MARK LABELS   Tick-mark labels describe the categories or values. Excel automatically adds tick-mark labels to a chart if they are included in the left row or top row of the selected range of your worksheet. Excel also determines the format of tick-mark labels along the value axis based on their format in the worksheet. For example, if your worksheet entries have dollar signs, the labels along the value axis will also have dollar signs.

GRIDLINES   Gridlines are reference lines that extend the tick marks across the entire area of the graph.

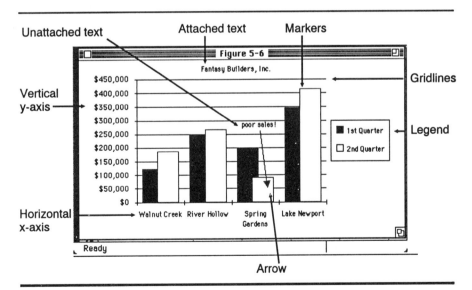

FIGURE 5-2.   Parts of a chart

MARKERS Markers are the bars, lines, points, or pie wedges that represent the actual data in the chart. The form of the markers depends on the type of chart you choose. In a pie chart, the markers are wedges, or slices, of the pie. In a line chart, the markers are solid lines, although at some sharp angles, the lines in a line chart may appear jagged or broken; this is due to the limitations of the screen. In a column chart, such as the one shown in Figure 5-2, the markers appear as columns.

Note that each set of markers in the chart represents a set of values within the worksheet. The set of values represented by the markers is referred to as a *data series*. If a chart displays data from more than one data series, each data series will be represented by a different pattern or symbol. In Figure 5-2, for example, the first-quarter data is one data series and the second-quarter data is another. Data series are further differentiated by the pattern or shadings of the columns.

If you selected a range in the worksheet that contains only one row or column of data, the chart contains only one data series. In a chart with a single data series, Excel takes any label in the extreme left column or top row of the selected range and automatically inserts that name as a title for the chart.

SERIES NAMES Series names can be assigned to each series of data contained in a chart. Excel automatically assumes series names based on the headings in your worksheets.

LEGENDS A legend defines the patterns (shadings) in the chart. It consists of a sample of the pattern followed by the series name (or the category name, if the chart displays only one data series). If you include labels as series names in the top row or left column of the selected worksheet range, Excel automatically uses those names in the legend.

ATTACHED TEXT Text can be attached to different portions of the chart. You can attach text to the value axis, the category axis, or to an individual data series or data point. Attached text can also take the form of a title, which can appear at the top or bottom of the chart.

UNATTACHED TEXT You can place unattached text, usually pertinent notes about your data, anywhere in the chart.

ARROWS Excel lets you add arrows to a chart to highlight particular information.

TYPES OF CHARTS

Excel offers eleven types, or *galleries,* of charts: area, bar, column, line, pie, scatter, 3-D area, 3-D column, 3-D line, and 3-D pie, as well as combinations of these types. Another type of chart, known as *high-low-close,* is commonly used to track investments. It can be created by using one of the options within the Line gallery.

You can choose any of Excel's available chart formats from the Gallery menu. For each format, the process of selection is the same. First you choose a chart type from the available options in the Gallery menu. When you do so, a gallery of formats for that type of chart appears on the screen. You then choose the desired format from the gallery and select the OK button. The chart is then drawn according to the data series selected within your worksheet.

The eleven galleries provide numerous style options for a total of 68 different chart formats. In addition, you can customize these formats to develop your own. Figure 5-3 shows the eleven different types of charts available from the Gallery menu. The potential uses for each type of chart are described here:

- Area charts show the importance of data over a period of time. Visually, area charts are cumulative in nature; they highlight the magnitude of the change instead of the rate of change.

- Bar charts provide a horizontally oriented visual emphasis of different values.

- Column charts are similar to bar charts, but they provide a vertical emphasis for the different values, which is suitable for showing comparisons among various units of data. Any passage of time is more visually evident with a column chart. It is common to place earlier data to the left and later data to the right, when you are representing data such as figures from successive months or years.

- Line charts are suited for showing a particular trend across a period of time. Line charts are visually similar to area charts, but line charts highlight the magnitude of the change rather than the rate of the change. Included in this category are high-low-close charts for stocks and for volume, which are used for showing relationships among the prices of securities over a period of time.

- Pie charts show a relationship between the parts of a "picture" or between one part and the entire picture. Because each section of the pie represents a portion of a total series, a pie chart can only represent a single data series.

- 3-D charts (available in area, column, line, or pie format) add a three-dimensional appearance to the types of charts described previously.

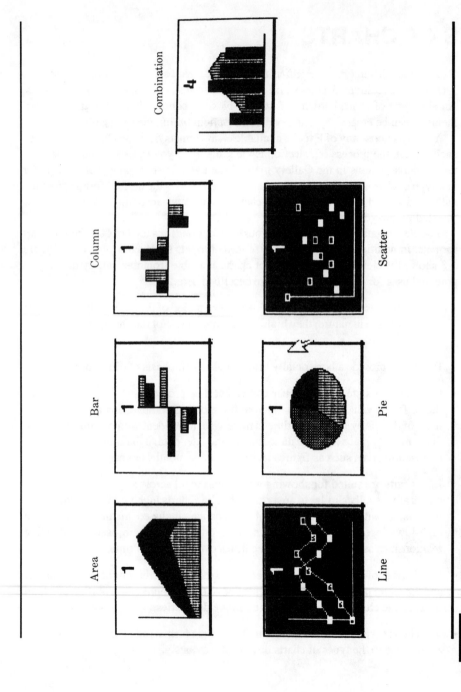

FIGURE 5-3. Types of charts

- Scatter charts show the relationship among various points of data. They are quite useful in scientific applications and for x-y axes charts that plot the coordinates of x and y data points.

- Combination charts combine several chart types in a single chart. This special feature of Excel's graphics can be quite useful for showing relationships between different types of data. For example, a combination chart might be used to emphasize the difference between sales and net profits. Combination charts are standardized versions of overlay charts, which are explained in detail later in this chapter.

Open the Gallery menu now and choose Area. The Gallery menu for area charts, shown here, appears instantly on the screen.

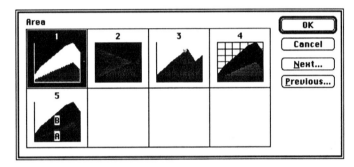

This menu offers five designs for area charts. You can select a gallery option in one of two ways: by entering the number of the desired choice, or by clicking the desired choice to select it. Once a particular choice has been selected, you can press RETURN or click the OK button to implement the choice. (As with most selections, you can also double-click on any desired choice to select it and confirm the selection simultaneously.)

The Gallery menu has two useful buttons: Next and Previous. These can be used to switch between the next and previous gallery styles. You can repeatedly click the Next or the Previous button to move among the galleries.

Experiment with this feature by selecting different types of charts from the Area menu and from the other Gallery commands. Afterwards, return to a column chart by choosing the Column command from the Gallery menu.

CHART MENUS

Excel provides seven chart menus: File, Edit, Gallery, Chart, Format, Macro, and Window. The following sections explore these menus.

The File Menu

The File menu contains commands that are, for the most part, identical to those used with worksheets. Two commands differ slightly from their counterparts in the worksheet File menu—the Page Setup and the Print commands. The Page Setup command used with charts lacks the Gridlines and Row and Column Headings options, because these are not needed with charts. The Print command lacks the options for printing notes, because notes cannot be attached to a chart. A Print Using Color option appears in the Print dialog box that you see when the Print command is chosen. This option allows color printing on hardware that supports the use of color.

The Edit Menu

The chart Edit menu is similar to the worksheet Edit menu, although it lacks the Delete, Insert, Fill Right, and Fill Down commands. All other commands in the Chart Edit menu are identical to those in the Edit menu used with worksheets.

The Gallery Menu

The following Gallery menu is not included in worksheet menus.

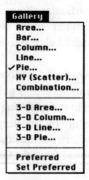

It provides eleven types of charts (galleries). In addition to the gallery types, the menu provides the Preferred command, which tells Excel to make the active chart follow a preferred format.

The preferred format is the highlighted format that appears by default in the Column gallery. You can use the Set Preferred command to make any style of chart the preferred format. To use this command, you simply change the format in the active chart to the desired format, and then select the Set Preferred command. From then on, each new chart created in Excel will assume that format. You can change the preferred chart back to the default (the first format in the Column gallery) by clearing the active chart window of any format, opening the Column gallery and choosing the first format, and then using the Set Preferred command.

The Chart Menu

Like the Gallery menu, the Chart menu, shown here, is used only with charts.

```
┌─────────────────────────┐
│ Chart                   │
├─────────────────────────┤
│ Attach Text...          │
│ Add Arrow               │
│ Add Legend              │
│ Axes...                 │
│ Gridlines...            │
│ Add Overlay             │
│ Edit Series...          │
├─────────────────────────┤
│ Select Chart        ⌘A  │
│ Select Plot Area        │
├─────────────────────────┤
│ Protect Document...     │
│ Color Palette...        │
├─────────────────────────┤
│ Calculate Now       ⌘=  │
│ Short Menus             │
└─────────────────────────┘
```

It provides a number of commands that affect the appearance of objects within the chart. This menu is of major importance in dealing with charts.

The Attach Text command lets you add text to a specific part of a chart. Text can be attached at the top of a chart as a title, along the category axis, along the value axis, or at a series or data point.

The Add Arrow command lets you add arrows to a chart. Arrows are useful for drawing attention to a particular portion of the chart. You can move an arrow or change the size of the arrow by using the Size and Move commands in the Format menu or by dragging the arrow with the mouse. When you select an existing arrow, the Add Arrow command changes to Delete Arrow. You can use the Delete Arrow command to remove arrows that are no longer needed, but you must select the arrow first. Selection techniques are covered later in this chapter.

The Add Legend command adds a legend to a chart. Once you add a legend, Excel reduces the size of the chart to make room for the legend. After you add a legend, the command changes to Delete Legend, which you can use to remove a legend if it is no longer needed.

The Axes command determines the visibility of chart axis lines. You can use it to display or remove the category axis or the value axis. The Gridlines command specifies whether gridlines appear in the chart. Using check boxes in a dialog box, you can display major or minor gridlines that extend from the value axis or the category axis.

The Add Overlay command lets you add an overlay chart to an existing chart. The existing chart (underneath) then becomes the *main chart,* and the added chart is the *overlay chart.* When you add an overlay chart, the menu command changes to Delete Overlay, which you can use to remove the overlay chart if desired. The Edit Series command lets you edit a data series used to compose the markers of a chart (this topic is covered later in this chapter).

The Select Chart command selects the complete chart. Once a chart has been selected, you can use the Copy command to copy the entire chart to another chart window, or you can use various commands in the Format menu to alter its appearance.

The Select Plot Area command selects the plot area, which is the area that falls within the axis boundaries. After selecting the plot area, you can use various commands in the Format menu to alter its appearance. Techniques for altering the appearance of the chart and the plot area are discussed later in this chapter.

The Protect Document command provides password protection for a chart's data series, formats, and windows. When you use this command, a dialog box requests a password. You are also given the option of protecting the chart's contents, the sizing and arrangements of the windows, or both. Once the password has been entered, all menu choices that would allow modifications to the chart become unavailable, and the Protect Document command changes to Unprotect Document. To allow changes to the chart, you must use the Unprotect Document command to remove the password protection. Note that there is no way to unprotect a chart without the password once one has been entered. If you use this command, you should make a written note of your password and keep it in a safe place.

The Color Palette command displays a palette of available colors that can be used for displaying or printing charts in color. (Your hardware must support color to display or print color charts.)

The Calculate Now command recalculates worksheets and redraws the charts that are dependent on those worksheets. If you turn off the Manual Calculation option in your worksheet, you must use the Calculate Now command to display a chart accurately after changes have been made to the corresponding worksheet values or formulas.

The Short Menus command lets you display only the most commonly used chart commands. Once you use this command, it changes to Full Menus, which you can use to restore the complete chart menus.

The Format Menu

The Format menu, shown here,

provides ten commands that affect the format of a chart in various ways. Most of these commands are dimmed on the menu until an applicable object on the chart has been selected. The commands in the chart Format menu operate very differently than the commands in the worksheet Format menu. The following sections describe how each of these commands work.

PATTERNS   The Patterns command is used to change the patterns and colors (on machines with color monitors) of the object selected within the chart. When you select all or part of a chart and then use the Patterns command, the dialog box shown here appears.

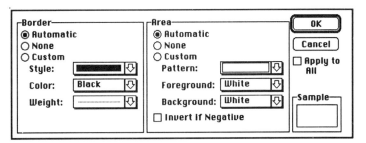

As the dialog box indicates, the Patterns command affects two general areas: the borders of the chart and the areas within the chart.

The Border Style, Border Color, and Border Weight options let you change the style, color, and thickness of the chart borders. The Automatic option, which applies to the borders of markers, tells Excel to apply the patterns to the data points or data series in the order in which the patterns are displayed in the dialog box. The Shadow option provides a shadow along the edges of the borders. The Apply to All option, which appears only when a data series or data point is selected, applies your chosen options to all of the data series or data points. Note that the Shadow, Font, and Apply to All options do not always appear in the dialog box; they appear only if your selection requires them to be included as options.

The Area Pattern, Foreground Color, and Background Color options let you change the appearance of the patterns in the plot area. The pattern and colors you choose apply to the object you have selected in the chart. The Automatic option applies to data points and series. This option tells Excel to apply the patterns to the data points or series in the order in which they appear in the dialog box. The Invert If Negative option, which appears if markers are selected, tells Excel to invert the pattern shading of negative values.

Selecting the Font button, if it is displayed in the dialog box, causes the Font dialog box to appear. This action is equivalent to choosing the Font command from the Format menu.

FONT   The Font command lets you change the style of the fonts used for the text and numbers displayed in the chart. When you select an object containing text and use the Font command, a Font dialog box like the one shown here is displayed.

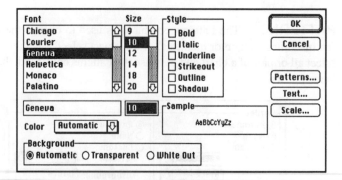

This box contains various options for font sizes and styles (and for font colors, when they are supported by the hardware.) Note that the fonts displayed in the list box depend on the system fonts you have installed on your startup disk.

Selecting the Patterns button in the Font dialog box causes the Patterns dialog box to appear. If a Scale button is available in the dialog box, selecting it makes the Scale dialog box appear. This is equivalent to selecting the Scale command from the Format menu.

TEXT   The Text command is used to format attached or unattached text contained within a chart. When you select a text object and use the Text command, the dialog box shown here appears.

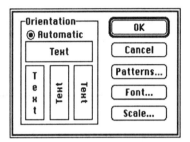

Using the options provided in this box, you can change the horizontal or vertical alignment of the text. The Vertical Text option formats the text vertically. The Automatic option aligns the text automatically, using Excel's best guess. The results of this command vary according to the type of chart and chart text you select.

The Show Value and Show Key options appear when the selected text is attached to a data point. When chosen, Show Value replaces the attached text with the value of the data point. Show Key, when selected, shows the pattern used by the data point beside the attached text.

SCALE   The Scale command lets you change the specifications behind the scales that appear along the value and category axes. When you select a chart axis and use the Scale command, one of two possible dialog boxes appears, depending on whether you have selected the Category Axis or the Value Axis option (see Figure 5-4).

From the Category Axis Scale dialog box, you can choose

- The number at the point where the value and category axes intersect

- The number of categories between tick labels or tick marks

- Whether the value axis crosses the category axis between the categories

- Whether a value axis crosses the category axis after the maximum or last category

- Whether categories are presented in the same order as is shown on the worksheet, or in reverse order (right to left instead of left to right)

From the Value Axis Scale dialog box, you can choose

- The minimum and maximum values for the axis

- The values used to determine the major and minor units

- A logarithmic scale

- Whether the values are displayed in reverse order (lowest value at the top of the chart, rather than at the bottom)

- Where the category axis crosses the value axis

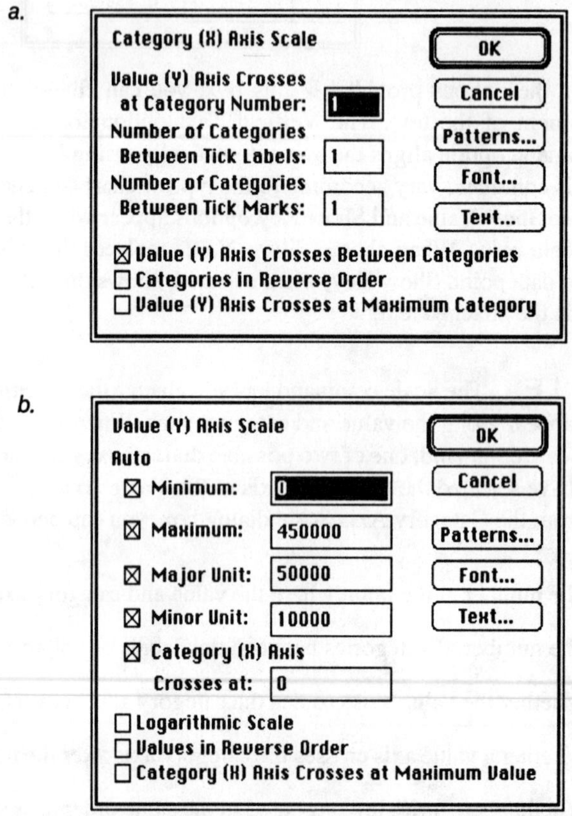

a.

Category (X) Axis Scale

Value (Y) Axis Crosses
at Category Number: `1`

Number of Categories
Between Tick Labels: `1`

Number of Categories
Between Tick Marks: `1`

[OK]
[Cancel]
[Patterns...]
[Font...]
[Text...]

☒ Value (Y) Axis Crosses Between Categories
☐ Categories in Reverse Order
☐ Value (Y) Axis Crosses at Maximum Category

b.

Value (Y) Axis Scale

Auto

☒ Minimum: `0`

☒ Maximum: `450000`

☒ Major Unit: `50000`

☒ Minor Unit: `10000`

☒ Category (X) Axis

Crosses at: `0`

[OK]
[Cancel]
[Patterns...]
[Font...]
[Text...]

☐ Logarithmic Scale
☐ Values in Reverse Order
☐ Category (X) Axis Crosses at Maximum Value

FIGURE 5-4.   (*a*) Category Axis Scale and (*b*) Value Axis Scale dialog boxes

The Patterns and Font buttons can be used to switch to the Pattern or Font dialog boxes, respectively. The Text button can be used to switch the Text dialog box.

LEGEND   The Legend command lets you change the position of the legend on the chart. (To add a legend to a chart, choose Add Legend from the Chart menu.) The Legend command displays a dialog box containing five possible positions: bottom, corner, top, right, or left. The Top option places the legend directly above the chart, and the Bottom option places the legend directly below the chart. The Right option places the legend to the right of the chart in a vertical format, while the Left option places the legend to the left of the chart in a vertical format. The Corner option places the legend in the upper-right corner of the chart. The Legend dialog box also contains Patterns and Font buttons, which can be used to switch to the Pattern or Font dialog boxes, respectively.

MAIN CHART   The Main Chart command allows you to change the format of a chart, such as its style, whether it is stacked, or whether markers in the chart overlap other markers. Many gallery options accomplish the same results as the Main Chart command. The important difference is that the Gallery command lets you choose from among 68 standard choices for chart formats, while the Main Chart command lets you design a custom format of your own.

When you select the Main Chart command, the dialog box shown here appears:

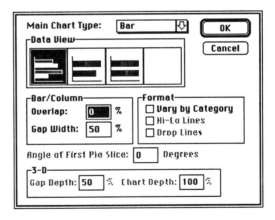

The available options depend on the type of chart selected. Bar and column charts, for example, can be stacked, but pie charts cannot.

The Type option lets you select one of ten types of charts. The Stacked option lets you stack the markers that represent different data series. In a stacked chart, the values from the first data series appear at the bottom, the values from the second data series appear above the first, and so on.

The 100 Percent option causes the values in each category to add up to 100 percent. The Vary by Category option is used when the chart plots just one data series. The resulting patterns in the chart markers will be different for each data point.

The Overlapped option lets you overlap the markers within bar or column charts. If you select this option, the Percent Overlap option can then be used to control the amount of overlap. In the two column charts shown in Figure 5-5, for example, the columns in the top chart overlap by 30 percent, and the columns in the bottom chart overlap by 70 percent.

a.

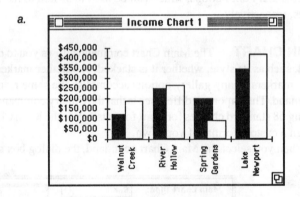

b.

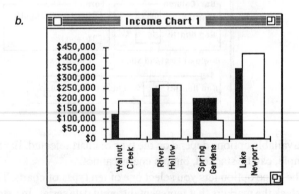

FIGURE 5-5. Chart columns overlapped (*a*) 30% and (*b*) 70%

Choosing the Drop Lines option results in vertical lines being drawn from the category axis to the highest value in that category. This style of chart is similar to options 7 and 8 in the Line gallery.

The Hi-Lo Lines option results in lines that extend from the lowest category value to the highest category value. This style of chart is similar to option 1 in the Line gallery.

The Gap Width option controls the spacing between the sets of markers in a bar or column chart. When you enter a number to represent a percentage of the width of a

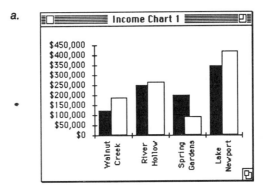

a.

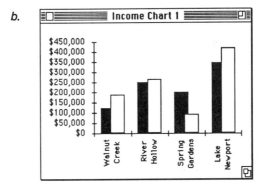

b.

FIGURE 5-6.   Cluster spacing of (a) 50% and (b) 90%

marker, the space equivalent to that percentage appears between the sets of markers. For example, Figure 5-6 shows two column charts; the first uses 50 percent Gap Width—or half the width of a column—between sets of markers, and the second uses 90 percent Gap Width—or nearly a full column width—between the sets of markers.

The Angle of First Pie Slice option applies only to pie charts. The value entered here represents the number of degrees from the "12 o'clock" position at which the top edge of the first pie slice will be placed.

OVERLAY The Overlay command is very similar to the Main Chart command—both are used to change the format of the chart. The Overlay command is available only if your chart contains an overlay chart. (Use the Add Overlay command from the Chart menu to add an overlay.) When you select the Overlay command, the dialog box that appears

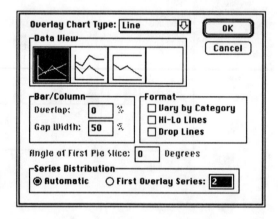

is nearly identical in operation to the one that appears for the Main Chart command. Only two options are new: First Overlay Series and Automatic. Both of these options appear at the bottom of the dialog box.

The First Overlay Series option lets you change the series that appears in the overlay chart. The number you enter for this option refers to the plot order number, contained within the series formula. For example, if a chart contains five data series and you enter **3** for this option, Excel will begin plotting the overlay chart with the third series and then continue plotting all successive series. Overlay charts are discussed in detail later in this chapter.

The Automatic option automatically divides the number of data series between the main chart and the overlay chart. If the chart contains an odd number of data series, the main chart is assigned one more series than the overlay chart.

MOVE AND SIZE   The last two commands within the Format menu, Move and Size, let you move or size selected objects (parts) of a chart by using the keyboard instead of the mouse. However, many users find such tasks easier to accomplish with the mouse, so you may not wish to use these commands.

Once you select an object and choose the Move or Size command, you can use the arrow keys to change the size or location of the particular object. After completing the changes, press RETURN to implement them. Note that not all objects in a chart can be moved or sized. If you cannot move or size an object, these menu options remain dim when the object is selected.

The Window Menu

The chart Window menu commands operate similarly to the worksheet Window menu commands. The Help command accesses the help system. The Show Clipboard command brings up the Macintosh Clipboard; you can copy portions of a chart into the Clipboard for later use in other programs. The Arrange All command lets you rearrange all open windows in a neat, layered pattern. The Hide command is used to hide an active window from view. The Unhide command displays a list of hidden windows, from which you can choose to bring a hidden window back into view.

The bottom of the Window menu contains a list of all open windows. You can make any window the active window by selecting that window from the list. Chapter 8 explains in detail how to use the Window commands effectively with charts and worksheets.

The Macro Menu

The chart Macro menu is used for the same purpose as the corresponding worksheet menu. The commands available in this menu are discussed in a later chapter.

SELECTING PARTS OF A CHART

Before applying menu selections to the parts of a chart, you must first select those parts. For example, if you want to change the way the text in a legend is displayed, you must first select the legend. Mouse users can select objects with relative ease by pointing at the desired object and clicking the mouse button to select it. If you prefer to use the keyboard, you can select objects in a chart window with the arrow keys. The LEFT ARROW and RIGHT ARROW keys move you among items in the same "class" of objects (such as markers). The UP ARROW and DOWN ARROW move you from class to class (such as from the markers, to the legend, to the axis, to the arrows, and so on). When you start working with these keys, you may find you can use the same key to select certain objects. For example, you can sometimes make the same selection with either the DOWN ARROW or the RIGHT ARROW key, depending on what class of objects is selected and how many objects are in the class.

When an object is selected, it is marked with white or black squares, depending on the type of object. Unattached text, arrows, and wedges in a pie chart are marked with black squares; other objects are marked with white squares. When an object in a chart is selected, the name of the object appears on the left side of the formula bar. Try pressing the arrow keys now, and you will see portions of the existing chart selected. An entire chart can be selected by using the Select Chart option of the Chart menu. You can also select the plot area of a chart with the Select Plot Area command in the Chart menu.

HOW EXCEL PLOTS A CHART

When you select a group of cells and open a new chart, Excel follows very specific steps to plot the chart. It first organizes the values in the marked cell range into a data series; then it plots the data series in the chart window.

Consider the chart shown in Figure 5-7. In this chart, the darker markers are based on one series of data, the sales for the first quarter. The lighter markers are based on another series of data, the sales for the second quarter. In the same chart, dollar amounts are plotted along the value axis, and subdivision names are plotted along the category axis. The chart values appear as dollars because the worksheet values are formatted in dollars. Excel obtains the category axis labels from cells A7 through A10, which contain the names of the subdivisions.

At this point, the column chart you created earlier (similar to the one in Figure 5-9) should still be open on your screen. If it isn't, plot the chart again by selecting cells A7 through C10 on the worksheet, choosing the New command from the File menu, and selecting Chart.

The exact points used to graph the data are contained in a *series formula*, which Excel builds for you. A series formula is similar to other formulas in that it can be edited from within the formula bar. To see the formula, you must first select the chart marker that is obtained from the series formula. You can select markers by using the UP ARROW or DOWN ARROW key until a small white rectangle appears within the

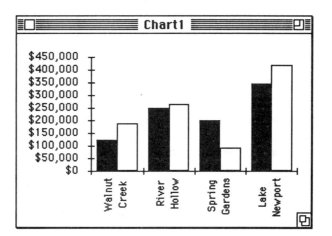

FIGURE 5-7.   Chart based on two data series

desired marker, or by clicking a marker to select that set of markers. Note that when you select a set of markers, Excel places a small rectangle in most, but not all, of the markers.

As an exercise, select the markers that represent the first-quarter sales either by pressing the DOWN ARROW key until all first-quarter markers are selected or by clicking any of the first-quarter markers. When the markers are selected, the series formula will appear in the formula bar, as shown here:

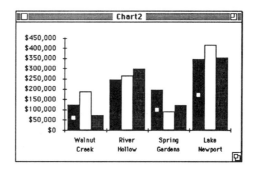

Excel uses a special function called the SERIES function to build the data series for each set of markers in the chart. The formula that results follows this general format:

=SERIES(*series name, categories reference, values reference, plot order argument*)

The series name is optional; if used, it appears in the legend when you add a legend to the chart.

The series formula currently shown in the formula bar on your screen does not contain a series name; instead, the formula starts with a comma. The next portion of the formula, Income!$A$7:$A$10, is the categories reference. Chart references always begin with an external reference, which is indicated by the name of the worksheet, followed by an exclamation point. The external reference is necessary because Excel can store worksheets and charts in separate files, so it must know which worksheet file to use when finding the data for a chart that is stored separately. Chart references also use absolute cell references, so dollar signs are included as a part of the cell ranges. As an option, you can use existing named ranges in place of the cell references.

The third portion of the formula, Income!$B$7:$B$10, is the values reference. Again, the reference must start with the name of the worksheet. The values reference tells Excel which worksheet values must be used to plot the markers. In this case, the values in cells B7 through B10 are used. The final part of the formula is the plot order argument. This integer (1, 2, 3, and so on) indicates the plot order of the markers. In this example, the number 1 indicates that the markers resulting from this formula will be the first in the series of markers. Click the second set of markers, and note the change in the series formula to reflect the points used for the second data series. Also note that the plot order argument is now 2, indicating that the resultant markers are the second markers in the series. Also notice that the values reference has changed, telling Excel to use cells C7 through C10 for plotting this set of markers. By editing the series formula, you can change the plot order argument and thus the order in which the markers appear in the chart.

═══*tip*═══ Excel can use named ranges from a worksheet in place of absolute cell references so you can make use of named ranges in your worksheets. If you create a chart that uses absolute references and you later insert rows or columns into the worksheet so that the data referred to by the chart is no longer in the same location, the chart will be unable to plot the data. The result will be a chart with zero values, or even worse, a chart with incorrect data. If you instead use named ranges in the series formula for the chart, Excel will find the data, even if you later insert rows or columns into the worksheet.

BUILDING YOUR OWN
SERIES FORMULAS

When you understand how Excel plots a chart data series, you can build your own series formulas. You can create or edit a series formula for a chart, just as you can create or edit formulas for a worksheet. You may decide to do this if you don't want to follow the assumptions Excel makes when it graphs your data.

For example, suppose you want to create a bar graph that displays the sales for your building company's first and last quarters only. You could go into the worksheet, copy the data from the first and last quarters to another area of the worksheet, redefine the range, and create a new chart. However, it would be far simpler to enter a series formula that plots the data across the desired quarters.

To do this, first click the set of markers for the first-quarter sales. Type the equal sign to begin a new formula, and enter

=SERIES(,Income!$A$7:$A$10,Income!$B$7:$B$10,1)

When you complete the entry, the graph will be redrawn, showing the markers for the new data series. Click the second set of markers, and start a new series formula for the fourth quarter by entering

=SERIES(,Income!$A$7:$A$10,Income!$E$7:$E$10,2)

The second set of markers are redrawn, reflecting the fourth-quarter sales figures.

Click on or select the third set of markers, and delete the entire formula from the formula bar. Press RETURN, and the unneeded third set of markers will be eliminated. Your chart should look similar to the one shown here:

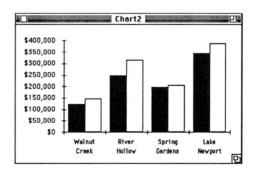

Editing a Series Formula

You can edit an existing series formula in the same way you edit any Excel formula. To edit a series formula, first select the desired markers within the chart. Then move the cursor into the formula bar, click the mouse, and use the BACKSPACE key to make the desired changes to the formula.

As an exercise, select the second set of markers, which currently represents the fourth-quarter sales. Click in the formula bar, and change the value reference from Income!$E$7:$E$10 to Income!$C$7:$C$10. When you press RETURN, the chart will be redrawn to represent the first- and second-quarter sales.

Note that most portions of a series formula are optional. The only information Excel actually needs to draw a chart is the values reference. (If you omit other information, you must include the commas that appear, or Excel will indicate an error in the series formula.) Of course, the more information you provide in the series formula, the more information Excel can make use of in plotting a detailed chart.

EXCEL'S ASSUMPTIONS

When you tell Excel to create a chart, it plots the data based on certain default assumptions. One significant decision that Excel makes is whether a data series should be based on the contents of rows or of columns. Excel assumes that a chart should contain fewer data series than data points within each series. When you tell Excel to create the chart, Excel examines your selected range of cells. If the selected range is wider than it is tall, Excel organizes the data series based on the contents of rows. On the other hand, if the selected range is taller than it is wide, Excel organizes the data series based on the contents of the columns.

To illustrate this operation, consider the chart shown in Figure 5-8. The selected range of cells to be charted is wider than it is tall. With this type of selection, Excel uses any text found in the left columns as series names. Text labels in the top row are used as categories, and each row becomes a data series in the chart.

If the data to be plotted is square (the number of rows is equal to the number of columns), Excel handles the orientation of the chart in the same manner. On the other hand, if the selected range is taller than it is wide, Excel orients the chart differently. In such cases, the text in the top row is used as the series names, text entries appearing in the left columns are used as categories, and each column becomes a data series. This type of worksheet, and the chart resulting from it, are shown in Figure 5-9.

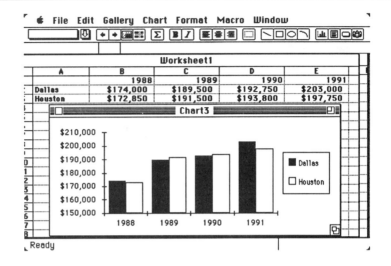

FIGURE 5-8.   Chart oriented by rows

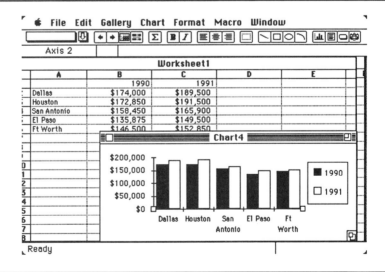

FIGURE 5-9.   Chart oriented by columns

Using Paste Special to Change Excel's Assumptions

You can use the Edit menu's Paste Special command to instruct Excel to handle these chart assumptions differently. To do so, select the range of data to be charted, and then use the Copy command from the Edit menu. Next, open a new chart with the New command from the File menu. Finally, use the Paste Special command from the Edit menu to paste the data into the chart, and indicate the orientation for the data in the appropriate dialog box.

As an exercise, consider the first- and second-quarter data in the Fantasy Builders worksheet that was charted in Figure 5-7. Since the range that was charted was taller than it was wide, each column became a data series in the resulting bar chart. Let's create another chart for the same data. First, select cells A6 through C10 on the worksheet. Open the Edit menu and choose the Copy command. The selected range is surrounded by a dotted line, indicating that the range has been copied into memory. Open the File menu and select the New command. From the dialog box that appears, choose Chart and then select OK. A chart window appears, but it is empty because you used the Copy command. The chart window is awaiting instructions from the Paste Special command.

Open the Edit menu and choose the Paste Special command. The dialog box shown here appears

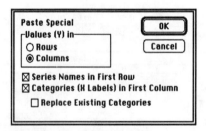

It lets you determine whether Excel should use the values in the rows or in the columns for the data series. You can also indicate whether Excel should use the names in the first row for series names, and whether labels in the first column should be used as categories.

For this exercise, choose the following options: Values in Rows, Series Names in First Column, and Categories in First Row. With these options selected, press RETURN or click the OK button. The chart is redrawn, using rows as the data series. To add a legend to the chart, open the Chart menu and select the Add Legend command. The results should resemble the chart displayed here:

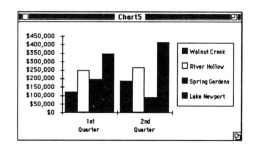

USING PASTE TO BUILD A CHART

You can also build a chart by pasting data from a worksheet into a chart window. By using Paste instead of simply selecting a range of cells, you can maintain more control over the data that is used in the chart.

To see how the Paste command works, open a new chart without selecting any data for inclusion in it. (Make sure that no area in the worksheet is currently selected; if necessary, use the Window menu to get to the worksheet and click in any blank cell to cancel a previous selection.)

Open the File menu and select the New command. From the dialog box that appears, choose Chart. When you select OK, a blank chart window appears on the screen. Remember the name assigned to the chart, because you will need to select that name to open the chart window.

You can now begin to copy and paste data into the chart; it will be graphed as you add the data. Click anywhere in the Income worksheet to switch back to the worksheet. Select cells B6 through B10. Open the Edit menu and choose Copy. Open the Window menu and choose the new chart by name. When the blank chart appears, open the Edit menu and choose Paste. You should see the data drawn in the chart.

Click anywhere in the Income worksheet to switch back to the worksheet. This time, select cells D6 through D10. Open the Edit menu and choose Copy. Open the Window menu, and again choose the chart by name. When the chart appears, open the Edit menu and choose Paste. The second range of data should be added to the chart.

Again, click anywhere in the Income worksheet to switch back to the worksheet. Select cells E6 through E10. Open the Edit menu and choose Copy. Open the Window menu and choose the chart by name. When the chart appears, open the Edit menu and choose Paste. The third range of data should be pasted into the chart. Finally, open the Chart menu and choose the Add Legend command to add a legend to the chart.

You may want to use the Paste command to chart multiple ranges of a worksheet. For example, a worksheet may contain values in rows 4 through 8 and in rows 12 through 15. This is a common business practice, because worksheet users often insert blank space between areas of similar data for visual clarity. The blanks can create a problem in a chart, because Excel interprets blank rows or columns to be zero values. Excel then adds a blank space for each blank row or column in the plotted range of data. If you care to see this problem, insert a blank row between any two housing subdivisions in your worksheet, and then create a new chart based on the range of all four subdivisions. Be sure to go back and delete the empty row when you're finished.

To avoid this problem, you can chart the areas as multiple ranges and use the Copy and Paste commands to plot each data series, one by one. Select the first desired range, and create the first chart in the normal manner. To add the next data series, return to the worksheet, select the next range to be charted, open the Edit menu, and choose the Copy command to copy the cells into memory. Then go back into the chart, and choose the Paste command from the Edit menu to paste the second set of data into the chart. You can perform this technique as many times as necessary to graph the desired data.

A solution to one problem sometimes creates another. If you included labels for category and value names in the first data area you plotted, these names may appear as labels in successive areas, even though you may not want them included in the other areas. To solve this problem when it occurs, you can edit the series formulas and insert your own desired text as a label.

USING LEGENDS

If a chart does not have a legend, you can add one at any time with the Add Legend command. Once you add a legend, you may want to change its appearance. The Format menu's Legend command can be used to change the appearance of a legend.

Select the legend in the currently active chart by pressing the DOWN ARROW key until the legend is selected or by clicking the legend with the mouse. Then open the Format menu and choose the Legend command. The dialog box containing the five position options for the legend should appear. Select Top and press RETURN or click the OK button. The legend appears at the top of the chart, as shown here:

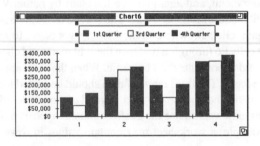

You can change a legend's font by using the Font command in the Format menu while the legend remains selected. Open the Format menu and choose the Font command. From the Font dialog box, select Italic. Then press RETURN or click the OK button. The legend text will reappear, this time in italic type.

ADDING TEXT AND ARROWS

Text and arrows are sometimes helpful for pointing out certain visual highlights of a chart (see Figure 5-2 for an example of an arrow in a chart). For example, you might wish to add a note emphasizing the poor third-quarter sales in the Spring Gardens development. Open the Chart menu and select the Add Arrow command. An arrow appears in the chart as the currently selected object. You can move it to a location of your choice.

Select the arrow by clicking it, and drag it to the desired location (pointing at the third-quarter sales for the Spring Gardens development). To change the arrow's length or its angle, place the mouse pointer at either end of the arrow, click and hold the mouse button, and drag or stretch the arrow to its new angle and size. You can move either end of the arrow with the mouse.

You can also change the style, color, weight (line thickness), and arrowhead width and length by selecting the arrow and then using the Patterns command from the Format menu. The Format dialog box provides all of the options for changing the appearance of the arrow.

Adding Unattached Text

To add unattached text to a chart, simply type the text. The text you type appears in the formula bar. Press RETURN when you are done, and the text should appear in a block somewhere in the chart. You must then use the mouse, or the Move command of the Format menu, to place the text where desired.

As an exercise, type **Unacceptable sales** and press RETURN. The text should appear in a selected box on the screen. Click in the center of the text, and drag the text to the desired location (above the end of the arrow you just added).

Keep in mind that Excel will not resize the text on its own, regardless of the size of the chart. If you resize a chart, you may want to select the text, choose the Text command from the Format menu, and pick an appropriate font, size, and type style.

ADDING GRIDLINES

If you prefer not to use the gridlines that accompany the standard chart choices in the Gallery menu, you can add gridlines to a custom chart with the Gridlines command of the Chart menu. Open the Chart menu and select the Gridlines command. The Gridlines dialog box provides a choice of major or minor gridlines along either the category axis or the value axis.

Major gridlines are heavier lines, widely spaced. Minor gridlines are fine lines, closely spaced. For this exercise, select the options for major gridlines along the value axis. Press RETURN or click the OK button, and the gridlines appear in the chart.

WORKING WITH PIE CHARTS

By their very design, pie charts are a different sort of chart. Because a pie chart shows the relationship between a whole and its parts, you can plot only a single data series in a pie chart. If the range that you select contains more than one data series, Excel uses the data in the first data series to build the chart.

Select the Income worksheet by opening the Window menu and choosing Income or by clicking in a portion of the Income worksheet with the mouse. Select cells A7 through B10 on the worksheet. The selected range includes the names of the housing subdivisions and the first-quarter sales figures. Open the File menu and choose the New command. Select Chart from the dialog box to draw a new chart.

Open the Gallery menu and choose the Pie command. From the gallery that appears, choose the last style by entering **6**. Then press RETURN or click the OK button to draw the chart.

You may want to make the chart larger in order to provide plenty of room for a legend. Drag on the Size box to increase the window size. Open the Chart menu and select the Add Legend command. A legend appears. Your pie chart should now resemble the one shown here:

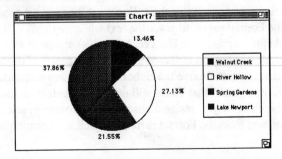

Excel can add visual emphasis to your pie charts by moving any slice out of the rest of the pie. Mouse users can click in the slice of the pie to select it, and with the mouse pointer inside the slice, click and drag the slice in or out of the pie. Keyboard users can move a slice by selecting the desired slice, selecting the Move command of the Format menu, and using the arrow keys to move the slice in or out.

As an exercise, select the pie slice representing the Walnut Creek subdivision. With the slice selected, click and drag outwards to move the slice. (Note that it is also possible to move the slice back in toward the center of the pie.) You can select other slices and move them for additional emphasis.

USING OVERLAY CHARTS

Excel offers a unique feature that provides another way of charting your data—overlay charts, which combine two types of charts. Overlay charts can be useful for giving a different perspective to a select set of values. As an example, you could highlight the sales for one quarter by showing those sales in an overlay chart.

You create standard overlay charts by using the Combination gallery (combination charts are actually overlay charts that use a standard format), or you can use the Overlay Chart command to create custom overlay charts. To see an example, select the Income worksheet by opening the Window menu and choosing Income or by clicking in a portion of the Income worksheet with the mouse. This time, select cells A6 through D10 in the worksheet. The selected range includes the names of the subdivisions and the sales figures for the first, second, and third quarters.

Open the File menu and choose the New command. Select Chart from the dialog box that appears and press RETURN or click the OK button to draw a new chart. The chart will be a column chart unless your preferred settings have been changed. To produce an overlay chart that superimposes third-quarter sales as a line chart on top of this column chart, open the Chart menu and choose the Add Overlay command. The chart will be redrawn and will be similar to the one shown here:

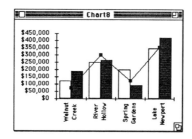

When you create an overlay chart, either by using the Overlay command or by selecting the Combination gallery, Excel evenly divides the number of data series in the selected range between the main chart and the overlay chart. If the range includes an odd number of data series (as in the example just used), Excel puts one more series in the main chart than in the overlay chart. To change this design, you can use the Overlay Chart command in the Format menu. Open the Format menu now and choose Overlay. When the dialog box appears, note the First Overlay Series option. Excel has entered the number 3 in this box, which means that the third data series is being used as the first series in the overlay chart. To change this design, click the box, enter **2**, and press RETURN. Excel redraws the chart, using figures from the second and third quarters in the overlay chart.

When you create your own charts, you should examine your data to determine whether overlay charts can be used effectively. Experimenting with the Combination gallery may give you some ideas about how you can design your own overlay charts.

CHANGING MARKER AND BACKGROUND PATTERNS

You can use the Format menu's Patterns command to change the patterns of the markers and backgrounds in your charts. Because these objects make up a major portion of your charts, changing their patterns and colors has a significant visual effect.

When you use the Patterns command, the dialog box that appears contains a variety of pattern and style options. The precise options depend on which chart object is selected. For example, when you select an axis and use the Patterns command, you are given the option of changing the axis weight (line thickness) and the types of tick marks. When you select a marker and use the Patterns command, you can use options for changing the area and border patterns, as well as the color and weight (line thickness) of the marker borders.

To change a marker pattern, first select the desired marker or series of markers. Then open the Format menu, select the Pattern command, and choose an appropriate pattern from the dialog box that appears.

CHANGING THE AXIS FORMATTING

You may find that the appearance of the axes is not precisely what you desire. For example, you may want to show a minor increase in sales in the best possible light, yet when you chart the data, the default formats used by Excel don't yield this result. You can select either axis and use the Patterns, Font, and Scale options of the Format command to change the scale and appearance of the axis and axis labels.

As an exercise, select the value axis with the arrow keys or by clicking the axis with the mouse. Open the Format menu. Note that when an axis is the selected object within the chart, the Format menu provides the Patterns, Font, and Scale commands for changing the appearance of the axis and its related parts. The Patterns command lets you change the style, color, and weight (line thickness) of the axis, as well as the types of tick marks used. The Font command lets you change the style and colors of the axis labels. The Scale command lets you change the numeric scale used for the axis.

Choose the Scale command now. The dialog box shown in Figure 5-4(b) appears. Perhaps you've determined that if the base of the chart represented $50,000 instead of zero, an increase in sales above that base would appear more pronounced. Change the Minimum option from the default of 0 to 50000 by typing **50000**. Click the Major Unit box and enter **25000**. The check marks will vanish from the column labeled "Auto" as you enter the value. (The Auto option check boxes let you tell Excel to determine the optimal values for these entries automatically.) Finally, click OK. The chart will appear with the new scale, starting at $50,000.

When you are implementing any general changes to a custom chart, keep in mind the availability of the Select Chart and Select Plot Area commands in the Chart menu. By selecting the entire chart or the entire plot area with these commands, you can apply pattern, font, and style changes to multiple objects. Experimentation is the best way to discover the flexibility of Excel's chart options.

CHANGING UNDERLYING VALUES BY DRAGGING CHART ITEMS

Excel lets you change the underlying values in a worksheet by dragging on a chart item. While this is a technique you'll probably want to use sparingly, it is useful to know that the capability exists. You can see how this works by creating a simple worksheet with a few figures, and a chart to support it.

Choose New from the File menu, and select Worksheet from the dialog box that appears. When the new worksheet appears, enter the following data in the cells noted:

A1   Widgets
A2   Gadgets
B1   170
B2   230

Next, select the range from A1 to B2, then choose New from the File menu. From the dialog box, select Chart. Assuming your default options have not been changed, a column chart will appear.

Select the column representing the sales of widgets, by pressing the LEFT ARROW or RIGHT ARROW key until only the Widgets column is highlighted by the small squares. Once you have selected the column, you can change its size by clicking and dragging on the black square (the one at the top center of the column). Try clicking and dragging on the column now. As you change its size, note that the value shown in the formula bar changes correspondingly.

Change the column to any new size you desire, and then click anywhere in the worksheet. Note that the value in cell B1, representing the sales of the widgets, has changed according to the changes made in the chart.

You may find this technique useful if you want to demonstrate the values needed to obtain a desired appearance on a chart. But since most business charts are based on numbers that are considered to be fixed, you'll want to be careful about using this technique; if you were to save the underlying worksheet after making such changes, you would probably invalidate the assumptions underlying the worksheet.

USING GRAPHIC IMAGES AS MARKERS

Excel has the ability to substitute graphic images (such as illustrations that you may have created in a painting program like MacPaint) in place of the normal markers used in bar and column charts. Since not everyone has images stored on their machines, this may or may not be of importance to you, but the basic technique is illustrated here. If you want to see how this works, and your Scrapbook contains graphic images, you can follow along. First, create a simple worksheet with a few figures. (If you created the worksheet described in the previous section of this chapter, you can use it.)

Choose New from the File menu, and select Worksheet from the dialog box that appears. When the new worksheet appears, enter the following data in the cells noted:

A1　Widgets
A2　Gadgets
B1　170
B2　230

Next, select the range from A1 to B2, and then choose New from the File menu. From the dialog box, select Chart. Assuming that your default options have not been changed, a column chart will appear.

Next, select the markers by clicking anywhere on either marker. Then, open the Scrapbook, by choosing Scrapbook from the Apple menu. Use the scroll bar to find a graphic image (the one of party balloons and champagne works well, if you have it). Open the Edit menu, and choose Copy to copy the graphic into memory.

Close the Scrapbook by clicking on the Close box. With the markers still selected, open the Edit menu, and choose Paste. Your markers will be replaced by the graphic image that you selected from the Scrapbook.

If you open the Format menu now and choose Patterns, you will see a Picture Format dialog box, with Stretch and Stack buttons. Because Stretch is chosen as the default, the graphic image is stretched as needed to create the columns. Try selecting the Stack button and choosing OK to see the different effect. With the Stack option, the markers will be composed of multiple graphic images, stacked atop one another.

If you decide to make use of this capability of Excel, you will find that some images work better than others. Software suppliers carry clip-art collections of graphic images that may prove helpful for use as chart markers.

WORKING WITH THREE-DIMENSIONAL CHARTS

As noted earlier, three-dimensional (3-D) charts are variations of area, column, line, and pie charts. You use the same techniques described throughout this chapter for building these charts; the only difference is the type choice that you make from the Gallery menu. 3-D charts are preferred by many people, particularly for business presentations. The added dimension provides visual interest that is hard to match with two-dimensional charts.

If you haven't already experimented with the 3-D options found in the Gallery example, consider a few examples now. Open the Income worksheet (if it is not already open), and select the range from cells A6 to C10. Choose New from the File menu, and choose Chart from the dialog box that appears; then click on OK to build the new chart. (You may want to expand the chart window when it appears, because 3-D charts tend to look odd in small windows.) Open the Gallery menu, and choose 3-D Area from the menu that appears. When the dialog box containing the seven possible 3-D area charts appears, select number 6. In a moment, the chart will be converted to an area chart like this one:

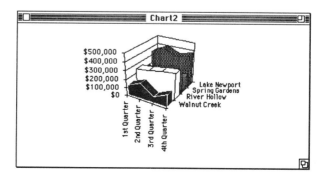

While you have a 3-D chart visible on the screen, you should familiarize yourself with the 3-D View command, a command that is available from the Format menu when you are working with 3-D Charts. Open the Format Menu, and choose 3-D View. In a moment, a dialog box will appear. In the dialog box are choices for elevation, rotation, perspective, and height (as a percentage of the base).

You can try changing the various values, by using the TAB key to reach a desired value, or by clicking on the entry box with the mouse. As you change the options, if you use the mouse or press the TAB key instead of RETURN, you will move to the next option while remaining within the dialog box. This lets you see a representation of the change in the small chart shown in the dialog box. If you do not like the change, you can tab back to the desired value, and change it back to the original value. When you are done with these options, press RETURN, or click on the OK button, and the changes will be applied to your chart.

The use of three dimensions adds to the challenge of finding a chart format that works best for visually displaying your data, so you will probably want to experiment with the 3-D formats on your own data. One very popular type of business presentation is the 3-D pie chart. Choose 3-D Pie from the Gallery menu, and select number 6 from the possible formats that appear in the dialog box. In a moment, the pie chart is drawn; it should resemble the example shown here:

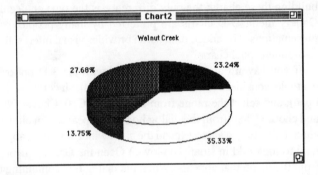

Keep in mind that, as with two-dimensional pie charts, you can emphasize a slice of the pie by selecting it, and then dragging it outwards with the mouse or the arrow keys. Of course, the primary restriction of pie charts (their ability to cover only one group of numbers at a time) also applies to 3-D pie charts.

WORKING WITH EMBEDDED CHARTS

As noted earlier in this chapter, you can attach charts directly to a worksheet when desired. If you are sure that a chart should always be displayed along with a worksheet, it works best to attach, or *embed,* the chart in the worksheet. To create embedded charts, use the Chart tool on the tool bar (it is the fourth tool from the right). The normal steps required to create an embedded chart are

1. Select the range of cells to chart. As with unembedded charts, be sure to include any labels that you plan to use to create legends in the chart.

2. Click on the Chart tool in the tool bar. (The mouse pointer will assume a crosshair shape.)

3. Position the pointer at the desired location for one corner of the chart.

4. Click and drag until the chart window is the desired size and shape; then release the mouse button. (If you hold the SHIFT key while dragging, the window will maintain the shape of a perfect square. If you hold the CTRL button while dragging, the window will align itself according to the grid formed by the cell borders.)

After you release the mouse button, Excel will create the chart according to the settings in the preferred chart format. You can use the Gallery menu as described earlier in this chapter to change the type of chart embedded in the worksheet, but note that you must select and open the chart first. This is done by double-clicking anywhere in the chart window.

An Example of an Embedded Chart

To try embedding a chart in a worksheet, select the range from A6 to E10 on the Income worksheet. With the range selected, click on the Chart tool in the tool bar. Click near the corner of cell B13, and drag down to approximately cell E28. (You will need this much room to display the labels that appear, without splitting words between syllables.) The embedded chart should resemble the example shown in Figure 5-10.

Keep in mind that you must select and open an embedded chart before you can change the chart type. Since the only document currently open is a worksheet, if the chart were not selected, Excel would have no way of knowing that you wanted to work with it. To see how this works, click anywhere in the worksheet. You'll see that the chart remains visible, but that there are no chart commands shown on the menu bar. Double-click the mouse anywhere in the Chart window to select and open the chart. The chart will take on the appearance of an unembedded chart, and the chart commands will appear in the menu bar.

Choose Area from the Gallery menu, and choose any format that appeals to you. After you make the selection and choose OK, the chart will be redrawn (but note, it still appears as an unembedded chart, because you have not deselected it). Click anywhere in the worksheet, and the chart will be redrawn as an embedded chart.

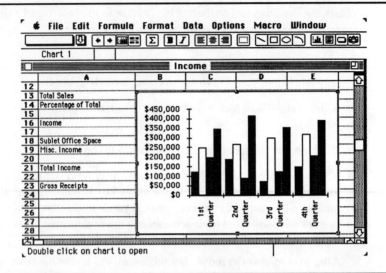

FIGURE 5-10. Embedded chart

One more point with regard to embedded charts: if you attach a chart to a worksheet and later decide that you want to save it separately, you can do so. Simply double-click on the chart to select and open it as an unembedded chart. You can then use the Save option of the File menu to save the chart to a separate file.

CREATING CHARTS OUTSIDE THE WORKSHEET ENVIRONMENT

You can use Excel to create charts that are based solely on data you enter into a series formula; a worksheet need not be open to create a chart. This feature can be very useful when a coworker or supervisor needs a chart in a hurry and all you have is a set of figures. You could open a worksheet, enter the data into the worksheet, and then create the chart, but a faster method would be to open a blank chart and simply type the data directly into the series formula. You could then use the Chart gallery to pick the desired chart.

If you do take this approach, you must follow a slightly different format for the series formula:

=SERIES(*series name*,{*category reference*},{*value reference*}, *plot order argument*)

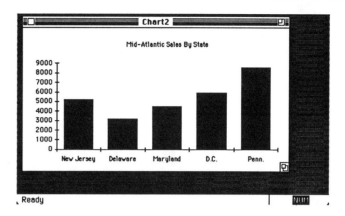

FIGURE 5-11.   Chart based on manual entry

The only difference between this formula and a series formula based on a worksheet is the presence of braces around the value and category references. This style must be followed when constants, rather than worksheet references, are entered for the values and categories within a series formula.

As an exercise, go back to the worksheet and click in any blank cell to ensure that no range is currently selected. Open the File menu and choose New; then select Chart for the type of file. A blank chart should appear on the screen. Type the following:

```
=SERIES("Mid-Atlantic Sales By State",{"New
Jersey","Delaware","Maryland","D.C.","Penn."},
{5200,3150,4500,5890,8550},1)
```

Press RETURN, and the chart will be drawn. If you resize the chart to provide room for the labels, it should resemble the one shown in Figure 5-11.

It is well worth your time to experiment with all of Excel's charting features. If you've followed all of the exercises in this chapter closely, you've probably realized that the graphics features alone could fill an entire book. Try the features with your own worksheets to develop proficiency in creating Excel charts.

chapter **6**

PRINTING
WORKSHEETS
AND CHARTS

At first glance, printing may seem like a simple procedure, but Excel provides numerous options for printing worksheets and charts. You can print an entire worksheet or just certain pages. You can also print selected ranges within a worksheet, and you can add headers and footers to a printed worksheet. In addition, you can change the width and height of charts.

The first time you use Excel to print a worksheet, you may want to make changes in some of the program's printing assumptions. Excel assumes that the worksheet should be printed with one-inch top and bottom margins, 3/4-inch left and right margins, page numbers, row and column headings, and cell gridlines. If any of these default values are not acceptable to you, you can change them with the Page Setup command of the File menu.

THE PAGE SETUP COMMAND

Because all print operations involve files, the print commands are accessed through the File menu. Open the File menu, shown here,

and note that two commands directly relate to printing: the Page Setup and Print commands.

The Page Setup command lets you change such page formatting features as margins, headers and footers, row and column headings, and gridlines. Once these options have been set, you can use the File menu's Print command to print the worksheet. Excel records the settings chosen with the Page Setup command, so you can change these settings and leave them until you find it necessary to change them again. The Page Setup settings are saved with each individual worksheet, so you can have different Page Setup values for different worksheets.

When you choose Page Setup from the File menu, the Page Setup dialog box appears. Figure 6-1 shows the Page Setup dialog box that appears when you are printing with an ImageWriter, and Figure 6-2 shows the one that appears when you are printing with a LaserWriter. (Note that the dialog box for the LaserWriter II SC differs slightly from the example in Figure 6-2.)

Paper Sizes

Your first choices in the Page Setup dialog box refer to paper sizes. With an ImageWriter, Excel lets you choose between the options U.S. Letter (8.5 × 11 inches), U.S. Legal (8.5 × 14 inches), A4 Letter (210 × 297 millimeters), International Fanfold (8.25 × 12 inches), and Computer Paper (15 × 11 inches). With a LaserWriter, the

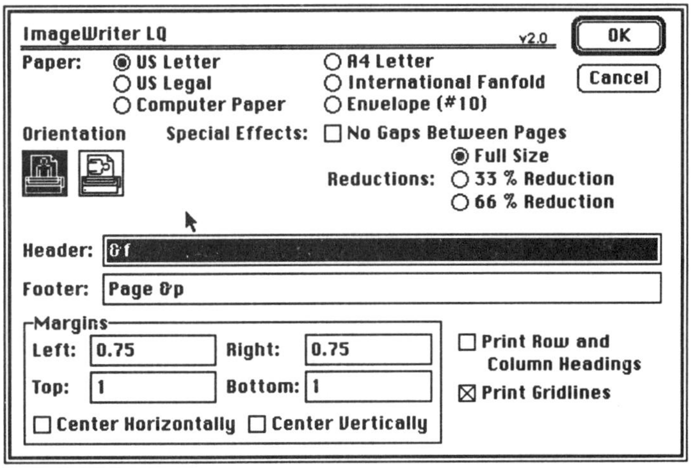

FIGURE 6-1.   Page Setup dialog box for ImageWriter

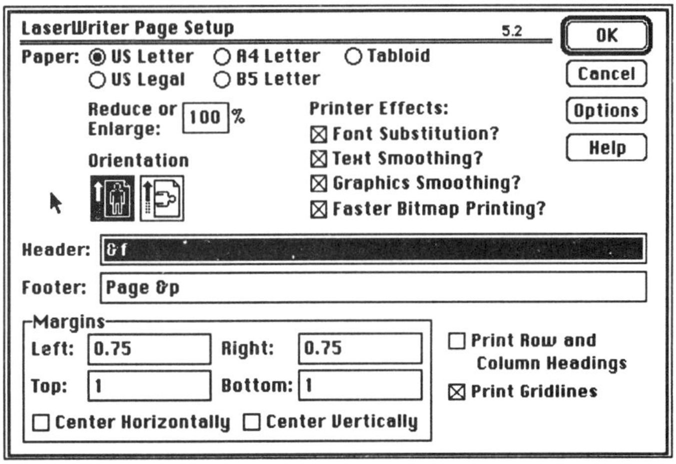

FIGURE 6-2.   Page Setup dialog box for LaserWriter

Computer Paper and International Fanfold options are omitted; however, there are additional options for European B5 size and Tabloid size, and for reducing or enlarging the printed image by a given percentage. Once you have chosen the appropriate paper size, you can proceed to select the desired orientation.

The Orientation option uses a visual symbol (an icon) to denote the choices of portrait and landscape orientation. (Portrait is the image of the person standing upright, and landscape is the image of the person lying sideways.) The difference between the two types of orientation is shown in Figure 6-3.

Choosing the Portrait icon results in a normal printing layout. Columns are printed across the page, and rows are printed with the first row at the top of the page, and each successive row underneath. When you choose the Landscape icon, the printed image is rotated 90 degrees from normal printing. The columns are printed horizontally down the paper, and the rows are printed vertically across the page. Landscape orientation can be useful for very wide worksheets. Users of earlier spreadsheet programs, when faced with the problem of printing wide spreadsheets, had to use an extra program such as Sideways to print the worksheets lengthwise, or had to tape printed pages together. With Excel, you avoid the frustration of either method.

Income

	A	B	C	D	E
1		Yearly Income Statement			
2	Income Worksheet				
3					
4					
5	Sales				
6		1st Quarter	2nd Quarter	3rd Quarter	4th Quarter
7	Walnut Creek	$123,000	$187,000	$72,750	$146,500
8	River Hollow	$248,000	$265,500	$297,800	$315,000
9	Spring Gardens	$197,000	$89,750	$121,000	$205,700
10	Lake Newport	$346,000	$416,000	$352,000	$387,600
11					
12					
13	Total Sales	$914,000	$958,250	$843,550	$1,054,800
14	Percentage of Total	24%	25%	22%	28%
15					
16	Income				
17					
18	Sublet Office Space	$1,800	$1,800	$1,800	$1,800
19	Misc. Income	$750	$750	$750	$750
20					
21	Total Income	$2,550	$2,550	$2,550	$2,550
22					
23	Gross Receipts	$916,550	$960,800	$846,100	$1,057,350
24					

FIGURE 6-3a. Portrait orientation

Income

	A	B	C	D	E
1	Yearly Income Statement				
2	Income Worksheet				
3					
4					
5	Sales				
6		1st Quarter	2nd Quarter	3rd Quarter	4th Quarter
7	Walnut Creek	$123,000	$187,000	$72,750	$146,500
8	River Hollow	$248,000	$265,500	$297,800	$315,000
9	Spring Gardens	$197,000	$89,750	$121,000	$205,700
10	Lake Newport	$346,000	$416,000	$352,000	$387,600
11					
12					
13	Total Sales	$914,000	$958,250	$843,550	$1,054,800
14	Percentage of Total	24%	25%	22%	28%
15					
16	Income				
17					
18	Sublet Office Space	$1,800	$1,800	$1,800	$1,800
19	Misc. Income	$750	$750	$750	$750
20					
21	Total Income	$2,550	$2,550	$2,550	$2,550
22					
23	Gross Receipts	$916,550	$960,800	$846,100	$1,057,350
24					

FIGURE 6-3b. Landscape orientation

Special Effects

The Special Effects portion of the dialog box contains check boxes for reduction, and a No Gaps Between Pages option. Depending on your ImageWriter model and version of system software, you may also see an option called Tall Adjusted. Clicking Tall Adjusted stretches the printout's width compared to its length to make charts print in correct proportions. Pie charts in particular may appear elongated if you do not use the Tall Adjusted option.

Choosing a reduction option causes the worksheet to be printed at a reduced size. This can prove useful when you want to present as much information as possible in a small space. Depending on your ImageWriter model and version of system software, you may have a 50% option, or you may have 33% and 66% options. Figure 6-4 shows two printed worksheets, one with the usual setting and one with 50% reduction.

The No Gaps Between Pages option causes each successive page of a worksheet to be printed immediately following the prior page, without the gaps usually left for fanfold paper. Note that you must also set the top and bottom margins to 0 to print across the breaks in fanfold paper. See "Changing the Margins" in this chapter for details on setting the margins.

The LaserWriter dialog box provides you with 50% and 75% buttons, which let you choose a percentage amount for reduction. (Depending on your model of Laser-Writer and your version of system software, you may see a percentage box; if you do, you can enter a desired percentage for reduction.) The ImageWriter offers only one reduction choice, 50%, but with a LaserWriter you can enter a size from 25% to 400% in 1% increments. If you are using a LaserWriter II SC, you can choose 50%, 75%, or 100%.

The LaserWriter also provides check boxes for font substitution, text and graphics smoothing, and for faster bitmap printing. (Users of versions of Apple System Software prior to 6.0 may lack the Faster Bitmap Printing option and may have only one smoothing option. Users of the LaserWriter II SC will not see these options.) If you check the Font Substitution box, the LaserWriter will substitute its built-in fonts for any stored Macintosh fonts used in a worksheet, rather than trying to imitate the standard fonts through graphics manipulation. When either of the smoothing options is selected, the LaserWriter will smooth jagged lines that may otherwise appear in the printout. The Faster Bitmap Printing option speeds up the printing of graphics, but with some loss of clarity. If you are using a LaserWriter II SC, options are provided for Exact Bit Images and Text Smoothing. Text Smoothing smooths jagged lines, and the Exact Bit Images option shrinks the image by about 4 percent.

a.   Income

	A	B	C	D	E
1		Yearly Income Statement			
2	Income Worksheet				
3					
4					
5	Sales				
6		1st Quarter	2nd Quarter	3rd Quarter	4th Quarter
7	Walnut Creek	$123,000	$187,000	$72,750	$146,500
8	River Hollow	$248,000	$265,500	$297,800	$315,000
9	Spring Gardens	$197,000	$89,750	$121,000	$205,700
10	Lake Newport	$346,000	$416,000	$352,000	$387,600
11					
12					
13	Total Sales	$914,000	$958,250	$843,550	$1,054,800
14	Percentage of Total	24%	25%	22%	28%
15					
16	Income				
17					
18	Sublet Office Space	$1,800	$1,800	$1,800	$1,800
19	Misc. Income	$750	$750	$750	$750
20					
21	Total Income	$2,550	$2,550	$2,550	$2,550
22					
23	Gross Receipts	$916,550	$960,800	$846,100	$1,057,350
24					

b.   Income

	A	B	C	D	E
1		Yearly Income Statement			
2	Income Worksheet				
3					
4					
5	Sales				
6		1st Quarter	2nd Quarter	3rd Quarter	4th Quarter
7	Walnut Creek	$123,000	$187,000	$72,750	$146,500
8	River Hollow	$248,000	$265,500	$297,800	$315,000
9	Spring Gardens	$197,000	$89,750	$121,000	$205,700
10	Lake Newport	$346,000	$416,000	$352,000	$387,600
11					
12					
13	Total Sales	$914,000	$958,250	$843,550	$1,054,800
14	Percentage of Total	24%	25%	22%	28%
15					
16	Income				
17					
18	Sublet Office Space	$1,800	$1,800	$1,800	$1,800
19	Misc. Income	$750	$750	$750	$750
20					
21	Total Income	$2,550	$2,550	$2,550	$2,550
22					
23	Gross Receipts	$916,550	$960,800	$846,100	$1,057,350
24					

FIGURE 6-4. (*a*) Normal printing and (*b*) reduced printing

Headers and Footers

The Header and Footer options control *headers* and *footers,* the lines of text that appear above and below the worksheet. Figure 6-5 shows a printed worksheet containing headers and footers. Headers are printed 0.5 inch from the top of the page, and footers are printed 0.5 inch from the bottom of the page. You generally use a name as the header (the name of the worksheet file or the name of your company, for example). A footer usually includes a page number, but footers are also used to provide other relevant information. You might, for example, decide to place the name of your department in the footer for a particular worksheet.

By default, Excel automatically adds headers and footers to your worksheets. The default value for the header is &F, which is an abbreviation for the current file name. This setting tells Excel to print the name of your file as a header above the worksheet. The default value for footer is Page &p, which tells Excel to print the word *Page,* followed by the page number, at the bottom of each page of the worksheet.

You can replace the header and footer defaults with headers and footers of your own choosing. For example, if you were to delete the existing header and footer designations and then enter **Fantasy Yearly** for a header and **Sheet No. &p** for a footer, each printed worksheet would have "Fantasy Yearly" at the top of the page and "Sheet No. *x*" (where *x* is the page number) at the bottom of the page. If you prefer no headers or footers, simply delete the entries in these options.

1/26/89   *Builders Income Statement*   11:30 AM

	A	B	C	D	E
5	Sales				
6		1st Quarter	2nd Quarter	3rd Quarter	4th Quarter
7	Walnut Creek	$123,000	$187,000	$72,750	$146,500
8	River Hollow	$248,000	$265,500	$297,800	$315,000
9	Spring Gardens	$197,000	$89,750	$121,000	$205,700
10	Lake Newport	$346,000	$416,000	$352,000	$387,600
11					
12					
13	Total Sales	$914,000	$958,250	$843,550	$1,054,800
14	Percentage of Total	24%	25%	22%	28%
15					

Accounting Dept.   Page 1

FIGURE 6-5.   Worksheet containing headers and footers

You can insert special codes that affect the display of the headers or footers. Each code consists of an ampersand (&) followed by an appropriate letter. The special codes that can be used for headers and footers are as follows:

Code	Meaning
&B	Use bold font for text that follows
&C	Center text
&D	Print the system date
&F	Print the worksheet file name
&I	Use italic font for text that follows
&L	Left-justify text
&P	Print the page number
&R	Right-justify text
&T	Print the system time
&&	Print a single ampersand

These codes can be combined within a single header or footer. For example, a header such as

&B&IAccounting Report &D&T

results in a header in boldface italics that reads "Accounting Report," followed by the current date and then the current time. The Bold and Italic options apply to the specific portions of text that follow the options, and not necessarily to the entire header or footer. This gives you added flexibility in that you can print portions of a header or footer with different styles. For example, a page footer setting of

&bPage &p&c&f&r&i&d

would cause Excel to print a header like this:

Page 1   Worksheet 1   *02/14/89*

When you use headers and footers, Excel positions them in relation to the edges of your page, not your worksheet margins. This may result in headers or footers appearing in a different location than you desire. For example, you might use the &C code to center a header, hoping it will appear centered over the worksheet. Usually, it would, but if you had changed the left and right margins, the header wouldn't be centered visually over the worksheet because the worksheet is no longer centered with your modified margins.

If you need to align a header or footer with a worksheet that has customized margins, you can try inserting spaces in the header or footer until the text is aligned. For example, if the header

&CProfit and Loss Statement, 1991

appears a bit too far to the left of the visual center of the worksheet, you can insert spaces between the center code and the text to shift the header to the right by entering

&C   Profit and Loss Statement, 1991

You may need to try different amounts of spaces until you find the most appealing setting.

Changing the Margins

Within the Margins options, you can enter a whole or a decimal value to set the desired top, bottom, left, and right margins. For example, 1.5 sets a margin of one and a half

EMPLOYEE.XLS

Employee	6/3/91	6/4/91	6/5/91	6/6/91	Totals
Askew, L.	$1,672.80	$1,738.27	$1,637.10	$1,776.05	$6,824.22
Baker, B.	$2,121.50	$2,186.97	$2,085.80	$2,224.75	$8,619.02
Baker, J.	$1,715.10	$1,780.57	$1,679.40	$1,818.35	$6,993.42
Block, P.	$1,854.25	$1,919.72	$1,818.55	$1,957.50	$7,550.02
Brown, N.	$1,475.98	$1,541.45	$1,440.28	$1,579.23	$6,036.94
Harris, C.	$1,717.05	$1,782.52	$1,681.35	$1,820.30	$7,001.22
Hayes, C.	$1,658.55	$1,724.02	$1,622.85	$1,761.80	$6,767.22
Johnson, M.	$1,845.23	$1,910.70	$1,809.53	$1,948.48	$7,513.94
Jones, R.	$1,756.65	$1,822.12	$1,720.95	$1,859.90	$7,159.62
Mills, E.	$1,845.20	$1,910.67	$1,809.50	$1,948.45	$7,513.82
Roberts, J.	$1,458.33	$1,523.80	$1,422.63	$1,561.58	$5,966.34
Simpson, S.	$1,548.25	$1,613.72	$1,512.55	$1,651.50	$6,326.02
Walker, A.	$1,459.56	$1,525.03	$1,423.86	$1,562.81	$5,971.26
Young, R.	$1,258.23	$1,323.70	$1,222.53	$1,361.48	$5,165.94
Zykowski, B.	$1,895.52	$1,960.99	$1,859.82	$1,998.77	$7,715.10

FIGURE 6-6.   Worksheet without row and column headings

inches, while 0.75 sets a margin of 3/4 inch. Excel's default margins are 3/4 inch (0.75) on the left and right sides, and 1 inch on the top and bottom of the page. You can check either the Center Horizontally or the Center Vertically button, to have Excel automatically use whatever margins are necessary to center a worksheet on the printed page.

The actual printed worksheet may fall inside of the bottom and right margins, depending on how large the printed area is, but it will never print outside of the specified margins. If all of the columns or rows cannot fit within the specified margins, Excel moves some of the columns or rows to the next printed page.

Print Row and Column Headings/
Print Gridlines

The Print Row and Column Headings option can be turned on or off by clicking the box next to the option name with the mouse. When this option is turned on, an X appears in the box, and the row and column letters and numbers are printed along with the worksheet data. With the option turned off, only the worksheet data appears; the row and column designations are not printed. Figure 6-6 shows an example of a worksheet printed without the row and column headings.

You can turn the Print Gridlines option on or off in the same manner as the Print Row and Column Headings option. With Print Gridlines turned on, the lines separating the rows and columns are printed; with the option turned off, they are omitted. Figure 6-7 shows a worksheet without printed gridlines.

Once you have chosen all of your desired options, press RETURN or click the OK button to tell Excel to store these options as your new defaults.

PRINTING THE WORKSHEET

To print the worksheet, open the File menu and select the Print command. A Print dialog box similar to the ones shown in Figure 6-8 and Figure 6-9 appears. Figure 6-8 shows the Print dialog box for the ImageWriter printer, and Figure 6-9 shows the one for the LaserWriter printer.

If you wish to print one copy of the entire worksheet, you can press RETURN or click the OK button. The worksheet will be printed with the default setting of one copy of all of the pages in the worksheet. You can print more than one copy of the worksheet by changing the entry in the Copies box. With an ImageWriter, you can also choose from among three quality settings: Best, Faster, and Draft. Selecting the Draft option prints your worksheet in high-speed mode, without any fancy formatting such as bold type. The Best option provides the best possible quality, but at very slow printing

EMPLOYEE.XLS

	A	B	C	D	E	F
1	Employee	6/3/91	6/4/91	6/5/91	6/6/91	Totals
2	Askew, L.	$1,672.80	$1,738.27	$1,637.10	$1,776.05	$6,824.22
3	Baker, B.	$2,121.50	$2,186.97	$2,085.80	$2,224.75	$8,619.02
4	Baker, J.	$1,715.10	$1,780.57	$1,679.40	$1,818.35	$6,993.42
5	Block, P.	$1,854.25	$1,919.72	$1,818.55	$1,957.50	$7,550.02
6	Brown, N.	$1,475.98	$1,541.45	$1,440.28	$1,579.23	$6,036.94
7	Harris, C.	$1,717.05	$1,782.52	$1,681.35	$1,820.30	$7,001.22
8	Hayes, C.	$1,658.55	$1,724.02	$1,622.85	$1,761.80	$6,767.22
9	Johnson, M.	$1,845.23	$1,910.70	$1,809.53	$1,948.48	$7,513.94
10	Jones, R.	$1,756.65	$1,822.12	$1,720.95	$1,859.90	$7,159.62
11	Mills, E.	$1,845.20	$1,910.67	$1,809.50	$1,948.45	$7,513.82
12	Roberts, J.	$1,458.33	$1,523.80	$1,422.63	$1,561.58	$5,966.34
13	Simpson, S.	$1,548.25	$1,613.72	$1,512.55	$1,651.50	$6,326.02
14	Walker, A.	$1,459.56	$1,525.03	$1,423.86	$1,562.81	$5,971.26
15	Young, R.	$1,258.23	$1,323.70	$1,222.53	$1,361.48	$5,165.94
16	Zykowski, B.	$1,895.52	$1,960.99	$1,859.82	$1,998.77	$7,715.10

FIGURE 6-7. Worksheet without gridlines

speed. The Faster option is a compromise between quality and speed. Both the Best and Faster options support the use of bold and italic type. Depending on your version of software and your model of ImageWriter, you may have an option called Head Scan, as shown in Figure 6-8. With this option you can choose bidirectional or unidirectional (one-way) printing.

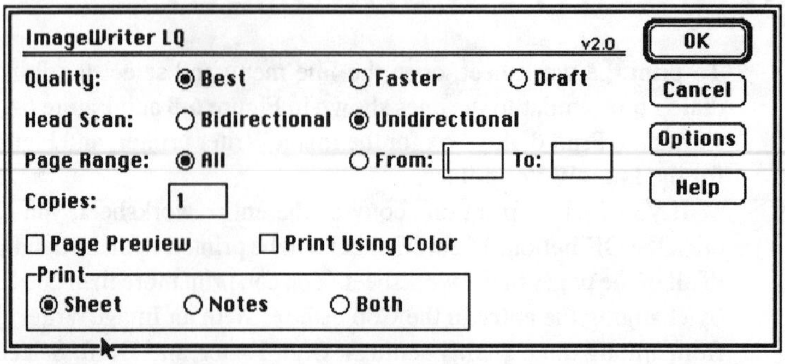

FIGURE 6-8. Print dialog box for ImageWriter

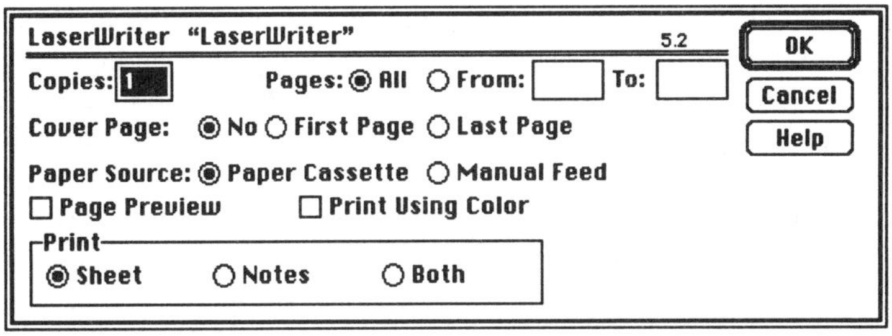

```
┌─────────────────────────────────────────────────────────────┐
│ LaserWriter "LaserWriter"                      5.2    ┌─────┐ │
│ Copies:[1]      Pages:◉ All  ○ From:[  ] To:[  ]      │ OK  │ │
│                                                       └─────┘ │
│ Cover Page:   ◉ No ○ First Page ○ Last Page        [ Cancel ] │
│                                                    [  Help  ] │
│ Paper Source: ◉ Paper Cassette ○ Manual Feed                 │
│ ☐ Page Preview      ☐ Print Using Color                      │
│ ┌Print─────────────────────────────────────────┐            │
│ │ ◉ Sheet       ○ Notes        ○ Both          │            │
│ └──────────────────────────────────────────────┘            │
└─────────────────────────────────────────────────────────────┘
```

FIGURE 6-9. Print dialog box for LaserWriter

To print a specific page or a range of pages, select the From choice in the Page Range option box and enter a starting page number in this box; then enter an ending page number in the To box. To print from the first page to a specific page, you can leave the From box empty and just enter a number in the To box. To print a single page, just enter the same number in both the From and To boxes. When you tell Excel to print a worksheet, it prints the entire worksheet unless you have previously defined only a part of the worksheet for printing. You can define a specific part for printing with the Set Print Area command of the Options menu; how to do so will be discussed later in this chapter.

Depending on the type of printer, you may also see options at the bottom of the dialog box for previewing the page, printing with Color, and printing the worksheet, notes, or both. The Sheet option tells Excel that only the worksheet should be printed, and the Notes option causes the contents of any notes stored within a worksheet to be printed. The Both option tells Excel to print both the worksheet and any notes.

LaserWriter users will also see the Cover Page and Paper Source options. You can choose not to include a cover page, to have the first page printed be a cover page, or to have the last printed page be a cover page. For the paper source, you can choose the Paper Cassette option (for normal paper feed) or the Manual Feed option. Print Using Color provides color printing on appropriate hardware.

Using the Print Preview Option

The Print Preview option provides an on-screen visual representation of the printed worksheet. This lets you see the overall appearance of your worksheet without wasting time or paper by printing it. To see an example, select the Print Preview option by choosing Print Preview from the File menu. Within a moment, a screen image resembling a fully printed worksheet will appear, as in Figure 6-10.

Because of the limitations of the screen, the preview image is not detailed enough to show you the actual data. However, you can use the Zoom option, selected with the Zoom button or with the mouse pointer, to select a portion of the image and enlarge it for full viewing. As you move the pointer over the worksheet, the pointer will assume the shape of a magnifying glass. By moving the magnifying glass to any portion of the worksheet image and pressing the mouse button, you can see a full-size image of that portion of the worksheet. Press the mouse button again to go back to the preview image. Note that you can also click the Zoom button to accomplish the same purpose.

Once you select the Zoom option by clicking the Zoom button, you can either use the arrow keys or drag the scroll bars with the mouse to move the image around the screen. Try using the Zoom option now by clicking the Zoom button. Press the arrow keys and note the movement of the print image around the screen. To get back to the full view, click Zoom again.

If you use the Zoom option to enlarge part of a multiple-page worksheet, you can advance page-by-page through the worksheet while viewing the same enlarged area by pressing the RETURN key. For example, say you have a five-page worksheet and you want to see how the area in the upper-left corner of each page will appear when printed. In this case, you would choose Print from the File menu, select the Print Preview command, and use the mouse or the Zoom button to enlarge the upper-left

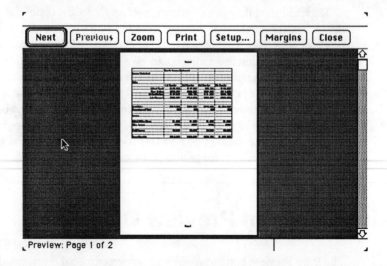

FIGURE 6-10.   Use of Print Preview

corner of the first page. Then, each time you pressed the RETURN key, the next successive page would appear, with the upper-left corner enlarged.

There are six additional options at the top of the screen: Next, Previous, Print, Setup, Margins, and Close. The Next option shows the next page in preview form; if you are on the last page of the worksheet, choosing this option tells Excel to exit Print Preview mode. As an alternative, you can press the RETURN key to move to the next page when in Print Preview mode. The Previous option displays the prior page of a worksheet in preview form. The Print option prints the worksheet with your chosen page settings and the Setup option displays the Page Setup dialog box, which allows you to change printer settings. The Margins option causes dotted lines that represent your existing margins to appear on the preview image. Finally, the Close option exits from Print Preview mode and returns you to the worksheet.

USING THE OPTIONS MENU PRINT COMMANDS

In addition to the print-related choices available in the File menu, you will find three print-related commands in the Options menu: Set Print Area, Set Print Titles, and Set Page Break. Open the Options menu, shown here, and note that these three commands appear as the first three available menu choices.

Setting a Print Area

When you issue a Print command from the File menu, Excel normally prints the entire worksheet. Sometimes, however, you may want to print a small portion of the worksheet. The Set Print Area command lets you specify a smaller area for printing. To use this command, you must first select the range of the worksheet you wish to print, and then choose the Set Print Area command from the Options menu.

As an exercise, select the range from cell A2 to cell E10. Open the Options menu and choose Set Print Area. You should see a dotted line around the selected area of the worksheet.

Open the File menu, choose Print, and then click OK to begin printing. Just the selected portion will be printed. If you choose the Print Preview mode, just a small portion of the worksheet appears on the screen, as shown in Figure 6-11.

Once you use this command to set an area for printing, it remains set for that worksheet range until you tell Excel otherwise. To go back to printing the entire worksheet, open the Formula menu and choose the Define Name command. Under the list of available names that appears, highlight Print_Area and choose the Delete option to delete the reference to the print area.

Setting a Page Break

Excel begins a new page automatically when the number of rows or columns on a printed sheet exceeds the margin settings. However, you may intentionally want to

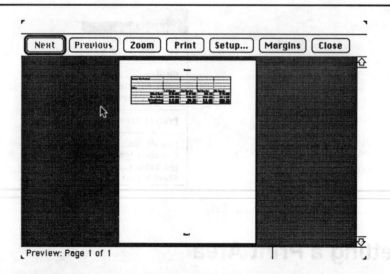

FIGURE 6-11. Previewing portion of page with Set Print Area

put one part of a worksheet on one page and the next part on the following page. You can do this with the Set Page Break command.

Set Page Break lets you put a *forced page break* at any location in the worksheet. A printed Excel worksheet can contain two types of page breaks: forced page breaks, which you can insert, and the page breaks that are inserted automatically by the program when a portion of a worksheet is too large for one page. The two types of page breaks look different. In Figure 6-12, the first dotted line is a page break inserted automatically by Excel, and the second dotted line is a page break inserted manually. As you can see, the manual page breaks are darker than the automatic ones.

To use the Set Page Break command, simply select the row or column at which you would like the page break to occur. If you want a vertical page break, click in a column heading; the break will be placed to the left of the chosen column. Then open the Options menu and select the Set Page Break command. A dotted line appears at the top of the selected row or to the left of the selected column.

Try placing a forced page break below the "Misc. Income" line of the worksheet by selecting cell A53 and selecting the Set Page Break command from the Options menu. Then open the File menu and choose the Print command. Turn on your printer and select the OK button. The document should be printed with a page break following row 52.

You can remove a page break by selecting any cell directly below or to the right of the page break, opening the Options menu, and selecting the Remove Page Break

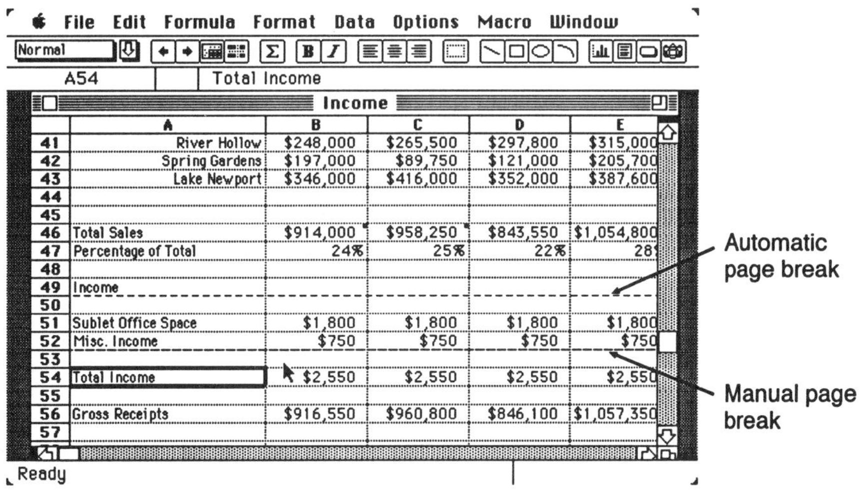

FIGURE 6-12.   Automatic and manual page breaks

command. Whenever the selection is below or to the right of a page break, the Remove Page Break command appears in the Options menu. Note that you cannot delete the page breaks that Excel automatically places in a document, although the location of these page breaks is affected by changing your paper size, orientation, margin settings, and manual page breaks. Also note that automatic page breaks won't be visible until you use either the Page Setup command, the Print Preview command, or the Print command. Once you use one of these commands, the dotted lines that indicate the presence of page breaks appear.

If you are printing a large worksheet for the first time, you may want to use the Print Preview command to see where the automatic page breaks appear. In general, it is a good idea to avoid including forced page breaks until you are working with the final version of your worksheet. If you insert a series of page breaks and then need to add new data, the page breaks you inserted will probably be in the wrong places, and you will have to go back and delete them.

Setting Print Titles

Excel lets you use specific rows or columns of a worksheet as titles on every page of a multiple-page worksheet—an extremely useful feature with large worksheets. For example, with the usual format of a large worksheet, the reader must flip back to page 1 to see the titles for certain rows or columns. With the Set Print Titles command, you can print the row or column titles on every page.

You identify titles by selecting the entire appropriate row or column and then choosing the Set Print Titles command within the Options menu. If you select a row of titles, the row appears at the top of each page of the worksheet; if you select a column of titles, the column appears at the left side of every printed page of the worksheet. You can also select more than one row or column of titles.

 When you use Set Print Titles to define titles for printing, you should also use Set Print Area to define the area to be printed as the data that falls beyond the titles. Otherwise, Excel will print the titles twice on the leading pages of the worksheet.

To see how the Set Print Titles feature works, select row 6 of the Income worksheet by clicking in the row 6 heading. Open the Options menu and choose the Set Print Titles command. If you removed the forced page break that you inserted earlier, replace it (at row 15) so that the Income worksheet prints as a two-page worksheet. Select the range from A7 to G23, and then open the Options menu and select Set Print

Area. Finally, open the File menu and select the Print command. When the document is printed, both pages will display the labels at the top of the worksheet, as shown in Figure 6-13.

You can select both rows and columns for use as titles on each page of a worksheet. To do so, first drag across the desired row or rows to select them. Next, hold down the COMMAND key and drag across the desired column or columns. The result is a multiple selection covering both rows and columns, as shown in the example in Figure 6-14. Choose Set Print Titles from the Options menu. When you print the worksheet, the headings in the selected rows and columns will appear as titles on each page of the worksheet, as shown in the example printout in Figure 6-15.

To cancel a print title, open the Formula menu and choose the Define Name command. Under the list of available names that appears, highlight Print Titles and choose the Delete option to delete the reference to it.

PRINTING CHARTS

The printing commands used with charts are nearly identical to those used with worksheets. Because the Set Print Area, Set Print Titles, and Set Page Break com-

a.

Income

	A	B	C	D	E	F
		1st Quarter	2nd Quarter	3rd Quarter	4th Quarter	
6						
7	Walnut Creek	$123,000	$187,000	$72,750	$146,500	
8	River Hollow	$248,000	$265,500	$297,800	$315,000	
9	Spring Gardens	$197,000	$89,750	$121,000	$205,700	
10	Lake Newport	$346,000	$416,000	$352,000	$387,600	
11						
12						
13	Total Sales	$914,000	$958,250	$843,550	$1,054,800	
14	Percentage of Total	24%	25%	22%	28%	

Income

b.

	A	B	C	D	E	F
		1st Quarter	2nd Quarter	3rd Quarter	4th Quarter	
6						
15						
16	Income					
17						
18	Sublet Office Space	$1,800	$1,800	$1,800	$1,800	
19	Misc. Income	$750	$750	$750	$750	
20						
21	Total Income	$2,550	$2,550	$2,550	$2,550	
22						
23	Gross Receipts	$916,550	$960,800	$846,100	$1,057,350	

FIGURE 6-13.   Printing titles on multiple pages with Set Print Titles

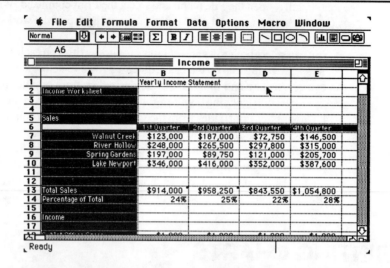

FIGURE 6-14.   Selecting both rows and columns for titles

Income

	A	B	C	D	E
6		1st Quarter	2nd Quarter	3rd Quarter	4th Quarter
7	Walnut Creek	$123,000	$187,000	$72,750	$146,500
8	River Hollow	$248,000	$265,500	$297,800	$315,000
9	Spring Gardens	$197,000	$89,750	$121,000	$205,700
10	Lake Newport	$346,000	$416,000	$352,000	$387,600
11					
12					
13	Total Sales	$914,000	$958,250	$843,550	$1,054,800
14	Percentage of Total	24%	25%	22%	28%

Income

	A	B	C	D	E
6		1st Quarter	2nd Quarter	3rd Quarter	4th Quarter
15					
16	Income				
17					
18	Sublet Office Space	$1,800	$1,800	$1,800	$1,800
19	Misc. Income	$750	$750	$750	$750
20					
21	Total Income	$2,550	$2,550	$2,550	$2,550
22					
23	Gross Receipts	$916,550	$960,800	$846,100	$1,057,350

FIGURE 6-15.   Printed worksheet with titles

mands apply only to worksheets, however, these commands are not available with charts. The File menu's Page Setup command performs a similar function with charts as it does with worksheets, but with some minor differences.

When a chart is active and you select the Page Setup command from the File menu, you see a dialog box like the one in Figure 6-16. All options in the dialog box, with the exception of the Size options, operate in the same manner as those used with worksheets. The Size options are Screen Size, Fit to Page, and Full Page.

If you turn on the Screen Size option, Excel prints the chart in the same dimensions as you see on your screen. If you select the Fit to Page option, Excel prints the chart using dimensions that fill your margin settings as much as possible, while maintaining the proper *aspect ratio* (height-to-width ratio). Before using the Fit to Page option, enter any desired changes to the left, right, top, and bottom margins. Then select the Fit to Page option. Excel prints the chart according to the settings you have specified.

The Full Page option tells Excel to fill the entire page with the chart. When this option is selected, Excel stretches the chart to fill the page, ignoring the aspect ratio. The printed chart that results is likely to be out of proportion with what is on the screen, but it will make maximum use of available printing space.

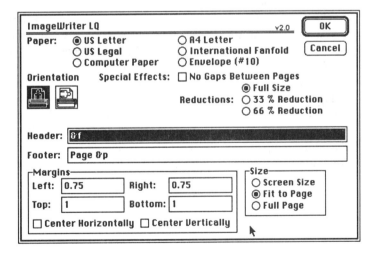

FIGURE 6-16.   Page Setup dialog box for charts

USING DIFFERENT PRINTERS

If you are using a printer other than the ImageWriter, you should be aware of the Chooser command on the Apple menu. If you open the Apple menu and select Chooser (you can do this inside or outside of Excel), you will see the Chooser dialog box, shown here, which contains a list box of available printers.

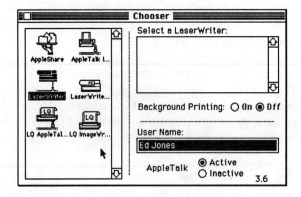

Your available printers may differ from those shown in the example, depending on what printers you have installed in your System Folder.

Click the desired printer name in the list box, and then click the correct printer port. If you are using an AppleTalk network, you should also click the AppleTalk Active button to tell your Macintosh to use the AppleTalk connection for printing.

If you have a printer installed that is not an ImageWriter or a LaserWriter, you will see one additional option in the File menu: the Printer Setup command. Use the Printer Setup command to display a dialog box showing possible choices for non-Macintosh printers. You can set the printer setup (Macintosh or TTY), the desired printer port (printer or modem connection), and the baud rate (from 300 to 9600). Once you change the printer setup to TTY, the other options (Printer Port and Baud Rate) are enabled. Refer to your printer manual for the correct baud rates and connection specifications.

chapter **7**

USING
A DATABASE

Excel lets you use all or part of a worksheet as a database for manipulating, retrieving, and reporting data. You can create a database, find specific information, extract certain information from the database, and sort a database. Figure 7-1 shows an example of an Excel database.

WHAT IS A DATABASE?

Although the term _database_ is often used in reference to computers, it also applies to any system in which information is catalogued, stored, and used. As you learned earlier, a database is a collection of related information grouped as a single item. Figure 7-1 shows an example of a simple database. A metal filing cabinet containing customer records, a card file of names and phone numbers, and a notebook filled with a handwritten list of store inventory are all databases. The physical container—the filing

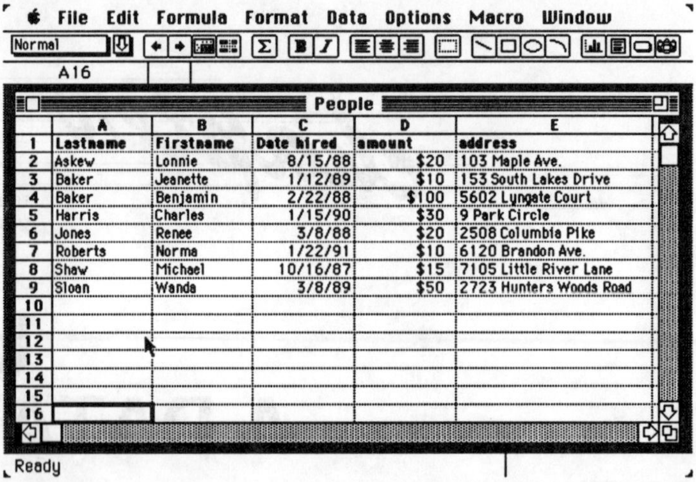

FIGURE 7-1. A sample Excel database

cabinet or notebook, for example—is not the database; what the container holds and the way in which the information is organized constitute the database. Objects like cabinets and notebooks are only tools in organizing information. Excel is one such tool for storing information.

Information in a database is usually organized and stored in a table by rows and columns. Figure 7-2, for example, shows a mailing list in database form. Each row contains a name, an address, a phone number, and a customer number. Because the mailing list is a collection of information arranged in a specific order—a column of names, a column of addresses, a column of customer numbers—it is a database.

Rows in a database file are called records, and columns are called fields. Figure 7-3 illustrates this idea by showing an address filing system kept on file cards. Each card in the box is a single record, and each category of information on that card is a field. Fields can contain any type of information that can be categorized. In the card box, each record contains six fields: name, address, city, state, ZIP code, and phone number. Since every card in the box contains the same type of information, the information in the card box is a database file. Figure 7-4 identifies a record and a field in the mailing-list database.

In Excel, you usually design a database in a row-and-column pattern, where each column of the spreadsheet contains a different field and each row contains an additional record. You can begin the design of any database by placing the cursor near

Name	Address	City	State	ZIP	Phone No.	Cust. No.
J. Billings	2323 State St.	Bertram	CA	91113	234-8980	0005
R. Foster	Rt. 1 Box 52	Frink	CA	93336	245-4312	0001
L. Miller	P.O. Box 345	Dagget	CA	93467	484-9966	0002
B. O'Neill	21 Way St. Apt. C	Hotlum	CA	92346	555-1032	0004
C. Roberts	1914 19th St.	Bodie	CA	97665	525-4494	0006
A. Wilson	27 Haven Way	Weed	CA	90004	566-7823	0003

FIGURE 7-2.   A simple database

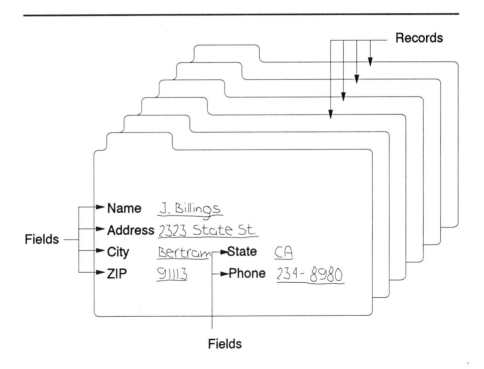

FIGURE 7-3.   Card-file database

Field

↓

Name	Address	City	State	ZIP	Phone No.	Cust. No.
J. Billings	2323 State St.	Bertram	CA	91113	234-8980	0005
R. Foster	Rt. 1 Box 52	Frink	CA	93336	245-4312	0001
L. Miller	P.O. Box 345	Dagget	CA	93467	484-9966	0002
B. O'Neill	21 Way St. Apt. C	Hotlum	CA	92346	555-1032	0004
C. Roberts	1914 19th St.	Bodie	CA	97665	525-4494	0006
A. Wilson	27 Haven Way	Weed	CA	90004	566-7823	0003

Record ⟶ C. Roberts

FIGURE 7-4. A record and a field of a database

the top of the worksheet and entering labels for the names of your fields in successive columns.

THE DATA MENU

To perform various database operations, you use the commands available from the Data menu, shown here:

The Find command lets you search for records that meet a specified set of conditions or criteria. Once the Find command has been chosen, the command changes to Exit Find. Choosing the Exit Find command cancels the find operation.

The Extract command finds records that meet a specified criteria and copies those records to another part of the worksheet. The Delete command deletes all records that meet a specified criteria. The Set Database command lets you define the area of the worksheet that will serve as a database. You can have multiple databases in one worksheet, but only one database can be defined at a time.

The Set Criteria command defines the area of the worksheet that contains the criteria Excel uses to qualify records. This area can contain the names of fields along with matching criteria for those fields, or it can contain formulas that test records for a specified condition. The Set Extract command lets you extract records from a database without having to select field names.

The Sort command sorts a database by the contents of one or more fields. Excel can sort by row or by column, in ascending or descending order. Up to three *sort keys,* or levels of sorting, may be specified.

The Series, Table, and Parse commands are found on the Data menu, but they can be used with regular worksheets as well as with databases. The Series command lets you fill a range of cells with a series of numbers or dates. It provides a simple way to enter progressive values automatically in dozens or hundreds of cells. The Table command is used to create tables. A *table* is a range of cells that contains the results of testing different values against one or two cells in the worksheet. The Parse command is used to transform portions of a file that are imported as ASCII text into values that can be used in an Excel worksheet. The Parse command is useful for converting data that has been downloaded from a mainframe into usable form. The Series command is discussed in this chapter, while the Table and Parse commands are covered in later chapters. Although it appears on the Data menu, the Consolidate option does not specifically apply to databases. This option is used to combine and summarize data from multiple worksheets.

CREATING A DATABASE

Creating a database in Excel consists of three steps:

1. Defining the fields

2. Entering the records

3. Defining the database range

Once you have decided on the fields, you can enter the field names in the field-name row, which is the first row of the database.

When constructing a database, you should leave approximately ten rows above the field-name row empty. This blank area serves as a convenient space for defining the criteria for the database, a topic that is covered shortly. The extra space also provides an area for tables and formulas that you may choose to use along with your database.

For the next example, a database that organizes purchases made by a building company initially contains five fields: Subdivision, Quantity, Description, Cost, and Category. You will create the database in a separate worksheet so that you can link the data in the database to other worksheets in later chapters.

Open the File menu and choose the New command. From the dialog box that appears, select Worksheet to bring a blank worksheet to the screen. In cell A10, enter **Subdivision** as the heading. In cell B10, enter **Quantity**. In C10, enter **Description**, in D10, enter **Cost**, and in cell E10, enter **Category**. Using the Format menu's Column Width command, change the column width for the description field to 20.

Once the fields have been defined, you can proceed to enter data. Excel lets you do so in one of two ways. The first is to use the data entry and editing techniques with which you are already familiar—that is, to select the desired cells, enter the data, and press RETURN upon completion of each entry. As an example, select cells A11 to E11 now. With the cursor at cell A11, enter the following data, and press RETURN upon the completion of each entry:

```
WC
5400
wall studs, 2 by 4
0.67
framing
```

To make data entry easier, the subdivision names are abbreviated. This manner of data entry is similar to that used by most spreadsheet programs that offer database capabilities. However, Excel offers another, easier method through the Data menu's Form command. Before you can use this command, however, you must tell Excel you are using a database. You can do this with the Data menu's Set Database command, which defines your database range, the third step in the process of creating a database. You do not need to enter all records in the database before you define a database range; the range can be defined either before or after the entry of the database records. However, the use of the Form command does require that the database range be defined. If the range is not defined, the Form command seems to work, but it may not be able to access all records in the database.

The range that will contain your initial records in this example covers 20 rows, from row 11 through row 30. The database will include data in columns A through E, so the database range is from cell A10 to cell E30. To define this area as the database range, you must select the area and then use the Set Database command from the Data menu.

Selecting a Large Area
Of a Worksheet

You could select the range by clicking and dragging, as you learned in earlier chapters. However, for very large areas, this can be an impractical method of selecting cells. Remember the Go To key, which can also be used to select a large area of a worksheet. To see how this is done, go to cell A10. Press the Go To key (COMMAND-G), and when the Go To dialog box appears, enter the lower-right coordinates of the range, **E30**, but don't press RETURN yet. To select all cells between the starting and ending coordinates, you simply press and hold down the SHIFT key while pressing RETURN in response to the Go To dialog box. Hold down the SHIFT key and press RETURN now. As a result of the SHIFT-RETURN combination, the Go To operation causes all cells between the starting and ending cells to be selected.

Defining the Database Range

Once you have selected the cells, you can use the Data menu's Set Database command to define the database range. Open the Data menu now, and choose the Set Database command. You won't see any visible evidence of the action, but Excel has assigned the name Database to the selected area. This name can be used like any assigned range name, even as a part of a formula if desired.

USING THE FORM COMMAND

Direct entry of the data into the cells is one method of data entry, but another method is to use the Form command to open on-screen forms for quick data entry. Remember, before a form can be fully utilized, you must define a database range. If you do not define the entire range, you may be able to use a form, but you may not be able to access and edit all of the records in the database.

Open the Data menu, and select the Form command. A data entry form for the database appears, as shown here:

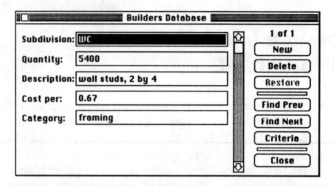

This form displays a box for each field in the defined database range, along with a number of option buttons. You can type new entries or edit existing entries in the boxes. The form is always in one of two modes: Criteria mode or Forms mode. Criteria mode is indicated by the presence of the word "Criteria" in the upper-right corner of the form (not in the option button). Forms mode is indicated by the presence of a record number, such as "1 of 2," or the term "New Record," in the upper-right corner. The Criteria/Form button, which is one of the buttons on the right side of the form, alternates between "Criteria" and "Forms" and is used to switch between the modes. Note that what is displayed on the button is the opposite of the mode you are in at the time. The button provides you with a convenient way to switch to the other mode.

If you click the Criteria button with the mouse, you enter Criteria mode, and the button changes to the Form button. Selecting the button again returns you to Forms mode, and the button changes back to the Criteria button. When you are in Criteria mode, you can enter a criteria in any of the appropriate boxes, and the Find Next and Find Previous buttons can then be used to jump to Forms mode and locate records that match the criteria. Once a desired record has been found and you are in Forms mode, you can use the Delete button to delete the record. The Clear button clears the entries from the fields. The Restore button restores entries that were previously deleted with the Clear button.

If you are not yet in Forms mode, click the Form button. (Remember, Forms mode is indicated by a record number or the "New Record" designation in the upper-right corner of the form.) Click the New button. The cursor will appear in the first field, Subdivision.

You can enter data in the fields by typing each entry and pressing the TAB key to move to the next entry. When you are within a data entry form, you cannot move to the next entry by pressing RETURN. If you press RETURN, you store the record in the database at that point.

Enter the following data for the next record, pressing TAB after each entry:

LN
3850
plywood sheets, 4 by 8
3.89
framing

When you complete the final field, press RETURN to store the entry and display a new blank form. Then enter the following, again pressing TAB after each entry:

RH
512
PVC pipe, 3′ length
1.27
plumbing

Press RETURN again to store the additions and display a new record. Continue entering each of the records listed in Figure 7-5. Press the TAB key following each entry, and press RETURN when the entry in the last field is complete to store the record and display a new one.

When you have entered the last field in the final record, be sure to store the record by pressing RETURN. Then click the Close button with the mouse to exit from the form. You should see the records in the database.

DEFINING THE CRITERIA

Once you have created a database and defined its range, you can search for and extract records that meet certain criteria. For example, you might need to see all expenses that fall in the "finish" category for the Walnut Hills and River Hollow subdivisions. Excel also lets you use computed criteria to find records that pass certain tests based on the contents of a formula. Using computed criteria, for example, you could locate all expenses that exceed $1000 for managerial approval of vendor payment.

To specify criteria that Excel uses in evaluating the records, you must define an area of the worksheet as a *criteria range*. The criteria range contains two types of items: field names and the matching criteria used to evaluate the contents of the field for each record in the database. The steps involved in creating criteria are similar to the steps for creating a database. They are

1. Enter the needed field names in a worksheet row.

2. Enter the desired matching criteria in the row below the field names.

3. Define the range that contains the names and matching criteria as the criteria range.

It is not necessary to include all field names of a database in the criteria, only the fields with which you want to use matching criteria. In this example, you'll perform several different matches, so all fields will be included in the criteria range.

A timesaving way to add field names to the criteria range is to copy existing field names from the database to an unused area of the worksheet with the Edit menu's Copy and Paste commands. This method can also minimize problems with misspellings, as the field names in the criteria range must be exact duplicates of the field names in the database. Select cells A10 to E10 now, and choose the Copy command from the Edit menu. Move the cursor to cell A2, open the Edit menu, and choose Paste to paste the field names into row 2. For your first search criteria, enter **finish** in cell E3. Once the criteria range has been defined, this criteria tells Excel to find only those records with the word "finish" in the category field.

To define the criteria range, you must first select the range and then use the Set Criteria command from the Data menu. Select cells A2 through E3 now. Then open the Data menu and choose the Set Criteria command. Although no change is apparent, Excel is ready to use the criteria along with the other Data commands: Find, Extract, and Delete.

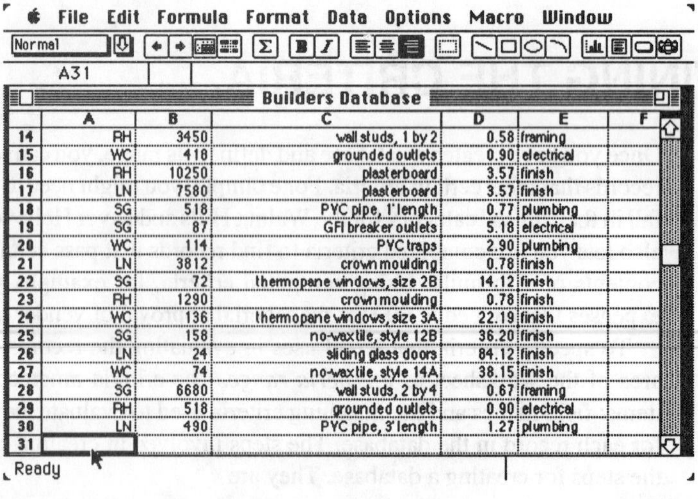

 File   Edit   Formula   Format   Data   Options   Macro   Window

	A	B	C	D	E	F
			Builders Database			
14	RH	3450	wall studs, 1 by 2	0.58	framing	
15	WC	418	grounded outlets	0.90	electrical	
16	RH	10250	plasterboard	3.57	finish	
17	LN	7580	plasterboard	3.57	finish	
18	SG	518	PVC pipe, 1' length	0.77	plumbing	
19	SG	87	GFI breaker outlets	5.18	electrical	
20	WC	114	PVC traps	2.90	plumbing	
21	LN	3812	crown moulding	0.78	finish	
22	SG	72	thermopane windows, size 2B	14.12	finish	
23	RH	1290	crown moulding	0.78	finish	
24	WC	136	thermopane windows, size 3A	22.19	finish	
25	SG	158	no-waxtile, style 12B	36.20	finish	
26	LN	24	sliding glass doors	84.12	finish	
27	WC	74	no-waxtile, style 14A	38.15	finish	
28	SG	6680	wall studs, 2 by 4	0.67	framing	
29	RH	518	grounded outlets	0.90	electrical	
30	LN	490	PVC pipe, 3' length	1.27	plumbing	
31						

Ready

FIGURE 7-5.   Remaining data

FINDING RECORDS

Once you have defined a database and a criteria range, you can use the Find command to find records that match your criteria. When you choose this command, Excel enters Find mode and remains in this mode until you select the Exit Find command from the Data menu, select a cell that resides outside of the database range, or select another command.

Open the Data menu now, and choose Find. The cursor should move to the first record in the database that contains "finish" in the category field (see Figure 7-6). If Excel displays a warning message indicating that it can find no match, you have probably misspelled the word "finish" in cell E3. Unlike some database software packages, Excel is not case-sensitive; it does not matter whether you use uppercase or lowercase letters in specifying the criteria.

You can find the next matching record by using the DOWN ARROW key. You can move to the prior matching record with the UP ARROW key. Also, note that Excel displays the record number on the extreme left side of the formula bar. If Excel cannot find any additional matching records when you press the UP or DOWN ARROW key, it will beep, or flash the menu bar if the sound is off.

You may note some changes in the appearance of the worksheet while Excel is in Find mode. Both scroll boxes have changed from solid colors to striped bars. When

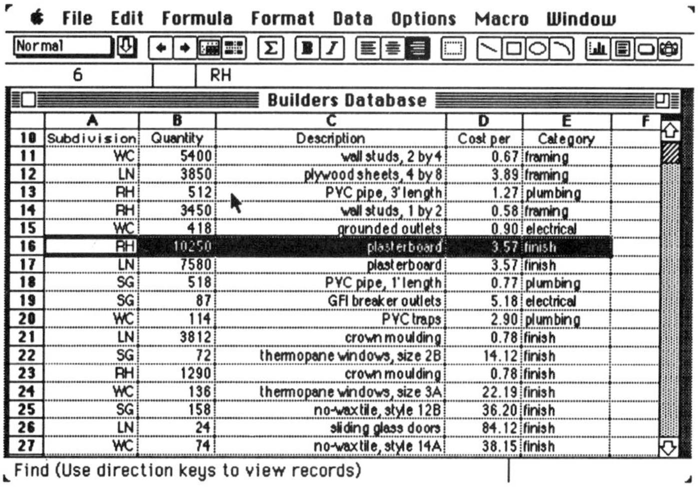

FIGURE 7-6. Data form containing existing record

Excel is in Find mode, the scroll bars operate differently. The scroll boxes now indicate your position within the database range, not within the entire worksheet. Clicking the up or down arrow in the scroll box moves you to the next or prior matching record, respectively. Dragging the scroll box causes Excel to move to the nearest matching record in the relative area indicated by the location of the scroll box. You can make any needed changes to a record, but once you enter the changes, you exit from Find mode.

Exit from Find mode now by opening the Data menu and selecting the Exit Find command.

EDITING A DATABASE

Because the database is a portion of an Excel worksheet, you are already familiar with many of the commands that can be used to edit a database. You can add records by inserting new rows or columns and filling in the new cells with the desired data. You can also use the Data menu's Form command to display and edit a form for a record. A word of caution is advised, however. If you add new records or fields by inserting new rows or columns at the end of a database, you must use the Set Database command to refine the database range after the rows or columns have been added. This is not necessary if you insert the new rows or columns in the middle of the worksheet, because Excel automatically adjusts the database range when rows or columns are inserted inside the range.

To delete records, you can select the rows containing the records to be deleted and then use the Delete command from the Edit menu. (To try this, save the completed database first with the File menu's Save command.) An alternative method of deleting records is to open a form with the Form command, find the desired records with the methods outlined in the next section of this chapter, and delete the record by selecting the Delete button on the form. When you delete records, any records remaining below the deleted ones will move up to close the space left by the deleted records.

All commands in the Edit menu, including the Copy and Paste commands, work exactly the same with a database as they do with other worksheets. You may find the Copy, Paste, Fill Down, and Fill Right commands quite useful for reducing the tedium of data entry. For example, if you are entering a mailing list containing dozens of customers who reside in the same city, you could use the Fill Down command to copy the city and state names to a range of cells, leaving only the names, addresses, and ZIP codes to be entered.

How to Edit in a Form

You can use the Form command to edit the contents of a database. To do so, define the database range if you have not already done so. Then choose the Form command from the Data menu.

Open the Data menu now, and choose the Form command. A form that contains an existing record in the database appears, and you are placed in Forms mode as shown here:

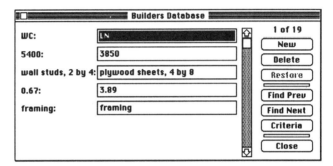

You can now use the Find Next and Find Previous buttons to move forward and backward in the database. You can also drag the scroll box within the form's scroll bar to navigate among the records. As the box is moved, the record number appears in the upper-right corner of the form. Clicking the up or down arrows at the top and bottom of the scroll bar moves you up or down by one record. To make any changes to records on the screen, click the appropriate box, enter the desired change, and press RETURN to store the record.

You can limit the records you view to specific criteria. This powerful feature of the Form command is similar to the Find command in the Data menu, but it works through the forms. You do this by switching to Criteria mode, entering the desired criteria, and then switching back to Forms mode to edit the desired records.

To try this, switch to Criteria mode by clicking the Criteria button. Click in the Category field, and enter **finish**. Then click the Forms button to switch back to Forms mode.

You can now use the Find Next and Find Previous buttons, or the scroll bar with the mouse, to find and edit records matching the criteria. Try selecting Find Next now by clicking the button. Each time you do this, you should see the next available record in the "finish" category. When you choose Find Next and no additional records are available, Excel beeps or flashes the menu bar.

To clear the criteria and resume full editing of the database, select the Criteria button to switch back to Criteria mode. Then delete the entry in the Category field by selecting it and pressing BACKSPACE. Finally, select the Form button to resume editing in Forms mode.

While in Forms mode, you can delete any record by choosing the Delete button as the record is displayed within the form. (If you wish to try this, be sure to save the database first.) When you select the Delete option, a dialog box appears, warning you that the deletion will be permanent. Click the OK button in the dialog box or press RETURN, and the record is deleted. The form then displays the next record in the database.

The New button can be used at any time to display a blank form for adding new records to the database. Simply select the New button and enter the desired data, pressing TAB after each entry. If you edit a field in an existing record and then change your mind, choosing the Restore button will restore the previous entry. When you are finished editing, choose the Close command to leave the form.

EXTRACTING RECORDS

Using the Data menu's Extract command, you can extract all records matching your criteria and store those records in another part of the database. The Extract command actually copies records, so the original records are left intact within the database. To extract matching records from the database, perform the following steps:

1. Locate a blank area of the worksheet that will contain the extracted data, and enter (or copy) the desired field names to the beginning of this area.

2. Select the field names, or a range that includes the field names, for the extracted records. If you select only the field names, Excel clears all cells below the field names and fills as much space as needed. If you select a range, Excel extracts only as many records as fit in that range.

3. From the Data menu, choose the Extract command.

When you choose the Extract command, Excel searches through the database range, comparing each record to the matching criteria specified in the criteria range. It then copies each matching record to the extract range. Note that any existing information in the extract range is overwritten as needed by the results of the Extract command.

As an exercise, let's extract all records of expenses for the Walnut Creek subdivision. First clear any existing entries of matching criteria underneath the field

To do this, select the cells containing any criteria and press COMMAND-B. Next, enter **WC** in cell A3.

Copy the field names to a blank area below the database. To do this, select cells A2 to E2. Open the Edit menu and choose Copy. Move to cell A35, open the Edit menu, and choose Paste. The field names will be copied into row 35 of the worksheet. With cells A35 to E35 still selected, open the Data menu and choose Extract. Within a moment, the following dialog box appears:

Extract
OK
Unique Records Only
Cancel

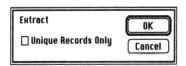

The dialog box provides an option named Unique Records Only. You can use it to eliminate the appearance of duplicate records in the extract range, which means that identical records will not appear twice in the extract range, even though they may be duplicated in the database.

For the present example, the Unique Records Only option isn't needed, so press RETURN or click the OK button to implement the Extract command. As a result, all

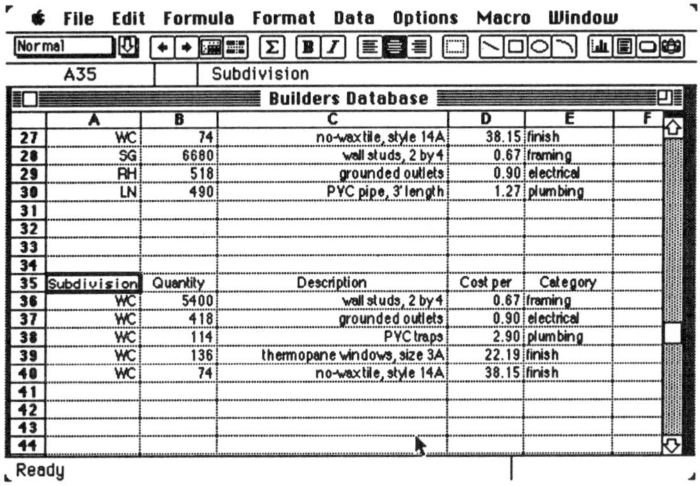

File Edit Formula Format Data Options Macro Window
Normal
A35
Subdivision
Builders Database
A B C D E F
27 WC 74 no-wax tile, style 14A 38.15 finish
28 SG 6680 wall studs, 2 by 4 0.67 framing
29 RH 518 grounded outlets 0.90 electrical
30 LN 490 PVC pipe, 3' length 1.27 plumbing
31
32
33
34
35 Subdivision Quantity Description Cost per Category
36 WC 5400 wall studs, 2 by 4 0.67 framing
37 WC 418 grounded outlets 0.90 electrical
38 WC 114 PVC traps 2.90 plumbing
39 WC 136 thermopane windows, size 3A 22.19 finish
40 WC 74 no-wax tile, style 14A 38.15 finish
41
42
43
44
Ready

FIGURE 7-7. Results of extract

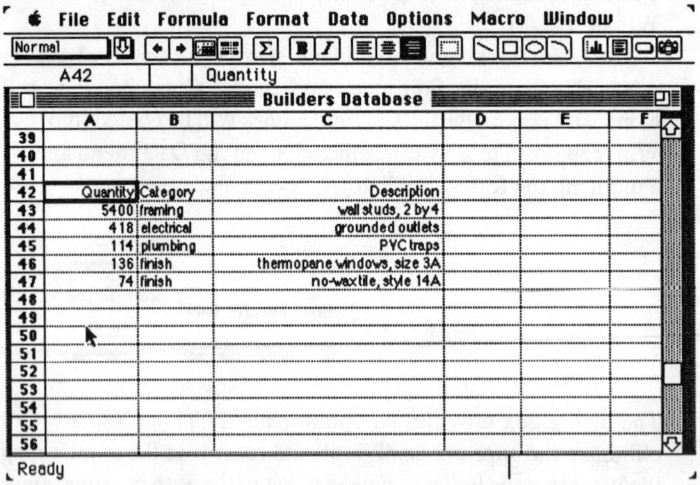

★ File Edit Formula Format Data Options Macro Window					

		Quantity			

Builders Database

	A	B	C	D	E	F
39						
40						
41						
42	Quantity	Category	Description			
43	5400	framing	wall studs, 2 by 4			
44	418	electrical	grounded outlets			
45	114	plumbing	PVC traps			
46	136	finish	thermopane windows, size 3A			
47	74	finish	no-wax tile, style 14A			
48						
49						
50						
51						
52						
53						
54						
55						
56						

Ready

FIGURE 7-8. Extract of selected fields

records with WC in the subdivision field appear in the cells below row 35, as shown in Figure 7-7. If your results don't match the results described here or if you see error messages such as "Extract range not valid," make sure you have correctly defined your database range and criteria range.

It is not necessary to use all of your field names in the extract range. You can limit the extracted data to certain fields by including only those fields at the top of the extract range. For example, enter the heading **Quantity** in cell A42, **Category** in cell B42, and **Description** in cell C42. Next, select this range of cells (from A42 to C42). Open the Data menu and choose Extract. When the dialog box appears, press RETURN to accept the default values. The records for Walnut Creek that contain only the specified fields listed in the extract range appear below row 42, as shown in Figure 7-8.

You should keep some points in mind when you are extracting records. First, if you define the extract range by selecting just one row, as you did in this exercise, Excel clears all information between that row and the bottom of the worksheet. This will happen even if only a single record is extracted as a result of the command. If you care about any data below the extract range, you should either define a specific range of cells for the extracted information or find an unused area of the worksheet. Second, when you perform an extract, Excel extracts the resultant values from the selected records, and not the contents of any formulas.

DELETING RECORDS BY MATCHING CRITERIA

The Delete command can be used to delete all records that match specific criteria. To delete records matching certain criteria, perform the following steps:

1. Select the database range containing the records to be deleted.

2. Define the criteria range containing the field names and the matching criteria.

3. Select the Delete command from the Data menu.

If you want to try this, be sure to save the database first. The effects of the Delete command cannot be reversed with the Undo command, so it is a good idea to use the Find or Extract command first to see just what records will be deleted when you use the Delete command. When you use the Delete command, a dialog box warns you that such deletions are permanent. You must then press RETURN or click the OK button to proceed with the deletion of the records.

USING CRITERIA CREATIVELY

By structuring your criteria in different ways, you can find, extract, or delete records that fulfill a variety of conditions. You can select records based on multiple criteria (for example, records of expenses between $500 and $1000). You can select records based on a combination of fields (for example, records with expenses over $500 that are in the River Hollow subdivision). You can also use *computed criteria,* which are criteria used to find records that pass certain tests based on a formula.

Matching on Two or More Fields

To find records that fulfill criteria in two or more fields, simply enter the information in the proper format below the names for each desired field. For example, say you wish to find all expenses in the River Hollow subdivision that are classified in the "finish" category. To try this, place the cursor in cell A3 and enter **RH**. Next, move to cell E3 and enter **finish**. Open the Data menu and choose Find. The first record in the database meeting these conditions appears (see Figure 7-9). Press the DOWN ARROW key (or click the down arrow in the scroll bar once), and the cursor moves to

❤ File Edit Formula Format Data Options Macro Window

| Normal | ⟨U⟩ | ← | → | ▦ ▦ | Σ | B | I | ▤ ▤ ▤ | ▢ | ◥ ▢ ◯ ◥ | ▦ ▦ ◯ ◉ |

| | 6 | | RH |

▢ Builders Database ▢

	A	B	C	D	E	F
10	Subdivision	Quantity	Description	Cost per	Category	
11	WC	5400	wall studs, 2 by 4	0.67	framing	
12	LN	3850	plywood sheets, 4 by 8	3.89	framing	
13	RH	512	PVC pipe, 3' length	1.27	plumbing	
14	RH	3450	wall studs, 1 by 2	0.58	framing	
15	WC	418	grounded outlets	0.90	electrical	
16	RH	10250	plasterboard	3.57	finish	
17	LN	7580	plasterboard	3.57	finish	
18	SG	518	PVC pipe, 1' length	0.77	plumbing	
19	SG	87	GFI breaker outlets	5.18	electrical	
20	WC	114	PVC traps	2.90	plumbing	
21	LN	3812	crown moulding	0.78	finish	
22	SG	72	thermopane windows, size 2B	14.12	finish	
23	RH	1290	crown moulding	0.78	finish	
24	WC	136	thermopane windows, size 3A	22.19	finish	
25	SG	158	no-waxtile, style 12B	36.20	finish	
26	LN	24	sliding glass doors	84.12	finish	
27	WC	74	no-waxtile, style 14A	38.15	finish	

Find (Use direction keys to view records)

FIGURE 7-9. Record with criteria match for two fields

the next record matching the criteria. Choose Exit Find from the Data menu to cancel the search.

Matching on Multiple Criteria

Suppose you want to find records that meet more than one criterion in the same field, such as all expenses in the plumbing or electrical categories. This can be done by entering each required criterion below the appropriate field name and by including all the entries in the criteria range. First clear the previous criteria by selecting cells A3 to E3 and pressing COMMAND-B. Move to cell E3 and enter **plumbing**. Next, move down one cell to E4 and enter **electrical**. Select cells A2 to E4 so that both possible entries for criteria are included in the range of selected cells. Open the Data menu and choose Set Criteria. In this case, you need to reset the criteria range to include both entries; otherwise, Excel would only include the entry that was within the range of the previously defined criteria.

Open the Data menu and choose Find. Pressing the DOWN ARROW key or clicking the down arrow in the scroll bar repeatedly displays the records meeting either condition you specified: those that have either "electrical" or "plumbing" in the category field. Note that because you placed more than one criterion below the field

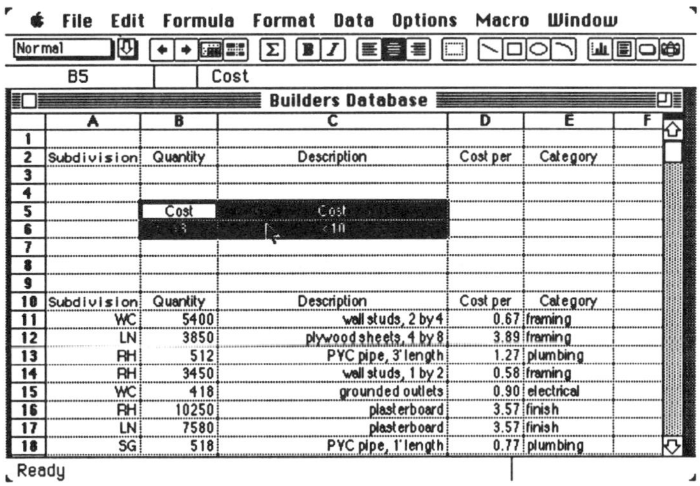

FIGURE 7-10.   Multiple criteria for the "and" condition

name, Excel found records that met either condition: electrical or plumbing. Whenever you list multiple criteria for the same field directly below a single field name, Excel follows *Boolean "or" logic:* If either qualification is met, Excel finds the record.

By contrast, you may want *Boolean "and" logic;* you may need to find records that match all criteria. To qualify records in this manner, you enter the same field name in more than one cell, but on the same row, and place the respective criteria below each field name. An example is shown in Figure 7-10. To find all records with an item cost of over $3.00 but under $10.00, enter **>3** in cell B6 directly below the first Cost field name and **<10** in cell C6 directly below the second Cost field name. Then set the criteria range to include the headings in B5 and C5 along with both criteria, and Excel locates all records that fall within this range. When you enter the criteria on the same row in this fashion, Excel places an "and" condition on the search; both criteria must be met before the record is selected.

COMPARING VALUES

The symbols =, <, and > can be used alone or in combination to build comparisons that cover a range of values, dates, times, or letters of the alphabet. The comparison operators are as follows:

<	Less than
>	Greater than
=	Equal to
<=	Less than or equal to
>=	Greater than or equal to
<>	Not equal to

Some examples illustrate the use of comparison operators. Figure 7-11 shows an extract of the database for the records from the Walnut Creek subdivision, where the cost per item was greater than $10.00. In this figure, the window containing the worksheet is split into two "panes" so that both the criteria range and the extracted data are visible at the same time. You will learn how to split windows to provide a better view in Chapter 8.

The example shown in Figure 7-12 illustrates an extract for all records in either the Walnut Creek or the River Hollow subdivisions, where the item quantity exceeded 600 units. Note that the data extracted as a result of this criteria includes only those records in either the Walnut Creek or the River Hollow subdivisions that had over 600 items in the Quantity field.

Now compare the criteria shown in Figure 7-12 with the criteria shown in Figure 7-13 and the results of the extracted data. In this case, the records extracted for the Walnut Creek subdivision are only the records with over 600 items in the Quantity field, but the extracted records for the River Hollow subdivision include all records

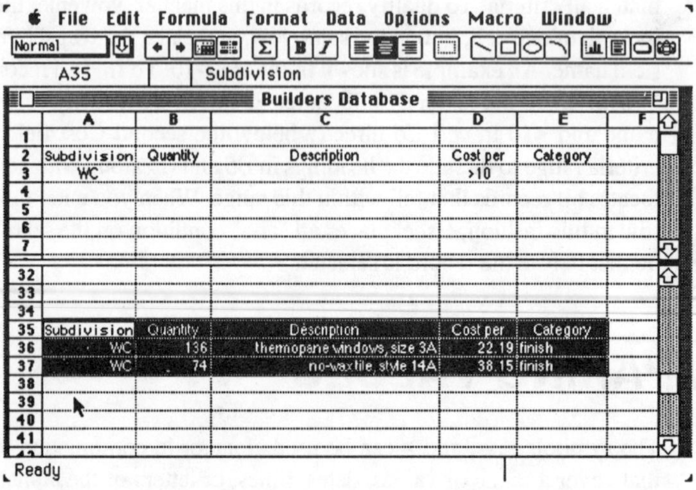

FIGURE 7-11. Walnut Creek cost comparison

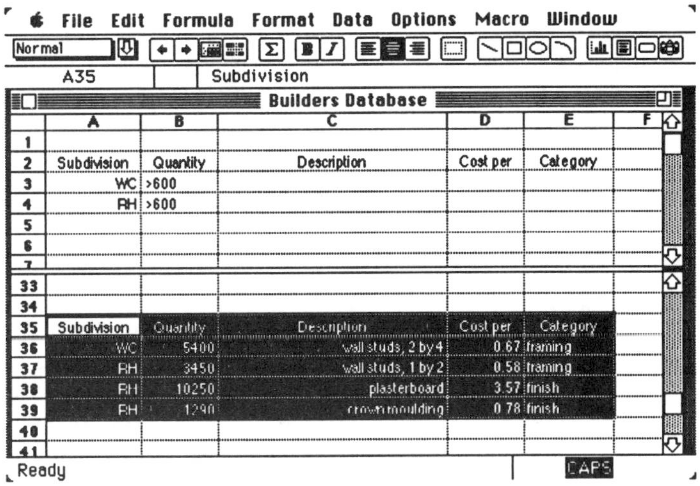

FIGURE 7-12.　Use of multiple criteria

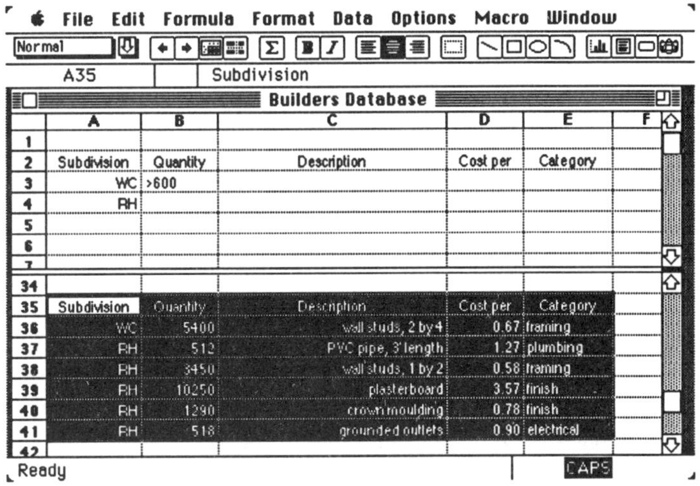

FIGURE 7-13.　A different result from multiple criteria

for that subdivision, not just those with 600 or more in the Quantity field. Excel derives its and/or logic, or the way it interprets multiple criteria, from the structure of that criteria. You must exercise care in designing complex criteria so that your results match your needs. Also make sure your ranges are properly defined, or you may encounter error messages or incorrect results from an extract.

Specifying Exact Searches

Excel finds the text that you enter as criteria if the contents of the cell begin with the text you've entered. Sometimes, this may not be what you want. In searching the City field in a sizable database, for example, you may want to find persons living in a town named Atlantic. The problem is that if you enter **Atlantic** in the cell used as the criteria for the City field, you will extract the names of persons living in Atlantic, Atlantic Beach, Atlantic Bay, Atlantic City, and Atlantic Island.

To locate text containing only the specified word in the field, surround the text with quotation marks, and surround the beginning quotation mark with two equal signs. To specify the town of Atlantic, for example, you would enter

="=Atlantic"

as the matching criteria for the City field.

Using Wildcards

As a part of the criteria, you can use *wildcards,* which are characters used as symbols for one or more characters. Excel permits two wildcards: the question mark, which stands for any character, and the asterisk, which represents any number of characters in the same position. For example, the criteria H?ll locates the names Hall, Hill, and Hull. The search text *der locates all strings of text ending in the syllable "der."

To see an example, clear any existing criteria currently below the field names in the criteria range. Then enter *ing in cell E3. Select cells A2 to E3 again, open the Data menu, and choose the Set Criteria command. (Specifying the criteria range again is necessary because the last operation you performed expanded that range to more than one row. For this example, only one row is desired.)

Open the Data menu and select Find. As you repeatedly press the DOWN ARROW key, notice that only those records with a category entry that ends in "ing" (as in "framing" and "plumbing") are selected. Choose Exit Find from the Data menu to leave Find mode.

Excel considers a blank cell in a criteria range to be a wildcard for that field. If your defined criteria range contains your headings, a row with criteria, and an extra blank row underneath the criteria, you may be surprised to discover that Excel selects every row in the database. Redefine your criteria range to omit any blank rows, and the problem disappears.

Using Computed Criteria

Excel lets you use formulas as criteria for selecting records. The formula that you enter can refer to one or more fields within the database. During a Find, Extract, or Delete operation, Excel evaluates each record to see if the formula results in a logical value of TRUE. Records that result in a logical value of FALSE are ignored.

For example, you might need to see all records in which the total cost of items purchased was over $1000. The database does not contain a field for total cost. You could add one by inserting a column and a formula and by using the Fill Down command to copy the formula into all of the cells. However, it is probably easier to use a computed criteria, which will be based on the values of the Cost and Quantity fields.

To perform the needed calculation, you can use this formula:

=COST*QUANTITY > 1000

This formula evaluates whether the cost multiplied by the quantity exceeds 1000. If it does, Excel returns a logical value of TRUE for the record in question; otherwise, it returns a logical value of FALSE. For the cell references that represent the Cost and Quantity amounts, you can enter relative references for the first record in the database. As Excel tests each record in the database, it adjusts the formula references to correspond to the row in question.

To enter a computed criteria, you enter a description of the criteria in a blank cell and enter the formula below the description. You then select those cells and use the Set Criteria command to define the selected area as the criteria range. For an example, go to cell C5 and enter the description

Is cost * quantity > 1000?

Move to cell C6 and enter the formula

=D11*B11>1000

When you finish entering the formula, the value of TRUE appears in the cell, because the formula is testing the first record in the database for the specified condition. Once you select a Find, Extract, or Delete command, Excel tests all records in the database range against the formula. Select cells C5 to C6, open the Data menu, and choose the Set Criteria command. (Note that you must always include the cell directly above the formula in the criteria range, even if you do not include a description. If you do not include this cell in the range, Excel displays an "Invalid range" error message when you try the Find command.)

Next, select cells A35 to E35, which are the headings for the extract range below the database. Open the Data menu and choose Extract. Press RETURN to accept the defaults when the dialog box appears. All records with a total cost that exceeds $1000 appear in the extract range below row 35, as shown in Figure 7-14.

Note that if you use the Define Name command to assign names to areas of a worksheet, you can use those names within your computed criteria formulas. If, for example, you give the name Cost to cells D11 to D30 and the name Quantity to cells B11 to B30, you can then use the formula

=COST*QUANTITY>1000

to select the desired records.

Before proceeding, clear the range that you just extracted. Then save the database.

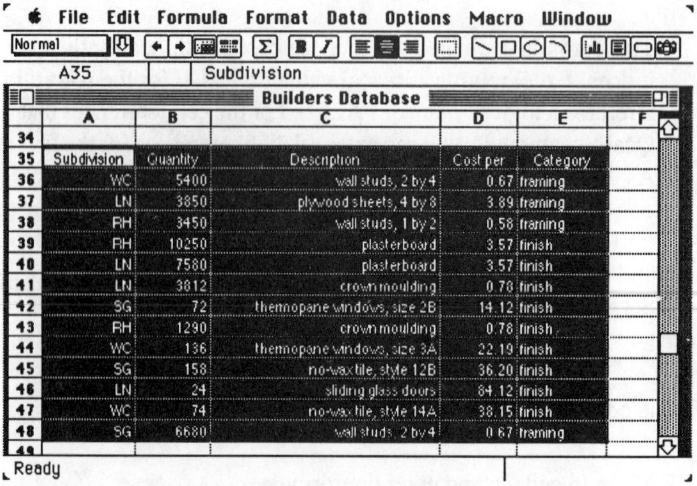

FIGURE 7-14. Extract resulting from computed criteria

SORTING A DATABASE

After you compile a database, you may need to arrange it in various ways. For example, consider the needs of the staff at the building company. Frank, who is the construction foreman, often needs a list of expenses by subdivision, while Jennifer, who is the accounting manager, is more interested in the cost of each item. You can arrange a database by *sorting*, which means changing the order of the records.

When Excel sorts a database, it rearranges all records in the database according to a specified new order. If you were to alphabetically sort a database of names arranged in random order, the sorted database would contain all the records that were in the old database, but they would be arranged in alphabetical order (see Figure 7-15).

When Excel sorts a database in ascending order, it sorts by numbers first, followed by text, the logical values TRUE or FALSE, and finally by error values. Excel is not case-sensitive; it ignores both case and accent marks while sorting. Blank cells appear at the end of the sort, whether you are sorting in ascending or descending order.

You must choose a field on which to sort. The chosen field is often referred to as the *key field.* In some cases, you might need to sort a database on more than one field. For example, if you sort a database alphabetically, using last names as the key field, you might get groups of records with the last names arranged alphabetically but with the first names in random order. In such a case, you can sort the database by using last names as the first key field and first names as the second key field.

To sort a database, you use the Data menu's Sort command. Before using this command, however, you must redefine the database range to exclude the row that contains the field headings. If you include the field headings in the database range, Excel sorts that row along with the other records, and your headings may be in the wrong location when the sort is completed.

As an exercise, go to cell A11. Press the Go To key (COMMAND- G) and type **E30** in the dialog box, but don't press RETURN. Instead, press SHIFT-RETURN to move to cell E30 and select the entire range. Open the Data menu, and choose the Set Database command to define the range to be sorted. Open the Data menu, and choose Sort. The following dialog box appears

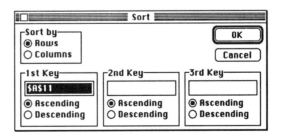

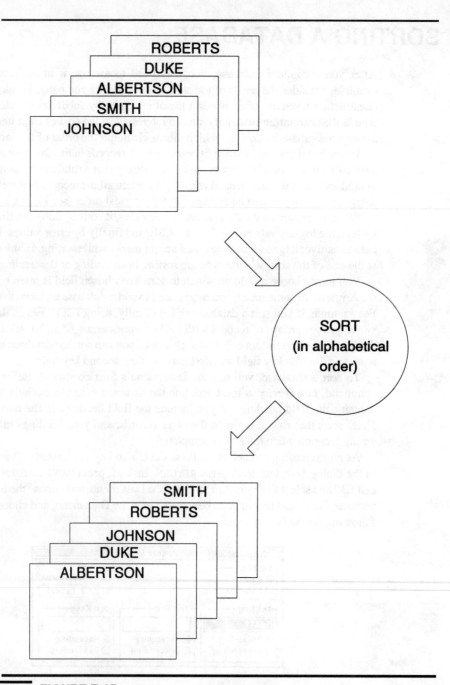

FIGURE 7-15. Sorting records in a database

The Sort dialog box lets you sort a database using any field, or a combination of up to three fields, in ascending or descending order. Databases can be sorted by rows or by columns.

Because this database contains records arranged in rows, it makes more sense to sort the database by rows. To choose the field for the sort, simply enter in the First Key box a cell reference that is in your chosen field. (You can select a default entry by clicking anywhere in the desired field on the worksheet before you select the Sort command). For example, if you want to sort by category, you enter a cell reference for any cell in column E within the First Key box. The Second and Third Key boxes are needed only for sorting on multiple fields, a topic that is discussed shortly. A choice of ascending or descending order is entered by selecting the Ascending or Descending button.

To satisfy Frank's request for a list of expenses for each subdivision arranged in alphabetical order, you need to enter a cell in column A as the First Key entry, which is currently highlighted. Excel has placed the current cursor location, $A$11, in this box, so in this case you can let the entry stand. (It is not necessary to use absolute references; Excel simply enters the reference in this fashion.)

The First Key designation indicates the priority of fields, in order of importance, that determines the sort. When a database is sorted on a single field, this order has no real meaning. However, when you sort a database on more than one field, you use the First, Second, and Third Key entries to choose the fields that will take priority in determining the order of the sort.

The First Key box also contains the Ascending button, which is chosen as a default entry. Excel assumes you wish to sort databases in ascending order. Ascending order means from A through Z if the sorted field contains text; from the lowest to the highest number for numeric fields; and from the earliest to the latest date for date fields. In most cases, this is how you want the database to be sorted. Ascending order is correct for this example.

Once the criteria for the sort have been entered in the dialog box, you can perform the sort by pressing RETURN or by clicking the OK button. Press RETURN now, and the database will be sorted. When it reappears it is arranged by subdivision in alphabetical order, as shown in Figure 7-16.

Note that if records are added to a database following a sort, the new records are not automatically sorted. If you want those records to fall into proper order, you must again sort the database after adding the records.

Sorting on Multiple Fields

Now you've printed the database and given it to Frank, who immediately decides that within each subdivision, the categories should appear in alphabetical order. Looking

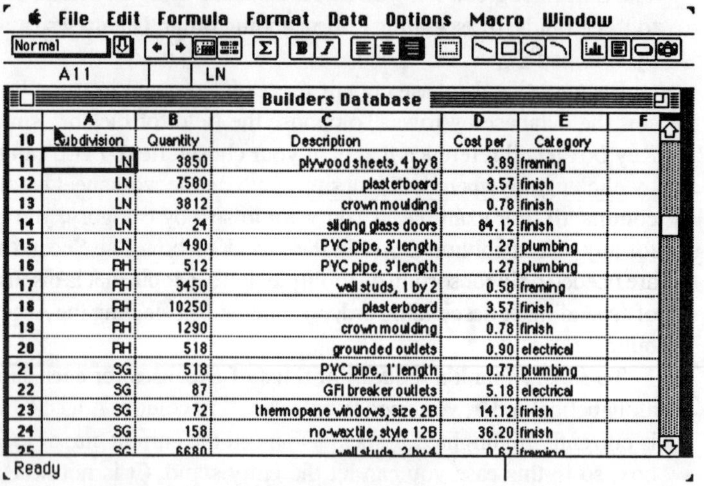

 File   Edit   Formula   Format   Data   Options   Macro   Window

| Normal | | ← | → | | | Σ | B | I | | | | | | ⟍ | ▢ | ◯ | ⟍ | | ⊞ | ▤ | ▭ | |
| A11 | | | LN | | | | | | | | | | | | | | | | | | | | | |

Builders Database

	A	B	C	D	E	F
10	Subdivision	Quantity	Description	Cost per	Category	
11	LN	3850	plywood sheets, 4 by 8	3.89	framing	
12	LN	7580	plasterboard	3.57	finish	
13	LN	3812	crown moulding	0.78	finish	
14	LN	24	sliding glass doors	84.12	finish	
15	LN	490	PYC pipe, 3' length	1.27	plumbing	
16	RH	512	PYC pipe, 3' length	1.27	plumbing	
17	RH	3450	wall studs, 1 by 2	0.58	framing	
18	RH	10250	plasterboard	3.57	finish	
19	RH	1290	crown moulding	0.78	finish	
20	RH	518	grounded outlets	0.90	electrical	
21	SG	518	PYC pipe, 1' length	0.77	plumbing	
22	SG	87	GFI breaker outlets	5.18	electrical	
23	SG	72	thermopane windows, size 2B	14.12	finish	
24	SG	158	no-wax tile, style 12B	36.20	finish	
25	SG	6680	wall studs, 2 by 4	0.67	framing	

Ready

FIGURE 7-16.   Sorted database

at Figure 7-16, it is easy to see that for each group of subdivisions, the records are not in alphabetical order by category. To make them so requires a sort on more than one field.

Select the range from A11 to E30 (if it is not still selected). Open the Data menu and select Sort. When the dialog box appears, click the Second Key box and enter **E11** as a cell reference for the second key. Press RETURN to implement the changes, and sort the database again. The database will now look like the one in Figure 7-17.

The references that you have entered within the sort keys indicate that the database should be sorted in two ways. First the records are arranged by subdivision in ascending alphabetical order. Second, within the same subdivision, the records are sorted by category in ascending alphabetical order.

Changing the Sort Direction

Frank is happy with the new database, but Jennifer would like to see a list of records arranged by cost per item, with the lowest costs at the bottom of the list. To sort in descending order, you need to change the direction of the sort.

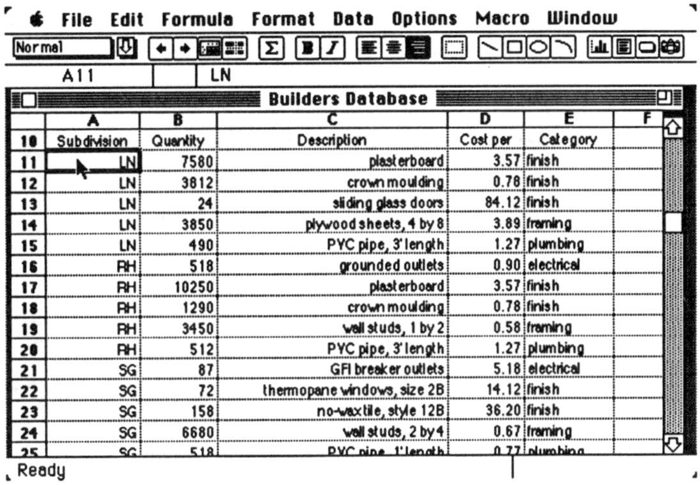

 ` ⚫ File Edit Formula Format Data Options Macro Window ⌐

| Normal | | | | Σ | | | | | | | |

| A11 | | LN |

Builders Database

	A	B	C	D	E	F
10	Subdivision	Quantity	Description	Cost per	Category	
11	LN	7580	plasterboard	3.57	finish	
12	LN	3812	crown moulding	0.78	finish	
13	LN	24	sliding glass doors	84.12	finish	
14	LN	3850	plywood sheets, 4 by 8	3.89	framing	
15	LN	490	PYC pipe, 3' length	1.27	plumbing	
16	RH	518	grounded outlets	0.90	electrical	
17	RH	10250	plasterboard	3.57	finish	
18	RH	1290	crown moulding	0.78	finish	
19	RH	3450	wall studs, 1 by 2	0.58	framing	
20	RH	512	PYC pipe, 3' length	1.27	plumbing	
21	SG	87	GFI breaker outlets	5.18	electrical	
22	SG	72	thermopane windows, size 2B	14.12	finish	
23	SG	158	no-wax tile, style 12B	36.20	finish	
24	SG	6680	wall studs, 2 by 4	0.67	framing	
25	SG	518	PYC pipe, 1' length	0.77	plumbing	

Ready

FIGURE 7-17. Database sorted by subdivision and category

Open the Data menu and select Sort. When the dialog box appears, enter **D11** as a reference in the First Key box. (You may notice that the Sort dialog box returns to the default choices; it does not retain the options used for the previous sort.) Select the Descending option by clicking its button. Press RETURN or click the OK button to implement the changes, and sort the database again. The database will be sorted by costs in descending order, as shown in Figure 7-18.

Sorting on More Than Three Fields

Occasionally, you may need to sort a database on more than three fields. For example, you might have a large mailing list in Excel, and you might wish to sort the database by state, then by city within each state, then by last name within each city, and then by first name within each group of last names.

Because Excel provides only three sort keys, this type of sort might sound impossible. In fact, Excel can handle such a task, if you break the job down into multiple sorts. Begin with the least important group of sorts and progress towards the most important group of sorts, and list the more important key first within each group of sorts. For example, you would first sort with the Last Name field as the first key and the First Name field as the second key. You would then perform another sort, this

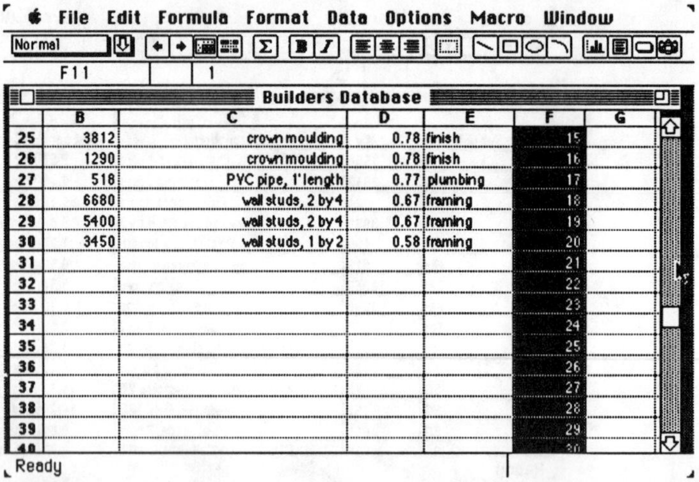

FIGURE 7-18.   Database sorted in descending order

time using the State field as the first key, the City field as the second key, and the Last Name field as the third key.

Sorting by Columns

With some databases, you may find it helpful to perform a *columnar* sort. An example of such a database is shown in Figure 7-19. The steps for sorting this database by columns are nearly identical to the steps for sorting a database by rows. The only difference is that you should select the Columns option from the Sort dialog box that appears when the Sort command is selected.

For the database shown in Figure 7-19, you would set the database range to cells B2 to F8. Choose the Sort command, and use cell B2 as the sort key. This indicates a sort by name, since all the employee names are in row 2. Select the Columns option within the Sort By area of the dialog box. Press RETURN to sort the database, and the results should be similar to those in Figure 7-20.

Because Excel has a columnar sort capability does not mean you should design your databases in a horizontal fashion. The Find, Extract, and Delete commands are designed to work effectively with criteria ranges that follow a vertical format. If you

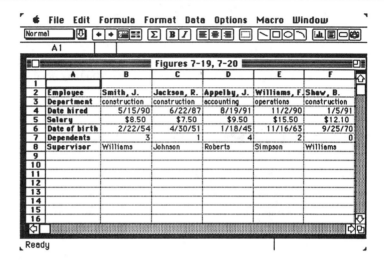

FIGURE 7-19. Sample personnel database

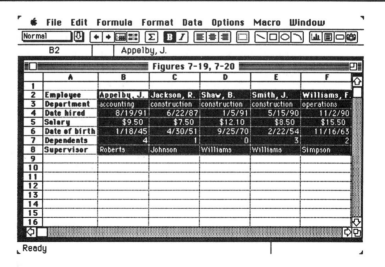

FIGURE 7-20. Database after columnar sort

try to use the Find or Extract command along with a criteria range for the database shown in Figure 7-19, you will run into difficulty. Excel will look down the rows of the database, trying to find a match that isn't there, because the database is arranged in a horizontal format. The columnar sort capability is simply an additional tool, provided by Excel for those instances in which you may need to sort by columns.

Recreating the Pre-Sort Original

You *cannot* undo the effects of a sort. If you want to retain your database in the manner in which the records were originally entered, you have two options. You can save the file under another file name and then recall that file if you want to see how the file was originally organized. This approach has problems, however, because it is difficult to keep two databases containing the same data updated.

A better approach is to add a column of record numbers to the database. The first record entered becomes record 1, the second record entered becomes record 2, and so on. If you ever want to reorganize the database in the order in which the records were originally entered, you can simply sort on the field that contains the record numbers.

USING THE SERIES COMMAND

You can use the Series command to create record numbers in a database automatically. The Series command fills any selected range of cells with values that increase or decrease at a rate that you specify. The first cell in the range must contain the starting value for the series. As an exercise, move to cell F11 and enter **1**. Then select the range from F11 to F40. Open the Data menu and choose Series. The following dialog box will appear

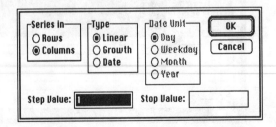

The choices in this box permit you to determine whether the series appears along a row or down a column, and whether the series increases in a linear fashion, a growth fashion, or by dates. The Linear option causes the values in the series to increase by

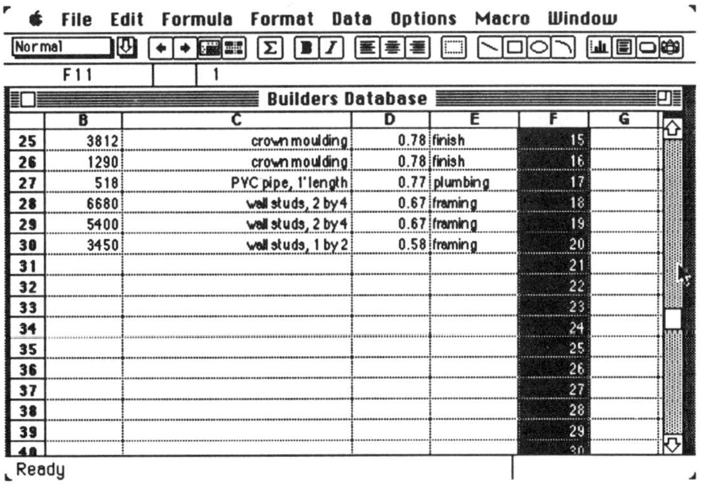

FIGURE 7-21.   Effects of Series command

the number you enter in the Step Value box. The Growth option multiplies the values in the series by the number you enter in the Step Value box. Choosing the Date option lets you select whether the value should be increased by day, weekday, month, or year. (If you select the Date option, the corresponding Date Unit options are made available.)

In this example, you want to increase the series values by 1 in a linear fashion. Because these are the default options, press RETURN or click the OK button. The selected cells are filled with values that increase by 1, as you can see in Figure 7-21.

Before proceeding, you may want to close the database without saving the sorted examples. The database in its current form will not be needed elsewhere in the book.

chapter 8

WORKING WITH MULTIPLE DOCUMENTS

Until now, you've been doing most of your work in a single window. Whenever a document is opened in Excel, it resides in a window. Since an unlimited number of windows can be open at the same time, you can make the most of Excel's capabilities by working with multiple windows.

Multiple windows are useful with large worksheets, letting you view different strategic areas of the worksheet at the same time. With databases, you can open multiple windows to view criteria in one window and records in another.

Excel's windows can also be used to work more effectively with *linked documents*—documents that are linked by external references or by references to a different worksheet. A major limitation of many older spreadsheets is that they are two-dimensional. Older spreadsheets can analyze data that is laid out down columns and across rows, but when you need to integrate numerous worksheets (for example, using a row of totals from one worksheet as starting values in another worksheet), you are faced with a three-dimensional problem. Second-generation spreadsheet users have found two ways around this problem: combining the worksheets into a single large worksheet, or manually copying the row containing the totals into the worksheet with the cumulative totals. Neither solution is entirely satisfactory; combining large worksheets takes too much memory, and copying rows by hand takes too much time. With a worksheet that is truly three-dimensional like Excel, you can link a summary worksheet with individual worksheets by referring to the cells on the individual worksheets when you create formulas in the summary worksheet.

SPLITTING A WINDOW

Because most worksheets are too large to fit on one screen, it is difficult to keep titles in view while you scroll to a different part of the worksheet. Excel lets you split a window into two or more "panes," which scroll independently of each other in one direction but are aligned with each other in another direction. A window can be split along a horizontal axis, a vertical axis, or both axes. To split a window, you drag the split bars with the mouse. The locations of the split bars are shown in Figure 8-1.

Open the Income worksheet you created in the earlier chapters. To split the worksheet window horizontally into two panes, move the mouse pointer to the split bar at the bottom of the worksheet. The pointer will change to a thin cross with arrows pointing to the right and left. Click the mouse, and drag the split bar until the shaded

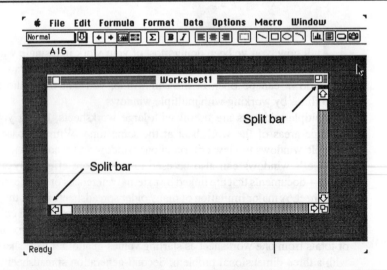

FIGURE 8-1. Split bars

bar is just past the width of the first column. (If you don't go past the column, you will still split the worksheet, but the two worksheets will both contain the same column.) When you release the mouse button, a solid double line between columns A and B indicates that the worksheet has been split into two panes (see Figure 8-2).

Try moving the cursor to the right. As you do so, you will see that the worksheet on one side of the split remains stationary while the worksheet on the other side of the split bar moves. You can move the active cell from one pane to another by clicking the mouse in any cell within the desired pane.

Try using the UP ARROW and DOWN ARROW keys or the vertical scroll bar. Although the worksheets are independent in terms of horizontal movement, you will see that they remain linked vertically. Also note the presence of added scroll bars at the bottom of the screen for each pane. These bars can be used independently to scroll the contents of either pane in the horizontal direction.

To close the pane, drag the split bar back to the far left edge of the worksheet, past the row numbers. Use this technique to close the pane now.

Opening a pane along a horizontal axis is a similar process. You place the mouse pointer near the split bar located at the right side of the worksheet, drag the split bar down to the desired location, and release the mouse. Use this technique now to split the worksheet just below the headings for each quarter. The results are shown in Figure 8-3 (depending on where you released the mouse, your screen may look different).

As you move the cursor to the right past the edge of the screen with the RIGHT ARROW key, you can see that the panes are linked in terms of horizontal movement.

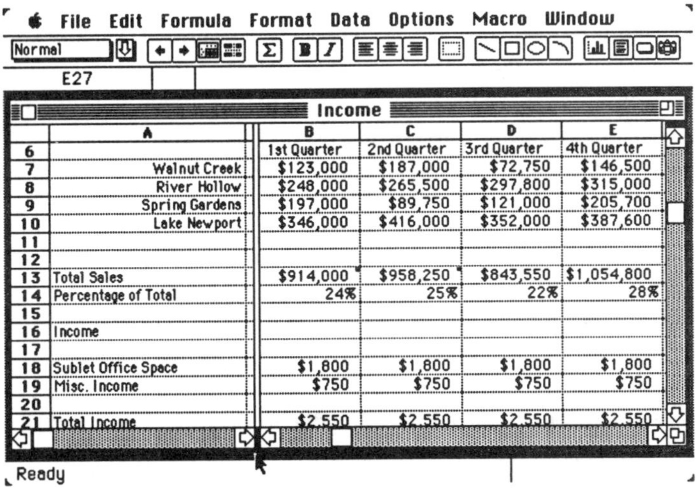

FIGURE 8-2.   Window split into two panes

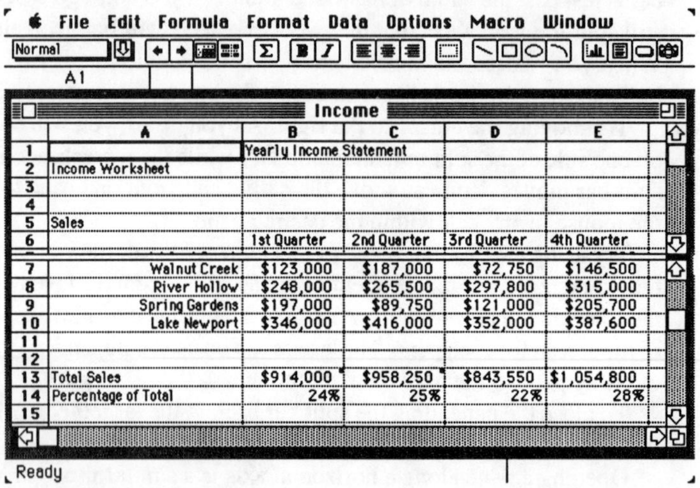

FIGURE 8-3. Window split along a horizontal axis

If you drag the boxes in either vertical scroll bar, however, it becomes apparent that the panes are independent of each other when it comes to vertical movement. Again, you can move between panes by clicking in any cell in the desired pane.

Either of the two scroll bars at the right edge of the worksheet can be used to scroll the contents of its respective windows. When you are in a small window, be careful with the scroll bars; a small amount of movement of the boxes can result in a large movement of the worksheet.

You can split a window along both the horizontal and vertical axes simultaneously. This can be helpful for keeping titles that appear along the top and left edges of a worksheet in view. To see how this works, first use the scroll bars to bring the top left corner of the worksheet back into view. Then drag the split bar at the bottom of the worksheet until the shaded line appears just to the right of the first column, and release the mouse button. The result is a worksheet split into four panes, as shown in Figure 8-4.

Try pressing the RIGHT ARROW and DOWN ARROW keys repeatedly. As the worksheet scrolls to the left or right, the pane directly below continues to be linked in its movement. When you use the UP ARROW and DOWN ARROW keys, the pane to the right continues to be linked also. In your worksheets, you can size the panes to gain the most benefit. Close the panes now by dragging the split bars back to the upper and left edges of the worksheet.

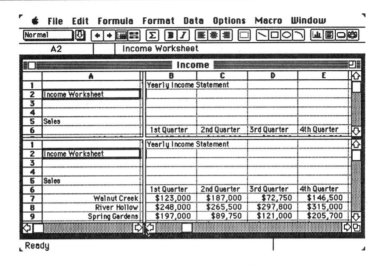

═══ **FIGURE 8-4.** Worksheet split into four panes

THE WINDOW MENU

Excel provides the Window menu, shown here, to help you manage your windows:

The first command in the menu, Help, displays the help screens you learned about in Chapter 2. The New Window command lets you open another window for the document you are currently using. The Show Clipboard command displays the contents of the Macintosh Clipboard. Details on how you can use the Clipboard with Excel can be found in Chapter 12.

The Show Info command displays information about the active cell, including the contents of any formulas and notes that are associated with the cell. The Arrange All command can be thought of as a housekeeper for a messy desk—it rearranges all open windows neatly on the screen in a layered fashion. The Workgroup command is used to select multiple worksheets for editing as a group. The Hide and Unhide commands can be used to temporarily place a window out of view or to bring a hidden window back into view.

In addition to providing these commands, the Window menu also lists all open windows by the name of the document at the bottom of the menu. You can select any document from the list to make that window the active window.

OPENING MULTIPLE WINDOWS FOR THE SAME DOCUMENT

Opening several windows for the same document lets you see different areas without having those areas linked in a scrolling direction, as is the case with panes. To open a second window for a document, use the New Window command of the Window menu. Open the Window menu now and choose New Window. In a moment, you should see a second window open for the Income worksheet, as shown in Figure 8-5.

When you use the New Window command, the newly created window automatically becomes the active window and lies on top of the existing window. If you want

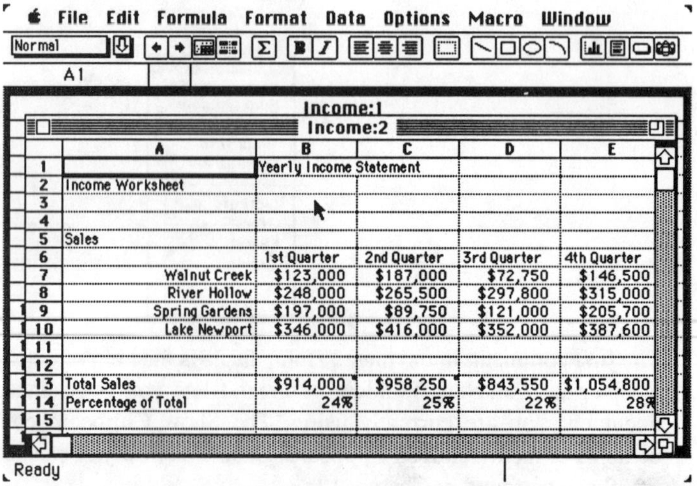

FIGURE 8-5. New window for Income worksheet

to see more of both windows, you must move and size the windows to your preference by dragging the size box in the lower-right corner of the window. Figure 8-6 shows both windows sized and moved to opposite corners of the screen.

When two windows of the same document are open, Excel differentiates between the two by adding a colon and a number to the document name; thus, one window on your screen is called Income:1, and the other is called Income:2. Each window moves independently of the other and has separate scroll boxes and cursors. Both windows still refer to the same file, so any changes you make in either window that are later saved with the Save command are saved to the same file.

Only one window can be the active window (the window within which you are working) at any one time. To change the active window, click anywhere within the desired window, or open the Window menu and choose the desired window from the list of window names that appears at the bottom of the menu.

Using Arrange All

When you are working with a number of windows and you can't see a particular window, you can use the Window menu's Arrange All command to organize your

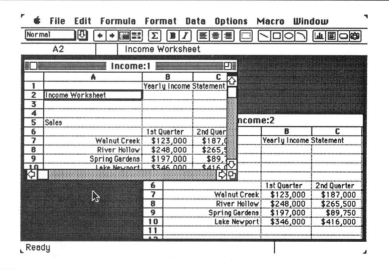

FIGURE 8-6.   Windows after sizing and moving

desktop. The Arrange All command quickly resizes and moves all open windows, rearranging them in a tiled fashion. Figures 8-7 and 8-8 demonstrate the effects of the Arrange All command.

Formula Editing Through an Active Window

When you are editing formulas, you can refer to cells that are visible in another window of the same worksheet. You begin by editing the formula in the usual manner, clicking in the formula bar and starting to enter the desired formula. However, when you need to include a cell reference that is in another window, instead of entering that reference, you open the Window menu and choose that window by name. Doing this makes that window partially active.

You cannot perform complete worksheet operations in the partially active window, but you can move the cursor around and select cells for inclusion in the formula. As you select the other cells, their references, including the worksheet names, appear within the formula bar.

Complete the formula in the usual manner. When you finish constructing the formula and press RETURN, you are returned to the active window.

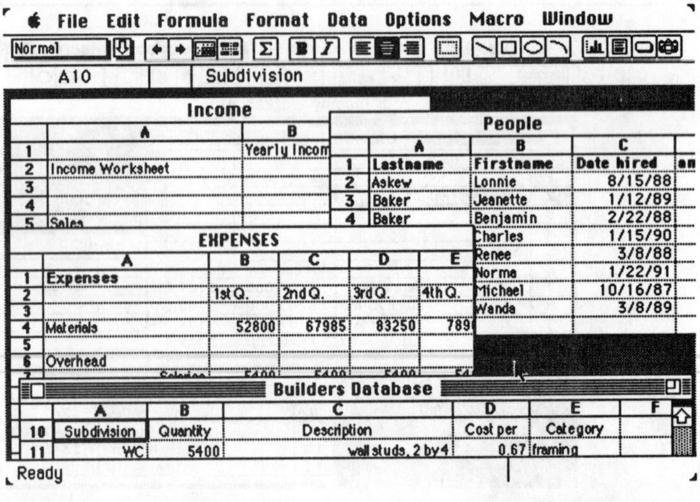

FIGURE 8-7.   Windows before choosing the Arrange All command

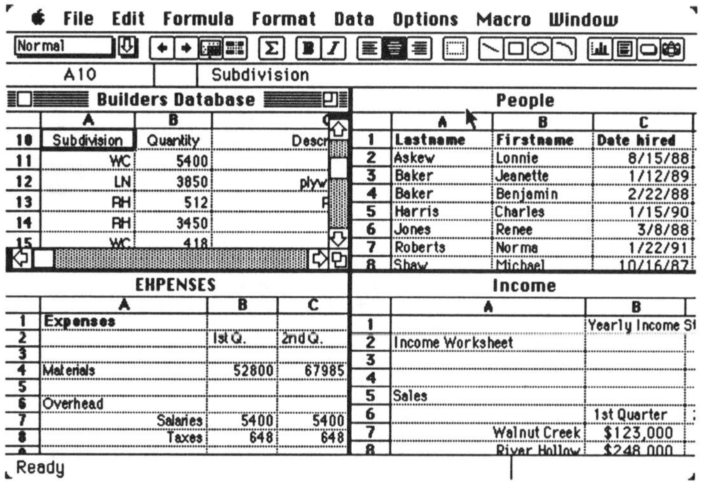

FIGURE 8-8.   Windows after choosing the Arrange All command

LINKING WORKSHEETS

In an Excel worksheet, you can refer to another cell or group of cells located on a different worksheet. Whenever you enter a cell reference that refers to another worksheet, Excel automatically links the active worksheet with the worksheet to which you are referring. Excel does this in such a simple, straightforward fashion that it seems transparent at times.

Cell references that refer to other worksheets are called *external references*. Like other references, external references can be relative or absolute. An external reference can refer to a single cell, a range of cells, or a named range on another worksheet. In Figure 8-9, cell B4 in the National Sales worksheet contains a formula with an external reference. The formula is displayed in the formula bar. The total units for the Mid-Atlantic region in the National Sales worksheet is calculated by adding the separate Mid-Atlantic state figures in the Regional Sales worksheet.

When worksheets are linked, the worksheet that refers to another is called the *dependent worksheet,* and the worksheet that is being referred to is called the *supporting worksheet.* In Figure 8-9, the National Sales worksheet is the dependent worksheet, and the Regional Sales worksheet is the supporting worksheet.

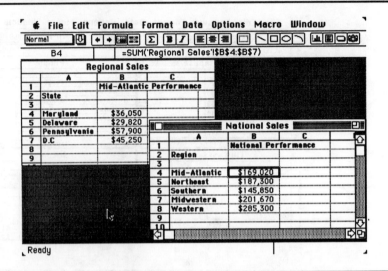

FIGURE 8-9.   Example of dependent and supporting worksheets

Creating External References

You can place an external reference within a formula in one of two ways: by manually entering the reference, or by selecting the cell that is referred to in the other worksheet as you are building the formula. External references are indicated by including the worksheet name surrounded by quotes, followed by an exclamation point, prior to the cell reference. In Figure 8-9, for example, the formula

   =SUM('Regional Sales'!$B$4:$B$7)

tells Excel that the reference is an external one and that the required values can be found in the range from cells B4 to B7 in the Regional Sales worksheet.

Here are some additional examples of external references:

='Region5'!C14	Relative reference to cell C14 in Region 5 worksheet
=SUM('Income'! B7:B10)	Relative reference to a range of cells in the Income worksheet

=SUM('Income'! Walnut_Creek: River_Hollow)	Reference to a named range within the Income worksheet

Dependencies

When you start working with dependent and supporting worksheets, you should keep the overall picture in mind. The values on your dependent worksheet may not be correct if you make certain changes to a supporting worksheet or if Excel cannot locate the supporting worksheet. Whenever you open a dependent worksheet, Excel looks to see if the supporting worksheets are open. If they are open, Excel updates the values in the dependent worksheet by getting the current values from the supporting worksheet. If you have not removed or changed these values since the last time the supporting worksheet was opened, Excel can update the values correctly. If you have made radical changes to the supporting worksheet, such as moving entire rows or columns, Excel probably won't find the proper data and will instead display an error message. Even worse, Excel may find data that is incorrect and display incorrect results based on that data.

Let's continue with an exercise. If the second window for the Income worksheet (Income:2) is not closed, close that window now by clicking the Close box. The first window containing the Income worksheet should remain open. If it is not open, open the Income worksheet now; doing so will avoid dependency problems later.

To demonstrate Excel's capacity to link multiple worksheets, you need another worksheet that lists the expenses for our fictitious building company. To simplify the task of data entry, let's enter some categories and data that are illustrative of an actual worksheet of this type.

Open the File menu and select New. Choose Worksheet from the dialog box to create a new worksheet. Enter the following data in the appropriate cells:

Cell	Entry
A4	Materials
A6	Overhead
A7	Salaries
A8	Taxes
A10	Office Rent
A11	Utilities
A12	Advertising
A13	Supplies
A14	Misc.
A16	Total Expenses

B2	1st Quarter
C2	2nd Quarter
D2	3rd Quarter
E2	4th Quarter
B4	52800
B7	5400
B8	=B7*0.12
B10	1200
B11	100
B12	550
B13	75
B14	110
B16	=SUM(B4:B14)
C4	67985
D4	83250
E4	78900

Select the cells from B7 to E16. Open the Edit menu and choose Fill Right to fill in the values and formulas for the second, third, and fourth quarters.

Select cells A7 to A14, open the Format menu, and choose Alignment, and then Right. Press RETURN to implement the change. Use the Column Width command from the Format menu to change the width of column A to 15 characters.

At this point, your worksheet should resemble the one shown in Figure 8-10. Open the File menu and choose the Save command. Enter **Expenses** as the worksheet name. *Do not* close the worksheet; you need to keep it open, because the Profits worksheet will be dependent on both the Expenses and Income worksheets.

At this point, the Expenses and Income worksheets should both be open on your screen. Create another new worksheet by using the New command from the File menu. This worksheet will serve as a profit-and-loss sheet, showing the income and expenses from the other worksheets. Enter this data in the appropriate cells:

Cell	Entry
A4	Gross Sales
A5	Other Income
A7	Total Income
A9	Less Expenses
A11	Net Profits
B2	1st Quarter
C2	2nd Quarter
D2	3rd Quarter
E2	4th Quarter

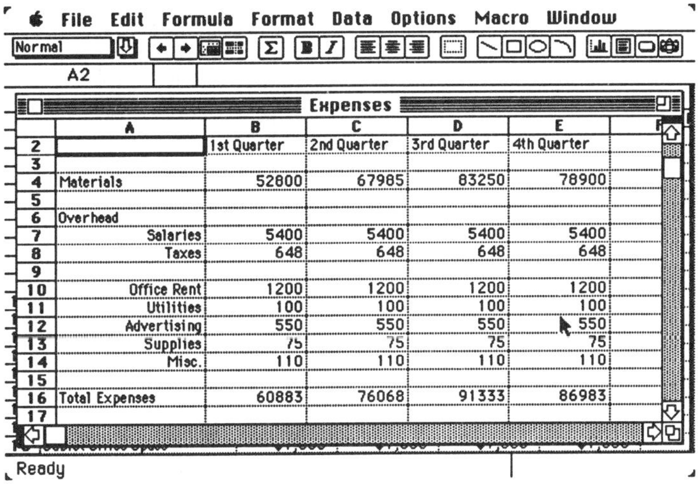

	A	B	C	D	E
2		1st Quarter	2nd Quarter	3rd Quarter	4th Quarter
3					
4	Materials	52800	67985	83250	78900
5					
6	Overhead				
7	Salaries	5400	5400	5400	5400
8	Taxes	648	648	648	648
9					
10	Office Rent	1200	1200	1200	1200
11	Utilities	100	100	100	100
12	Advertising	550	550	550	550
13	Supplies	75	75	75	75
14	Misc.	110	110	110	110
15					
16	Total Expenses	60883	76068	91333	86983
17					

FIGURE 8-10. New worksheet containing expenses

Select any cell in column A, and use the Column Width command from the Format menu to set the column width to 15.

At this point, you are ready to link the Income and Expenses worksheets to the Profits worksheet. Before doing so, consider exactly what information will be needed in the Profits worksheet, and from where that information will come. Row 4 of the Profits worksheet, Gross Sales, will come from the Total Sales row of the Income worksheet. The figures in Row 5, Other Income, are derived from the Total Income row in the Income worksheet. Row 7 is simply an addition of rows 4 and 5.

Row 9, Less Expenses, is derived from the Total Expenses row in the Expenses worksheet. Finally, row 11 provides the net profits by subtracting row 9 from row 7. Figure 8-11 shows the conceptual basis for the linking of the worksheets.

Go to cell B4, and start a formula with the equal sign. You could simply enter the rest of the formula, but for experience, try the method of selecting the cells in another worksheet. Open the Window menu and choose the Income worksheet to make that worksheet partially active. Next, go to cell B13 of the Income worksheet. If you need to move the cursor quite a distance, you can make use of the Go To (COMMAND-G) key. While the cursor is at B13, it is surrounded by a moving broken line, and you should see the external reference automatically entered in the formula bar. Press RETURN to complete the formula. The window containing the Profits worksheet becomes fully active, and the value appears in cell B4.

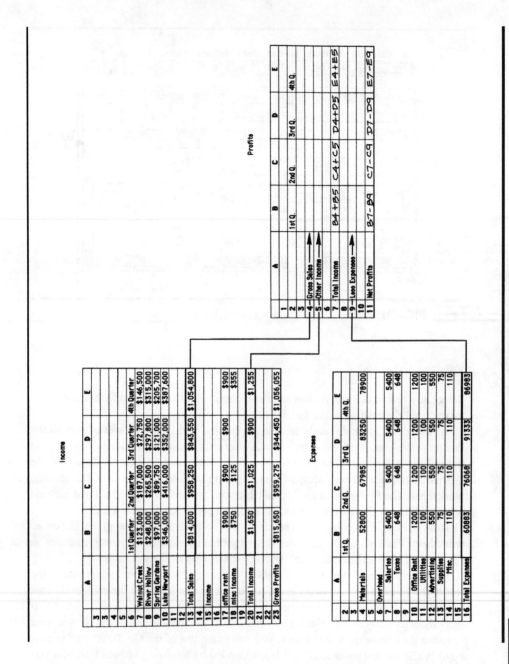

FIGURE 8-11. Links between Profits and supporting worksheets

Notice that when you select a cell in another worksheet to build an external reference, Excel assumes that the reference should be an absolute one. This is a wise assumption because using absolute references tends to avoid problems when worksheets become more complex. However, there may be times when you don't want an absolute reference.

In this example, relative references serve a better purpose because the references could later be copied into adjoining cells with the Fill Right command. With the cursor in cell B4, click in the formula bar to edit the contents of the cell, and then remove the dollar signs from the formula. When you press RETURN to store the change, the results are the same, but the formula is now a relative reference to cell B13 on the Income worksheet. Using the Fill Right command later will change the cell references as desired.

Move to cell B5, and enter

=Income!B21

Move to cell B7 and enter

=B4+B5

In cell B9, enter

=Expenses!B16

Finally, move to cell B11, and enter

=B7–B9

Select the range of cells from B4 to E11. Open the Edit menu and choose Fill Right. The results should resemble the worksheet shown in Figure 8-12.

Open the File menu and save the worksheet, entering **Profits** as its name. Don't close the Profits worksheet yet; you will use it later.

 It is always a good idea to save supporting worksheets before saving dependent worksheets. Excel assists you in this area by displaying an Alert box if you try to save a dependent worksheet before the supporting worksheet has been saved for the first time. The danger in not saving the supporting worksheet first is that you might save the dependent worksheet and later abandon the unsaved supporting worksheet in favor of a different worksheet design. The dependent worksheet would then be unable to update its references correctly.

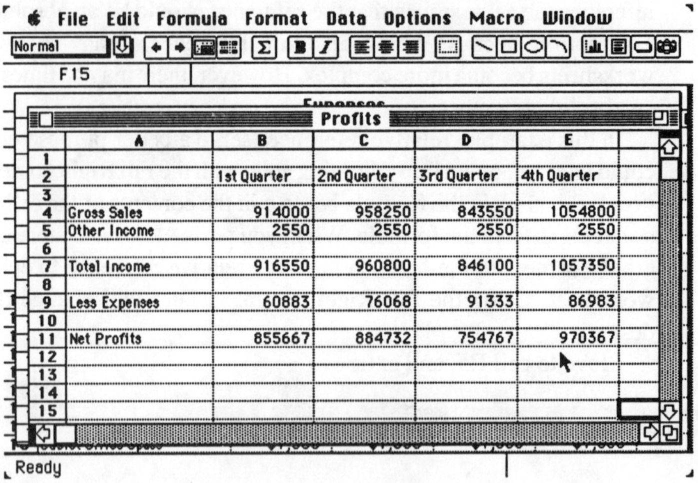

	A	B	C	D	E
1					
2		1st Quarter	2nd Quarter	3rd Quarter	4th Quarter
3					
4	Gross Sales	914000	958250	843550	1054800
5	Other Income	2550	2550	2550	2550
6					
7	Total Income	916550	960800	846100	1057350
8					
9	Less Expenses	60883	76068	91333	86983
10					
11	Net Profits	855667	884732	754767	970367
12					
13					
14					
15					

FIGURE 8-12. Completed Profits worksheet

Linking a Range of Cells

One common use for Excel's linking capabilities is to link a range of cells to another range of cells. For example, you may want to bring an entire row of cells containing totals over to a different worksheet. One method is to enter the first cell in the row as a relative reference, as you just did with the Profits worksheet, and later use the Fill Right command to create additional references along that row. However, this method is useless if you want to maintain the absolute references that Excel normally inserts when you point to cells in another worksheet.

What you can do instead is to link ranges of equal size on both worksheets. For example, consider the need to link the group of cells from B13 to E13 in the Income worksheet to cells B4 to E4 in the Profits worksheet. In each of the cells from B4 through E4 on the Profits worksheet, you can refer to the same formula:

=Income!$B$13:$E$13

As a result of this formula, Excel would use the individual cells in the range B13 to E13 and put the values in cells B4 to E4 in the Profits worksheet. To see how this works, make the Profits worksheet the active window if it isn't already. Go to cell B4 and type an equal sign to begin a formula.

Open the Window menu, and choose Income from the list of worksheets to make the Income worksheet partially active. Go to cell B13 and select the range B13 to E13. Press RETURN to enter the formula and remain in cell B4.

With the cursor still in B4, open the Edit menu and choose Copy to copy the cell's formula into memory. Then select cells C4 through E4. Open the Edit menu and choose Paste to copy the formula into these three cells.

The resultant values that appear are unchanged from those supplied by the formulas you entered previously. However, note that the formulas now in these cells all contain a common formula, with absolute references to the range of cells from B13 to E13 in the Income worksheet. When using this technique to refer to rows in another worksheet, make sure that the range of cells containing the formula in the dependent worksheet is the same size as the range of cells in the supporting worksheet, and make sure you are referring to the proper worksheet.

 When building formulas to link worksheets, you can use the Go To (COMMAND-G) key to go to a cell located in another worksheet. After pressing COMMAND-G, enter both the worksheet name and the cell reference, separated by an exclamation point, as shown here:

Income!A5

When you press RETURN or click the OK button, the cell on the worksheet you referred to by name becomes the active cell.

WORKING WITH DEPENDENT WORKSHEETS

When you open a dependent worksheet and one or more of the supporting worksheets is not open, Excel displays the following dialog box, which asks if you want to update the references to nonresident worksheets:

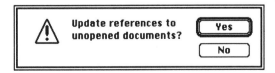

If you answer Yes to this question, Excel gets the needed values from the supporting worksheets, assuming they can be found on the disk. If you answer No, simple formulas are updated with the most recent values they contained, and complex formulas display the error message "REF!".

Note that if a worksheet is dependent on another worksheet and the dependent worksheet cannot be located, Excel will use the last values displayed by the supporting worksheet for the calculations. To avoid possible errors in your dependent worksheets, the latest copy of all needed supporting worksheets should be available on your hard disk.

WORKING WITH INTERDEPENDENT WORKSHEETS

You must be particularly careful of interdependencies when the same worksheet is both a supporting and a dependent worksheet. For example, consider a corporation with three divisions, each division having three departments, and each department having a projected budget. The department totals are fed into the division budgets, and the divisional totals are fed into the corporation budget. If you use the linking capabilities of Excel to plot the budgets for the departments, the divisions, and the corporation as a whole, the divisional worksheets will be both dependent (on the departmental worksheets) and supporting (of the corporate worksheet).

Just when you think all of the worksheets are complete, one of the department heads adds some additional sales figures to that department's budget. You open the corporate worksheet, and when the dialog box asks if you wish to update the references, you answer Yes. You haven't changed the location of any cells, so you assume that the corporate worksheet will be updated properly. However, that assumption is wrong. When you answer Yes to the dialog box, it tells Excel to update references to nonresident sheets, but Excel only looks downward one level. In other words, Excel checks the actual references for the active worksheet.

In this example, the corporate worksheet contains references to the divisional worksheets, and the divisional worksheets contain references to the departmental worksheets. When you tell Excel to update references to nonresident sheets, it does so, but all of those references were to the divisional worksheets, not to the departmental worksheets. Because one of the departmental worksheets has changed, one of the divisional worksheets now contains incorrect data, which means that the corporate worksheet gets updated with incorrect data. This kind of problem can force you to search through generation after generation of worksheets, looking for obscure errors. To get an accurate recalculation of the corporate worksheet in this scenario, the divisional worksheets and the departmental worksheets would have to be open.

chapter 9

USING MACROS

Macros are combinations of keystrokes that automate many of the tasks you normally perform with a program. Macros allow you to record a sequence of characters as a single key combination. Later, you can play back the character sequence by pressing the same key combination. When the macro is played back, Excel performs as if you had manually typed the characters contained within the macro. If you must produce daily reports or perform similar repetitive tasks, you can save many keystrokes with macros.

Excel's macros can also be very complex programs that make decisions based on user input. Excel's rich macro language has capabilities that most programmers are already familiar with. Excel macros can also call other programs outside of the Excel environment and work with ASCII text files.

If you have no interest in becoming a programmer, you needn't worry about macros. Unlike some popular spreadsheets that force you to create macros by typing obscure codes into cells, Excel provides a Macro Recorder feature. You can turn on the Macro Recorder and perform the same steps in your worksheet as you normally do manually. When you are finished with the task, you can simply turn off the Macro Recorder and have a complete macro that performs those steps for you.

TYPES OF MACROS

Excel provides two types of macros: *command macros* and *function macros*. Command macros carry out a series of commands. For example, you can create a command macro that marks a specific range of a worksheet, opens the Print menu, and chooses the Print command to begin printing. You can also create a macro that applies a preferred format to an entire worksheet. Command macros can range from the very simple to the extremely complex.

Function macros are very similar to Excel's functions in that they act upon values, perform calculations, and return a value. For example, you can create a function macro that takes the dimensions of an area in feet and returns the area in square yards.

It's easier to remember the difference between the two types of macros if you keep these points in mind:

- Command macros are similar to commands—they do tasks.

- Function macros are stored in formulas and accept and return a value, like functions.

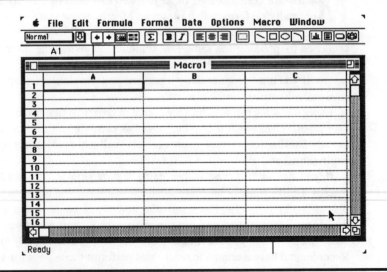

FIGURE 9-1. Macro sheet

MACRO SHEETS

Excel uses *macro sheets* to contain the macros that you create. A macro sheet looks much like a worksheet, as you can see from the macro sheet in Figure 9-1. Because macro sheets are so similar to worksheets, you are already familiar with many tasks that can be performed with macros. Making entries, editing cells, using Copy and Paste, and most other operations are identical to the same operations in worksheets.

Like worksheets, macro sheets are saved as individual files. This approach has significant advantages over storing macros within a worksheet, the approach of Lotus 1-2-3 and other spreadsheets. First, the common practice of storing Lotus 1-2-3 macros in a remote corner of the worksheet wastes memory. Second, if you use similar or identical macros with different worksheets, you must duplicate the macros in each worksheet. With Excel, an unlimited number of worksheets can make use of the same macro.

Inside the cells of the macro sheet are the formulas that make up the macros. These formulas are composed mostly of *macro functions,* a special type of function used only in macros. Excel has dozens of macro functions for performing a variety of tasks.

THE MACRO MENU

Many macro commands can be accessed from the Macro menu, shown here:

The menu contains six commands: Run, Record, Start/Stop Recorder, Set Recorder, Absolute/Relative Record, and Assign to Object.

The Run command is used to run (execute) an existing macro. The Record command prepares a new or existing macro sheet to begin recording the macro. The Start Recorder command starts the Macro Recorder. Once the Macro Recorder is recording your keystrokes, this command changes to Stop Recorder, which you use to turn off the Macro Recorder when you are finished recording keystrokes. The Set Recorder command lets you define a particular macro sheet, or a portion of a particular macro sheet, as the area that will contain the commands recorded by the Macro Recorder. The Absolute/Relative Record command lets you designate whether the Macro Recorder should use relative or absolute references in its macros. The Assign to Object command lets you assign a macro to be run when an object on a worksheet is selected with the mouse.

CREATING A MACRO SHEET

You can create a macro in one of two ways:

- By turning on the Macro Recorder (in which case Excel opens a macro sheet automatically when it is needed)

- By opening a new macro sheet with the New command of the File menu

Open the File menu now and choose New. From the dialog box that appears, select Macro Sheet. Press RETURN or click the OK button to create the new macro sheet, which should resemble the one in Figure 9-1.

Note that the macro sheet has much wider columns than a worksheet does. The additional width is provided to accommodate the functions that constitute the macro formulas. Excel displays formulas in macro sheets by default. Worksheets, by comparison, display values by default. (You can force worksheets to display formulas instead of values by using the Formulas setting of the Options menu's Display command.) Another difference between a macro sheet and a worksheet is that on a macro sheet, if the contents of a cell are wider than the cell width and the cell to the right is empty, the contents of the first cell do not run over into the adjacent cell.

CREATING YOUR FIRST MACRO

Excel lets you build a macro in one of two ways: by manually entering the desired macro in a macro sheet, or by turning on the Macro Recorder, performing the required steps in a worksheet, and then turning off the Macro Recorder. You'll gain a better appreciation for the second method if you are familiar with the first; also, you must know how to create macros manually if you want to perform more complex, programming-like tasks with macros. Some complex functions can't be done from a worksheet.

Creating a macro manually requires three steps:

1. Open a new macro sheet.

2. Enter in a single column the macro functions that make up the macro.

3. Use the Formula Define Name command to assign a name to the macro and to designate it as a command macro or a function macro. If you choose a COMMAND-OPTION key combination to start the macro, note that Excel distinguishes between upper- and lowercase. For example, COMMAND-OPTION-A and COMMAND-OPTION-a are two different keys.

With the cursor in cell A1 of the macro sheet, enter as a heading

First_Macro

Although this title is not actually a part of the macro, it does identify the macro by name. Next, enter the following in the cells indicated:

Cell	Entry
A2	=SELECT(!$C$5)
A3	=FORMULA(12345)
A4	=RETURN( )

These entries will be explained shortly, but for now, go back to cell A2. Open the Formula menu and choose the Define Name command. You'll see the dialog box shown here:

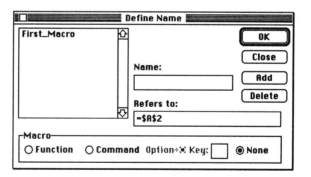

Note one significant difference between this dialog box and a worksheet dialog box for the Define Name command. At the bottom of the macro dialog box are buttons that let you indicate whether the macro is a command macro or a function macro. In the case of command macros, you can also designate a COMMAND-OPTION key combination to be used as a shortcut for starting the macro.

In the Define Name dialog box, you must enter a name for the macro and a reference indicating where the macro begins. Because you placed the cursor at cell A2 before you used the Define Name command, Excel assumes that you want to start the macro at that cell; therefore, =$A$2 already appears in the Refers to: box. The cursor is currently in the Name box because Excel needs a name for the macro. First_Macro (including the underline) appears as the default name in the box. Excel assumes that this is the name you want by checking the cell directly above the current cursor location for a text entry. If you enter a name manually, keep in mind that underlines are necessary for names composed of more than one word, because spaces can't be used in a macro name.

Since the Refers to: box has been filled in as a result of your previous selection of the starting cell on the macro sheet, all that remains is to tell Excel that this macro is a command macro. Click the Command button, and then click the OK button. (Use of the COMMAND+OPTION Key button in the dialog box will be discussed shortly.) You now have a macro available for use in any worksheet. If you wished, you could save this macro by saving the macro sheet, using the same commands that you use for saving worksheets and charts. It is not necessary to save the example macro sheet at this time; just leave it open on your screen.

Open a new worksheet now with the New command of the File menu, or switch to a blank worksheet if one is already available. Once the worksheet appears, you can run the macro with the Macro menu's Run command. Open the Macro menu and choose the Run command. The Run dialog box, shown here, appears:

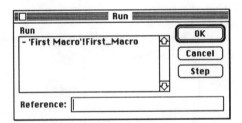

The list box within this dialog box displays the names of all available macros. (A macro becomes available as soon as you create one or open one that was saved earlier.) If many macros are available, you can select from among the various titles with the scroll bar just as you do with other dialog-box scroll bars.

Notice that the macro name has two parts: the name of the macro sheet followed by the name assigned to the macro. The two parts are always separated by an exclamation point. Click the name, and then click the OK button. The macro runs, with the results shown in Figure 9-2. Following your entries in the macro, Excel selected cell C5 and entered the value 12345. The instructions that you entered in the macro sheet are translated by Excel as follows:

=SELECT(!$C$5)	Selects cell C5 of the current worksheet
=FORMULA(12345)	Enters any value, formula, or text enclosed in quotes within the parentheses
=RETURN( )	Indicates the end of the macro (all macros must have this function at the end, or an error message will appear when the macro is run)

Although this macro is extremely simple, it demonstrates the central concept behind all macros. By storing special macro functions within a macro sheet, you can build a macro that will perform a series of keystrokes for you in any Excel worksheet.

Note that absolute cell references were used in this example. You do not have to use absolute cell references in your macros; like worksheets, macros can contain relative or absolute cell references. Also, you will soon have a chance to use the Multiplan (R1C1) style of referencing, because the Macro Recorder feature normally stores cell references in this fashion.

USING THE MACRO RECORDER

If you took the time to type the previously described macro, you'll have a good idea why Excel's Macro Recorder is such a useful option. You can build macros similar

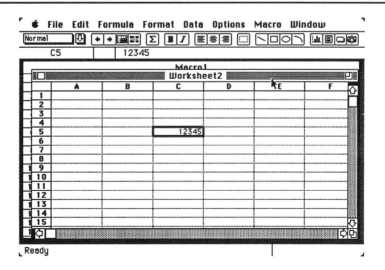

FIGURE 9-2.   Results of first macro

to the one you just entered manually by turning on the Macro Recorder as you perform the necessary steps.

To quickly see how this can be done, first clear the cell in the worksheet with COMMAND-B. Use the Window menu to switch to the Macro window, and close that window without saving it. With just the worksheet remaining open, move the cursor back to cell A1.

Next, open the Macro menu and choose Record. Accept the default name given to the new macro by clicking OK in the dialog box that appears. The dialog box will close, and the message "recording" at the bottom of the screen will indicate that the Macro Recorder is recording your keystrokes.

Move the cursor to cell C5, and enter the value 12345. After entering this value, choose Stop Recorder from the Macro menu.

Clear the entry in the worksheet cell and move back to cell A1. Open the Macro menu and choose Run. From the dialog box that appears, choose the new macro by clicking its name (it should be the only one in the list box if you've been following this example). Click OK to run the macro. The results should be identical to those in the macro you created manually. This time, however, instead of typing the macro functions, you've let Excel's macro recorder do the work for you.

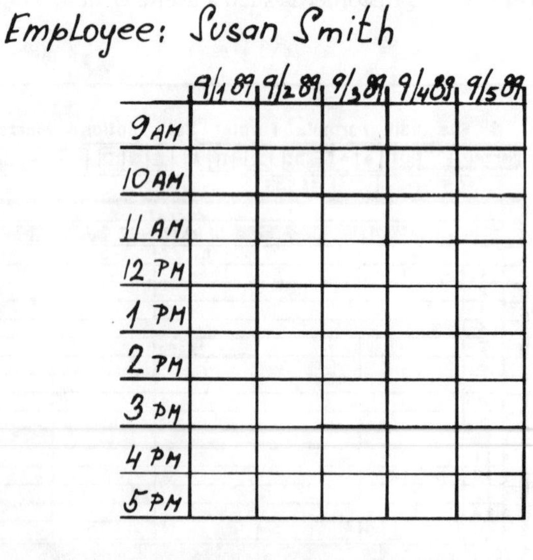

Employee: Susan Smith

	9/1 89	9/2 89	9/3 89	9/4 89	9/5 89
9 AM					
10 AM					
11 AM					
12 PM					
1 PM					
2 PM					
3 PM					
4 PM					
5 PM					

═══ **FIGURE 9-3.**   Design for sample timesheet

Now let's consider a more complex example, typical of the kinds of repetitive tasks for which macros are used. Perhaps each Monday morning you prepare a form for tracking some sort of activity throughout the week. In this example, the form is a timesheet used to track hours spent on a particular task (it could just as easily be daily expenses by categories, or sales generated in the course of a day). This timesheet, if laid out on paper, would look like the one in Figure 9-3.

Using the paper-and-pen approach, one could lay out a form with ruled lines, run multiple copies of the form, and fill in the employee names and dates each week. However, this sort of repetitive work is precisely what Excel's macros can reduce. A macro can direct Excel to construct the form and to format it as you desire, including the entry of the current dates. With the Macro Recorder, you can create such a macro with no programming; you just turn on the recorder and let Excel do the work for you.

Try the timesheet example by performing these steps. Close all worksheets and macro sheets that are currently open without saving them. Next, open a new worksheet. Choose Record Macro from the Macro menu to start the recorder. When the dialog box appears, enter **TIMESHEET** as a macro name and press RETURN or click OK.

Press COMMAND-G, and then enter **B3** as a cell reference. (It's a good idea to use the Go To key or the mouse instead of moving the cursor with the arrow keys when you are recording macros; you may not always be at the same worksheet location when you play back the macro.) With the cursor now in B3, enter the following, pressing RETURN or DOWN ARROW after each entry to move the cell to the next successive row:

9 AM
10 AM
11 AM
12 NOON
1 PM
2 PM
3 PM
4 PM
5 PM

Press COMMAND-G, and then enter **C2** as a cell reference. Once you are at cell C2, open the Formula menu and choose Paste Function. When the dialog box appears, click in Paste Arguments to turn off the check box. From the list of available functions that appears, select NOW and click OK. Then press RETURN to complete the entry and remain in cell C2. (The NOW function is discussed in more detail in Chapter 11; it causes Excel to retrieve the current date stored in the computer's clock.)

Open the Format menu, choose Number, and select the d-mmm-yy date format. Press COMMAND-G, and type **G2,** but don't press RETURN. Instead, press SHIFT-RETURN to select the cells from C2 to G2.

Choose the Series command from the Data menu. Make sure that Date is selected as the type, and then click the OK button. The selected range of cells will be filled in with dates.

Open the Edit menu and choose Copy. Then, without moving the cursor, open the Edit menu again and choose Paste Special. Click the Values option button in the dialog box that appears, and then click OK. This action will "freeze" the values so that the dates will not change from day to day.

With the cells still selected, choose Font from the Format menu. Select Bold, and then click OK. Press COMMAND-G, and enter **A1** as a reference. With the cursor in cell A1, enter the following:

NAME:

After pressing the RETURN key, choose Stop Recorder from the Macro menu.

Now close the worksheet without saving it. (It's all right to throw away this worksheet without saving it, because you have a macro that will rebuild it at a moment's notice.) You should, however, save the macro sheet before running it, since an error in the macro could make it difficult to save later. When you close the worksheet, you will see the macro sheet, containing the formulas and functions needed to create the worksheet. Choose Save from the File menu to save the macro sheet; call it Time Macro.

Open a new worksheet by choosing New from the File menu. Choose Run from the Macro menu, and select Timesheet in the dialog box. Click OK. If all goes well, you'll see Excel duplicate the timesheet in a few moments; it will look similar to the example in Figure 9-4.

Close the worksheet to take a closer look at the macro sheet constructed by Excel. The macro sheet should resemble the one in Figure 9-5. Because a macro sheet was not open when you used the Macro Recorder, Excel stored the macro in a new macro sheet. Because you used the Go To key while Excel was recording your actions, the Macro Recorder has used the FORMULA.GOTO function in cell B2. The FORMULA.GOTO function causes the active cell to move to the cell reference indicated within parentheses.

Notice that Excel's Macro Recorder uses the R1C1 style of cell referencing. Recall from Chapter 1 that this style of referencing uses numbered rows and columns; for example, R3C2 refers to row 3, column 2 (cell B3 under the A1 style of referencing). Macro cell references entered with the R1C1 style of referencing are surrounded by quotation marks. When you manually enter a macro, you can use either style of cell referencing, but omit the quotation marks if you use the A1 referencing style.

Other functions perform the other tasks needed to construct the timesheet. (Scroll down in the macro sheet to see the remaining functions.) The FORMULA function inserts values just as if you had typed them into the worksheet cells. The FORMAT.NUMBER function formats a cell (which is equivalent to choosing the Number

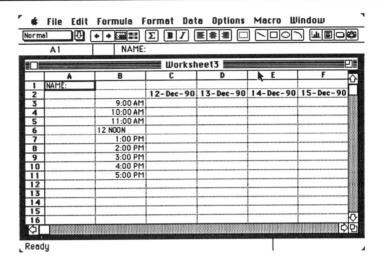

FIGURE 9-4.   Results of sample timesheet macro

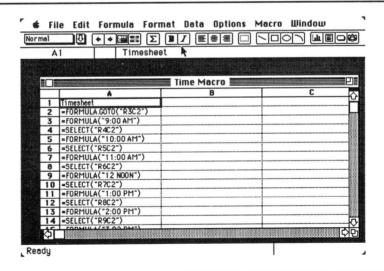

FIGURE 9-5.   Timesheet macro created with Macro Recorder

command from the Format menu). The DATA.SERIES, COPY, and PASTE.SPE-CIAL functions also imitate the similarly named menu commands. Like all macros, this one ends with the RETURN function, located in the last filled-in cell of the macro sheet.

Comparing this macro with the ones built manually in earlier parts of this chapter, it should be obvious that much can be accomplished with the macro language provided by Excel, although it takes time to become familiar with all of the available macro functions. The more commonly used macro functions are identified in detail at the end of the next chapter. If you plan to develop applications using Excel, you might also want to consult other programming-oriented references, such as the macro directory included in Excel's documentation.

One useful way to become more accomplished with macros is to use the Macro Recorder to build macros that mimic your common tasks. Then edit those macro sheets, adding options and additional capabilities, as you become more familiar with the language.

Excel's Macro Recorder offers one design feature that you may not immediately notice but will come to appreciate in time. Unlike the macro recorders found in many programs, Excel's Macro Recorder adds your steps to the macro sheet only after you have completed an action. This means that if you make a mistake and choose Cancel, or make an incorrect selection and change that selection, the mistake does not appear in your macro sheet along with the desired keystrokes.

ASSIGNING A COMMAND-OPTION KEY TO A MACRO

With any command macro, you can include a COMMAND-OPTION-key designation that can be used to start the macro. You do this by including a letter or number in the COMMAND + OPTION Key text box when you name the macro. The letter or number, when used with the OPTION and COMMAND keys, will start the macro from your active worksheet. For example, if you click the COMMAND + OPTION Key button after naming the macro and then enter the letter *a* in the text box, you can call that macro at any time by pressing COMMAND-OPTION-a.

Remember the case of the letters you use, because this is one of the few times when Excel is case-sensitive. For a macro key, COMMAND + OPTION + w is not the same as COMMAND + OPTION + W. Excel offers this flexibility so that you can define dozens of different macro command keys by assigning them uppercase letters, lowercase letters, or numbers.

CREATING FUNCTION MACROS

Although you will probably spend much of your time working with command macros, you should not ignore function macros, which you can use to create your own customized functions. You can use these customized functions in the same way that you use Excel's standard functions (to provide sums or averages, or payments on a loan, for example).

Function macros are entered manually on a macro sheet; you cannot use the Macro Recorder to build them. To build a function macro, you begin by entering a name for the macro in the first row as you do with command macros. You then enter formulas for the arguments in the cells below the heading. *Arguments* are functions that pass values to the macro and provide results. You also enter formulas to perform calculations, and you end the macro with a RETURN function.

Arguments

The ARGUMENT function assigns names to values that are passed to the function macro. For example, a function macro can be designed to calculate the area of a room based on its length and width. Values for the length and width are passed to the function macro in the form of arguments. The syntax for the ARGUMENT function is

=ARGUMENT(*name, type, reference*)

where *name* is the name that is to be assigned to the value passed to the macro, *type* is the type of value, and *reference* denotes an optional cell reference in which the value is stored. The type is represented by certain numbers, from 0 to 64, as indicated in the following table:

Type	Type of Data
0	Formula
1	Number
2	Text
4	Logical
8	Cell reference
16	Error
64	Array

For example, examine the following macro function used within a formula:

=ARGUMENT("length",1)

This function tells Excel that the argument to be passed to the function macro is called "length," and the data to be passed must be numeric data (type 1). The ARGUMENT function lets you exercise tight control over the types of data handled by your customized functions.

Once you have constructed the function macro, you must name the macro using the Define Name command of the Formula menu. Since function macros are used like other functions, you cannot assign a COMMAND key to a function macro. You can only use function macros within other formulas to return a value.

To try a simple function macro, consider the problem of computing the area of a room in square yards, given the length and width of a room in feet. Excel has no standard function that does this task, but a function macro can be built to perform the job. Open an existing macro sheet (it doesn't matter which one), and move the cursor to a blank column. For this example, use column M. With the cursor in cell M1, enter **Area** as the heading. Then, in cells M2 to M5, type the following entries:

Cell	Entry
M2	=ARGUMENT("length",1)
M3	=ARGUMENT("width",1)
M4	=(length*width)/9
M5	=RETURN(M4)

Go to cell M2, open the Formula menu, and choose Define Name. Note that in the dialog box, "Area" appears as a default name for the macro. Select Function from the Macro box to define this macro as a function macro. Press RETURN to accept the options in the dialog box. Like any other function, this macro can now be used in any worksheet.

There is one point you must remember with macro functions: you must include the name of the macro sheet containing the function when you try to use the function name in a formula. For example, you can get away with using only the name of the SUM function in a formula because it is a standard function; that is, you can enter the formula **=SUM(B7:B25)** and Excel will perform the calculation. However, if you enter the formula **=AREA(12,27)** after building a macro function named Area, Excel cannot use the function, because the worksheet has no way of knowing on which macro sheet the function resides. You must enter **=Macro2!AREA(12,27)** to be successful, assuming the function is stored on a macro sheet called Macro2. Before leaving this macro, note the name of the macro sheet that contains the AREA macro. You'll need this name to use the function.

Switch to any worksheet, or open a new one if none is currently open. Find a blank area, and enter the following formula in a cell (assuming that the macro sheet containing your AREA function is called MACRO3):

=MACRO3!AREA(60,12)

(If the AREA function is stored on some other macro sheet, use the name of that macro sheet in place of "Macro3" in this example.) Once you enter the formula, your customized function calculates the square yardage of the 12-by-60 foot area and displays a total of 80 square yards in the active cell.

As with standard functions, function macros can be accessed from the Paste Function command of the Formula menu. The macro functions will always appear at the end of the list of functions displayed in the Paste Function dialog box.

WHAT TO DO WHEN THINGS GO WRONG

As soon as you start building macros of any complexity, you will probably make errors. Even the most expert programmers spend a great deal of time debugging program code. However, Excel does offer you help by displaying a dialog box with the location of the error and options for continuing the macro, halting the macro, or using Step mode to continue execution one step at a time.

When Excel encounters a bug in a macro, it displays a dialog box containing an error message, as shown here:

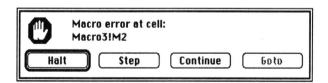

The dialog box presents three choices: Halt, Step, and Continue. Of the three, Continue is likely to be the least useful option. Choosing Continue tells Excel to ignore the problem and finish executing the macro. In most cases, this option lets you see if the macro contains other errors (so you can correct more than one typo at a time), but it isn't going to lead to acceptable results, because one error usually causes a host of problems down the line.

The Step option lets you go through the macro a step at a time. This can be helpful for finding hard-to-trace errors in a macro. If you want to execute the entire macro one step at a time before the error occurs, you can choose Run from the Macro menu, and click on the Step button instead of the OK button. Or, you can simply insert

```
=STEP()
```

following the heading and before the first instruction in the macro. The Step function turns on Step mode through the entire macro. You can watch the results at each phase to find the source of the problem.

The Halt option suspends the processing of the macro. You can then switch to the window that contains the macro and make the necessary changes to the desired cells. Most errors in your macros are likely to be syntactical in nature. Excel lets you know when you enter wrong cell references or when you leave out exclamation points, quotation marks, and parentheses, so these types of problems are relatively easy to find. Errors in logic, however, can be very difficult to track down, and they often do not stop processing; you simply get the wrong results from your macro. You can hold logic errors to a minimum by carefully planning your macros, on paper first if necessary, before building them.

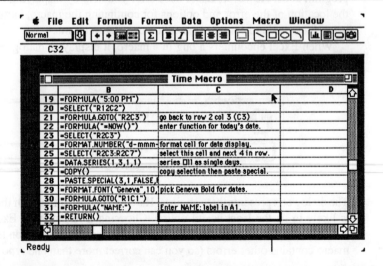

FIGURE 9-6. Documented macro

DOCUMENTING YOUR MACROS

One technique that will improve your macros is documentation. Good documentation serves as a valuable guide during macro design and also helps others to understand the philosophy behind your macros.

Documentation for macros can take the form of comments, names, or notes entered in cells in the macro sheet. One common method of documenting macros is to include remarks in the column adjacent to the macro statements. Figure 9-6 shows such an approach. If you prefer, you can also include comments within the macro itself. During execution of a macro, Excel ignores cells that do not contain formulas. You can enter comments in the form of text or as cell notes that provide a detailed explanation for the different steps in the macro.

The exercises in this chapter have suggested ideas for developing your own macros. Due to the complexity and flexibility of Excel's macro language, this chapter has only been able to scratch the surface of Excel's macro capabilities.

Different readers will develop different levels of macro expertise. Some readers may feel that the Macro Recorder is all they need to know about macros; others will want to know much more, such as the possibility of calling assembly language programs from within a macro. The more study you devote to this rich feature of Excel, the better it will serve you.

chapter 10

USING FUNCTIONS

Excel offers numerous functions, which are built-in shortcuts for performing specialized operations. In earlier chapters, you made regular use of the SUM function to calculate the total of values within a range of cells quickly. Excel has functions for tasks that range from calculating the square root of a number to finding the future value of an investment.

Although the various functions perform a wide range of tasks, nearly all functions share certain traits: They accept a value or values, perform an operation based on those values, and return a value or values. (A few functions do not require values but nevertheless return a value.) The values that you supply the function are called *arguments.* The values that the functions return are called *results.*

You use functions by including them within a formula in a worksheet cell. All functions follow a common format, or syntax, which is illustrated in Figure 10-1.

There are two ways to enter functions in a formula. You can manually type the entire function into the formula, or you can select the desired function from the list of functions that appears when you use the Paste Function command from the Formula menu. As you saw in Chapter 3, the Paste Function command displays a list box

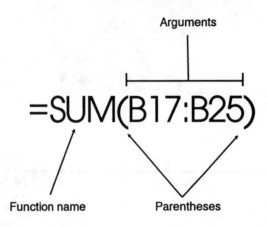

FIGURE 10-1.   Syntax for functions

containing all available functions. You can quickly press one or more letters in the name of the function, or you can use the scroll bars to find and select the desired function. Once you select the function from the list box, it is pasted into the formula you are building.

The kind of arguments you can use in a function depend on the type of function. Some functions accept numeric arguments, others accept text strings as arguments, and still others accept different types of arguments. Excel functions use six types of arguments: numbers, text, logical values, arrays, error values, and references. (Arrays are discussed in Chapter 11.) If you leave the Paste Arguments box checked when you paste a function into a cell, Excel will paste a description of the type of argument needed in the cell. A function can have from 0 to 14 arguments. If the function contains more than one argument, the arguments are separated by commas.

In addition to the functions described in this chapter, Excel also offers a number of functions that are designed to work with dates and times. These functions are detailed in Chapter 11 under "Working with Dates and Times."

This chapter cannot cover every available function offered by Excel; to do so would require a book in itself. In addition, some functions (such as the EXEC macro function, which calls other Macintosh applications) are clearly beyond the scope of this book. Refer to your Excel documentation for a complete listing of all available functions.

MATH FUNCTIONS

You can use Excel's math functions to perform various specialized numeric operations, such as finding the square root of a number or rounding off a fractional value.

ABS(*number*)   The ABS function provides the absolute value of a number, in effect canceling a negative value. For example, =ABS(–36) returns a value of 36.

EXP(*number*)   The EXP function returns E raised to the power of the number provided as the argument. (E is 2.71828183, or the base of the natural logarithm.) For example, =EXP(10) returns the value 22026.4658, while =EXP(1) returns the value 2.71828183.

INT(*number*)   The INT function returns the integer value of the argument, rounding fractional values down to the nearest integer. For example, =INT(5.002) returns the value 5, and =INT(11.9998) returns the value 11.

MOD(*number,divisor*)   The MOD function returns the *modulus,* or remainder, of a division operation. For example, MOD(10,3) returns a value of 1, the remainder after 10 is divided by 3.

PI( )   The PI function, which requires no argument, returns the value of pi carried to nine digits, or 3.14159265.

RAND( )   The RAND function, which requires no argument, returns a random number that ranges from 0 to .99999999999999. Each time the worksheet is recalculated, a new random number is generated. If you need random numbers that are integers, simply multiply the result by another number and use the INT function to convert the value to an integer. For example, =INT(RAND( )*11) returns a random value between 0 and 10.

ROUND(*number,number of digits*)   The ROUND function rounds off a number by the specified number of digits. The argument provided by *number of digits* is 0 to round to the nearest integer, a positive number to round off digits that appear to the right of the decimal point, and a negative number (with a minus sign) to round off digits that appear to the left of the decimal point. The following statements demonstrate the results of the ROUND function:

=ROUND(857.1579,2)	Returns the value 857.16
=ROUND(857.1579,-2)	Returns the value 900
=ROUND(857.1579,-1)	Returns the value 860
=ROUND(857.1579,0)	Returns the value 857

SIGN(*number*)   The SIGN function returns the sign of a number, expressed as 1 if a number is positive, –1 if a number is negative, and 0 if the number is 0. For example, the expression =SIGN(34) returns a value of 1, and the expression =SIGN(-9) returns a value of –1.

SUM( )   The SUM function provides a sum of a list of values, commonly indicated by referencing a range of cells. For example, the expression =SUM(5,10,12) provides a value of 27. The expression =SUM(B5:B60) provides the sum of all numeric values contained in the range of cells from B5 to B60.

SQRT(*number*)   The SQRT function returns the square root of the number specified by the argument. For example, =SQRT(16) returns the value 4 and =SQRT(120) returns the value 10.9544512. The argument must be a positive number. If a negative number is supplied, the SQRT function returns a #NUM! error value.

STATISTICAL FUNCTIONS

You will probably use Excel's statistical functions more than any other group of functions. Many of these functions were introduced in earlier chapters, but are repeated here for easy reference. Using these functions, you can calculate the sum of a range of values or find the average, minimum, or maximum value in a range of values.

AVG(*1st value, 2nd value, 3rd value,...last value*)   The AVG function takes a series of values and returns an average of those values. For example, the expression =AVG(6,12,15,18) yields the value 12.75. The expression =AVG(B10:B15) provides the average of the values from cells B10 through B15.

COUNT(*1st value, 2nd value, 3rd value,...last value*)   The COUNT function returns a count of the numeric values contained in the list of arguments. The list of arguments is usually a worksheet range, and the COUNT function returns the number of cells that contain values that are in that range. For example, if a range of ten cells from B5 to B14 on a worksheet contains six cells with text strings and four cells with numbers, the expression =COUNT(B5:B15) returns the value 4.

MAX(*1st value, 2nd value, 3rd value,...last value*)
MIN(*1st value, 2nd value, 3rd value,...last value*)   The MAX and MIN functions provide the maximum and minimum values, respectively, of all values in the specified range or list of numbers. For example, the expression =MIN(120,180,900) returns the value 120. The expression =MAX(B5:B25) returns the highest value in the range of cells from B5 to B25 in the active worksheet.

STDEV(*numbers1,numbers2,numbers3,...numbersX*)   The STDEV function provides the standard deviation for the numbers provided in the list of arguments. For proper results, the arguments should be values or references that contain values. Standard deviation is a statistical measurement that indicates the dispersion of a select group of numbers. The larger the standard deviation, the broader the variance in the population you are measuring; the smaller the standard deviation, the more closely packed the population being measured.

For example, if cells A1 to A10 contain a random sampling of ages that are 27, 29, 35, 43, 18, 56, 39, 54, 33, and 19, the formula

=STDEV(A1:A10)

returns a standard deviation of 13.03883 years between the samples of this population, indicating a fairly wide age spread within the sample.

TRIGONOMETRIC FUNCTIONS

Excel offers standard trigonometric functions that are helpful for scientific and engineering applications.

ACOS(*number*)   The ACOS function returns the arc cosine of the value specified as the argument. The arc cosine is the angle, measured in radians, whose cosine is equal to the argument. The argument must fall in the range from –1 to +1. For example, =ACOS(-0.3) returns 1.87548898.

ASIN(*number*)   The ASIN function returns the arc sine of the value specified as the argument. The arc sine is the angle, measured in radians, whose sine is equal to the argument. The argument must fall in the range from –1 to +1. For example, =ASIN(0.3) returns 0.30469265.

ATAN(*number*)   The ATAN function returns the arc tangent of the value specified as the argument. The arc tangent is the angle, measured in radians, whose tangent is equal to the argument. The argument must fall in the range from –1 to +1. For example, =ATAN(0.3) returns 0.29145679.

COS(*number*)   The COS function returns the cosine of the value specified as the argument. The value provided is the cosine of the angle, as measured in radians. For example, =COS(1.0) returns 0.54030231.

SIN(*number*)   The SIN function returns the sine of the value specified as the argument. The value provided is the sine of the angle, as measured in radians. For example, =SIN(1) returns 0.84147098.

TAN(*number*)   The TAN function returns the tangent of the value specified as the argument. The value provided is the tangent of the angle, as measured in radians. For example, =TAN(0.5) returns 0.54630249.

LOGICAL FUNCTIONS

Excel's logical functions perform conditional tests and return values based on the results of those tests.

IF(*conditional test,value if true,value if false*)   The IF function performs a conditional test and returns one value if the test is true and another value if the test is false. For example, the expression =IF(C5=100,275,400) returns the value 275 if the amount in cell C5 is equal to 100; otherwise, the function returns the value 400.

You can also use text as the values to be provided. In the formula

=IF(B2>10000,"credit approved","credit denied")

the value in cell B2 is used to determine whether the message "credit approved" or the message "credit denied" is displayed. If the value is greater than 10000, the message "credit approved" is displayed.

AND(*logicals–1,logicals–2,...logicals–x*)   The AND function returns a logical value of TRUE if all logical values in the list of arguments are true. For example, the expression =AND(5+5=10,8–3=5) returns a value of TRUE. For another example, if the values in cells B3 and B4 of a worksheet are not equal, the expression =AND(B3=B4,B5=B7) returns a value of FALSE.

ISERROR(*value*)   The ISERROR function looks for error values and returns a value of TRUE if the cell contains an error value. For example, if cell C4 of a worksheet contains a formula that attempts to divide by zero, the "#DIV/0!" error message appears in that cell, and the expression =ISERROR(C4) would return a value of TRUE. The ISERROR function can be useful for presenting clear, unthreatening error messages. In the example just used, the formula

=IF(ISERROR(C4),"You tried to divide by zero!")

displays the message "You tried to divide by zero!" in the current cell.

OR(*logicals-1,logicals-2,...logicals-x*)   The OR function returns a logical value of TRUE if any logical value in the list of arguments is true. For example, the expression =OR(5+5=10,8-3=2) returns a value of True. For another example, if the values in cells B3 and B4 of a worksheet are not equal, and the values in cells B5 and B7 of the same worksheet are not equal, the expression =OR(B3=B4,B5=B7) returns a value of FALSE.

NOT(*logical*)   The NOT function evaluates a logical argument for a TRUE or FALSE value. If the logical argument is true, the NOT function returns a value of FALSE. If the logical argument is false, the NOT function returns a value of TRUE. For example, the expression =NOT(2+2=4) would return a value of FALSE, and the expression =NOT(2+2=5) would return a value of TRUE.

TRUE( ) and FALSE( )   The TRUE and FALSE functions, which require no arguments, always return the logical values of TRUE and FALSE, respectively. These functions are usually combined with other functions in formulas to return logical TRUE or FALSE values in response to a specified condition. For example, the expression

=IF(Balance>1000,TRUE( ),FALSE( ))

returns a logical value of TRUE if the value in the named range Balance is greater than 1000, and a logical value of FALSE if the value is equal to or less than 1000.

TEXT FUNCTIONS

You use text functions to perform various manipulations on strings of text. You can extract parts of a string, or substrings, from a string of text. You can also convert text strings containing numbers into values, and you can convert values into text strings composed of numbers.

DOLLAR(*number,number of digits*)   The DOLLAR function formats a value as dollars and rounds off the value by a specified number of digits. If the argument for *number of digits* is omitted, Excel defaults to two decimal places. If the argument for *number of digits* is negative, Excel rounds off the values to the left of the decimal point. The following examples illustrate the use of the DOLLAR function:

=DOLLAR(2857.23,2)	Displays as $2,857.23
=DOLLAR(2857.23,4)	Displays as $2,857.2300
=DOLLAR(2857.23,0)	Displays as $2,857
=DOLLAR(2857.23,-1)	Displays as $2,860

FIXED(*number,number of digits*)   The FIXED function rounds off a number by a specified number of digits. The result is displayed as a text string. For example, the expression

=FIXED(102.784,2)

returns the text string 102.78.

LEN(*text*)   The LEN function returns the length of the value provided in the argument. For example, if cell E12 contains the text string "North Carolina," the expression =LEN(E12) returns the value 14. If cell F2 contains the value 1024, the expression =LEN(F2) returns the value 4, the number of characters in the value. Note that spaces within a text string are counted as a part of the length.

MID(*text,starting position,number of characters*)   The MID function is used to extract a substring from a text string. The first argument, *text,* is a value containing a text string. The *starting position* argument identifies the starting point in the text. The *number of characters* argument indicates the number of characters in the extracted substring. The value specified for *starting position* must be a value of 1 or more. The value specified in *number of characters* must be a value of 0 or more. If the value specified for the starting position is greater than the number of characters in the string, the MID function returns an empty value. For an example of the MID function, the expression

=MID("first second third",7,6)

returns a text value of "second."

REPT(*text,number of times*)   The REPT function repeats a text string by the number of times specified in the argument. The argument specified by *number of times* can range from 0 to 255. If the argument is omitted, the function returns an empty string. For example, the expression =REPT("*",20) returns a text string consisting of 20 asterisks.

TEXT(*value, format*)   The TEXT function converts a numeric value into a text string that follows the format specified by the argument. The *format* argument is a text string that uses any valid Excel formatting characters used by the Format Number command. (Note that you cannot specify the General format as the format argument.)
    The following examples demonstrate the use of the TEXT function:

    =TEXT(89989.5,"$#,##0.00")   Returns $89,989.50
    =TEXT(12.5*5,"0.00")   Returns 62.50
    =TEXT(.63680556,"HH:MM:SS")   Returns 15:17:00

In the last example, a fractional number representing a portion of one day is used with the time format to return a time. See Chapter 2 for more details on how Excel uses values to represent times and dates.

VALUE(*"text string"*)   The VALUE function converts a text string into a value if that text string consists of a number, a date, or a time. For example, the expression =VALUE("102.567") returns the numeric value 102.567. The expression =VALUE("12/02/87") returns the value 30651. The expression =VALUE("3:17 PM") returns the value 0.63680556.

FINANCIAL FUNCTIONS

Financial functions are useful to anyone who deals with currency on a regular basis. They let you quickly perform common business calculations, such as the future value of an investment or loan amortization amounts.
    A number of common arguments are used by the financial functions:

- The *rate* argument is the interest rate for the loan or investment in question. Excel expects the rate to be in the form of a percentage. If you supply it as a whole number, you get unusually large (and incorrect) returns on your investments.

- The *number of periods* argument is the number of periods for the investment or loan. The frequency of this argument and *rate* should be based on the same method of measurement; otherwise, you will get erroneous results. For example, you cannot combine an annual interest rate with monthly payment periods in a financial function and expect to obtain the proper results. You must first divide the annual percentage rate by 12 to come up with a monthly interest rate, and then use the monthly interest rate along with the number of monthly periods.

- The *payment* argument represents the amount of the payment made during each period of the loan or investment.

- The *present value* argument is simply the value of an investment that has already been received.

- The *future value* argument is the value of an investment at some future date.

- The *type* argument, which is always optional, is a useful feature that lets you specify whether payments will be received at the beginning or the end of each period. A *type* of 1 calculates the values based on the payments being received at the start of each period. A *type* of 0 causes the calculation to be based on payments made at the end of each period. If *type* is omitted, Excel assumes that the payments are made at the end of each period.

PV(*rate,number of periods,payment, future value,type*)   The PV function returns the present value of an investment, based on an interest rate, payment amount, and number of payments. (When the *future value* argument is supplied and the *payment* argument is omitted, Excel calculates the value of a balloon payment.) As an example of the PV function, the formula =PV(1.8%,36,–500) takes 36 payments of $500 each at a rate of 1.8% per month (or 21.6% per year) and returns a value of $13,163.50, assuming the cell is formatted to display the value as dollars and cents.

NPV(*rate,1st value,2nd value,3rd value,....x value*)   The NPV function returns the net present value of a series of payments or investments made in an uneven fashion. Within the arguments, payments received can be signified by positive numbers, while investments made can be signified by negative numbers.

As an example, consider a rental condo that you purchase for $50,000 and sell six years later for $76,000. The condo generates a cash flow of –$1050 the first year, $800 the second year, $2000 the third year, $3500 the fourth year, and $5100 the fifth year. By comparison, you could have invested the $50,000 in a money market account paying 9% interest, so you want to see if the net present value exceeds the 9% return on investment rate. The expression

=NPV(9%,–50000,–1050,800,2000,3500,5100,76000)

returns a positive value of 2169.60. If the NPV exceeds 0, the investment has exceeded your comparison rate of 9%. A net present value of less than 0 indicates that you would have been better off not making the investment.

FV(*rate,number of periods,payment,present value,type*)   The FV function returns the future value of an investment, based on an interest rate, payment amount, and number of payments. (As an option, the *present value* argument can be supplied and the *payment* argument omitted; Excel would then calculate the future value of a balloon payment.) For an example of the use of the FV function, the formula =FV(.9%,12,–1000) takes 12 payments of $1000 each at a rate of 0.9% per month (or 10.8% per year) and returns a future value of $12,612.19.

PMT(*rate,number of periods,present value,future value,type*)   The PMT function calculates the payment for a loan amortization based on the number of payment periods, the interest rate, and the total amount specified. For example, if you need to know the amount of the payments on a 48-month car loan for $17,000 at an annual percentage rate of 14.5, you could divide 14.5 by 12 to come up with a monthly percentage rate of 1.2083%. Then use the expression

=PMT(1.2083%,48,17000)

to return a value of –468.8217, or a cash payment of $468.82 as your monthly car payment.

RATE(*number of periods,payment,present value,future value,type,guess*)   The RATE function computes the rate of return on an investment. The *future value, type,* and *guess* arguments are options. (You can indicate *future value* and omit *payment* to compute the rate on a balloon payment.) The *guess* option, a value between 0 and 1, provides a starting point for a series of iterations that Excel must process to perform the calculation.

As an example of the RATE function, to find the rate of return on a $10,000 investment that pays you in five payments of $3000 each, use the expression

=RATE(5,–3000,10000)

which returns 0.152382, or roughly 15%, as the rate of return. Excel goes through an iterative process to come up with this value, repeating a calculation over and over again until it arrives at a conclusion. If Excel cannot reach a satisfactory conclusion within 20 tries, it displays the #NUM! error value. If you get this error when you are using the RATE function, you can supply a value for the *guess* argument, enabling

Excel to begin the iteration process more accurately. A guess between 10% (0.1) and 90% (0.9) usually suffices.

IRR(*values,guess*)   The IRR function calculates the internal rate of return for an investment. The *values* argument refers to a range of cells containing the numbers used to calculate the internal rate of return. Payments received can be signified by positive numbers, while investments made can be signified by negative numbers within the arguments.

An example of the use of the IRR function appears in Figure 10-2. In this worksheet printout, cell C12 contains the formula =IRR(C2:C9). It calculates the internal rate of return by comparing the original investment cost (entered as a negative value in cell C2) and the resultant cash flows (in cells C3 through C9).

The *guess* argument, which is optional, performs the same purpose as it does in the RATE function. If your use of the IRR function results in a #NUM! error message, try adjusting the guess rate.

MIRR(*values,safe,risk*)   The MIRR function calculates the modified internal rate of return. It is similar to the IRR function, except that MIRR also considers the cost of the funds borrowed to finance the investment (the *safe* argument) and the reinvestment rate for the funds generated by the investment (the *risk* argument). In using a reinvestment rate, the MIRR function takes into account the fact that you are likely to

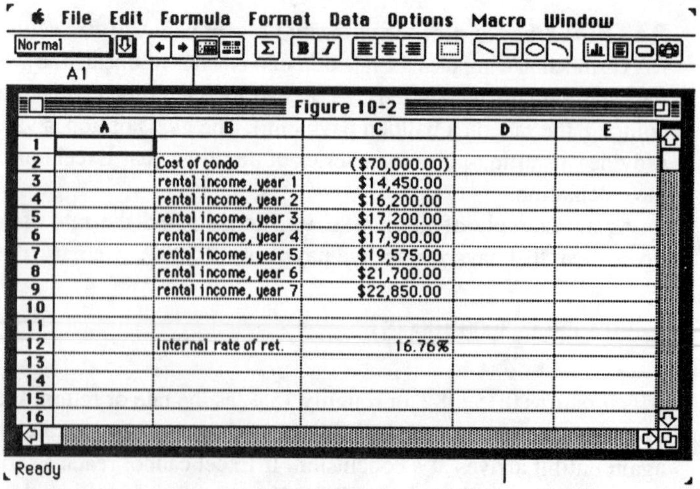

FIGURE 10-2.   Example of IRR function

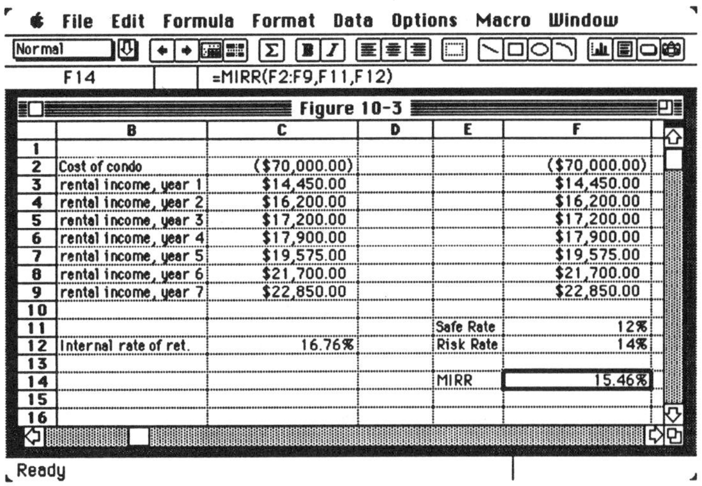

	B	C	D	E	F
1					
2	Cost of condo	($70,000.00)			($70,000.00)
3	rental income, year 1	$14,450.00			$14,450.00
4	rental income, year 2	$16,200.00			$16,200.00
5	rental income, year 3	$17,200.00			$17,200.00
6	rental income, year 4	$17,900.00			$17,900.00
7	rental income, year 5	$19,575.00			$19,575.00
8	rental income, year 6	$21,700.00			$21,700.00
9	rental income, year 7	$22,850.00			$22,850.00
10					
11				Safe Rate	12%
12	Internal rate of ret.	16.76%		Risk Rate	14%
13					
14				MIRR	15.46%
15					
16					

FIGURE 10-3. Example of MIRR function

reinvest the cash produced by the investment. The *risk* argument is the rate of return for the reinvested funds.

Figure 10-3 shows the use of the MIRR function. Using the same figures as in the IRR example, this example of the MIRR function takes into account the cost of the financing for the condo at 12%, and assumes a reinvestment rate of 14%. The formula =MIRR(F2:F9,F11,F12) compares the original investment cost in cell F2, the cash flows in cells F3 through F9, the safe rate in cell F11, and the risk rate in cell F12 to arrive at the modified investment rate of return of 15.46%.

DATABASE FUNCTIONS

Excel offers database functions that are nearly identical in nature to statistical functions. The database functions provide sums, averages, minimum and maximum values, and standard deviations just as the statistical functions do. The difference is that the database functions apply only to database records that have been selected based on a set criteria. You must specify a database range and a criteria range before using any of the database functions.

Database functions use the following arguments:

- The *database* argument is a reference to a valid database range. If you have used the Set Database command to define the database range, you can use the word "database" as this reference.

- The *criteria* argument is a reference to a valid criteria range. If you have used the Set Criteria command to define the criteria range, you can use the word "criteria" as this reference.

- The *field name* argument is the name of the field that supplies the average values.

- As an option, you can specify a *field index value,* which is the number of the field in the database; the first field is field 1, the second is field 2, the third is field 3, and so on.

DAVERAGE(*database,field name,criteria*)
DAVERAGE(*database,field index value,criteria*) The DAVERAGE function takes a series of values in records of the database range that satisfy the given criteria and returns an average of those values. In the example shown in Figure 10-4, the database range has been defined with the Set Database command. This range includes the data and the column headings. The criteria range (cells A5 to E6) has been defined

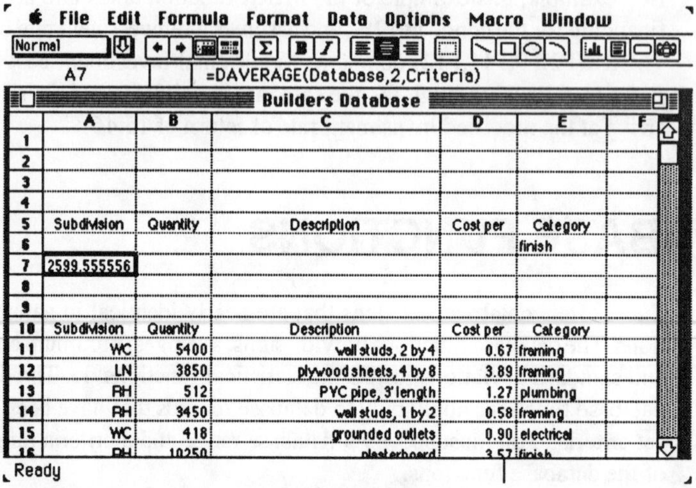

FIGURE 10-4. Example of DAVERAGE function

with the Set Criteria command. The specified criteria result in the inclusion of all records containing the word "finish" in the Category field. In cell A7, the formula

=DAVERAGE(Database,2,Criteria)

returns the value of 2599.55556, which is the average of the Quantity fields for all records with "finish" in the Category field.

DCOUNT(*database, field name, criteria*)
DCOUNT(*database, field index value, criteria*)   The DCOUNT function returns a count of the numeric values contained in the database records that meet the specified criteria. In the example shown in Figure 10-5, the database range has been defined with the Set Database command. The specified criteria, included as a range in the formula in this example, result in the inclusion of all records that are in the Walnut Creek (WC) subdivision. In cell A7, the formula

=DCOUNT(database,2,$A$5:$E$6)

returns the value 5, indicating that five records in the database match the specified criteria and have a value in the Quantity field.

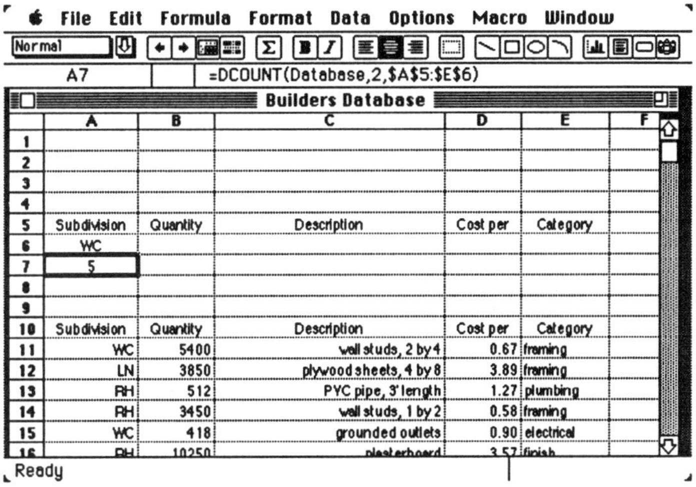

	File	Edit	Formula	Format	Data	Options	Macro	Window	

Normal					Σ									

A7		=DCOUNT(Database,2,$A$5:$E$6)

Builders Database

	A	B	C	D	E	F
1						
2						
3						
4						
5	Subdivision	Quantity	Description	Cost per	Category	
6	WC					
7	5					
8						
9						
10	Subdivision	Quantity	Description	Cost per	Category	
11	WC	5400	wall studs, 2 by 4	0.67	framing	
12	LN	3850	plywood sheets, 4 by 8	3.89	framing	
13	RH	512	PVC pipe, 3' length	1.27	plumbing	
14	RH	3450	wall studs, 1 by 2	0.58	framing	
15	WC	418	grounded outlets	0.90	electrical	
16	RH	10250	plasterboard	3.57	finish	

Ready

FIGURE 10-5.   Example of DCOUNT function

DMAX(*database, field name, criteria*)
DMAX(*database, field index value, criteria*)

DMIN(*database, field name, criteria*)
DMIN(*database, field index value, criteria*)   The DMAX and DMIN functions provide the maximum and minimum values, respectively, in a specified field for all
records in the database that meet the specified criteria. In the example shown in Figure
10-6, the database range and the criteria range (cells A5 to E6) are specified as ranges
within the formulas. The specified criteria result in the inclusion of all records that are
in the River Hollow (RH) subdivision. In cell C7, the formula

=DMAX($A$10:$E$30,4,$A$5:$E$6)

returns the value of 3.57, indicating that among the records for the River Hollow
subdivision, 3.57 is the highest amount in the Cost field. In cell C8, the formula

=DMIN($A$10:$E$30,4,$A$5:$E$6)

returns the value of $0.58 as the lowest amount in the Cost field for any of the records
that are in the River Hollow subdivision.

	A	B	C	D	E	F
1						
2						
3						
4						
5	Subdivision	Quantity	Description	Cost per	Category	
6	RH					
7			3.57			
8			0.58			
9						
10	Subdivision	Quantity	Description	Cost per	Category	
11	WC	5400	wall studs, 2 by 4	0.67	framing	
12	LN	3850	plywood sheets, 4 by 8	3.89	framing	
13	RH	512	PYC pipe, 3' length	1.27	plumbing	
14	RH	3450	wall studs, 1 by 2	0.58	framing	
15	WC	418	grounded outlets	0.90	electrical	
16	RH	10250	plasterboard	3.57	finish	

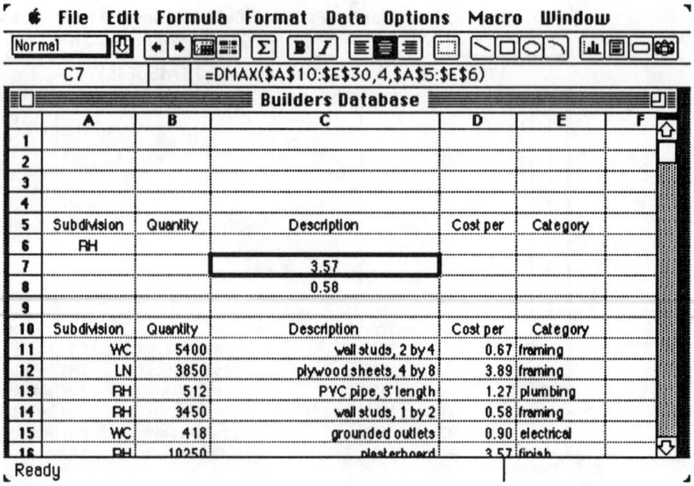

FIGURE 10-6.   Example of DMAX and DMIN functions

DSUM(*database,field name,criteria*)
DSUM(*database,field index value,criteria*)   The DSUM function returns the sum of the numbers in a specified field for all records in the database that meet the specified criteria. In the example shown in Figure 10-7, the database range has been defined with the Set Database command, and the criteria range (cells A5 to E6) has been defined with the Set Criteria command. The specified criteria result in the inclusion of all records that are in the Walnut Creek (WC) subdivision. In cell A7, the formula

   =DSUM(database,2,criteria)

returns the value of 6142, indicating that among the records for the Walnut Creek subdivision, the Quantity amounts total 6142.

DSTDEV(*database,field name,criteria*)
DSTDEV(*database,field index value,criteria*)   The DSTDEV function returns the sample standard deviation for the numbers in the specified field for all database records that satisfy the given criteria. The function is the database version of the STDEV function (see the discussion of STDEV in the "Statistical Functions" section earlier in this chapter).

```
 ⬥  File  Edit  Formula  Format  Data  Options  Macro  Window

[Normal]  [ ] [←|→|▦▦|Σ|▣I|≣≣≣|▱|◥□○◝|▥▤□⬡]
      A7          =DSUM(Database,2,Criteria)
▦□▦▦▦▦▦▦▦▦▦▦ Builders Database ▦▦▦▦▦▦▦▦▦▦
         A          B              C              D        E       F
  1
  2
  3
  4
  5   Subdivision  Quantity       Description    Cost per  Category
  6      WC
  7     6142
  8
  9
 10   Subdivision  Quantity       Description    Cost per  Category
 11      WC        5400      wall studs, 2 by 4     0.67  framing
 12      LN        3850      plywood sheets, 4 by 8  3.89  framing
 13      RH         512      PYC pipe, 3' length    1.27  plumbing
 14      RH        3450      wall studs, 1 by 2     0.58  framing
 15      WC         418      grounded outlets       0.90  electrical
 16      RH       10250      plasterboard           3.57  finish
 Ready
```

FIGURE 10-7.   Example of DSUM function

MACRO FUNCTIONS

The remainder of this chapter describes the most commonly used macro functions. Use these functions inside a macro sheet to perform the desired action. You place the desired functions, in the desired order, in the macro sheet; then close the macro sheet, open a worksheet if necessary, and run the macro to achieve the desired results. Additional macro functions designed for working with dates and times are covered in Chapter 11. For a complete listing of all macro functions, refer to the macro directory included with your Excel documentation.

File Menu Macro Functions

These macro functions have the same effect as the commands from the File menu.

FILE.DELETE(*name text*)
FILE.DELETE?( )   This function is equivalent to the Delete command of the File menu. Specifying a file name between the parentheses deletes the file. If the second form of the function is used, a dialog box prompts the user for a file name, and that file is then deleted.

NEW(*type number*)
NEW?( )   This function is equivalent to the New command of the File menu. Specifying a type of 1, 2, or 3 between the parentheses opens a new file. Type 1 corresponds to a worksheet, 2 corresponds to a chart, and 3 corresponds to a macro sheet. If the second form of the function is used, a dialog box prompts the user to choose a worksheet, a chart, or a macro sheet.

OPEN(*file,update,read-only,format,password*)   This function is equivalent to the Open command of the File menu. The *file* argument represents a file name, which can include an optional path and drive identifier. The *update* argument is a logical value of TRUE or FALSE. This value determines whether any external references in the worksheet are to be updated when the file is opened. If you enter TRUE, the references are updated; if you enter FALSE, the references are not updated. The *read-only* argument also corresponds to a logical value. If TRUE, the file is set to read-only. If FALSE, the file may be changed.

The *format* option is used with text files. A value of 1 for this option specifies a text file containing tab-separated values, while a value of 2 specifies a text file containing comma-separated values. The *password* option specifies the password if any is needed to open the file. For details on protecting files with passwords, see Chapter 11.

PAGE.SETUP(*head,foot,left,right,top,bottom,heading,grid,h_center,v_center***)**
PAGE.SETUP?( )   This function is equivalent to the Page Setup command of the File menu. The *head* and *foot* arguments are headers and footers that are entered as text. The arguments *left, right, top,* and *bottom* are margin settings entered as numeric values; the *heading* and *grid* arguments are both logical arguments that correspond to the Row and Column Headings and Gridlines options in the dialog box for the Print command. Entering TRUE for either argument is equivalent to choosing the option in the dialog box. *H_center* and *v_center* are logical arguments that correspond to the Horizontal Centering and Vertical Centering options.

Choosing the second syntax for this function, PAGE.SETUP?( ), causes the dialog box for the Page Setup command to appear. The user can then select the appropriate response from the dialog box.

PRINT(*range, from,to,copies,draft,preview,parts,color, feed***)**
PRINT?( )   This function is equivalent to choosing the Print command from the File menu. The *range* argument can be 1 (to print all pages) or 2 (to print a specified page range). The *from* and *to* arguments are numeric values indicating the starting and ending page; the *copies* argument is also a numeric value indicating the number of copies to be printed. The *draft* and *preview* arguments are logical arguments. Note that *draft* is provided only for compatibility with Windows Excel for the IBM PC and compatibles. Entering TRUE in the *draft* or *preview* arguments is equivalent to choosing the corresponding option in the Print command dialog box. The *parts* argument specifies what to print; 1 is a document, 2 is notes, or 3 is both. The *color* argument corresponds to the Print Using Color check box. *Feed* is a numeric argument of 1 for continuous or 2 for manual paper feed.

The second syntax for this function, PRINT?( ), causes the dialog box for the Print command to appear. The user can then select the appropriate response from the dialog box.

SAVE( )   This function, which has no arguments, is equivalent to the Save command from the File menu.

SAVE.AS(*name,type,password,backup***)**
SAVE.AS?( )   This function is equivalent to choosing the Save As command from the File menu. The *name* argument identifies the file name in the form of a text string; it can include an optional path and drive specifier such as HARDDISK:EXCEL:Accounts 1. The *type* argument is a number from 1 to 25, identifying the file format according to the following table:

Type	File Format
1	Excel
2	SYLK (Excel 1.5 or below, Multiplan, Chart)
3	ASCII text
4	WKS (Lotus 1-2-3, release 1a or 1.1)
5	WK1 (Lotus 1-2-3, release 2)
6	CSV (comma-separated values)
7	DBF2 (dBASE II)
8	DBF3 (dBASE III/III PLUS)
9	DIF (Data interchange format)
10	Not used
11	DBF4 (dBASE IV)
12-14	Not used
15	WK3 (Lotus 1-2-3, release 3)
16	Excel 2.2
17	Template
18	Add-in macro
19	Text (Macintosh)
20	Text (Windows)
21	Text (OS/2 or DOS)
22	CSV (Macintosh)
23	CSV (Windows)
24	CSV (OS/2 or DOS)
25	International macro

The *backup* argument is a logical argument; if TRUE is supplied, a backup file is created. The *password* argument is an optional password entered as a text string. This argument can only be used with Excel files; you cannot password-protect foreign files from within Excel.

Edit Menu Macro Functions

The following functions parallel the commands from the Edit menu.

CLEAR(*number*)
CLEAR?( ) The CLEAR function is equivalent to the Clear command from the Edit menu. The *number* argument is a value from 1 to 4, indicating whether all entries

(1), formats only (2), formulas only (3 or blank), or notes (4) shall be cleared from the selected cells. If the second form of the function, CLEAR?( ), is used, the dialog box is displayed, and the user can then select the types of information that should be cleared.

EDIT.DELETE(*number*)
EDIT.DELETE?( )   The EDIT.DELETE function is equivalent to selecting the Delete command from the Edit menu. The *number* argument is a value of 1 to 4, indicating whether the remaining cells should be shifted to the left (1) or up (2) after the deletion, or whether the entire row (3) or entire column (4) should be deleted. If the second form of the function, EDIT.DELETE?( ), is used, the dialog box containing the Shift Cells Left and Shift Cells Up options appears.

INSERT(*number*)
INSERT?( )   The INSERT function is the equivalent of selecting the Insert command from the Edit menu. The *number* argument is a value of 1 or 2, indicating whether the adjacent cells should be shifted to the right (1) or down (2) after the insertion. If the second form of the function, INSERT?( ), is used, the dialog box containing the Shift Cells Right and Shift Cells Down options appears.

FILL.RIGHT( )
FILL.DOWN( )   These functions, which use no arguments, are equivalent to the Fill Right and Fill Down commands of the Edit menu.

UNDO( )   The UNDO function, which uses no arguments, is identical in operation to the Edit menu's Undo command.

Formula Menu Macro Function

This macro function imitates a command from Excel's Formula menu.

DEFINE.NAME(*name,refers to,macro type,shortcut key*)   This function is equivalent to the Define Name command of the Formula menu. The *name* argument identifies a name to be assigned to the range, entered as a text string; the *refers to* argument provides a reference to which the name should apply. That reference can be a cell, a group of selected cells, a value, formula, or an external reference in another worksheet. References used with this function must be in R1C1 style.

The *macro type* argument, which is optional, applies only to macros. It can be 1 for a command macro or 2 for a function macro. The *shortcut key* argument is a letter key, which can be designated as a COMMAND-OPTION key in the case of command macros.

Format Menu Macro Functions

These functions are equivalent to commands from the Format menu.

ALIGNMENT(*number,wrap*)
ALIGNMENT?( )   This function is the equivalent of the Format menu's Alignment command. The *number* argument is a value from 1 to 5 representing different types of alignment. The choices are 1 for general, 2 for left, 3 for centered, 4 for right, and 5 for fill. *Wrap* is a logical argument that corresponds to the Wrap Text check box. If the second form of the function, ALIGNMENT?( ), is used, a dialog box containing the Alignment choices appears.

BORDER(*outline,left,right,top,bottom,shade*)
BORDER?( )   This function is equivalent to the Border command from the Format menu. The *outline, left, right, top, bottom,* and *shade* arguments are logical arguments; specifying TRUE for any of these arguments results in that type of border at the selected cells. If the second form of the function, BORDER?( ), is used, a dialog box appears from which the user can select the desired options.

COLUMN.WIDTH(*number,reference,standard,type_number*)
COLUMN.WIDTH?( )   This function is the equivalent of the Column Width command. The *number* argument is a numeric value indicating the desired width for the selected columns; the *reference* argument indicates the column to which the new width applies. If omitted, the cell width applies to the column containing the active cell. *Standard* is a logical argument that corresponds to the Standard Width check box. *Type_number* is a numeric argument from 1 to 3: 1 hides the column, 2 unhides the column by restoring it to its prior width, and 3 sets the column to the best width. If the second form of the function, COLUMN.WIDTH?( ), is used, a dialog box containing the Column Width options appears.

FORMAT.NUMBER(*format string*)
FORMAT.NUMBER?( )   This function is equivalent to the Number command of the Format menu. The *format string* argument is a string of text representing a valid Excel format. If the second form of the function, FORMAT.NUMBER?( ), is used, a

dialog box containing the Format Number choices appears. As an example of FOR-MAT.NUMBER, the statement

=Formula(Format.Number("$#,##0.00"))

formats the active cell in the dollar format indicated.

ROW.HEIGHT(*number, reference, standard height, type_number*)
ROW.HEIGHT?( )   This function is equivalent to the Format menu's Row Height command. The *number* argument is a value indicating the new height of the rows; the *reference* argument is a reference to a row or group of rows that are to be adjusted in height; and the *standard height* argument is a logical argument. If TRUE, row height is controlled by the standard font size, and if FALSE, row height is the same regardless of the font size. *Type_number* is a number from 1 to 3 that corresponds to the Hide/Unhide button: 1 hides the row (sets row height to 0), 2 unhides the row (restores row height to its prior setting), and 3 sets the row to a "best-fit" height. If the second form of the function, ROW.HEIGHT?( ), is used, a dialog box containing the Row Height entries appears.

Data Menu Macro Functions

The functions listed here parallel commands from the Data menu.

DATA.DELETE( )
DATA.DELETE?( )   This function, which uses no arguments, is equivalent to the Delete command of the Data menu. The first syntax for the command, DATA.DELETE( ), deletes the selected record. The second form, DATA.DELETE?( ), displays a dialog box asking for confirmation to delete the record. Once the OK button is selected, the record is deleted.

DATA.FORM( )   This function, which uses no arguments, is equivalent to the Data menu's Form command. When it is used, a form for the defined database appears, and the user can then use all of the normal features of the form (see Chapter 7 for an explanation of forms). When the user chooses the Exit button on the form, control returns to the macro.

DATA.FIND(*logical value*)   This function is equivalent to the Data Find and Data Exit Find commands of the Data menu. If the *logical value* argument provided is

TRUE, Excel executes a Data Find command. If the logical value is FALSE, Excel executes a Data Exit Find command to exit an existing Data Find operation.

DATA.FIND.NEXT( )
DATA.FIND.PREVIOUS( )   The DATA FIND NEXT and DATA FIND PRE-VIOUS functions find the next or previous records in a database that match the database criteria identified previously by a Set Criteria command or SET.CRITERIA function. If a matching record cannot be found, the function returns a logical value of FALSE.

EXTRACT(*logical value*)
EXTRACT?( )   This function is equivalent to the Data menu's Extract command. The *logical value* argument controls the setting of the Unique check box, either to extract all records or only unique ones (thereby filtering out all duplicate records). If the argument is TRUE, Excel performs an extract of unique records; if it is FALSE, Excel performs an extract of all records meeting the specified criteria. When the EXTRACT?( ) syntax for the command is used, a dialog box displays the Unique Records check box.

SET.DATABASE( )
SET.CRITERIA( )   These functions, which use no arguments, are equivalent to the Set Database and Set Criteria commands of the Data menu. For proper results, the macro should select the desired range prior to the use of these functions.

SORT(*sort by,key1,order1,key2,order2,key3,order3*)
SORT?( )   This function is equivalent to the Data menu's Sort command. The *Sort by* argument is 1 or 2, indicating whether you want to sort by rows (1) or by columns (2). The *key* and *order* arguments are used to identify the desired sort keys and to specify whether the sorts will be in ascending or descending order. The *key* arguments are entered as R1C1-style cell references, in the form of text, or as an external reference to an active worksheet. The *order* arguments consist of the number 1 or 2, indicating an ascending order sort (1) or a descending order sort (2).

Options Menu Macro Functions

This group of functions has the same effect as commands from Excel's Options menu.

DISPLAY(*formula,gridlines,headings,zero value,color,reserved,***
outline,page_breaks,object_number)
DISPLAY?( )   The first format of this function is equivalent to the Display command of the Options menu. The *formula, gridlines, headings,* and *zero value* arguments are logical arguments; specifying TRUE for any of these arguments results in the chosen option being selected. The *color* argument is a numeric value, and color choices are indicated by numbers from 1 to 8, which correspond to the numbered color choices that appear in the dialog box for the Display command.

The *reserved* option is reserved for some international versions of Excel. *Outline* is a logical argument that corresponds to the Outline Symbols check box. *Page_breaks* is a logical argument that corresponds to the Page Breaks check box. *Object_number* is a numeric argument from 1 to 3, corresponding to the display options in the Object box.

The second format of this function, DISPLAY?( ), causes the Options/Display dialog box to appear. The user can then fill in the desired options.

SET.PRINT.AREA( )
SET.PRINT.TITLES( )   These functions, which use no arguments, are equivalent to the Set Print Area and Set Print Titles commands of the Options menu.

SET.PAGE.BREAK( )
REMOVE.PAGE.BREAK( )   These functions, which use no arguments, are equivalent to the Options menu's Set Page Break and Remove Page Break commands.

Macro Menu Macro Function

This function imitates a command from the Macro menu.

RUN(*reference,step***)**
RUN?( )   The RUN function is equivalent to the Macro menu's Run command. The *reference* argument can be an external reference to a macro, an R1C1-style reference to a macro, or the text of a name assigned to the macro that is to be run. *Step* is a logical argument that denotes whether the macro should be run in single-step mode. The second form of the function, RUN?( ), displays the Run dialog box, and the user can then choose the desired macro to run.

Chart-Related Macro Functions

The macro functions described in this section relate specifically to charts.

COMBINATION(*number*)
COMBINATION?( ) The COMBINATION function selects a type of combination chart from the Combination gallery. This function is identical in operation to the Combination command of the Gallery menu. The number specified must correspond to one of the available types of combination charts. If the second format of the function is used, COMBINATION?( ), a dialog box allows the user to select the desired combination.

GALLERY.*XXXX*(*number,delete overlay*)
GALLERY.*XXXX*?( ) The GALLERY function selects a gallery from the Chart gallery. The argument *XXXX* specifies one of the available chart types: area, bar, column, line, pie, scatter, 3-D area, 3-D column, 3-D line, and 3-D pie. The *number* argument specifies a format available in the chosen gallery. The *delete overlay* argument is a logical value; if TRUE, the function deletes any overlay charts and applies the new format to the main chart. Note that the *delete overlay* option does not apply to 3-D charts.

As an example of GALLERY, the statement

    =GALLERY.COLUMN(3)

selects the third format of column chart from the Column gallery. The statement

    =GALLERY.PIE(1)

selects the first format of pie chart from the Pie gallery. If the second format of the function is used, GALLERY.XXXX?( ) the appropriate Gallery menu is displayed, allowing the user to select the desired chart. For example, the statement

    =GALLERY.LINE?( )

displays the Gallery menu for line charts, and the user can then select the desired option from the menu.

PREFERRED( ) The PREFERRED function, which has no arguments, is identical in operation to the Set Preferred command from the Gallery menu.

SELECT.CHART( )　　The SELECT.CHART function, which uses no arguments, selects the entire chart as an object. Note that this function is provided for compatibility with Windows Excel for the IBM PC and compatibles and for compatibility with macros written in Excel version 1.5 or earlier. This command is identical in function to the Chart menu's Select Chart command.

chapter **11**

ASSORTED FEATURES

By now, you know how to make Excel work for you and you feel comfortable with its basics. This chapter covers a variety of more advanced topics that you may find useful as you work with Excel. Read through the sections in this chapter, and then use whichever features suit your needs.

WORKING WITH DATES AND TIMES

Excel can work with values expressed in date or time formats. Cells can contain dates, times, or a combination of a date and a time. You can also change the way dates and times are displayed.

Like other popular worksheets, Excel stores date and time entries as numbers. Excel uses a range of numbers from 0 to 63918 to store the dates and times. It considers 0 to be equivalent to January 1, 1904, and 63918 equivalent to December 31, 2078. Each integer between 1 and 63918 represents a day that falls somewhere in this range. Times are represented by fractional values. A combination of a day and a time can be represented by the sum of the whole number that represents the date and the fractional number that represents the time.

To see how this works, open a blank worksheet. In cells C5 to C9, enter these values:

Cell	Entry
C5	1
C6	63918
C7	30782
C8	0.65625
C9	=C8+C7

After entering the data, select the range C5 to D9, open the Edit menu, and select Fill Right to copy the data into the adjacent columns. Select cells D5 to D9, choose Column Width from the Format menu, and set the column width to 18. Open the Format menu again and select Number. Use the scroll bars to bring the date and time formats, shown here, into view:

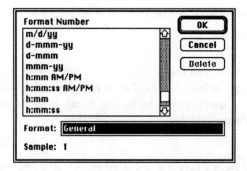

Select the last available format, m/d/yy h:mm. Then press RETURN or click the OK button. The figures in the worksheet should resemble the ones in Figure 11-1. The choice of formats from the Number command on the Format menu determines how the data will be displayed.

Select several individual cells and use various choices of the Format Number command to see how the values are displayed. Figure 11-2 shows examples for each standard date and time format. As with other formats discussed in earlier chapters, you can add a custom date and time format if the standard ones do not fit your needs.

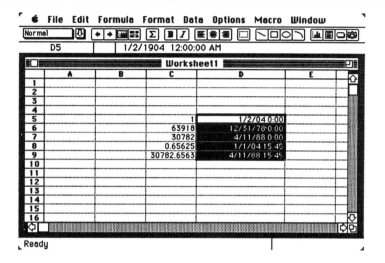

FIGURE 11-1.   Values displayed in date and time format

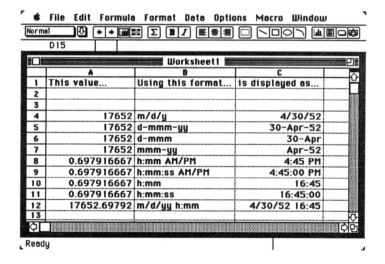

FIGURE 11-2.   Types of date and time formats

To add a custom date or time format, enter the format in the Format text box using the symbols of the date and time formats.

For example, say you want a combined date and time format with the European (dd-mmm-yy) date display and the military (hh:mm:ss) time display. Because this format is not included in the standard choices, you must create your own. To do this, you would select the cell or cells to be formatted, choose the Number command from the Format menu, and enter the following in the Format box:

dd-mmm-yy hh:mm:ss

With this format, the date and time of 04/30/52, 4:45:02 P.M. would be displayed as 30-Apr-52 16:45:02.

Once you create a custom format, it is added to the list box that appears when you select the Number command from the Format menu.

You can display dates and times in various formats by using the symbols shown here:

Symbol	Display
d	Day without leading zero
dd	Day before 10th with leading zero
ddd	Day displayed as a three-letter abbreviation (Sun, Mon, and so on)
dddd	Day completely spelled out
m	Month without leading zero
mm	Month with all months prior to October displaying a leading zero
mmm	Month spelled as a three-letter abbreviation (Jan, Feb, and so on)
mmmm	Month completely spelled out
yy	Year as a two-digit number
yyyy	Year as a four-digit number
h	Hours without leading zeros
hh	Hours with leading zeros
m	Minutes without leading zeros
mm	Minutes with leading zeros
s	Seconds without leading zeros
ss	Seconds with leading zeros
AM/PM	Time using AM/PM designation
A/P	Time using A/P designation

Note that there is a quick way to create a custom date or time format. First select from the list box the format that is closest to your desired format. When you select a format from the list box, it appears in the entry box at the bottom of the dialog box. You can then edit the entry, adding the symbols you want. Once you press RETURN or click OK, the custom format is added to the list box.

Entering Dates and Times

If Excel freed you to enter dates and times as obscure numbers like 17652.697939815, the program's ability to display dates and times would be of limited use. The real advantage Excel offers over many spreadsheets when dealing with dates and times is that it can accept the data in a standard date or time format, and then format the cell automatically (if it has not yet been formatted) to display the data as a date or time. For example, if you enter **4/15/91** in any empty cell on the worksheet, Excel stores the value 31881 but displays 4/15/91. This means you can enter dates and times in ordinary date and time formats and change the format of the display later if desired.

Excel accepts date and time entries in any of these formats:

Dates	Times
4/15/91	7:02:05 PM
15-Apr	7:02 PM
15-April-91	19:02:05
April-91	19:02

You can use slashes or hyphens to separate the parts of a date. Colons are always used to separate the parts of a time. Capitalization can be used, but is purely optional. If you enter a date and a time in the same cell, always separate the two with a space. Note that if you omit the year during data entry, Excel assumes the current year, as indicated by the system's clock.

Excel's ability to work with dates and times can prove useful in tracking chronological data. Because dates and times are serial numbers, you can use them in your worksheet calculations. You can subtract one day from another to find the number of days between two dates, and you can subtract one time from another to calculate the hours and minutes between two times.

Figure 11-3 shows an example of the use of dates and times in a worksheet. The example uses a worksheet to calculate an employee's weekly hours. The start and stop times are entered directly into the cells in the formats shown. The figures in the Total Hours row are calculated by subtracting the Start Time from the Stop Time and multiplying the result by 24. (Since the time values are measured in days, you must multiply by 24 to convert to hours.)

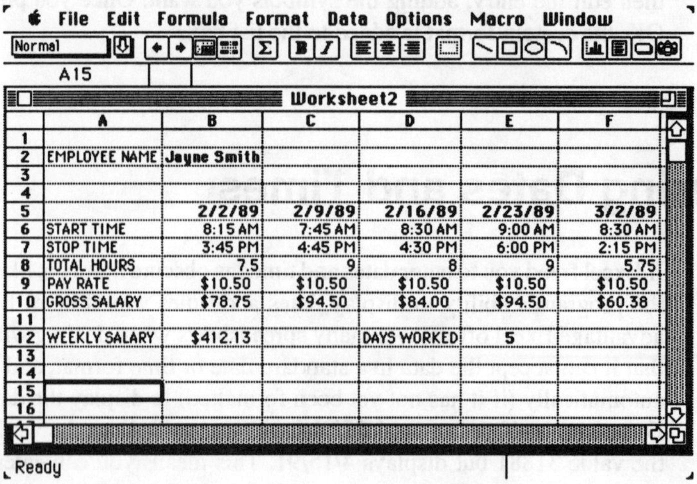

🍎 File Edit Formula Format Data Options Macro Window

A15

Worksheet2

	A	B	C	D	E	F
1						
2	EMPLOYEE NAME	Jayne Smith				
3						
4						
5		2/2/89	2/9/89	2/16/89	2/23/89	3/2/89
6	START TIME	8:15 AM	7:45 AM	8:30 AM	9:00 AM	8:30 AM
7	STOP TIME	3:45 PM	4:45 PM	4:30 PM	6:00 PM	2:15 PM
8	TOTAL HOURS	7.5	9	8	9	5.75
9	PAY RATE	$10.50	$10.50	$10.50	$10.50	$10.50
10	GROSS SALARY	$78.75	$94.50	$84.00	$94.50	$60.38
11						
12	WEEKLY SALARY	$412.13		DAYS WORKED	5	
13						
14						
15						
16						

Ready

FIGURE 11-3.   Example of using dates and times

You can automate this kind of application by developing macros to prompt for the start and stop times. Total hours for each employee could then be linked to another worksheet to form the basis of a payroll system.

Using the Series Command with Dates

The Data menu's Series command saves you considerable time and effort when you are setting up worksheets based on chronological data. It is used to fill a range of data with a series of values that increase or decrease by a set amount. You can use the Series command to fill a range of cells with successive days, weekdays, months, or years. The data can be filled into rows or columns.

To see an example, enter **4/15/91** into a blank cell in the worksheet. Select that cell and the next dozen or so below it. Open the Data menu and choose Series. Because a value formatted as a date was already present in the first cell, the Series dialog box that appears already has date chosen as the type, as shown here:

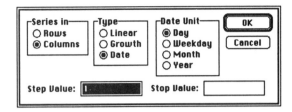

All options in the Series dialog box work in the same manner discussed in Chapter 7. When filling a range with a series of dates, you can choose Day (which fills the range with successive days), Weekday (which omits Saturdays and Sundays when filling the range), Month, or Year. For this exercise choose Day, and then press RETURN or click the OK button. Your screen should resemble the one shown in Figure 11-4.

As an option, you can enter a date in a cell and select just that cell, choose the Series command from the Data menu, and then enter another date in the Stop Value entry box. Be sure to choose Rows or Columns from the Series In box so Excel knows whether to fill the series across a row or down a column. Because you have not selected a range, Excel cannot guess whether you want rows or columns, and defaults to rows unless told otherwise.

FIGURE 11-4. Range filled with days

Large ranges take some time to fill. If you specify a very large range, don't be surprised to see a "Not enough memory" dialog box. The most direct solution to this problem is the rather expensive one of adding additional memory. Short of that, there are a number of ways to economize on memory. The last section in this chapter offers some memory-saving ideas.

The Series command gives you slightly bizarre but understandable results if you ask it to fill in a series of months based on a day that does not exist in every month. For example, if you enter **05/31/91** in a cell, select that cell and the next eleven cells below it, and use the Data Series command to fill in a series of months, you get the following entries in the selected range:

5/31/91

6/30/91

7/31/91

8/31/91

9/30/91

10/31/91

11/30/91

12/31/91

1/31/92

2/29/92

3/31/92

4/30/92

Because many months of the year don't contain 31 days, Excel returns date values that may not be what you had in mind for the range. Using a step value other than 1 along with the Weekday option selected in the Series dialog box may also give you strange results, because Excel skips numbers along the range set by the step value that happen to fall on a weekend.

Commonly Used Date and Time Functions

Excel's date and time functions can be used to return parts of values based on dates and times. The functions are listed in this section.

DATE(*year,month,day*)   The DATE function returns the serial value representing the date specified by the arguments. The *year* argument can be entered as a four-digit number or as a number from 0 (representing 1904) to 178 (representing 2078). The *month* argument is a number from 1 to 12, and the *day* argument is a number from 1 to 31. For example, the statement

    =DATE(1967,12,23)

returns the value 23367, the serial number that corresponds to December 23, 1967.

DAY(*serial number*)   The DAY function returns a number between 1 and 31, representing the day of the month specified by *serial number*. The argument can be in the form of a number between 1 and 63918, or it can be entered as text following a valid date format. For example, both of these statements return the value of 17, for the seventeenth day of May, 1981.

    =DAY(28261)
    =DAY("05/17/81")

HOUR(*serial number*)
MINUTE(*serial number*)
SECOND(*serial number*)   The HOUR, MINUTE, and SECOND functions return a number representing the hour, minute, and second, respectively, for the time specified by the argument *serial number*. This argument can be a fractional number between 1 and 63918, or it can be entered as text following a valid time format. Examples of these functions are shown here:

    =HOUR(0.75)   Returns 18
    =HOUR("6:00 PM")   Returns 18
    =MINUTE(.83995)   Returns 9
    =MINUTE("8:09 PM")   Returns 9
    =SECOND("7:12 AM")   Returns 0
    =SECOND("7:12:32 AM")   Returns 32

MONTH(*serial number*)   The MONTH function returns a number between 1 and 12 representing the month of the year specified by *serial number*. The argument can be a number between 1 and 63918, or it can be entered as text following a valid date format. For example, both of these statements return the value 5 for the fifth month of the year:

=MONTH(28261)
=MONTH("05/17/81")

NOW( )   The NOW function returns a serial number that represents the current date and time, based on the PC's internal clock. This value is updated each time a worksheet is recalculated. The NOW function is handy for keeping a simple clock in an unobtrusive corner of a worksheet. Just enter **=NOW( )** into an unused cell and format the cell using the Format Number command to display as a date and time. Each time you press Calculate Now (COMMAND-=) or perform any operation that recalculates the worksheet, the current time is displayed in the cell.

    The TODAY( ) function performs the same task as the NOW( ) function.

TIME(*hour,minute,second*)   The TIME function returns a serial number that represents a specific time, designated by the arguments *hour, minute,* and *second.* For example, the statement

=TIME(18,30,42)

returns the value 0.771319, which is equivalent to 6:30:42 PM. This function can be useful for converting time data from other programs, which often represent such data as separate fields for the hours and minutes. For example, you might import a text file containing times from a mainframe application. In Excel, that file might appear with the time data in two columns; cell B2 might contain 18 as the hour, and cell C2 might contain 37 as the minutes. You could use the following formula in cell E2 to convert these values into a serial number representing a valid time:

=TIME(B2,C2,0)

You would then need to format the cells as desired to display the time in an acceptable manner.

WEEKDAY(*serial number*)   The WEEKDAY function returns a number between 1 and 7, representing the day of the week specified by *serial number*. Sunday corresponds to 1 and Saturday corresponds to 7. The argument can be a number between 1 and 63918, or it can be entered as text following a valid date format. For example, both of these statements return the value 1 for the first day of the week, a Sunday:

```
=WEEKDAY(28261)
=WEEKDAY("05/17/81")
```

YEAR(*serial number*)   The YEAR function returns a number between 1904 and 2078, representing the year in the argument specified by *serial number*. The argument can be a number between 1 and 63918, or it can be entered as text following a valid date format. For example, both of these statements return the value of 1981:

```
=YEAR(28261)
=YEAR("05/17/81")
```

CUSTOMIZING YOUR WORKSPACE

You can change the style of Excel with the Workspace command from the Options menu. You use the Workspace command to

- Change the style of references back and forth between A1 style and R1C1 style

- Control whether status bars, scroll bars, formula bars, and command underlines (underlined letters in the menu commands) normally appear

- Control cursor movement after pressing RETURN

- Decide what key is used as an alternate method of accessing menus

Selecting the Workspace command from the Options menu reveals the Workspace dialog box shown here:

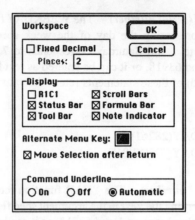

You can select the Fixed Decimal check box and enter the desired number of decimal places to display values as you choose. This affects the display of cells formatted with any of the numeric formats.

The Display box contains check boxes that let you turn on or off the display of the status bar, scroll bars, formula bar, tool bar, and note indicator, as well as selecting the R1C1 style of referencing. If Status Bar is turned off, a status bar only appears when a message is displayed in the bar and disappears afterwards. If Formula Bar is turned off, the formula bar only appears when you are entering a formula and disappears afterwards. If you don't use the scroll bars for navigation, you can provide more room for viewing cells by turning off the display of the scroll bars. The Tool Bar check box determines whether the tool bar appears. Turning off the tool bar will also provide more room for worksheet display. The Note Indicator check box determines whether the note indicator (a small square in the lower-right corner of a cell) appears when a note has been attached to the cell.

The Alternate Menu Key box lets you specify another key for accessing menus. The default alternative is the slash key, which is used by Lotus 1-2-3 and many other worksheets. If you want to specify a different key, type that key in this box. The Move Selection After Return check box determines whether the cursor moves after you press RETURN to complete a cell entry.

The Command Underline option buttons determine whether command letters are underlined in the pull-down menus. On causes the command letters always to appear underlined, while Off hides the underlining. Automatic hides the underlined letters until you use the slash key to display a menu; then the underlines appear.

SAVING AN ENVIRONMENT
WITH FILE WORKSPACE

You can save a list of all currently open windows and documents with the File menu's Save Workspace command. This helps you keep a record of files that are open on a desktop at the same time, so you can quickly open those same files at a later date.

For example, say you open the Profits, Income, and Expenses worksheets and a supporting macro sheet or two at the same time. Opening a large number of files like this on a regular basis can become tedious. To cure this minor headache, you could save all of the documents by selecting the Save Workspace command from the File menu. You will be asked to enter a name for the workspace in the dialog box that appears. (The default name is Resume Excel.) Each document will be saved in turn, and you will be prompted to confirm any overwrites of existing documents.

The resultant file, which you specify by name, contains the names of all open documents at the time you issued the Save Workspace command. When you next go into Excel, instead of loading each file separately, you can open the file named Resume Excel (or whatever name you assigned to the workspace). Doing so will tell Excel to open all documents named in that file.

CONTROLLING CALCULATION

All of the exercises in this book have been performed with Excel's automatic calculation turned on (unless you have turned it off). Excel automatically recalculates all dependent formulas within a worksheet each time you enter a value or change a formula that refers to values in the worksheet. Although this operation is generally useful, it sometimes becomes a major drawback. As your worksheets grow in size, recalculation takes longer and longer to perform. If you are making a series of small changes to a very large worksheet, automatic recalculation can be particularly annoying.

To turn off automatic recalculation, choose the Calculation command from the Options menu. When you choose this command, you'll see the Calculation dialog box, shown here:

```
┌─Calculation───────────────┐  ┌──────────┐
│ ⦿ Automatic               │  │    OK    │
│ ○ Automatic Except Tables │  └──────────┘
│ ○ Manual                  │  ┌──────────┐
│    ☒ Recalculate Before Save│  │  Cancel  │
│                           │  └──────────┘
│ ┌───────────────────────┐ │
│ │ ☐ Iteration           │ │
│ │ Maximum Iterations: ▐100▌│ │
│ │                       │ │
│ │ Maximum Change:  │0.001││ │
│ └───────────────────────┘ │
│ ┌─Sheet Options─────────┐ │
│ │ ☐ Precision as Displayed│ │
│ │ ☒ 1904 Date System    │ │
│ │ ☒ Save External Link Values│ │
│ └───────────────────────┘ │
└───────────────────────────┘
```

This dialog box provides options for making calculation automatic, manual, or automatic on all types of elements except tables. Select Manual to turn off automatic calculation, and then press RETURN or click the OK button. Thereafter, Excel will only calculate the worksheet when you press the Calculate Now key (COMMAND--) or choose the Calculate Now option from the Options menu. Saving a file forces Excel to perform a recalculation, but printing a file does not. If you turn on manual recalculation, be sure to recalculate the worksheet before printing, or you may get erroneous results.

When calculation is set to Manual, a Recalculate Before Save option also appears in the dialog box. If this option is enabled (the default), Excel will recalculate the worksheet whenever you save it.

The Precision as Displayed and Iteration options in the Calculation dialog box are discussed shortly. The 1904 Date System option tells Excel to use the Apple Macintosh numbering system for dates. Because the values on the IBM and Apple systems represent different dates, when you transfer an Apple Macintosh worksheet containing dates to an IBM or an IBM compatible, any dates will contain erroneous values. You can turn off this option to force the Macintosh to use the same date system the IBM PC version of Excel uses.

═══*note*═══ Excel uses a "smart" method of worksheet recalculation, which lets it perform most recalculations much faster than many spreadsheets. Unlike other worksheets (such as Lotus 1-2-3 version 2.0), Excel does not recalculate every cell in a worksheet each time you change a formula. Instead, Excel keeps a list of cells that are dependent on the formula or cell you are changing, and recalculates only those cells. This approach saves a considerable recalculation time.

RESOLVING CIRCULAR
REFERENCES WITH ITERATION

Circular references occur whenever two or more cells in a worksheet are dependent on each other for the results of a formula. When this situation occurs, Excel cannot properly resolve the formulas, so it displays an error message in a dialog box and places a value of 0 in the cell or cells containing the formula that is causing the circular reference.

Figure 11-5 shows an example of a circular reference. Cell B2 contains the value 29800. Cell B3 contains the formula =B2+(B3*0.05). In order to calculate the formula, Excel must refer to the value in B3, which is the cell that is occupied by the formula itself. As a result of this "chasing-its-tail" approach to calculation, Excel displays the dreaded "Can't resolve circular references" error message when the formula is first entered.

You may sometimes want Excel to resolve a circular reference. You can make Excel do this by telling it how many times it can repeat the calculation before using the result. The number of times a calculation is repeated is known as an *iteration*. You specify the acceptable number of iterations from the Calculation dialog box.

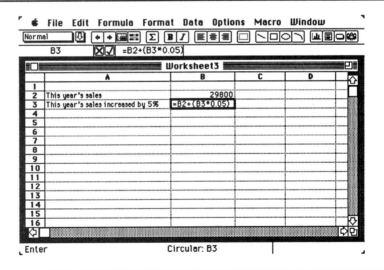

FIGURE 11-5. Example of circular reference

As an exercise, duplicate the example in Figure 11-5 in your own worksheet. Choose the Calculation command from the Options menu, select the Iteration box to turn on iteration, and enter **20** in the Maximum Iterations entry box. Excel recalculates the formula once you accept the options. The result is shown here:

Your Maximum Iterations entry in the Calculation dialog box tells Excel how many times you want the iteration completed. Excel will perform the iteration the specified number of times or until it resolves the calculation (which may be possible, depending on how your formula is structured). The Maximum Change entry tells Excel to consider a calculation to be resolved once the values in the cells that are dependent on each other change less than 0.001 between iterations. Excel stops the iterations when the cells differ by less than the indicated value in Maximum Change or when the number specified with Maximum Iterations has been reached, whichever comes first.

In this simple example, the cells would never contain values that are so close to each other, because one cell is directly dependent on the other and the formula is a simple multiplication. Therefore, Excel performs the specified number of iterations (in this case, 20) and then stops. With more complex circular references, the values in the dependent cells will probably change less and less as iterations are completed. You can specify up to 32,767 iterations. In most cases, the default value of 100 will be more than enough to resolve the circular reference.

USING PRECISION AS DISPLAYED

Formatting cells to provide a set number of decimal places occasionally results in apparently incorrect results. This occurs because Excel normally calculates formulas based on the actual contents of the cells, carried to 14 digits of precision, regardless of what appears in the cell because of its format. Usually, this is a desirable trait, but sometimes it creates a problem, as shown here:

File Edit Formula Format Data Options Macro Window

	A	B	C	D	E	F
1						
2						
3	Value A	87.445	87			
4	Value B	5.489	5			
5						
6	Total	92.934	93			

The cells in each row contain the same values, but the total in cell C6 appears incorrect: 87 plus 5 equals 92, not 93. The problem is that cells C3, C4, and C6 are formatted to display values as integers, but during the calculation process, Excel uses the actual value of the cells.

To solve this problem, you can use the Calculation command from the Options menu. When the dialog box appears, select Precision as Displayed. This option tells Excel to use a numeric precision that is equivalent to the chosen numeric format for that cell. If the cell is formatted to display two decimal places, Precision as Displayed applies a precision of two digits to the value. The results of the Precision as Displayed option when applied to cells C3 through C6 in the previous example are shown here:

File Edit Formula Format Data Options Macro Window

C6   =C3+C4

	A	B	C	D	E	F
1						
2						
3	Value A	87.445	87			
4	Value B	5.489	5			
5						
6	Total	92.934	92			

The Precision as Displayed option uses as many digits as are shown in the cell, which depends on your chosen format. If the cells are in the General format, the Precision as Displayed option has no effect.

Once you use the Precision as Displayed option, it remains in effect for all further work that you do in formatted numeric cells within the worksheet. To restore the normal precision of up to 14 digits, turn off the Precision as Displayed check box.

Keep in mind that Excel *permanently changes* the values of the cells it rounds off when you use the Precision as Displayed option. For example, if a cell contains the value 12.9175 and you select Precision as Displayed while that cell is formatted with a numeric format of 0.00, the value will be permanently changed to 12.90. Make sure this feature will not result in major inaccuracies before you use the Precision as Displayed option.

USING ARRAYS

Excel lets you use arrays—rectangular groups of cells that behave like a single cell—to save yourself time in formula entry. Using arrays, you can apply a formula to a range of cells and produce another range of cells as a result. You can also apply a formula to ranges of cells and produce a single result.

You create arrays by building formulas that identify a range of cells to serve as the input values for the array. This process is similar to the one you use to build formulas that work with a range of values. When you are using an array, however, you must always end the formula by pressing the COMMAND-RETURN key combination. Using COMMAND-RETURN tells Excel to calculate the formula as an array. The resultant formula will also be clearly visible as an array, because it will be enclosed in { } brace symbols.

Use the following steps to create an array:

1. Select a group of cells that will hold the result of the array calculation. If the result will be another array, the selected range should be the same size as the input values used to build the array.

2. Enter a formula that uses the input cells as a reference. You can type the references, or you can select the input range to enter the reference in the formula.

3. Press COMMAND-RETURN to create the array.

Using an Array Formula
To Produce an Array

An example will clarify how simple and timesaving arrays can be. Open the builder's inventory database that you created earlier. Notice that the database does not have a fiscal total of the cost for the items in the building company's inventory. If you wanted to add a column of values in column F to show the unit quantity (column B) multiplied by the unit cost (column D), at least two steps would be required. You would have to create a formula in a single cell that references two other individual cells; for example, in cell F11, you could place the formula =B11 * D11. That step would provide a total for only row 11 of the database. You would then have to duplicate the same formula in every row of the database either by selecting the range and using Fill Down or by using the Paste and Copy commands to copy the formula into the other cells.

Excel's array capability provides a better way to do this. In a single step, you can provide a column of values that shows the total inventory cost of each record in the database. You do this by building an array formula that specifies the ranges from B11 to B30 and D11 to D30 as input values, and the range from F11 to F30 as an output range for the resulting array. In calculating the values, Excel considers every cell in the input ranges and makes the same calculations to produce the values that appear in the output range. The design behind such an array formula would look like this:

F11:F30 = Array of [(range from B11:B30) * (range from D11:D30)]

First you need to select the group of cells that will be used to store the resultant array. Select cells F11 through F30 now. Start a formula with the equal sign, and select cells B11 through B30. This defines the first range of cells that will serve as an input value to the array. Type an asterisk (*) to insert the multiplication operand into the formula, and then select the range of cells from D11 to D30, but don't press RETURN. The formula in your formula bar should read

=B11:B30*D11:D30

Press COMMAND-RETURN to tell Excel to calculate the results as an array. Two things should happen. First, the formula in the formula bar should appear as

{=B11:B30*D11:D30}

Second, an array of values like the one in Figure 11-6 should appear in cells F11 through F30.

Try moving the cursor to any of the cells within the resultant array. Regardless of the cell you are in, the array formula remains the same. Excel treats the array range as if it were a single cell.

Using an Array Formula
To Produce a Single Argument

You can also use an array formula to produce a single value or argument. Functions with which you're already familiar, such as SUM and AVERAGE, can be used as part of an array formula. For example, suppose the accounting department would like to

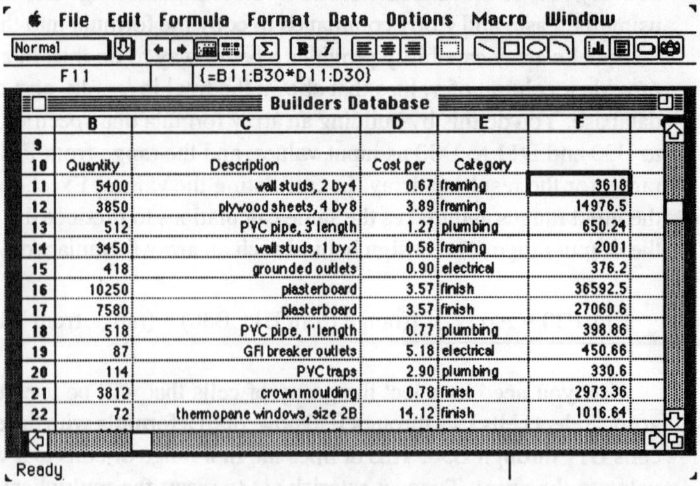

🍎 File Edit Formula Format Data Options Macro Window

| Normal | ⬆️ | ← → ▦ ▦ Σ **B** *I* ▤▤▤ ☐ ╲◻○◖ 📊🗐◻📷 |

| F11 | {=B11:B30*D11:D30} |

Builders Database

	B	C	D	E	F
9					
10	Quantity	Description	Cost per	Category	
11	5400	wall studs, 2 by 4	0.67	framing	3618
12	3850	plywood sheets, 4 by 8	3.89	framing	14976.5
13	512	PYC pipe, 3' length	1.27	plumbing	650.24
14	3450	wall studs, 1 by 2	0.58	framing	2001
15	418	grounded outlets	0.90	electrical	376.2
16	10250	plasterboard	3.57	finish	36592.5
17	7580	plasterboard	3.57	finish	27060.6
18	518	PYC pipe, 1' length	0.77	plumbing	398.86
19	87	GFI breaker outlets	5.18	electrical	450.66
20	114	PYC traps	2.90	plumbing	330.6
21	3812	crown moulding	0.78	finish	2973.36
22	72	thermopane windows, size 2B	14.12	finish	1016.64

Ready

FIGURE 11-6. Resultant array of values

know the total value of the company's current inventory. You can quickly produce an array representing the total of the values in cells B11 to B30 of the Expense database, multiplied by the values in cells D11 to D30.

First you need to place the cursor in the cell that is to contain the result of the array formula. Go to cell D32 and enter **Sum of inventory** as the label. Then place the cursor in cell F32, which will be used to store the results of the array. Start a formula with the equal sign. Choose Paste Function from the Formula menu and select the SUM function. (Turn off the Paste Arguments check box, to avoid having to delete the sample arguments.) Select cells B11 through B30 to define the first range of cells as an input value to the array. Type an asterisk (*) to enter the multiplication operand into the formula, and then select the range of cells from D11 to D30. The formula in the formula bar now reads "=SUM(B11:B30*D11:D30)." Press COMMAND-RETURN to tell Excel to calculate the results as an array. The total cash value of the inventory items appears in cell F32, as shown in Figure 11-7.

Rules for Arrays

When the data within a resultant range of values is an array, they are not truly separate values, so there are some things you cannot do with these numbers. You cannot edit or clear individual cells within an array, and you cannot move a group of cells within

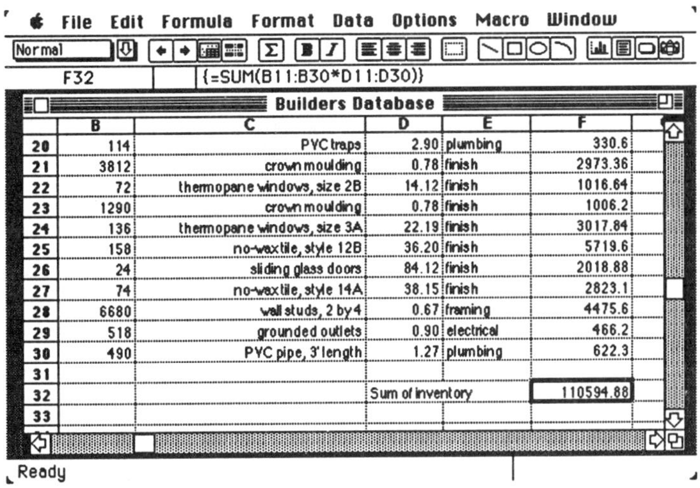

⊄ File Edit Formula Format Data Options Macro Window

| Normal | ⟨ | ◆ | ◆ | ⊞ | ⊞ | Σ | B | I | ≣ | ≣ | ≣ | ▢ | ◥◻◯◝ | ⊫ ▤ ▢ ▩ |

F32   {=SUM(B11:B30*D11:D30)}

Builders Database

	B	C	D	E	F	
20	114	PVC traps	2.90	plumbing	330.6	
21	3812	crown moulding	0.78	finish	2973.36	
22	72	thermopane windows, size 2B	14.12	finish	1016.64	
23	1290	crown moulding	0.78	finish	1006.2	
24	136	thermopane windows, size 3A	22.19	finish	3017.84	
25	158	no-wax tile, style 12B	36.20	finish	5719.6	
26	24	sliding glass doors	84.12	finish	2018.88	
27	74	no-wax tile, style 14A	38.15	finish	2823.1	
28	6680	wall studs, 2 by 4	0.67	framing	4475.6	
29	518	grounded outlets	0.90	electrical	466.2	
30	490	PVC pipe, 3' length	1.27	plumbing	622.3	
31						
32				Sum of inventory	110594.88	
33						

Ready

FIGURE 11-7.   Array formula result as a single value

the array to another location. You can, however, move or clear the entire array. You can also set individual formats, such as numeric, alignment, border, and shading formats, for separate cells within the array. You can also edit the array formula by placing the cursor at any cell in the array and editing the formula in the usual manner.

You cannot insert new rows or columns inside of an array. If you attempt to perform any of these operations, Excel displays a message box containing the message "Can't change part of array." Place the cursor at any of the cells between F11 and F30 now, and try to enter a number. When you press RETURN to enter the value, you'll see the error message. To exit the Edit mode, press RETURN again (to acknowledge the OK button in the message box) and click the Cancel box in the formula bar.

Because of these rules, an array may sometimes interfere with your work. For example, if you wanted to add three rows to the database, you could not insert them inside the existing rows. You could, of course, clear the entire array range, add the new rows, and build a new array range later. However, you may want to consider another option: converting the values in the array to actual values. You can do this by selecting the array range, choosing the Copy Command from the Edit menu, and then choosing the Paste Special command from the Edit menu. When the Paste Special dialog box appears, select Values and press RETURN or click OK. Each cell within the array will be converted to values, and you can perform all normal worksheet operations on those values.

Arrays can provide many ways to analyze your worksheet data, and they can be used within certain types of functions that support arrays. Such topics are beyond the scope of this book, but you may want to investigate additional resources to decide whether you want to use the full capabilities of arrays.

PROTECTING A DOCUMENT

You can protect a document from unauthorized changes with the Protect Document command of the Options menu. You can protect the contents of a document, the window size and shape, or both. You can assign an optional password to the document so the document cannot be changed without the password. There is no way around this password protection if you use it, so be careful not to lose the password.

To protect the active document, open the Options menu and choose the Protect Document command. You should see the dialog box shown here:

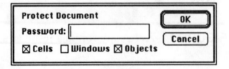

You can enter the desired password, which may consist of any combination of letters, numbers, and symbols, in the Password box. Selecting the Cells box tells Excel to protect the cells of the document from any changes. Selecting the Windows box tells Excel to protect just the size and shape of the window for the document. Selecting Objects protects any objects (such as embedded charts) from changes. You can select one or more of the three options. When you have entered the password and selected the desired options, press RETURN or click the OK button to protect the document.

Once a document has been protected, any attempt to change the cell contents (if Cells was selected), the window (if Windows was selected), or any object (if Objects was selected), results in a message box containing "Locked cells can't be changed." To make any changes, the document must be unprotected. When a protected document is in the active window, the Protect Document command in the Options menu changes to Unprotect Document. Select this command from the Options menu to remove protection, and enter the password exactly as it was entered when the document was protected.

Assigning a password to a document during the protection process is optional. If you do not enter a password, the document will still be protected, and any attempted changes will display a "Locked cells" message box. The document can be unprotected by choosing the Unprotect Document command shown in the Options menu when a protected document is active. If the password was omitted during the protection process, you won't need to enter any password to unprotect the document. This can serve as an excellent method of protecting a worksheet from accidental change, while leaving it open for intentional changes.

Unlocking or Hiding Cells

You can also specify that certain cells should remain unlocked or hide their formulas from view when a document is protected. Before protecting the document, select the cell or range of cells in question. Then open the Format menu and choose Cell Protection. You should see the dialog box displayed here:

As a default, Excel assumes that you want to protect all of the cells in a document and that all formulas should remain visible. You can remove the check mark from the Locked option to unprotect a selected range of cells. The Hidden option lets you hide formulas in selected cells from view. Remove the check mark from Locked or add a check mark to Hidden as desired, and then use the Protect Document command from the Options menu to protect the document.

 If you need to hide just a column of values from view—for a column containing employee review ratings or other such sensitive data—you can easily do so by moving the cursor to that column and using the Column Width command from the Format menu to set the column width to 0. The column will still exist, but with a width of 0 it will not be visible. You will not be able to move to the hidden column using the mouse or the cursor keys. To return the column to view, use Go To (COMMAND-G) to go to any cell in the hidden column, and then use the Format Column Width command to set the column width back to a normal value.

FREEZING WINDOW PANES

When you are using the split bars to split an active window into panes, you can choose the Freeze Panes option from the Options menu to "freeze" the location of the cells inside a pane. When you split a window into panes, you can still scroll the work areas inside of each pane, but when you freeze a pane, the work area inside the frozen pane remains stationary. Remember, the split bars are the rectangular black boxes at the top right and bottom left corners of the worksheet. (Splitting windows is discussed in Chapter 8.)

Figure 11-8 shows the Income worksheet split into two panes. Both worksheets can be scrolled by clicking in the scroll bars with the mouse.

By opening the Options menu and choosing the Freeze Panes command, you can freeze the pane to the left of the split (see Figure 11-9). The Freeze Panes command freezes the window to the left or above the split. After you freeze a pane, the Freeze Panes command changes to Unfreeze Panes. You can use this command to restore the split, allowing both panes to be scrolled.

USING TABLES

Worksheets are often needed to perform "what if" exercises. Suppose you create a worksheet that provides projections based on your best guess regarding prevailing market conditions. What if sales exceed or fall short of expectations by a given percentage? It is often helpful to see the net effect of different conditions on the bottom line.

You could provide answers to "what if" questions by creating a separate formula for each projection, but this can be a lengthy process, particularly if you want to compare many possible conditions. For example, you might want to know what effect

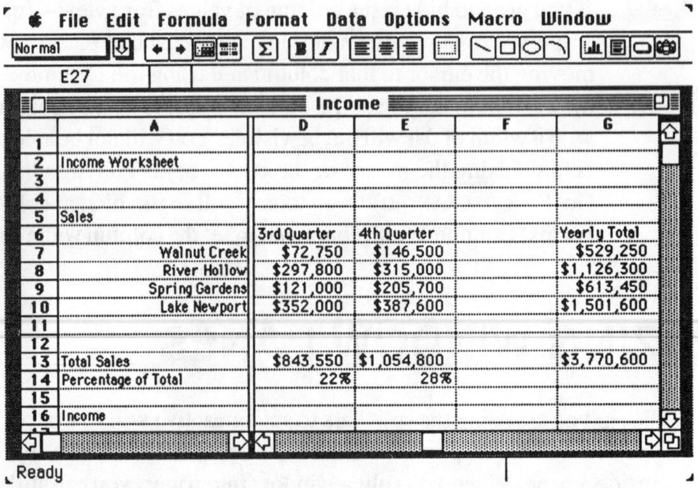

FIGURE 11-8. Income worksheet split into two panes

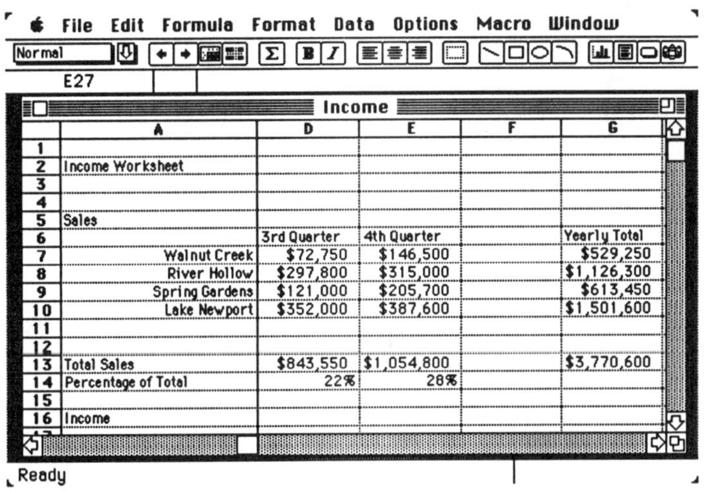

	A	D	E	F	G
1					
2	Income Worksheet				
3					
4					
5	Sales				
6		3rd Quarter	4th Quarter		Yearly Total
7	Walnut Creek	$72,750	$146,500		$529,250
8	River Hollow	$297,800	$315,000		$1,126,300
9	Spring Gardens	$121,000	$205,700		$613,450
10	Lake Newport	$352,000	$387,600		$1,501,600
11					
12					
13	Total Sales	$843,550	$1,054,800		$3,770,600
14	Percentage of Total	22%	28%		
15					
16	Income				

Ready

FIGURE 11-9.   Income worksheet with left pane frozen

a series of different sales increases might have on your company's bottom line. Excel lets you build tables that are ideal for "what if" analysis.

With a single-input table, you can determine how changes in a certain value will affect the values of a series of formulas. You use the Data menu's Table command to create a table. Before using the command, you need the following:

1. A cell that contains the value you wish to change (referred to as the input cell).

2. A column or row that contains the values you will apply to the input cell. When the Table command is used, these values will replace the values in the input cell, one at a time, producing the result determined by your formulas.

3. A row or column that contains the formulas to be used to produce the values.

Open a blank worksheet and build the structure for a table by entering the following data:

Cell	Entry
B2	Monthly Sales
B4	Increase Rate
B7	Projected Sales

Cell	Entry
B8	What-If Rate
C8	5%
C9	6%
C10	7%
C11	8%
C12	9%
C13	10%
D2	120000
D4	6%
D7	=D2+(D2*D4)

At this point, your worksheet should resemble the one shown in Figure 11-10. The simple formula in cell D7 projects a sales increase by multiplying current sales in cell D2 by a projected increase rate of 6% in cell D4, and adding the result to the current sales.

A table is a handy way of figuring different alternatives quickly. The alternative percentages entered in cells C8 through C13 are the input values for the table. To create the table, follow these steps:

1. Choose the range of cells that contains the row or column of input values, and the column or row of formulas will be provided with the input values.

2. Open the Data menu and choose Table.

3. If the input values occupy a row, enter the reference for the input cell in the Row Input Cell box. If the input values occupy a column, enter the reference for the input cell in the Column Input Cell box.

4. Press RETURN or click the OK button.

Perform the first step now by selecting the range from cell C7 to D13. This range contains both the input values (in cells C8 to C13) and the formula (in cell D7). Next, open the Data menu and choose Table. You should see a dialog box similar to the one shown here:

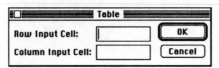

Because the input values are arranged in a column, the input cell reference should be entered in the Column Input Cell box. Move the cursor to the Column Input Cell

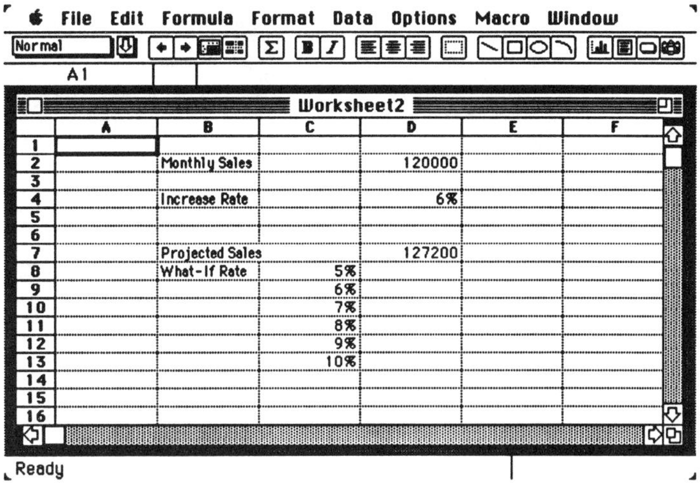

FIGURE 11-10. Structure for table

box now. You can manually enter the reference, or you can do so by selecting the cell. In this case, enter **$D$4** to tell Excel that the input cell is D4 on the worksheet. Press RETURN or click the OK button. The table is filled with the respective "what if" values, as shown in Figure 11-11.

The range of values created by the Table command shares some similarities with an array's values. Like an array, a table does not consist of separate values, but rather of numbers generated by a single formula. You cannot edit or clear an individual cell within a table, and you cannot insert space, rows, or columns anywhere inside a table. If you attempt any of these operations, Excel displays a "Can't change part of table" error message. You can, however, insert space in the top row or left column of a table with the Insert command. Doing so provides room for adding new comparison values or formulas. To delete or cut and paste a table, you must select the entire table before using the Delete, Cut, or Copy command.

USING THE FIND COMMAND

Excel's Find command, located on the Formula menu, can be used to locate a particular portion of text, a value, or a formula anywhere in the worksheet. Although this may sound like a feature that belongs in a word processor, there are times when

```
 ⌘  File  Edit  Formula  Format  Data  Options  Macro  Window
┌─────────┐  ┌──┐ ┌─┬─┬──┬──┐ Σ B I ┌─┬─┬─┐ □ ◇□○┐ ╔═╦═╗
│Normal   │  │↧ │ │←│→│▦ │▦▦│       │▤│▥│▦│        ┌▪▪┐▣□✿
└─────────┘  └──┘ └─┴─┴──┴──┘       └─┴─┴─┘        └──┘
      D10              {=TABLE(,D4)}
┌────────────────────────── Fig11-21 ═══════════════════════┐
│□│                                                        │⌐│
│   │    A    │    B    │   C   │    D    │   E   │   F   │ ⌂
│ 1 │         │         │       │         │       │       │
│ 2 │         │Monthly Sales│   │ 120000  │       │       │
│ 3 │         │         │       │         │       │       │
│ 4 │         │Increase Rate│   │   6%    │       │       │
│ 5 │         │         │       │         │       │       │
│ 6 │         │         │       │         │       │       │
│ 7 │         │Projected Sales│ │ 127200  │       │       │
│ 8 │         │What-If Rate│ 5%│ 126000  │       │       │
│ 9 │         │         │  6%   │ 127200  │       │       │
│10 │         │         │  7%   │ 128400  │       │       │
│11 │         │         │  8%   │ 129600  │       │       │
│12 │         │         │  9%   │ 130800  │       │       │
│13 │         │         │ 10%   │ 132000  │       │       │
│14 │         │         │       │         │       │       │
│15 │         │         │       │         │       │       │
│16 │         │         │       │         │       │       │⌄
│◇│                                                        │◇▯
│ Ready                                    │                │
└────────────────────────────────────────────────────────────┘
```

FIGURE 11-11.   Results of Table command

the Find command proves invaluable. For example, you may use a particular formula a number of times at different locations in a worksheet. Later, if you discover a flaw in the logic of that formula, you would be forced to search for every occurrence of the formula. With the Find command, you can quickly search for the problem entries instead of performing a tedious manual search.

When you choose Find from the Formula menu, the Find dialog box, shown here, appears:

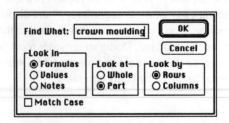

You simply type what you are looking for—values, text, or all or part of a formula—into the Find What text box. Once you have made the entry, use the option buttons to make the appropriate choices for the Find command's operation; then click OK. Excel will search for the first occurrence of the entry. Once it has been found, you can again choose Find from the Formula menu (or use the COMMAND-H key combination) to make Excel search for the next occurrence of the desired entry. Note that the SHIFT-COMMAND-H key combination will perform the search in reverse.

The Look In option box tells Excel whether it should search within formulas, values, or notes. Choosing Formulas causes Excel to search within the cell formulas, and choosing Values causes Excel to search the actual values displayed on the screen. Choosing Notes limits the search to all notes attached to cells.

The Look At option box tells Excel to find the entry either when it exists as a whole word or when it is part of a cell's contents. For example, if you search for the value 36 and use the Part option, it would be found in cells containing 36, 36.7, 369, and 2362. If you used the Whole option for this same search, only cells containing 36 would bc found.

The Look By option tells Excel whether to perform the search by rows or by columns. Choosing Rows causes Excel to look for the data starting at the top row, and moving down row by row. Choosing columns makes Excel start in the first column and look for the data column by column, from left to right.

Note that you can use the ? and * wildcard characters with the Find command. The ? replaces any one character, and the * replaces one or more characters. For example, entering **At*** would find Atlantic City, Atwater, and Atkinson in a column of names. Entering **10**? would match 101, 102, 103, and so forth up to 109.

MANAGING MEMORY

Computer memory is much like most people's salaries; there just never seems to be quite enough. As your worksheets grow in size, your system's memory may begin to limit what you can accomplish. Each cell containing an entry, whether the entry is a value or a formula or simply a cell format, consumes memory. Excel uses *sparse memory management,* a major improvement over earlier spreadsheets. With this memory technique, empty cells do not consume memory, so Excel will probably store much larger worksheets than you may be used to working with. Nevertheless, you will want to conserve memory wherever possible to avoid running short and to speed the recalculation of your worksheets.

Good worksheet design helps consolidate the amount of memory consumed by a worksheet. By using Excel's multidimensional worksheet capability, you should be able to avoid single worksheets littered with data representing different areas. Instead, you should use multiple linked worksheets and simple external references wherever possible so that Excel can update the worksheets without having to open supporting documents.

Unneeded data and text labels are a tremendous waste of computer memory, and should be deleted, but the memory is not recovered until you exit the document. To recover memory after the deletion of unneeded data, you must save the worksheet and load it again.

How you store data also affects memory usage. You can conserve memory by using arrays wherever possible; arrays use less memory than equivalent formulas stored in separate cells. Constant values also use less memory than formulas, so you may be able to gain memory by converting the results of formulas into constant values using the Copy and Paste Special commands. Be judicious about using cell formats; these also use memory. In large worksheets, avoid formatting large blocks of unused cells. Instead, add the formatting after the cells are filled with other data.

If you attempt an operation that cannot be performed because you simply do not have sufficient memory, Excel displays the "Not enough memory" message box, shown here:

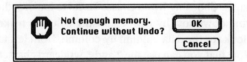

You can select OK to continue the attempted operation without the ability to undo the results, or you can choose Cancel. (The Cancel option may be the wiser choice, because the results of an operation may be uncertain if you run out of memory.) Memory shortages may not be this dramatic. Excel makes very flexible use of memory, going so far as to remove portions of the program temporarily from memory to clear space for data, reloading the program code as it is needed. This sophisticated technique is known as *dynamic memory management.* Although this technique lets you build bigger worksheets, it also slows program operation noticeably. If the speed of program operation (particularly any changes that force a recalculation) begins to slow dramatically, it is a sign that Excel is approaching the limits of your computer's memory, and you should begin looking for ways to boost the available memory.

One drastic but very effective solution to a memory shortage is to add memory to your system. Excel will use all available memory in your computer for your worksheets.

USING OUTLINES

Spreadsheet outlines are a significant feature added to version 3.0 of Excel, and many users find them helpful for looking at the "big picture" while maintaining the ability, to highlight smaller parts of a worksheet. The concept is the same as it is for outlining used in word processing, where less important levels of information can be hidden while more important levels are still displayed. Because words are processed on a horizontal plane, word processing outlining is, in effect, limited to "rows" (the lines of words that appear on a page). Worksheets span more than one dimension, however, so Excel outlines can take on a horizontal or a vertical orientation, depending on how the numbers on your worksheet are arranged.

You use various outline tools on the tool bar to create an outline based on an existing worksheet, or to build a new worksheet in outline form. Once an outline based on a worksheet exists, you can collapse or expand rows or columns of the worksheet, to display or hide data stored in the less important levels. Outlining makes it particularly easy to manage large, departmental worksheets.

To see how outlining works, open the Income worksheet. You can use Excel's outlining tools to collapse the individual sales for the subdivisions and the individual expenses for the company. Before proceeding, you should know where the outlining tools that you will need are. They are located on the tool bar, as follows:

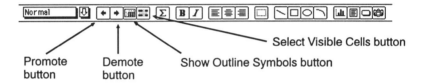

Promote button   Demote button   Show Outline Symbols button   Select Visible Cells button

(If the tool bar is not visible, choose Workspace from the Options menu, and turn on the Tool Bar check box in the dialog box that appears.) As you can see, the first group of four tools on the left are all related to outlines. The left-pointing arrow is the Promote button, and the right-pointing arrow is the Demote button. These are used to promote (raise) or demote (lower) selected rows or columns to a higher or lower level in an outline. To the right of these buttons is the Show Outline Symbols button; and the rightmost button in the group is the Select Visible Cells button. The Show Outline Symbols button will display or hide outline symbols on the worksheet. The Select Visible Cells button will select the visible cells in an outline range. This is useful when you want to work with just the cells that are visible in an outline, when copying data or building charts.

For the Income worksheet, the first step in building the outline is to use the individual sales for the subdivisions as a lower level of the outline. Select rows 7 through 10 by clicking on row 7 in the row border, and dragging down to row 10. Then, click on the Demote button in the tool bar. Your worksheet should resemble the example shown in Figure 11-12.

Don't be concerned because the individual subdivisions are still visible. They will be hidden later, when you click on the collapse button. (The small rectangle at the end of the line that just appeared beside the highlighted columns is a collapse button.)

Next, the income needs to be selected as a lower level in the outline. Select rows 18 and 19. Again, click on the Demote button (remember, it is the right-pointing arrow) in the tool bar. A collapse button, similar to the one that appeared in the previous step, will appear beside the selected rows.

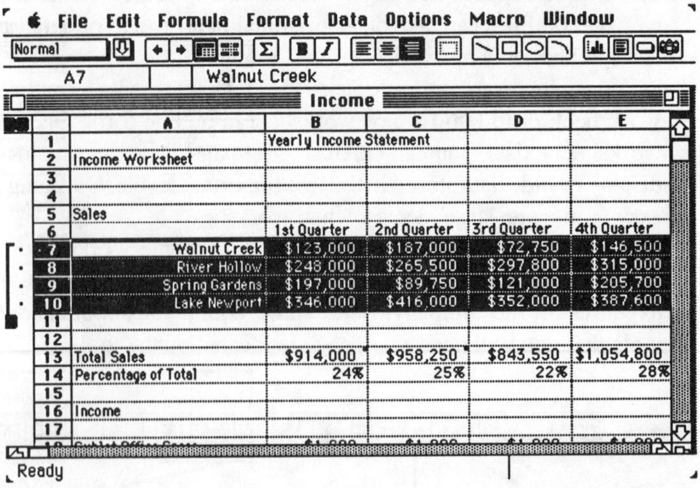

FIGURE 11-12. Income worksheet with subdivisions demoted

The outline now exists as part of the Income worksheet, and you can reduce it into outline form by clicking on the collapse buttons. Click on both collapse buttons, and your worksheet should resemble the example shown in Figure 11-13.

In outline form, the individual sales and income sources are hidden; only the totals are visible. Either the sales or the income figures can be made visible as desired, by clicking on the expand buttons. (The expand buttons take the place of the collapse buttons when a section has been collapsed. They appear beside the collapsed rows or columns as rectangular buttons containing a plus symbol. You may want to try alternately clicking on the collapse and expand buttons, to see their effects.)

Choose Close from the File menu now (or click on the worksheet's Close box), and answer No when the "Save changes to Income" message appears in the dialog box. You will need the Income worksheet without the outline for one more example in this chapter.

Notes About Outlines

You are not limited to a single level when creating outlines. You can select a large group of rows to demote, select a smaller group of rows inside the large group to demote further, and select a smaller group of rows to demote further still.

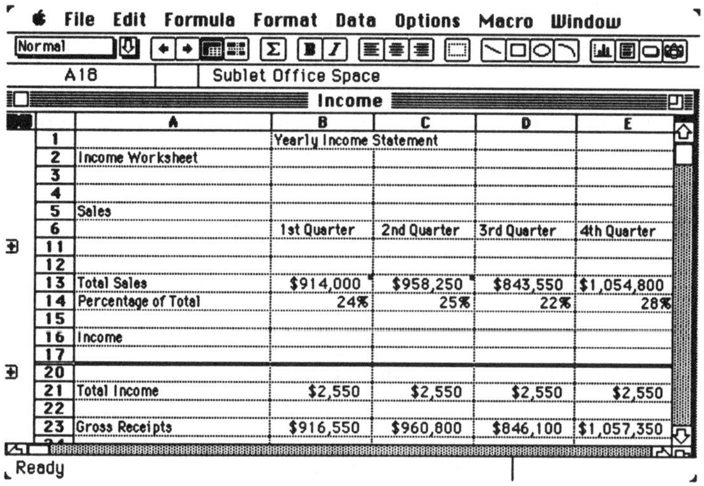

═══════ **FIGURE 11-13.**   Income worksheet in outline form

If you are sure you no longer need an outline, you can clear the outline. To do so, first select the entire worksheet. Then, click on the Promote button in the tool bar. A dialog box appears, asking if you want to promote all rows or all columns. Choose Rows (if your outline is row based), or columns (if your outline is column based). You will need to repeat these steps for all multiple levels in the outline.

Finally, keep in mind that you can create outlines based on existing worksheets automatically. Excel makes some assumptions when you do this, and you may or may not like these assumptions; nevertheless, automatic outline creation can be a useful and timesaving tool.

To automatically create an outline, choose Outline from the Formula menu. The following dialog box will appear:

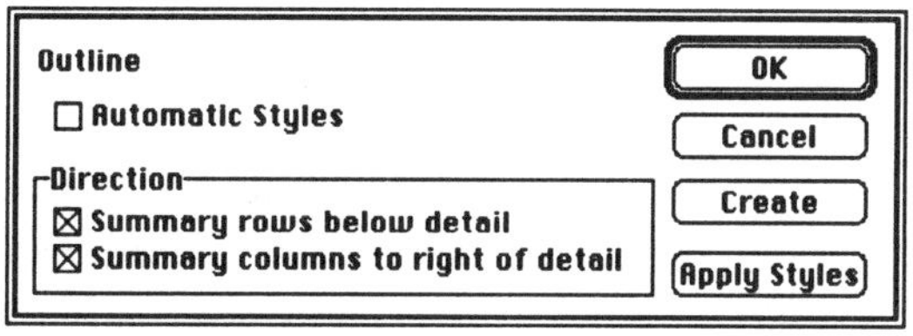

If you check the Automatic Styles box, Excel will apply default styles to the indentations of the outline. Excel also assumes that summary rows appear below detail rows, and summary columns appear to the right of detail columns. If either of these

assumptions is incorrect, you should turn off the applicable check box. Finally, click on the Create button (*not* the OK button!) to create the outline. (All the OK button does here is store settings; it cannot create an outline.)

As an example of automatic outline creation, open the Income worksheet now. Choose Outline from the Formula menu, and then click on the Create button. In a moment, the Income worksheet will reappear, complete with outline collapse buttons, resembling the example shown in Figure 11-14. If you examine the top of the worksheet, you will notice that Excel has created a columnar outline, as well as row outlines. Because the "Yearly Total" label in the top row was separated by a blank column, Excel assumed that it could consider the prior columns to be lower levels. If you click on the collapse button at the top of the worksheet (you'll need to scroll to the right to see it), you will find that only the subdivision names and yearly totals are displayed. Scroll back to the far left, and click on the expand button to restore the lower-level columns to full view. This demonstrates a point about designing worksheets in advance to facilitate outlining. If you are going to make use of automatic outlining, try to indent your labels in a manner that will help Excel determine the difference between higher- and lower-level data. Doing so will save you time later, because you won't have to make changes because of incorrect assumptions.

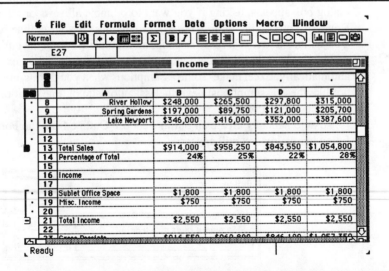

FIGURE 11-14.   Outline created automatically

USING GOAL SEEKING

Another improvement present in versions of Excel from 3.0 on is Goal Seeking, a feature that lets you enter a desired result, and calculate backwards to find the initial values needed to reach that result. (At the risk of sounding facetious, this is a great tool for sales managers who need to obtain certain results from the sales staff on a regular basis!) With goal seeking, Excel will change the value in a selected cell, until a formula dependent on the selected cell returns the desired value. Goal seeking is a powerful tool designed to aid in "what-if" analyses; with it, you can greatly reduce the amount of work necessary to find a desired result.

If you want to see how goal seeking works, duplicate the worksheet shown in Figure 11-15. Be sure to enter the value in cell B14, $103,920.00, as an actual value, and *not* as the result of a formula. (The reason for this will be discussed shortly.) The contents of cell B16 can be entered as the formula

=B14/SUM(B5:B7)

All other entries are simply values or labels.

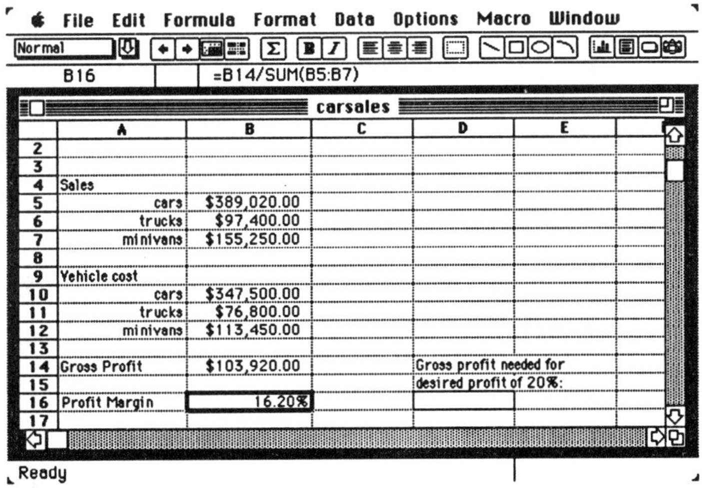

FIGURE 11-15.   Car sales worksheet

First, let's outline the steps in goal seeking. They are as follows:

1. Select the cell with the formula for which you need to find the desired solution.

2. From the Formula menu, choose Goal Seek. A dialog box will appear.

3. In the To Value box, enter your desired result.

4. In the By Changing Cell box, enter the reference for the cell that contains the value to be changed to produce your desired result. You can select the cell or type a cell reference. *Note:* You *must* enter the reference of a cell that contains a value the original formula depends on (directly or indirectly). Also, you *cannot* enter the reference of a cell that contains a formula. (This is why the entry in B14 was entered as a number, and not as a formula.)

5. Choose OK. Excel will display a status box reporting the progress of the goal-seeking operation. When the operation is complete, Excel will display the results.

6. If the desired solution has been reached, you can choose OK, and it will replace the old value in the worksheet. If the desired solution has not been reached, choose Cancel, and the old values will be retained.

An Example of Goal Seeking

In the case of the previous example, what's desired is a dollar amount (as gross profits) that will produce a profit margin of 20%, instead of the existing profit margin of 16.2%. With the example in Figure 11-15 created, the first step is to move to cell B16, because this cell contains the formula that produced the current profit margin.

With the cursor at B16, choose Goal Seek from the Formula menu. The Goal Seek dialog box appears, as shown here:

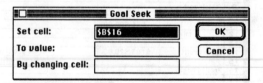

The first box, Set cell, already contains the proper entry (cell B16), because it was selected when you chose Goal Seek from the menu. Tab or mouse down to the next box, To value. Here, you must enter the value you are seeking. In this case, 20% is desired, so enter **20%** (as with cells, you can enter the value using the percent sign).

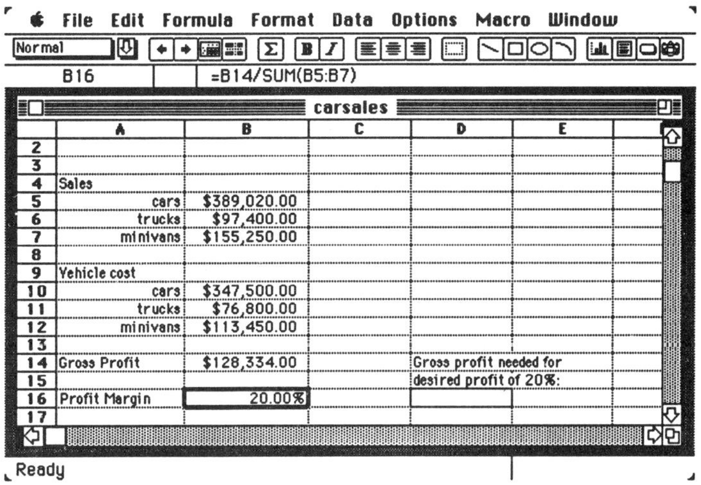

FIGURE 11-16.   Solution using goal seeking

Tab or mouse down to the next box, By changing cell. In this box, you enter the reference for the cell that must be changed to achieve your desired value. Since the gross profit must be increased to achieve a profit margin of 20%, enter B14 in this box.

Finally, click on OK to begin the goal-seeking process. If all entries have been made correctly, Excel will quickly find a solution. Click on OK in the dialog box. Your worksheet should resemble the example shown in Figure 11-16.

Note that Excel came up with a figure of $128,334.00 needed for the dealership to achieve a profit margin of 20%. If you choose OK when a goal-seeking operation is complete, and then decide that you want to go back to the earlier worksheet figures, you can choose Undo Goal Seek from the Edit menu (as long as this is the very next edit operation you do).

chapter **12**

USING OTHER
SOFTWARE
WITH EXCEL

The success of Excel has proven that it is a capable product; understandably, however, there are some tasks that it does not do well or does not do at all. These tasks fall in the areas outside of Excel's design: word processing, communications, relational database management, desktop publishing or page layout, and so on. There may be times when you need to do some of these tasks along with the work that you do with Excel. Perhaps you need to insert a spreadsheet and corresponding graph into a document created with Microsoft Word or MacWrite, or you need to transfer a database of store sales kept in FoxBase Mac to an Excel spreadsheet so a chart can be created. Perhaps stock prices retrieved from an on-line database like CompuServe need to be transferred to an Excel spreadsheet, so that high-low-close charts can be created. You can do all of these tasks, and more, using Excel's capabilities to transfer data to and from other software.

TRANSFERRING EXCEL DATA WITH THE MACINTOSH CLIPBOARD

The easiest way to transfer small or moderate amounts of data (a page or less) to and from Excel and other applications is to use the Copy and Paste commands to move data between the applications.

To move data from Excel to another application, select the desired data in the worksheet, chart, or macro sheet, open the Edit menu, and choose Copy. This action copies the selected item into a portion of your system's memory and onto the Clipboard. (Choosing Show Clipboard from the Window menu will reveal the Clipboard and its copied contents.) Exit Excel, open the other application in the normal manner, and use the Paste command from that application's Edit menu to paste the data to the desired location. (You can do this without exiting Excel if you use MultiFinder or System 7.0. See the next section for details.)

Figure 12-1 shows a document containing a chart in MacWrite, a word processor. The text was originally created in MacWrite with one line of space between the first and second paragraphs. The first step was to load Excel in the usual manner. In Excel, the Income worksheet was loaded, and a chart of the quarterly sales figures was drawn.

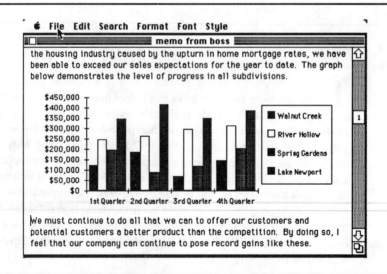

FIGURE 12-1. Excel chart pasted into MacWrite document

The next step was to select the chart by using the Select Chart command from the Chart menu, or by clicking on the entire chart. (If worksheet data were needed in the document instead of a chart, you could simply select the cells containing that data.) The Copy command from the Edit menu was then used to copy the selected chart into memory. The final step was to quit Excel and to get back into MacWrite. With the MacWrite document on the screen, the cursor was placed between the two paragraphs; the Edit menu was opened, and the Paste command was selected. That's all there was to it.

Your ability to manipulate the pasted data once it is in the other application depends on the capabilities of that application. Some word processors (including MacWrite and Microsoft Word) and most desktop publishing programs let you move and size objects pasted in them from Excel. Other applications may or may not offer these capabilities.

You can also move data in the other direction with the Clipboard—from another application (such as a word processor or database) into Excel. For example, you can select a paragraph of text while you are in your word processor and choose the Copy command from the Edit menu to copy the paragraph into the Clipboard. You then exit the word processor and load Excel. Once you are in the desired worksheet, place the cursor at the location where the text is to appear and choose Paste from the Edit menu. With most foreign software, the textual data will appear as one long label within the cell of the worksheet. If you want to transfer data from a database manager, it usually makes more sense to do this by loading a foreign file. See "Loading and Saving Foreign Files" later in this chapter.

Transferring Data with MultiFinder Or System 7.0

You can use a technique that is nearly identical to the one just described if you are using MultiFinder or System 7.0. The only difference is that MultiFinder or System 7.0 saves you the hassle of exiting Excel and loading the other application. To use this technique, you run both Excel and the other application. (For details on installing and selecting MultiFinder on your startup disk, see your Macintosh system software user's guide.) Get into the Excel worksheet or chart, select the desired data, and choose Copy from the Edit menu. Then click the application icon at the right side of the menu bar until the other application becomes the active one. Place the cursor in the document at the desired location for the data, and choose Paste. The Excel data will appear in your document as a result.

LOADING AND SAVING FOREIGN FILES

Excel uses a familiar and fairly painless approach for transferring files to other software packages that use different file formats. Many software programs force you to use conversion utilities to work with files written in a different program's file format, but Excel loads and saves foreign files with the same File Open and File Save commands used for Excel documents. Any file you want to load must first be in Macintosh disk format, however; the end of this chapter gives you tips on getting files from IBM PC disk format into Macintosh format.

To open a file that is in another file format, you simply use the Open command and provide the name of the file, including the folder name and hard drive name (if any). Excel analyzes and converts the contents of the foreign file. To save a file in a foreign file format, simply select the Options button in the Save As dialog box, click on the Options button, and choose one of the listed formats in the File Format list box. The file will be saved in the chosen format.

The only limitation of Excel's foreign file capability is that the foreign format must be one of the types shown in the list in the "Saving Files in Foreign Formats" section of this chapter. If Excel cannot convert the file, it still tries to load it. This operation can have strange and unpredictable results, so it is a good idea to stick with the file types shown in the list.

Opening Files in Foreign Formats

To open a foreign file, use the File menu's Open command. Next, choose the file by name from the list box that appears. If the file is in a different folder, you can click the folder name, and the files located in that folder will appear in the list box.

If the file is a text file, click the Text button, and choose Tab or Comma as the column delimiter from the dialog box that appears. Then select the file and press RETURN or click the OK button to load the file. Excel can load files that are in DBF (dBASE II, III/III PLUS, dBASE IV), WKS (Lotus 1-2-3 release 1A), WK1 (Lotus 1-2-3 release 2), WK3 (Lotus 1-2-3 release 3), DIF, Microsoft SYLK, CSV (comma-separated values), and ASCII text formats.

Saving Files in Foreign Formats

To save a file in a foreign format, open the File menu, choose the Save As command, and select the Options button that appears in the dialog box. An expanded dialog box containing additional choices for saving files appears, as shown here:

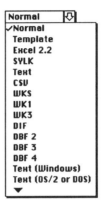

The File Format list in the box that appears within the expanded dialog box contains the types of file formats acceptable to Excel; simply select the desired option. Here is an explanation of each choice:

File Type	Description
Normal	Excel format
Excel 2.2	Excel version 2.2 format
SYLK	Symbolic link format; can be used by other Microsoft programs, including Multiplan and earlier versions of Excel
Text	ASCII text in tabular form (also called SDF by some software packages)
CSV	Comma-separated values
WKS	Lotus 1-2-3, release 1A
WK1	Lotus 1-2-3, release 2

File Type	Description
WK3	Lotus 1-2-3, release 3
DIF	Data interchange format
DBF 2	dBASE II format
DBF 3	dBASE III/III PLUS
DBF 4	dBASE IV format
TEXT (Windows)	ASCII text from Windows software (IBM-PC)
TEXT (OS/2 or DOS)	ASCII text from OS/2 or DOS (IBM-PC)
CSV (Windows)	CSV from Windows software (IBM-PC)
CSV (OS/2 or DOS)	CSV from OS/2 or DOS (IBM-PC)

The Password space in the dialog box applies only to Excel and Lotus 1-2-3; you cannot create other types of password-protected foreign files within Excel. The Create Backup File check box can be used with any type of file; if you select this box, a backup file is created each time you overwrite an existing file. Once the file has been saved, you can use the other software's normal method of file retrieval to open and work with the file.

Once Excel loads a foreign file in an acceptable format, it leaves the file in that format unless you tell it otherwise by saving the file in a different format. This lets you work with foreign files in Excel while leaving the foreign file formats intact for users of other software. For example, if you are using Excel and some of your coworkers are using Lotus 1-2-3, you can load a 1-2-3 file and work with the file while you are in Excel. When you save the file, it will be saved as a 1-2-3 file automatically. It must then be converted to IBM disk format before it can be loaded on an IBM compatible; see the end of this chapter for suggestions on conversion.

If a software package that you want to use with Excel does not use one of the acceptable formats just listed, you can probably still transfer files, although the process becomes a little more complex. First you must translate a file from its own format to one of the acceptable formats as an "intermediary" file format. For example, if your database manager were dBASE Mac, you could use the Datafile/Export command within dBASE Mac to translate the dBASE Mac database file to tab-delimited file format. You could then load the translated file into Excel. Most other general-purpose software products on the market can export a file in a common file format, often as DIF, WKS (Lotus), DBF (dBASE II/III/IV), or tab-delimited or comma-delimited ASCII text format.

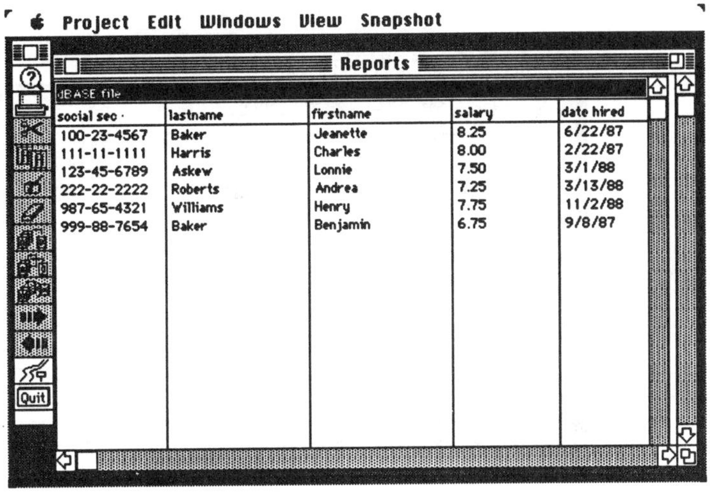

FIGURE 12-2. dBASE Mac database

ASCII text files separated only by spaces present a special problem because they are imported as labels. Such text labels can be converted into usable values with the Parse command (see "Using Parse to Convert ASCII Text to Values" later in this chapter). Excel can import ASCII text files that are separated by tabs or commas or files that are in DIF, dBASE, or Lotus 1-2-3 format with better results, because these files all have clearly defined fields that Excel stores in separate columns.

Figure 12-2 shows a dBASE Mac database exported in tab-delimited format, which contains text fields, a date field, and a numeric field. The file was loaded directly into an Excel worksheet by using the Open command and specifying the full name of the file. Figure 12-3 shows the resultant worksheet. Note that the translation process is quite complete in the conversion of the types of fields. The text fields containing the names were converted into labels in Excel. The fields containing the hire dates were converted into serial numbers representing dates in date format. The fields containing the salary amounts were converted into numeric values.

Users who import Lotus 1-2-3 files encounter a similar "seamless" translation. Because Lotus 1-2-3 is a popular offering in the IBM-compatible world, the latter portion of this chapter contains additional tips for Excel users who must deal with Lotus 1-2-3 files on a regular basis.

```
      File  Edit  Formula  Format  Data  Options  Macro  Window
 Normal       🔽  ◆  ➔  ▦ ▦  Σ  B I  ▤▦▤  ▢  ◜◻◯◠  📊▣◻📷
         A1              111-11-1111
```

	A	B	C	D	E
1	111-11-1111	Harris	Charles	$8.00	2/21/83
2	222-22-2222	Roberts	Andrea	$7.25	3/12/84
3	987-65-4321	Williams	Henry	$7.75	11/1/84
4	999-88-7654	Baker	Benjamin	$6.75	9/7/83
5	100-23-4567	Baker	Jeanette	$8.25	6/21/83
6	123-45-6789	Askew	Lonnie	$7.50	2/29/84
7					
8					
9					
10					
11					
12					
13					
14					
15					
16					

Ready

FIGURE 12-3.   Worksheet data imported from database software

Exporting Excel to Word Processors

If you want to export Excel data (minus any graphics) to your word processing software and you prefer not to use the copy and paste techniques of the Clipboard, MultiFinder, or System 7.0, select Save As from the File menu and click Options. Then choose the Text button in the File Types portion of the dialog box. Save the file under a desired file name, and use the usual commands of your word processor to import the file.

More advanced users may benefit from knowing that an Excel worksheet exported as text uses the ASCII value 009 (Tab) to separate the columns. Each row exported to a text file ends with a hard carriage return, or ASCII 013 followed by ASCII 010. Most word processors recognize the ASCII 009 code as a valid tab character; however, you may need to set your tabs so that the columns line up properly once the data is in your word processor. Also, if you are exporting to Microsoft Word, you should use the Clipboard. Cells pasted into the Clipboard will become tables when pasted into a Microsoft Word document.

USING PARSE TO CONVERT ASCII TEXT TO VALUES

Because Excel can read text files, it is a relatively simple matter to insert a text file containing data separated by spaces into an Excel worksheet. What you can do with the file at that point is a different matter, since each line of text appears as one long label. Mainframes that transfer data to your PC often display a text file in tabular form, with the data separated by spaces instead of tabs. This type of data may be valuable in a worksheet if you are able to convert the labels to individual cells containing values. Fortunately, the Parse command from the Data menu lets you do just that.

The worksheet in Figure 12-4 contains a typical example. The worksheet is a file of labels that resulted from a text file being loaded by Excel. This particular text file of stock trends was downloaded from CompuServe, an on-line database and information service. The contents of each cell appear in the formula bar as one long label composed of various numbers and text. In this form, you cannot graph any of the values or use them in any calculations.

The solution to this dilemma is to use the Parse command to convert the labels to cells of values. The Parse command works on a single column of cells and divides the data according to its best guess as to how the data should be arranged, or according

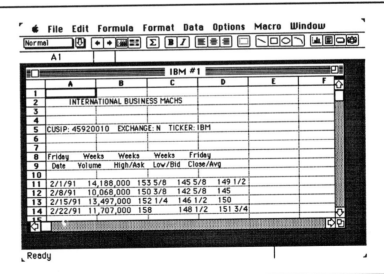

FIGURE 12-4. Worksheet data downloaded from CompuServe

to a format that you specify. To perform this conversion, select the column of cells containing the labels. Then open the Data menu and choose Parse. In the dialog box that appears, you can define a format or select the Guess button to tell Excel to make its best guess on the parsing of the data. When you select OK, the data is converted into values.

In this example, cells A11 through D11 were selected and the Parse command was chosen, resulting in the dialog box shown here:

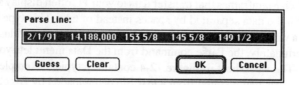

The dialog box's parse line contains the data that is stored in the worksheet as a long label. Using the ruler at the bottom of the parse line as a reference, you can place delimiters (left and right bracket symbols) at the start and end of the respective fields to tell Excel how to convert each line of text into separate fields of data. When this dialog box appears, enter the bracket symbols around the fields of data. Use the mouse to position the cursor and add the brackets where needed. Another alternative is to select the Guess option, letting Excel handle the placement of the brackets. In this example, the Guess option was chosen, and Excel placed the brackets as shown here:

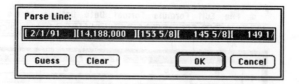

If you disagree with Excel's parsing, you can change it by selecting the Clear button, which clears all of the brackets from the parse line. You can then use the mouse to place the cursor at any location on the parse line and manually enter the left and right bracket symbols around each data field. When you are satisfied that the brackets are in the right places, select OK, and the parsing will take place. In this example, manual entry of the brackets resulted in the worksheet shown in Figure 12-5.

The format of the particular data downloaded in this example still presents one small problem. Because the stock quotes were displayed as fractional numbers, the columns of cells containing the fractions translate as dates; for example, 3/8 is translated as 8 March, or the eighth day of the third month. There is no simple way to solve this problem. The fractions were converted by the addition of a macro that read the contents of each cell, used functions to return the values representing the month

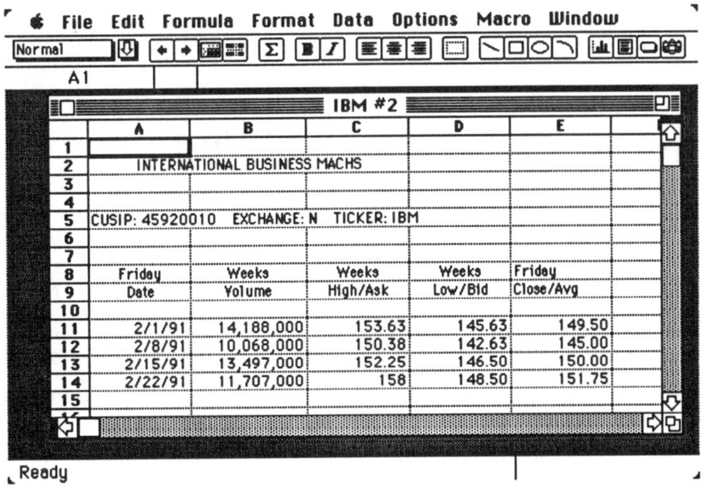

FIGURE 12-5.   Results after parsing manually

and day, converted those values to individual divisors and dividends, and performed the calculation to return the actual value. When you work with mainframe data that may not always be in the right format, you may have to tinker with the data to get it into a format that works for you. The Parse command is just one aid to help you perform this task.

EXCEL FOR LOTUS USERS

If you've been using Lotus 1-2-3, you'll be pleased to learn that Excel provides an extremely smooth transition between Lotus spreadsheet products and Excel. Excel can load and save Lotus products files directly: the same Open and Save commands from the File menu are used for Lotus files as are used for Excel files. There are some differences, however, between 1-2-3 and Symphony worksheets and similar Excel worksheets, and you should be prepared to deal with these differences.

Most of the differences are related to Excel's expanded capabilities, which exceed those of Lotus 1-2-3 release 2. As a result, you should encounter fewer problems when taking worksheets from the 1-2-3 environment into Excel than vice versa. For example, references to linked worksheets do not convert from Excel to 1-2-3 format, because you cannot link worksheets with release 1.1A or release 2 of Lotus 1-2-3.

Loading Lotus-Format Files

To load a file produced by Lotus 1-2-3, select the Open command from the File menu and enter the name of the 1-2-3 file. (As with any foreign files created on the IBM PC, it is up to you to first transfer the IBM PC worksheet file to a Macintosh disk in Macintosh format.) Under the PC-DOS or MS-DOS file-naming conventions, Lotus 1-2-3 release 1A files have extensions of .WKS, release 2 files have extensions of .WK1, release 3 files have extensions of .WK3, and Symphony files have extensions of .WR1.

Symphony files should be converted to Lotus 1-2-3 format before loading them in Excel. Symphony users can use the File Translate utility in Symphony to convert the files to Lotus 1-2-3 format. See your Symphony documentation for more details on this topic.

Once you've manually entered a file name or chosen one from the list box, press RETURN or click the OK button, and the file will be loaded. Excel automatically recognizes the file type, based on the contents of the file.

PROBLEMS   If Excel encounters a formula it cannot convert during the translation process, a dialog box containing a "Can't read record" error message is displayed. The dialog box shows the cell reference of the cell causing the error. Excel also asks if you want it to continue reporting each error, or if the translation process should continue without reporting errors. Select the desired option as indicated by the option buttons to continue the translation process.

SAVING LOTUS FILES   To save a file in Lotus 1-2-3 format, open the File menu, choose the Save or Save As command, and select the Options button that appears in the dialog box. Once you do this, an expanded dialog box containing additional choices for saving files appears (you saw it earlier). Select the desired option. Use WKS to save a file in 1-2-3 release 1A or Symphony format. Use WK1 to save a file in 1-2-3 release 2 format. Use WK3 to save a file in 1-2-3 release 3.0 format. The Password option in the dialog box applies only to Excel, 1-2-3 release 2.0, and 1-2-3 release 3.0 files, although you can protect the worksheet with the Protect Document command. A protected Excel worksheet translates to a protected Lotus 1-2-3 worksheet, and vice versa. The Create Backup File check box can be used with Lotus files; if you select the box, a backup file is created each time you overwrite an existing file.

Once the file has been saved in the respective file format and transferred to an IBM-compatible disk format, you can use the usual commands in Lotus 1-2-3 or in Symphony to open and work with the file.

Remember, once Excel loads a Lotus 1-2-3 file, it leaves the file in that format unless you tell it otherwise by saving the file in a different format. This feature lets you work with Lotus-type files in Excel while leaving the file formats intact for users of Lotus 1-2-3 or Symphony. If you are using Excel and some of your associates are using Lotus 1-2-3, you can load a 1-2-3 file and work with the file while you are in Excel. When you save the file, it is saved automatically in 1-2-3 file format.

The 1-2-3 Conversion Process

Whenever Excel cannot convert a formula because of a difference in Lotus 1-2-3 and Excel capabilities, you are warned of this fact by the appearance of a dialog box containing a "Can't write record" error message. In most cases, this error message indicates that Excel has encountered a cell reference or a function within a formula that has no direct equivalent in Lotus 1-2-3; therefore, the cell cannot be properly converted.

FORMULA CONVERSION   Numbers in formulas convert as numbers, and text converts as text. However, Excel lets you build formulas that use text as constants, or formulas that produce text as a result. Lotus 1-2-3 does not permit this, so any Excel cell that contains a formula with a text argument cannot be converted to 1-2-3.

Logical values are handled differently in the two packages, although the net result is similar. Lotus 1-2-3 uses @TRUE and @FALSE functions, which produce values of 1 and 0 representing logical true and logical false. Excel uses the logical values TRUE and FALSE within cells. The conversion process converts the 1-2-3 @TRUE and @FALSE functions to Excel's logical TRUE and FALSE values.

Error values are also handled differently, because 1-2-3 supports only two types of errors, @NA and @ERR, while Excel supports seven types of error values, as discussed in Chapter 3. The #N/A error value in Excel is converted to 1-2-3's @NA function. All other error values in Excel are converted to 1-2-3's @ERR function. When 1-2-3 worksheets are converted to Excel format, all @NA error functions are converted to #N/A error values, and all @ERR error functions are converted to #VALUE! error values.

Arrays in an Excel worksheet cannot be converted to 1-2-3 format because 1-2-3 version 2.0 does not support arrays, and version 3.0 handles arrays in a substantially different fashion (through the use of multiple worksheets). Cell references are also an area to watch. You should not encounter any problems in going from 1-2-3 to Excel, but you may encounter some in going from Excel to 1-2-3. Since 1-2-3 version 2.0

does not support linked worksheets, Excel references to a linked worksheet do not convert in version 2.0 of 1-2-3. In Lotus 1-2-3, external references appear as cells full of asterisks. If these cells are later converted back into Excel format, they will contain meaningless numeric values.

Also, a 1-2-3 worksheet has a maximum of 2048 rows, so any cell references to a cell higher than row 2048 do not convert. If you make extensive use of named ranges in Excel worksheets, you may have a problem when you go to 1-2-3 format, because 1-2-3 supports named references to single cells and to ranges, but not to multiple ranges.

Excel supports union and intersection operators. (These are advanced topics not covered in detail in this book.) Lotus 1-2-3 does not support these types of operators, so any formulas containing them do not convert to 1-2-3 format. Other operators usually convert without a problem. Areas of major differences between the two packages include the treatment of percentages and logical AND, OR, and NOT values. Lotus 1-2-3 does not have a percentage operator; Excel does. A percentage in Excel converts to a fractional value in 1-2-3; for example, 9.5% in Excel converts to .095 in 1-2-3. Also, 1-2-3 uses #NOT#, #AND#, and #OR# operators; Excel uses NOT, AND, and OR functions. The Excel functions convert to their respective 1-2-3 operators, and vice versa.

1-2-3 Format	Excel Format
General	General
+ or −	General
Text	General
Fixed, 0 decimals	0
Fixed, 2 decimals	0.00
Currency, 0 decimals	$#,##0;($#,##0)
Currency, 2 decimals	$#,##0.00;($#,##0.00)
Exponential, 0 decimals	0E + 00
Exponential, 2 decimals	0.00E + 00
Percent, 0 decimals	0%
Percent, 2 decimals	0.00%
Comma, 0 decimals	#,##0;(#,##0)
Comma, 2 decimals	#,##0.00;(#,##0.00)
D1 date format	d-mmm-yy
D2 date format	d-mmm
D3 date format	mmm-yy

TABLE 12-1.   Format Conversion

FORMAT CONVERSION   Excel converts 1-2-3 cell and range formats into their closest equivalents in Excel. In nearly all cases, the conversion provides satisfactory results. Table 12-1 shows how formats convert between Excel and 1-2-3. Any 1-2-3 formats not listed in the table convert to Excel's General format.

Both Lotus 1-2-3 and Excel support left, right, and general alignment, so these formats translate between 1-2-3 and Excel. Lotus 1-2-3 also allows text to be repeated to fill a cell. This technique translates to the Fill format in Excel.

FUNCTION CONVERSION   Common functions convert between 1-2-3 and Excel. Note that some Excel functions are not available in 1-2-3, and Excel handles 1-2-3 functions as operators. If an Excel function is not available in 1-2-3, the function does not convert. Table 12-2 shows a comparison between 1-2-3 functions and Excel functions. Note that Excel's statistical functions (MAX, MIN, AVG, SUM, COUNT, STDEV, and VAR), while similar to 1-2-3's, are limited to 14 arguments. For example, you may have a formula containing more than 14 values in an AVG function in 1-2-3, but such a formula would not convert properly to Excel because of Excel's 14-argument limit.

Also note that Excel and 1-2-3 treat empty cells that are a part of statistical functions very differently. Lotus 1-2-3 counts blank cells as zeros, while Excel ignores blank cells. This could cause major differences, depending on the worksheet's design. If, for example, a range of ten cells contains five values, a formula in Lotus to find the average value would total the values and divide by 10 (the number of cells in the range). Excel is more accurate in that it would divide by 5 (the number of cells that actually contain values in the range).

How Other Properties Convert

Lotus worksheets, when converted to Excel, appear without gridlines. Use the Options Display command to turn gridlines on, if desired.

Cell and worksheet protection are supported by both 1-2-3 and Excel. Cells and worksheets that are locked in one format will be locked in the other format. Note that 1-2-3 does not support hidden formulas. If you use the Cell Protection command to hide cell formulas, those cell formulas will not be hidden when the worksheet is converted to 1-2-3 format.

Database ranges and criteria ranges do convert between the packages. Lotus 1-2-3 uses Input Ranges, which correspond to Excel's Database Range. Also, 1-2-3 uses Criterion Ranges, which correspond to Excel's Criteria Range. Lotus 1-2-3 also uses an Extract range to extract qualified data from the database. Excel uses the Extract command along with the Criteria range for the same purpose, so the Extract Range in 1-2-3 does not convert to the Excel worksheet.

Excel Function	Lotus Equivalent
ABS(*number*)	@ABS
ACOS(*number*)	@ACOS
AND(logical,logicals2...)	Converts to x#AND#y operators
AREAS(reference)	Not available
ASIN(number)	@ASIN
ATAN(number)	@ATAN
ATAN2(x number,y number)	@ATAN2(x,y)
AVG(*numbers1,numbers2...*)	@AVG(*list*)
CHOOSE(*index,value1,value2*)	@CHOOSE(a,V0,V1)
COLUMN(*reference*)	Converts to column number of the active cell
COS(*number*)	@COS(*x*)
COUNT(*numbers1,numbers2...*)	@COUNT(*list*)
DATE(*year,month,day*)	@DATE(*year,month,day*)
DAVERAGE(*database, field index,criteria*)	@DAVG(*input,offset,criteria*)
DAY(*serial number*)	@DAY(*date*)
DCOUNT(*database, field index,criteria*)	@DCOUNT(*input,offset,criteria*)
DMAX(*database, field index,criteria*)	@DMAX(*input,offset,criteria*)
DMIN(*database, field index,criteria*)	@DMIN(*input,offset,criteria*)
DOLLAR(*number, no of digits*)	Not available
DSUM(*database, field index,criteria*)	@DSUM(*input,offset,criteria*)
DVAR(*database, field index,criteria*)	@DVAR(*input,offset,criteria*)
EXP(*number*)	@EXP(*x*)
FALSE( )	@FALSE
FIXED(*number, no of digits*)	Not available
FV(*rate,nper,pmt,pv,type*)	@FV(*payment,interest,n*) [a]
GROWTH(*Y-array, x-array,y-array*)	Not available
HLOOKUP(*lookup value,compare array,index no*)	@HLOOKUP(*x,range,offset*)
HOUR(*serial number*)	Not available
IF(*logical,true val, false val*)	@IF (*a, vtrue, vfalse*)
INDEX(*array,row,col*)	Not available
INDEX(*ref,row,col,area*)	Not available

TABLE 12-2.   Lotus 1-2-3 Versus Excel Functions

Excel Function	Lotus Equivalent
INT(*number*)	@INT(*x*) [b]
IRR(*values,guess*)	@IRR(*guess,range*)
ISERROR(*value*)	@ISERR(*x*)
ISNA(*value*)	@ISNA(*x*)
ISREF(*value*)	Not available
LEN(*text*)	Not available
LINEST(*Y-array,X-array*)	Not available
LOGEST(*Y-array,X-array*)	Not available
LOOKUP(*lookup value,compare array*)	Not available
LOOKUP(*lookup value,compare vector,result vector*)	Not available
LN(*number*)	@LN(*x*)
LOG10(*number*)	@LOG(*x*)
MATCH(*lookup,compare,type*)	Not available
MAX(*numbers1,numbers2...*)	@MAX(*list*)
MID(*text,start pos,no chars*)	Not available
MIN(*numbers1,numbers2...*)	@MIN(*list*)
MINUTE(*serial number*)	Not available
MIRR(*values,safe,risk*)	Not available
MOD(*number,divisor number*)	@MOD(*x,y*) [c]
MONTH(*serial number*)	@MONTH(*date*)
NA( )	@NA
NOT(*logical*)	#NOT#x
NOW( )	@TODAY
NPER (*rate, pmt, pv, fv, type*)	Not available
NPV(*rate,values1,values2*)	@NPV(*x,range*) [d]
OR(*logicals1,logicals2...*)	Converts to x#OR#y operators
PI( )	@PI
PMT(*rate,nper,pv,fv,type*)	@PMT(*payment,interest,n*) [a]
PV(*rate,nper,pmt,fv,type*)	@PV(*payment,interest, term*) [a]
RATE(*nper,pmt,pv,fv,type,guess*)	Not available
REPT(*text,no of times*)	Not available
ROW( )	Converts to the row number of the active cell

TABLE 12-2. Lotus 1-2-3 Versus Excel Functions (*continued*)

Excel Function	Lotus Equivalent
ROWS(*array*)	Not available
RAND( )	@RAND
ROUND(*number, no of digits*)	@ROUND(*x,no-digits*)
SECOND(*serial number*)	Not available
SIGN(*number*)	Not available
SIN(*number*)	@SIN(*x*)
SQRT(*number*)	@SQRT(*x*)
STD(*numbers1,numbers2...*)	@STD(*list*)
SUM(*numbers1,numbers2...*)	@SUM(*list*)
TAN(*number*)	@TAN(*x*)
TEXT(*number,format text*)	Not available
TIME(*hour,minute,second*)	Not available
TRANSPOSE(*array*)	Not available
TREND(*Y-array,x-array,y-array*)	Not available
TRUE( )	@TRUE( )
TYPE(*value*)	Not available
VALUE(*text*)	Not available
VAR(*numbers1,numbers2...*)	@VAR(*list*)
VLOOKUP(*lookup value,compare array,index no*)	@VLOOKUP(*x,range,offset*)
WEEKDAY(*serial number*)	Not available
YEAR(*serial number*)	@YEAR(*date*)

[a] If an Excel financial function has more than three arguments, it does not convert to 1-2-3.

[b] Negative numbers and divisors will provide different results in 1-2-3 and Excel due to differences in the way these functions are handled.

[c] Excel's INT function rounds down, while 1-2-3's rounds towards zero. This difference may result in different values when negative numbers are converted to integers.

[d] If an Excel NPV function contains more than one argument, it does not convert.

TABLE 12-2. Lotus 1-2-3 Versus Excel Functions (*continued*)

Users of databases should note that database commands in 1-2-3 and Excel behave in different ways, so databases may not provide identical results. You should refer to your 1-2-3 documentation, along with Chapter 7 of this book, to determine how the database commands compare and how the differences in operation may affect the way you use your databases.

Tables are supported by both 1-2-3 and Excel and therefore do convert between the two packages. Note that 1-2-3 handles tables slightly differently from Excel, in that you must use Recalc when in 1-2-3 to recalculate the table.

Window characteristics do not convert from Excel to 1-2-3 because 1-2-3 is not a graphics-oriented package (at least, not at the time of this writing). Also, most print settings, such as headers, footers, and margins, do not convert between Excel and 1-2-3. A defined print range in 1-2-3 does convert to a print area in Excel. Column widths convert, but row heights do not, because Lotus 1-2-3 does not let you change row heights.

TRANSFERRING DATA BETWEEN A MACINTOSH AND AN IBM

Overcoming the hurdle of disk formats is a problem often encountered when files are moved between 1-2-3 and Excel (or between any other IBM-compatible software and earlier models of the Macintosh). The 880K disk format used by the Apple Macintosh cannot be read on an IBM compatible without special hardware, even if the IBM compatible has 3.5-inch disk drives like those on the Macintosh. There are a number of proven ways around this obstacle; in general, the less troublesome these methods are, the more expensive they become. Newer Macintosh models (those with the Apple Superdrive) can directly read IBM-format disks, so transferring files on these machines is not a problem. These models include the Mac Classic, Macintosh LC, Macintosh II SI, Macintosh II CI, and Macintosh II FX.

The least expensive (and most troublesome) method is to use a null modem and communications software to transfer the files. Null modems are special serial cables that act electrically as two modems connected by a phone line. They are available at electronics stores like Radio Shack. Connect one end of the null modem cable to the serial port on the Macintosh, and connect the other end of the cable to the serial port on the IBM compatible. Load the communications software on each machine, set the baud rates to the fastest possible matching speeds, and set the parity and stop bit settings to the same parameters on each computer. To transfer the desired file, set one computer to transmit and the other to receive.

Slightly more expensive and slightly less troublesome are cable and software kits like MacLink. These consist of a prepared null modem cable and special software for both the Macintosh and the IBM compatible. The software is already set for transmission speeds and settings, so all you have to do is provide the name of the file to be transferred and indicate the direction in which it is going. Another advantage of kits like MacLink is that they use compression techniques and higher speeds than ordinary communications software, so it takes much less time to transfer the files.

Next up the ladder in cost are add-on disk drives for IBM compatibles, which can read and write disks in Macintosh formats. Dayna Communications makes a line of such drives; you can attach one of these to any IBM compatible with an available expansion slot.

Finally, if saving money is not your utmost concern, you can use a local area network that is compatible with both machines, such as Sun Microsystems' TOPS network, and move the files over the network. Another method is to use a Mac Plus, Macintosh II, IIx, or IIcx with the Superdrive. This disk drive reads and writes files in either Apple Macintosh or IBM PC disk formats.

chapter 13

EXAMPLE MODELS

This chapter will get you started on your own applications by providing some examples of worksheets for various tasks. It provides models for IRS tax calculation, mortgage loan calculation and amortization, break-even analysis, cash flow management, IRA calculations, and personnel tracking. Complete instructions for building each worksheet are provided.

The worksheets in this chapter are also available on disk for readers who would rather save the time and effort of inputting. See the order form at the front of this book for details.

CASH FLOW ANALYSIS

Managing cash flow—or your accounts receivable and accounts payable—is a basic task facing virtually every business. The following cash flow worksheet is relatively simple to set up, yet it presents a clear picture of available funds. It is patterned after the common single-entry debits and credits bookkeeping system. A starting balance

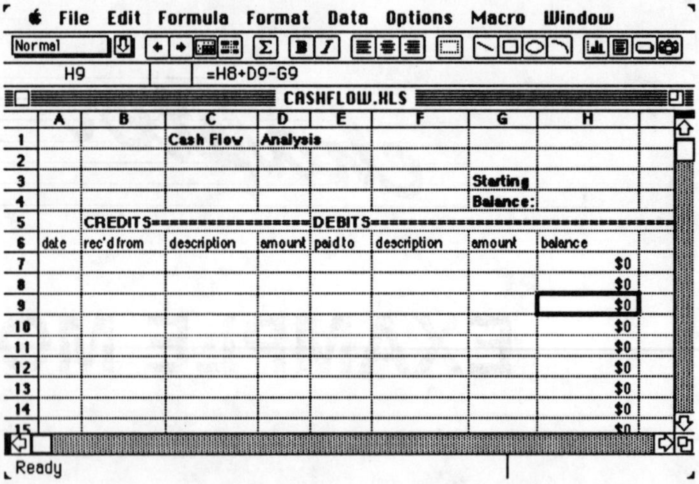

FIGURE 13-1. Cash Flow worksheet

is entered into cell H4. Column A is used to record the date of each transaction and whether it is a credit or a debit. Columns B, C, and D are used to record credits by listing the creditor, the description, and the amount. In columns E, F, and G, debits are recorded, by listing whom the amount is paid to, the description, and the amount. Column H contains the formulas that are used to keep a running total of cash on hand. This amount is computed by taking the previous entry's running balance, adding the credits, and subtracting the debits.

This type of system can be maintained by creating a separate worksheet for each month. At the end of the year, the totals can be consolidated into another worksheet to show yearly figures for cash flow. The worksheet is shown in Figure 13-1.

To build the worksheet, enter the following labels and formulas into the cells:

Cell	Entry
A6	Date
B5	CREDITS============================
B6	rec'd from:
C1	Cash Flow
C6	description
D6	amount

E5	DEBITS===============================
E6	paid to:
F6	description
G3	Starting
G4	Balance:
G6	amount
H6	balance
H7	=H4+D7–G7
H8	=H7+D8–G8

To copy the formula into successive cells in column H, select the range of cells from H8 to H40, open the Edit menu, and choose Fill Down.

Select the range of cells from H4 to H40, open the Format menu, choose Number, and select the dollars-and-cents format, $#,##0.00; ($#,##0.00) from the list. Using the same steps, choose the same format for cells D7 to D40 and G7 to G40. Select the range of cells from A7 to A40, and using the Format menu's Number command, format these cells to display dates in dd-mmm-yy format.

The worksheet is ready to use at this point. Although you may want to use your own figures, Figure 13-2 shows part of the Cash Flow worksheet filled in with figures from a typical small business.

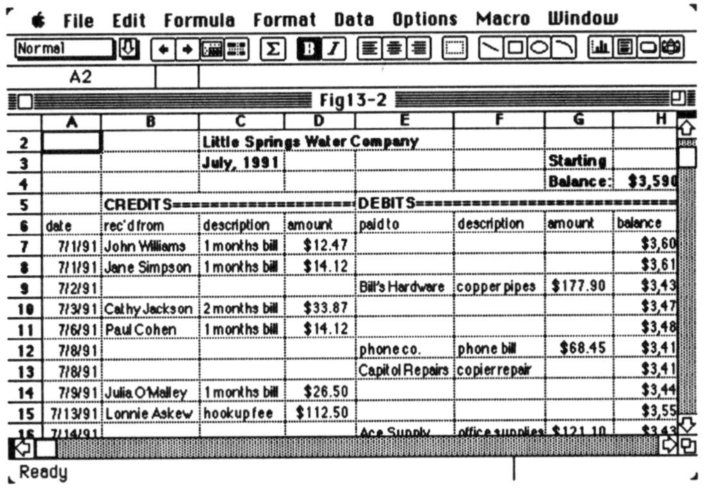

File   Edit   Formula   Format   Data   Options   Macro   Window

Normal   Σ B I

A2

Fig13-2

	A	B	C	D	E	F	G	H
2			Little Springs Water Company					
3			July, 1991				Starting	
4							Balance:	$3,590
5			CREDITS=============		DEBITS==============			
6	date	rec'd from	description	amount	paid to	description	amount	balance
7	7/1/91	John Williams	1 months bill	$12.47				$3,60
8	7/1/91	Jane Simpson	1 months bill	$14.12				$3,61
9	7/2/91				Bill's Hardware	copper pipes	$177.90	$3,43
10	7/3/91	Cathy Jackson	2 months bill	$33.87				$3,47
11	7/6/91	Paul Cohen	1 months bill	$14.12				$3,48
12	7/8/91				phone co.	phone bill	$68.45	$3,41
13	7/8/91				Capitol Repairs	copier repair		$3,41
14	7/9/91	Julia O'Malley	1 months bill	$26.50				$3,44
15	7/13/91	Lonnie Askew	hookup fee	$112.50				$3,55
16	7/14/91				Ace Supply	office supplies	$121.10	$3,43

Ready

FIGURE 13-2.   Filled-in Cash Flow worksheet

Form **1040** Department of the Treasury—Internal Revenue Service **1990** (P)
U.S. Individual Income Tax Return

For the year Jan.–Dec. 31, 1990, or other tax year beginning _____ , 1990, ending _____ , 19 ___ | OMB No. 1545-0074

Label
(See Instructions on page 8.)

Use IRS label. Otherwise, please print or type.

L A B E L H E R E	Your first name and initial	Last name	**Your social security number**
	If a joint return, spouse's first name and initial	Last name	**Spouse's social security number**
	Home address (number and street). (If you have a P.O. box, see page 9.)	Apt. no.	**For Privacy Act and Paperwork Reduction Act Notice, see Instructions.**
	City, town or post office, state, and ZIP code. (If you have a foreign address, see page 9.)		

Presidential Election Campaign
(See page 9.)
▶ Do you want $1 to go to this fund? . . . . | Yes | No
If joint return, does your spouse want $1 to go to this fund? | Yes | No

Note: Checking "Yes" will not change your tax or reduce your refund.

Filing Status

Check only one box.

1 ☐ Single. (See page 10 to find out if you can file as head of household.)
2 ☐ Married filing joint return (even if only one had income)
3 ☐ Married filing separate return. Enter spouse's social security no. above and full name here. ▶ _____
4 ☐ Head of household (with qualifying person). (See page 10.) If the qualifying person is your child but not your dependent, enter this child's name here. ▶ _____
5 ☐ Qualifying widow(er) with dependent child (year spouse died ▶ 19 ___). (See page 10.)

Exemptions
(See Instructions on page 10.)

If more than 6 dependents, see Instructions on page 11.

6a ☐ **Yourself** If your parent (or someone else) can claim you as a dependent on his or her tax return, do not check box 6a. But be sure to check the box on line 33b on page 2

b ☐ **Spouse** . . . .

c **Dependents:** (1) Name (first, initial, and last name)	(2) Check if under age 2	(3) If age 2 or older, dependent's social security number	(4) Dependent's relationship to you	(5) No. of months lived in your home in 1990

d If your child didn't live with you but is claimed as your dependent under a pre-1985 agreement, check here ▶ ☐

e Total number of exemptions claimed . . . .

No. of boxes checked on 6a and 6b ___
No. of your children on 6c who:
• lived with you ___
• didn't live with you due to divorce or separation (see page 11) ___
No. of other dependents on 6c ___
Add numbers entered on lines above ▶ ☐

Income

Attach Copy B of your Forms W-2, W-2G, and W-2P here.

If you do not have a W-2, see page 8.

Attach check or money order on top of any Forms W-2, W-2G, or W-2P.

7 Wages, salaries, tips, etc. *(attach Form(s) W-2)* | 7
8a **Taxable** interest income *(also attach Schedule B if over $400)* . | 8a
  b **Tax-exempt** interest income (see page 13). DON'T include on line 8a| 8b | |
9 Dividend income *(also attach Schedule B if over $400)* . . . . | 9
10 Taxable refunds of state and local income taxes, if any, from worksheet on page 14 | 10
11 Alimony received . . . . | 11
12 Business income or (loss) *(attach Schedule C)* . . . . | 12
13 Capital gain or (loss) *(attach Schedule D)* . . . . | 13
14 Capital gain distributions not reported on line 13 (see page 14). . . | 14
15 Other gains or (losses) *(attach Form 4797)* . . . . | 15
16a Total IRA distributions . | 16a | | 16b Taxable amount (see page 14) | 16b
17a Total pensions and annuities | 17a | | 17b Taxable amount (see page 14) | 17b
18 Rents, royalties, partnerships, estates, trusts, etc. *(attach Schedule E)* . | 18
19 Farm income or (loss) *(attach Schedule F)* . . . . | 19
20 Unemployment compensation (insurance) (see page 16) . . . . | 20
21a Social security benefits . | 21a | | 21b Taxable amount (see page 16) | 21b
22 Other income (list type and amount—see page 16) .... | 22
23 Add the amounts shown in the far right column for lines 7 through 22. This is your **total income** ▶ | 23

Adjustments to Income

(See Instructions on page 17.)

24a Your IRA deduction, from applicable worksheet on page 17 or 18 . | 24a | |
  b Spouse's IRA deduction, from applicable worksheet on page 17 or 18 . | 24b | |
25 One-half of self-employment tax (see page 18) . . . . . | 25 | |
26 Self-employed health insurance deduction, from worksheet on page 18 | 26 | |
27 Keogh retirement plan and self-employed SEP deduction . . | 27 | |
28 Penalty on early withdrawal of savings . . . . . | 28 | |
29 Alimony paid. Recipient's SSN ▶ | 29 | |
30 Add lines 24a through 29. These are your **total adjustments** . . . . ▶ | 30

Adjusted Gross Income

31 Subtract line 30 from line 23. This is your **adjusted gross income.** If this amount is less than $20,264 and a child lived with you, see page 23 to find out if you can claim the "Earned Income Credit" on line 57 . . . . ▶ | 31

FIGURE 13-3. IRS Form 1040

Form 1040 (1990) Page **2**

Tax Compu-tation	32	Amount from line 31 (adjusted gross income)	**32**	
	33a	Check if: ☐ **You** were 65 or older; ☐ Blind; ☐ **Spouse** was 65 or older ☐ Blind.		
If you want IRS to figure your tax, see Instructions on page 19		Add the number of boxes checked above and enter the total here . . . . . ▶	**33a**	
	b	If your parent (or someone else) can claim you as a dependent, check here . . ▶	**33b** ☐	
	c	If you are married filing a separate return and your spouse itemizes deductions, or you are a dual-status alien, see page 19 and check here . . . . ▶	**33c** ☐	
	34	Enter the larger of { • Your **standard deduction** (from the chart (or worksheet) on page 20 that applies to you), **OR** • Your **itemized deductions** (from Schedule A, line 27). If you itemize, attach Schedule A and check here. . . ▶ ☐	**34**	
	35	Subtract line 34 from line 32	**35**	
	36	Multiply $2,050 by the total number of exemptions claimed on line 6e	**36**	
	37	**Taxable income.** Subtract line 36 from line 35. (If line 36 is more than line 35, enter -0-.)	**37**	
	38	Enter tax. Check if from: **a** ☐ Tax Table, **b** ☐ Tax Rate Schedules, or **c** ☐ Form 8615 (see page 21) (If any is from Form(s) 8814, enter that amount here ▶ **d**	)	**38**	
	39	Additional taxes (see page 21). Check if from: **a** ☐ Form 4970 **b** ☐ Form 4972 . .	**39**	
	40	Add lines 38 and 39 . . . . ▶	**40**	
Credits (See Instructions on page 21.)	41	Credit for child and dependent care expenses (attach Form 2441)	**41**	
	42	Credit for the elderly or the disabled (attach Schedule R) . . .	**42**	
	43	Foreign tax credit (attach Form 1116)	**43**	
	44	General business credit. Check if from: **a** ☐ Form 3800 or **b** ☐ Form (specify) _____	**44**	
	45	Credit for prior year minimum tax (attach Form 8801) . . .	**45**	
	46	Add lines 41 through 45	**46**	
	47	Subtract line 46 from line 40. (If line 46 is more than line 40, enter -0-.) . . . . . ▶	**47**	
Other Taxes	48	Self-employment tax (attach Schedule SE)	**48**	
	49	Alternative minimum tax (attach Form 6251)	**49**	
	50	Recapture taxes (see page 22). Check if from: **a** ☐ Form 4255 **b** ☐ Form 8611 . .	**50**	
	51	Social security tax on tip income not reported to employer (attach Form 4137) . . .	**51**	
	52	Tax on an IRA or a qualified retirement plan (attach Form 5329)	**52**	
	53	Advance earned income credit payments from Form W-2 . . .	**53**	
	54	Add lines 47 through 53. This is your **total tax** . . . . ▶	**54**	
Payments Attach Forms W-2, W-2G, and W-2P to front	55	Federal income tax withheld **(if any is from Form(s) 1099, check ▶ ☐)** . .	**55**	
	56	1990 estimated tax payments and amount applied from 1989 return	**56**	
	57	**Earned income credit** (see page 23)	**57**	
	58	Amount paid with Form 4868 (extension request) . . .	**58**	
	59	Excess social security tax and RRTA tax withheld (see page 24)	**59**	
	60	Credit for Federal tax on fuels (attach Form 4136)	**60**	
	61	Regulated investment company credit (attach Form 2439) . .	**61**	
	62	Add lines 55 through 61. These are your **total payments** . . . . ▶	**62**	
Refund or Amount You Owe	63	If line 62 is more than line 54, enter amount **OVERPAID** . . . . ▶	**63**	
	64	Amount of line 63 to be **REFUNDED TO YOU** . . . . ▶	**64**	
	65	Amount of line 63 to be **APPLIED TO YOUR 1991 ESTIMATED TAX** ▶	**65**	
	66	If line 54 is more than line 62, enter **AMOUNT YOU OWE**. Attach check or money order for full amount payable to "Internal Revenue Service." Write your name, address, social security number, daytime phone number, and "1990 Form 1040" on it	**66**	
	67	Estimated tax penalty (see page 25)	**67**	

Sign Here
Keep a copy of this return for your records

Under penalties of perjury, I declare that I have examined this return and accompanying schedules and statements, and to the best of my knowledge and belief, they are true, correct, and complete. Declaration of preparer (other than taxpayer) is based on all information of which preparer has any knowledge.

Your signature	Date	Your occupation
Spouse's signature (if joint return, BOTH must sign)	Date	Spouse's occupation

Paid Preparer's Use Only

Preparer's signature	Date	Check if self-employed ☐	Preparer's social security no.
Firm's name (or yours if self-employed) and address		E.I. No.	
		ZIP code	

*U.S. Government Printing Office: 1990 — 265-058

FIGURE 13-3. IRS Form 1040 (*continued*)

SCHEDULES A&B	**Schedule A—Itemized Deductions**	OMB No. 1545-0074
(Form 1040)	(Schedule B is on back)	**1990**
Department of the Treasury Internal Revenue Service (P)	▶ Attach to Form 1040. ▶ See Instructions for Schedules A and B (Form 1040).	Attachment Sequence No. 07

Name(s) shown on Form 1040   Your social security number

Medical and **Dental Expenses**		**Caution:** *Do not include expenses reimbursed or paid by others.*	
	1	Medical and dental expenses. (See page 27 of the Instructions.)	1
	2	Enter amount from Form 1040, line 32 . 2	
	3	Multiply the amount on line 2 by 7.5% (.075). Enter the result .	3
	4	Subtract line 3 from line 1. Enter the result. If less than zero, enter -0- ▶	4
Taxes You **Paid**	5	State and local income taxes	5
	6	Real estate taxes	6
(See Instructions on page 27.)	7	Other taxes. (List—include personal property taxes.) ▶	7
	8	Add the amounts on lines 5 through 7. Enter the total . . . . . . ▶	8
Interest You **Paid**	9a	Deductible home mortgage interest paid to financial institutions and reported to you on Form 1098. Report deductible points on line 10 . .	9a
(See Instructions on page 27.)	b	Other deductible home mortgage interest. (If paid to an individual, show that person's name and address.) ▶	
		. . . .	9b
	10	Deductible points. (See Instructions for special rules.) . . .	10
	11	Deductible investment interest (attach Form 4952 if required). (See page 28.)	11
	12a	Personal interest you paid. (See page 28.) 12a	
	b	Multiply the amount on line 12a by 10% (.10). Enter the result .	12b
	13	Add the amounts on lines 9a through 11, and 12b. Enter the total . . ▶	13
Gifts to **Charity**		**Caution:** *If you made a charitable contribution and received a benefit in return, see page 29 of the Instructions.*	
(See Instructions on page 29.)	14	Contributions by cash or check	14
	15	Other than cash or check. (You **MUST** attach Form 8283 if over $500.)	15
	16	Carryover from prior year.	16
	17	Add the amounts on lines 14 through 16. Enter the total . . . . ▶	17
Casualty and **Theft Losses**	18	Casualty or theft loss(es) (attach Form 4684). (See page 29 of the Instructions.) ▶	18
Moving **Expenses**	19	Moving expenses (attach Form 3903 or 3903F). (See page 30 of the Instructions.). ▶	19
Job Expenses **and Most Other** **Miscellaneous** **Deductions**	20	Unreimbursed employee expenses—job travel, union dues, job education, etc. (You **MUST** attach Form 2106 if required. See Instructions.) ▶	20
	21	Other expenses (investment, tax preparation, safe deposit box, etc.). List type and amount ▶	
(See Instructions on page 30 for expenses to deduct here.)		. . . .	21
	22	Add the amounts on lines 20 and 21. Enter the total . . .	22
	23	Enter amount from Form 1040, line 32. 23	
	24	Multiply the amount on line 23 by 2% (.02). Enter the result .	24
	25	Subtract line 24 from line 22. Enter the result. If less than zero, enter -0-. . . . ▶	25
Other **Miscellaneous** **Deductions**	26	Other (from list on page 30 of Instructions). List type and amount ▶	
		. . . .	
		. . . . ▶	26
Total Itemized **Deductions**	27	Add the amounts on lines 4, 8, 13, 17, 18, 19, 25, and 26. Enter the total here. Then enter on Form 1040, line 34, the **LARGER** of this total or your standard deduction from page 20 of the Instructions . . . . ▶	27

For Paperwork Reduction Act Notice, see Form 1040 Instructions.   **Schedule A (Form 1040) 1990**

FIGURE 13-4. Schedule A (Form 1040)

Schedules A&B (Form 1040) 1990	OMB No. 1545-0074	Page **2**
Name(s) shown on Form 1040. (Do not enter name and social security number if shown on other side.)	Your social security number	

Schedule B—Interest and Dividend Income

Attachment Sequence No. **08**

Part I Interest Income

(See Instructions on pages 13 and 30.)

If you received more than $400 in taxable interest income, or you are claiming the exclusion of interest from series EE U.S. savings bonds issued after 1989 (see page 31), you must complete Part I. List ALL interest received in Part I. If you received more than $400 in taxable interest income, you must also complete Part III. If you received, as a nominee, interest that actually belongs to another person, or you received or paid accrued interest on securities transferred between interest payment dates, see page 31.

Interest Income	Amount
1 Interest income. (List name of payer—if any interest income is from seller-financed mortgages, see Instructions and list that interest first.) ▶	

Note: If you received a Form 1099-INT, Form 1099-OID, or substitute statement, from a brokerage firm, list the firm's name as the payer and enter the total interest shown on that form.

2 Add the amounts on line 1. Enter the total	**2**	
3 Enter the excludable savings bond interest, if any, from Form 8815, line 14. Attach Form 8815 to Form 1040	**3**	
4 Subtract line 3 from line 2. Enter the result here and on Form 1040, line 8a . ▶	**4**	

Part II Dividend Income

(See Instructions on pages 13 and 31.)

If you received more than $400 in gross dividends and/or other distributions on stock, you must complete Parts II and III. If you received, as a nominee, dividends that actually belong to another person, see page 31.

Dividend Income	Amount
5 Dividend income. (List name of payer—include on this line capital gain distributions, nontaxable distributions, etc.) ▶	

Note: If you received a Form 1099-DIV, or substitute statement, from a brokerage firm, list the firm's name as the payer and enter the total dividends shown on that form.

6 Add the amounts on line 5. Enter the total		**6**	
7 Capital gain distributions. Enter here and on Schedule D* .	**7**		
8 Nontaxable distributions. (See the Inst. for Form 1040, line 9.)	**8**		
9 Add the amounts on lines 7 and 8. Enter the total		**9**	
10 Subtract line 9 from line 6. Enter the result here and on Form 1040, line 9 . . ▶		**10**	

* *If you received capital gain distributions but do not need Schedule D to report any other gains or losses, see the Instructions for Form 1040, lines 13 and 14.*

Part III Foreign Accounts and Foreign Trusts

(See Instructions on page 31.)

If you received more than $400 of interest or dividends, OR if you had a foreign account or were a grantor of, or a transferor to, a foreign trust, you must answer both questions in Part III.

	Yes	No
11a At any time during 1990, did you have an interest in or a signature or other authority over a financial account in a foreign country (such as a bank account, securities account, or other financial account)? (See page 31 of the Instructions for exceptions and filing requirements for Form TD F 90-22.1.)		
b If "Yes," enter the name of the foreign country ▶		
12 Were you the grantor of, or transferor to, a foreign trust that existed during 1990, whether or not you have any beneficial interest in it? If "Yes," you may have to file Form 3520, 3520-A, or 926		

For Paperwork Reduction Act Notice, see Form 1040 Instructions.   Schedule B (Form 1040) 1990

*U.S. Government Printing Office: 1990 — 265-058

FIGURE 13-5. Schedule B (Form 1040)

IRS 1040 TAX WORKSHEETS

IRS 1040 tax worksheets are the only ones in this chapter that are not accompanied by a detailed discussion of logic; for most readers, the logic behind the worksheets is all too familiar. If you haven't had the pleasure of becoming familiar with IRS Form 1040 and schedules A and B, illustrations are provided in Figure 13-3, Figure 13-4, and Figure 13-5.

The Excel worksheets follow the structure of the IRS forms; part of one of the worksheets is shown in Figure 13-6. These IRS worksheets are an ideal use of Excel's three-dimensional capability, because figures from one form often are used on another, and some figures from nearly all forms must eventually appear on Form 1040.

If you want your worksheets to resemble the actual IRS forms, you must turn off the gridlines (use the Display command from the Options menu) and add borders around respective cells with the Border option of the Display command. You may or may not consider this to be worth the effort, since the worksheet provides perfectly acceptable results without these extra steps. The worksheets are linked, so they will reflect accurate figures only when all the worksheets are completed. You should create and fill in the worksheets for the schedules first and then create the worksheets for Form 1040, pages 1 and 2. If you don't follow this pattern, you may see #REF! errors in certain cells as you build the worksheets. This is no cause for concern; once all the

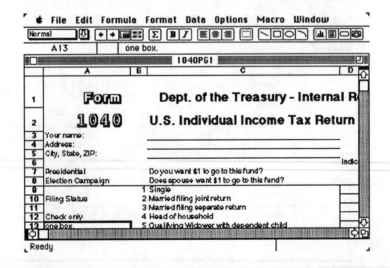

FIGURE 13-6.   Sample of Excel worksheet for Form 1040

worksheets are open, the dependent worksheet (usually Form 1040) will pull the necessary data from the schedules.

Note that these worksheets are based on the 1990 tax forms provided by the IRS. These forms are likely to change in the years ahead, so you should use them as guidelines only. Compare the design and formulas in your worksheet to the actual forms you receive from the IRS.

To build the Schedule A worksheet, open a new worksheet and define the column width. Set column A to 15, column B to 3, column C to 30, column D to 12, column E to 3, and column F to 12. Then enter the following formulas and values:

Cell	Entry
A1	Form 1040
A4	Medical and
A5	Dental Expenses
A8	(Do not
A9	include
A10	expenses
A11	reimbursed or
A12	paid by others.)
A14	(See P.23)
A17	Taxes You
A18	Paid
A21	(See
A22	instructions
A23	on P.27)
A25	Interest You
A26	Paid
A28	(See
A29	instructions
A30	on P.27)
A42	Gifts to
A43	Charity
A46	(See
A47	instructions
A48	on page 29)
A52	Casualty and
A53	Theft Losses
A54	Moving
A55	Expenses
A56	Job expenses
A57	and most other
A58	miscellaneous

A59	deductions
A62	(See
A63	Instructions
A64	on Page 30.)
A65	Other
A66	Miscellaneous
A67	Deductions
A71	Total Itemized
A72	Deductions
B4	1
B12	2
B13	3
B14	4
B19	5
B20	6
B21	7
B24	8
B30	9a
B32	9b
B36	10
B37	11
B38	12a
B40	12b
B41	13
B42	14
B48	15
B50	16
B51	17
B52	18
B54	19
B56	20
B59	21
B61	22
B62	23
B63	24
B65	25
B71	26
C1	Schedule A
C2	Itemized Deductions
C4	Medical and dental expenses

C5	(See page 27 of the instructions.)
C12	Enter amount from Form 1040, Line 32
C13	Line 2 multiplied by .075
C14	Line 3 subtracted from Line 1
C15	(but not less than zero)
C19	State and local income taxes
C20	Real estate taxes
C21	Other taxes (list- incl. pers.
C22	property taxes_____
C23	_____)
C24	Total of lines 5 through 7
C30	Deductible home mortgage
C31	interest paid to financial institutions
C32	Other deductible home mortgage
C33	interest paid (if to an individual, show
C34	person's name & address (_____
C35	_____
C36	Deductible points
C37	Deductible investment interest
C38	Personal interest you paid
C39	(See page 28)
C40	Line 12a multiplied by 20%
C41	TOTAL INTEREST:
C42	Contributions by cash or check.
C43	CAUTION: If you made a charitable
C44	contribution and received a benefit in
C45	return, see pg. 29 of instructions.
C48	Other than cash or check, (If over
C49	$500, attach Form 8283)
C50	Carryover from prior year
C51	TOTAL CONTRIBUTIONS:
C52	Casualty or theft losses.
C53	(Attach Form 4684)
C54	Moving Expenses
C55	(Attach Form 3903 or 3903F)
C56	Unreimbursed employee business expenses
C57	(You may need Form 2106;
C58	see instructions.)
C59	Other expenses (list type & amount)
C60	_____
C61	Total of lines 20 and 21
C62	Form 1040, line 32 × 2%:

C63	Line 22 less line 23
C64	(but not less than zero)
C65	Other (from list on page 26 of
C66	Instructions). Enter type and
C67	amount: _____
C68	_____
C69	_____
C70	_____
C71	Total of lines 4,8,13,17,18,19,24, & 25.
C72	This amount linked to Form 1040, line 34.
D2	1990
D13	=F12*0.075
D14	=IF(F4−D130,F4−D13,0)
D40	=20%*D38
D61	=D57+D60
D62	=2%*'Form 1040 Page 2'!$F$2
E4	1
E12	2
E13	3
E14	4
E19	5
E20	6
E21	7
E24	8
E30	9a
E32	9b
E36	10
E37	11
E38	12a
E40	12b
E41	13
E42	14
E48	15
E50	16
E51	17
E52	18
E54	19
E57	20
E60	21
E61	22

E62	23
E63	24
E69	25
E72	26
F12	'Form 1040 Page 2'! $F$2
F15	=D14
F24	=SUM(D19:D21)
F41	=D30+D32+D36+D37+D40
F51	=SUM(D42:D50)
F63	=IF(D61-D62>0,D61-D62,0)
F72	=F15+F24+F41+F51+F52+F54+F63+F69

Save the worksheet as Schedule A. The names of the worksheets are important, because cells in various worksheets refer to each other by name. If you use different file names, the links will not be made unless you also change the worksheet names where they are used in the formulas.

To build the Schedule B worksheet, open a new worksheet and define the column widths. Set column A to 15, column B to 3, column C to 30, column D to 12, column E to 3, and column F to 12. Then enter the following formulas and values:

Cell	Entry
A1	Form 1040
A2	If you received more than $400 in taxable interest income, or you are claiming the
A3	exclusion of interest from Series EE U.S. savings bonds issued after 1989 (see page
A4	31), you must complete Part 1. List ALL interest received as a nominee, interest that
A5	actually belongs to another person, or your received or paid accrued interest on
A6	securities transferred between interest payment dates, see page 31.
A8	Part 1
A9	Interest
A10	Income
A12	(See
A13	Instructions on
A14	pages 10 and 27.)
A16	NOTE: If you
A17	received a Form
A18	1099-INT or 1099-OID

A19	list the firm's name
A20	as the payer & enter
A21	the total interest on
A22	that form.
A26	If you received more than $400 in gross dividends and/or other dividends on stock, you
A27	must complete Parts II and III. If you received, as a nominee, dividends that actually
A28	belong to another person, see page 31.
A29	Part II
A30	Dividend
A31	Income
A35	NOTE: If you
A36	received a Form
A37	1099-INT or 1099-OID
A38	list the firm's name
A39	as the payer & enter
A40	the total interest on
A41	that form.
A52	Part III
A53	Foreign
A54	Accounts
A55	and
A56	Foreign
A57	Trusts
A60	(See
A61	Instructions on
A62	page 27.)
B8	1
B22	2
B23	3
B25	4
B29	5
B43	6
B44	7
B46	8
B49	9
B50	10
B57	10
B62	10B
B63	11

C1	Schedule B
C7	Interest and Dividend Income
C8	Interest income. (List name of payer—if any interest is from
C9	seller-financed mortgages, see instructions, and list that interest
C10	first.) _____
C12	_____
C13	_____
C14	_____
C15	_____
C16	_____
C17	_____
C18	_____
C19	_____
C20	_____
C21	_____
C22	Add the amounts on Line 1. Enter total:
C23	Enter the executable savings bond interest, if any, from
C24	Form 8815, Line 14. Attach Form 8815 to 1040.
C25	Line 3 subtracted from Line 2:
C29	Dividend income (list name of payer—
C30	include capital gain distributions,
C31	nontaxable distributions, etc._____
C32	_____
C33	_____
C34	_____
C35	_____
C36	_____
C37	_____
C38	_____
C39	_____
C40	_____
C41	_____
C42	_____
C43	Total of amounts on Line 5
C44	Capital gain distributions.
C45	Enter here and on Schedule D.
C46	Nontaxable distributions
C47	(See the instructions for
C48	Form 1040, Line 9.)
C49	Total of Lines 7 & 8

C50	Line 6 less Line 9
C51	(This amount linked to 1040, Line 9.)
C52	If you received more than $400 of interest or dividends, OR
C53	if you had a foreign account or were a grantor of, or a
C54	transferor to, a foreign trust, you must answer both
C55	questions in Part III.
C57	At any time during 1990, did you have an interest
C58	in or a signature or other authority over a financial
C59	account in a foreign country? See P. 31 of the instructions
C60	for exceptions and filing requirements for Form TD F90-22.1
C62	If "Yes," enter the name of the country:_____
C63	Were you the grantor of, or transferor to, a foreign trust
C64	which existed during 1990, whether or not you have
C65	any beneficial interest in it? If yes, you may have
C66	to file Forms 3520, 3520-A, or 926.
D56	Yes:_____
D61	Yes:_____
D67	Yes:_____
E8	1
E22	2
E23	3
E25	4
E43	5
E44	6
E46	7
E49	8
E50	9
E61	10
E67	11
F1	1990
F7	Amount
F22	=SUM(F8:F21)
F25	=F22-F23
F43	=SUM(F29:F42)
F49	=D44=D46
F50	=F43–F49
F61	No:_____

F67   No:_____

Save this worksheet as Schedule B.

To build page 1 of the Form 1040 worksheet, open a new worksheet and define the column widths. Set column A to 18, column B to 3, column C to 40, column D to 3, and column E to 12. Then enter the following formulas and values:

Cell	Entry
A1	Form
A2	1040
A3	Your name:
A4	Address:
A5	City, State, ZIP:
A7	Presidential
A8	Election Campaign
A10	Filing Status
A12	Check only
A13	one box.
A14	Exemptions
A24	Child not w/you but claimed under pre-1985 agreement:
A26	Income
A50	Adjustments
A51	To Income
A60	Adjusted
A61	Gross Income
B9	1
B10	2
B11	3
B12	4
B13	5
B14	6a
B16	6c
B27	7
B28	8a
B29	8b
B30	9
B32	10
B33	11
B34	12
B35	13

B36	14
B37	15
B38	16a
B39	16b
B40	17a
B41	17b
B42	18
B43	19
B44	20
B45	21a
B46	21b
B47	22
B48	23
B51	24
B52	25
B53	26
B54	27
B55	28
B56	29
B58	30
B60	31
C1	Dept. of the Treasury—Internal Revenue Service
C2	U.S. Individual Income Tax Return
C7	Do you want $1 to go to this fund?
C8	Does spouse want $1 to go to this fund?
C9	Single
C10	Married filing joint return
C11	Married filing separate return
C12	Head of household
C13	Qualifying Widow(er) with dependent child
C14	Yourself _____ 6b Spouse _____
C16	Dependents
C17	Name (first, initial, last name) & Soc Sec No.
C25	TOTAL EXEMPTIONS CLAIMED:
C27	Wages, Salaries, tips, etc.
C28	Taxable interest income
C29	Tax-exempt interest income
C30	Dividend income (make manual entry here
C31	if you don't fill out Schedule B.)
C32	Taxable refunds—state & local inc. taxes
C33	Alimony received

C34	Business income or loss (Attach Sched. C)
C35	Capital gain or loss (Attach Sched. D)
C36	Cap. gain not reported on line 13
C37	Other gains or losses (Attach form 4797)
C38	Total IRA distributions
C39	-taxable amt, if any, on above
C40	Total pensions & annuities
C41	-taxable amt, if any, on above
C42	Rents, royalties, partnerships, estates
C43	Farm income or loss (Attach Sched. F)
C44	Unemployment compensation (insurance)
C45	Social security benefits (see page 13)
C46	-taxable amount, if any, from p.13
C47	Other income
C48	TOTAL INCOME
C51	Your IRA deduction, from worksheet p.14 or 15
C52	Spouse's IRA deduction, from p.14 or 15
C53	Self-employed health ins. deduction (p.15)
C54	Keogh retirement plan and SEP deduction
C55	Penalty on early savings withdrawal
C56	Alimony paid (recipient's name
C57	and so. sec no:_____)
C58	TOTAL ADJUSTMENTS
C60	This is your ADJUSTED GROSS INCOME.
D6	Indicate Yes or No.
D27	7
D28	8
D29	8b
D30	9
D32	10
D33	11
D34	12
D35	13
D36	14
D37	15
D38	16a
D39	16b
D40	17a
D41	17b
D42	18
D43	19

D44	20
D45	21a
D46	21b
D47	22
D48	23
D51	24
D52	25
D53	26
D54	27
D55	28
D57	29
D58	30
D60	31
E2	1990
E14	No. of boxes checked on 6a & 6b
E18	No. of children on 6c
E19	who lived with you
E20	No. of children on 6c
E21	who didn't live with you
E22	No. of parents listed on 6c
E23	Other dependents listed on 6c
E25	Add numbers in boxes above
E28	"SCHEDULE B"!$F$25
E30	IF("SCHEDULE B"!$F$50>400,"SCHEDULE B"!f50,0)
E34	"SCHEDULE C"!f51
E48	=SUM(E27:E28)=SUM(E30:E37)=E39=SUM(E42:E44)=SUM(E46:E47)
E58	=SUM(E50:E57)
E60	=E48–E58

Save this worksheet as Form 1040 Page 1.

To build page 2 of the Form 1040 worksheet, open a new worksheet and define the column widths. Set column A to 15, column B to 3, column C to 30, column D to 12, column E to 3, and column F to 12. Then enter the following formulas and values:

Cell	Entry
A3	Tax
A4	Computation
A40	Credits
A41	(See instructions

A42	on Page 18.)
A50	Other
A51	Taxes
A53	(Including
A54	Advance EIC
A55	Payments)
A57	Medicare
A58	Premium
A61	Payments
A73	Refund or
A74	Amount
A75	You Owe
B2	32
B4	33a
B9	33b
B10	33c
B13	34
B22	35
B24	36
B27	37
B32	38
B35	39
B37	40
B38	41
B39	42
B42	43
B43	44
B46	45
B47	46
B48	47
B49	48
B50	49
B51	50
B53	51
B55	52
B56	53
B57	54
B58	55
B59	56
B60	57
B62	58

B63	59
B64	60
B66	61
B68	62
B70	63
B71	64
B72	65
B73	66
B75	67
C2	Amount from line 31 (adj. gross income)
C4	Check if: ____65 or over ____ blind
C5	Check if spouse is: ____65 or over ____ blind
C6	Add number of boxes checked.
C7	Enter total here:
C9	Check if:___someone can claim you
C10	Check if:___married filing separately, or
C11	you are a dual-status alien
C13	IF YOU ITEMIZE, this is amount from
C14	Schedule A, line 26.
C18	IF YOU DO NOT ITEMIZE,
C19	SEE PAGE 17 of the Form 1040 instructions
C20	for your standard deduction amount.
C22	This is line 34 subtracted from line 32.
C24	Total exemptions claimed × $2000
C25	(from line 6)
C27	Taxable Income (line 35 minus line 36)
C28	CAUTION: If under age 14 and you have over $1000
C29	of investment income, see pg 17 to see if you must
C30	use form 8615 to figure your tax.
C32	Enter tax. Check if from ___Tax Table,
C33	___Tax Rate Schedule, ___Schedule D, or
C34	___Form 8615 (Computation of children's tax)
C35	Additional taxes. Check if from:
C36	___Form 4970, ___Form 4972,
C38	Credit for child care (att. form 2441)
C39	Credit for the elderly or
C40	the disabled (Attach Sched. R)
C42	Foreign tax credit
C43	General business credit. From:
C44	( )Form 3800, ( )Form [specify] _____
C46	Credit for prior year minimum tax

C47	Sum of lines 41 through 45
C48	Line 46 subtracted from line 40
C49	Self-employment tax (Attach Sched. SE)
C50	Alternative minimum tax (Attach Form 6251)
C51	Tax from recapture of investment credit
C52	(Attach Form 4255 or Form 8611)
C53	Social Security tax on tip income not
C54	reported to employer (Attach Form 4137)
C55	Tax on IRA or retirement plans (Attach Form 5329)
C56	Sum of lines 47 through 52
C57	Supplemental Medicare premium
C58	TOTAL TAX:
C59	Federal income tax withheld
C60	1989 Estimated tax payments
C61	and amount applied from 1988 return
C62	Earned income credit(See P.19)
C63	Amount paid with Form 4868
C64	Excess social security tax
C65	and RRTA tax withheld (see page 20)
C66	Credit for Federal tax on
C67	fuels (attach Form 4136)
C68	Regulated investment company
C69	credit (attach Form 2439)
C70	Total of 56 through 62, TOTAL PAYMENTS
C71	Amount OVERPAID (if any)
C72	Amount to be REFUNDED TO YOU (if any)
C73	Amount of line 64 to be
C74	applied to your 1990 estimated tax
C75	Amount YOU OWE (if any)
D1	Form 1040, Page 2
D37	TOTAL TAX:
D47	=SUM(D38:D46)
E2	32
E13	34a
E19	34b
E22	35
E24	36
E27	37
E33	38
E36	39

E37	40
E38	41
E39	42
E42	43
E43	44
E46	45
E47	46
E48	47
E49	48
E50	49
E51	50
E53	51
E55	52
E56	53
E57	54
E58	55
E60	56
E61	57
E62	58
E63	59
E64	60
E66	61
E68	62
E70	63
E71	64
E72	65
E73	66
E75	67
F2	='Form 1040 Page 1'!$E$60
F13	='Schedule A'!$F$72
F22	=IF(F13>F19,F2-F13,F2-F19)
F24	='Form 1040 Page 1'!$D$25*2000
F27	=F22-F24
F37	=F33+F36
F48	=F37-D47
F56	=SUM(F47:F55)
F58	=F57+F56
F70	=SUM(D59:D68)
F71	=IF(F70>F58,F70-F58,0)
F72	=F71-D73
F75	=IF(F70<F58,F58-F70,0)

Save this worksheet as Form 1040 Page 2.

Once the worksheets are saved, you can enter the necessary figures to calculate your taxes. Open all four worksheets so that the references will update as you enter the values. If you want your worksheets to resemble the one shown in the earlier illustration, turn off the gridlines with the Options Display command. Use the Format Border command, as desired, to add borders around all cells that will contain entries.

BREAK-EVEN ANALYSIS

A common "what if" scenario for almost any firm is the break-even analysis, which determines how many units of a given product must be sold before the producer shows a profit. A break-even analysis requires the juggling of two groups of figures: fixed costs and variable costs. Fixed costs do not directly increase with each unit sold. Such costs include the costs of rental of the manufacturing plant, utilities to power the production line, and advertising expenses. Variable costs directly increase with each unit sold. Such costs include the costs of the materials to assemble each unit, labor costs per unit, packaging costs, and shipping costs.

A typical break-even analysis performs a one-time deduction of the fixed costs and then calculates the per-unit costs for each unit produced. These negative amounts are balanced against the net profits (or net sales cost times the number of units sold). As the number of units sold is increased, a break-even point is reached where the total profit equals the negative fixed and variable costs. The Break Even Analysis worksheet shown in Figure 13-7 illustrates the break-even point for a child's bicycle.

To build the model, open a new worksheet. Set the width of column A to 20 and of column C to 3. The other columns can remain at their default widths. Enter the following formulas into the cells:

Cell	Entry
A3	Break-even Analysis
A4	-------------------------
A5	Name of Product:
A6	Sales Price:
A8	FIXED COSTS
A9	Rent
A10	Telephone
A11	Utilities
A12	Advertising
A13	Miscellaneous

 File   Edit   Formula   Format   Data   Options   Macro   Window

Normal					
A4					

BRKEVEN.HLS

	A	B	C	D	E	FGHI
3	Break-even Analysis			Units Sold	Profit/Loss	
4						
5	Name of Product:	Child's Bicycle		15	($2,479.00)	
6	Sales Price:	$59.70		30	($2,158.00)	
7				45	($1,837.00)	
8	FIXED COSTS			60	($1,516.00)	
9	Rent	$1,500.00		75	($1,195.00)	
10	Telephone	$150.00		90	($874.00)	
11	Utilities	$500.00		105	($553.00)	
12	Advertising	$450		120	($232.00)	
13	Miscellaneous	$200.00		135	$89.00	
14	TOTAL Fixed Costs	$2,800.00		150	$410.00	
15				165	$731.00	
16	VARIABLE COSTS, PER UNIT			180	$1,052.00	
17	Manufacturing	$22		195	$1,373.00	

Ready

FIGURE 13-7.   Break-even Analysis worksheet

A14	TOTAL Fixed Costs
A15	-------------------------
A16	VARIABLE COSTS, PER UNIT
A17	Manufacturing
A18	Labor
A19	Packaging
A20	Shipping
A21	TOTAL Variable Costs
A22	---------------------------
A23	QUANTITY INCREMENT
A24	-------------------------
B4	------------------
B5	Child's Bicycle
B6	59.7
B9	1500
B10	150
B11	500
B12	450
B13	200
B14	=SUM(B9:B13)

B15	-----------------
B17	22.08
B18	8.07
B19	4.9
B20	3.25
B21	=SUM(B17:B20)
B22	-----------------
B23	15
B24	-----------------
D3	Units Sold
D4	------------
D5	=B23
D6	=D5+$B$23

The remaining formulas in column D can be created quickly by selecting the range from D6 to D41 and using the Fill Down command on the Edit menu.

D7	=D6+$B$23
D8	=D7+$B$23
D9	=D8+$B$23
D10	=D9+$B$23
D11	=D10+$B$23
D12	=D11+$B$23
D13	=D12+$B$23
D14	=D13+$B$23
D15	=D14+$B$23
D16	=D15+$B$23
D17	=D16+$B$23
D18	=D17+$B$23
D19	=D18+$B$23
D20	=D19+$B$23
D21	=D20+$B$23
D22	=D21+$B$23
D23	=D22+$B$23
D24	=D23+$B$23
D25	=D24+$B$23
D26	=D25+$B$23
D27	=D26+$B$23
D28	=D27+$B$23
D29	=D28+$B$23
D30	=D29+$B$23
D31	=D30+$B$23

D32	=D31+$B$23
D33	=D32+$B$23
D34	=D33+$B$23
D35	=D34+$B$23
D36	=D35+$B$23
D37	=D36+$B$23
D38	=D37+$B$23
D39	=D38+$B$23
D40	=D39+$B$23
D41	=D40+$B$23
D42	------------

In column E, enter the following values and formulas:

E3	Profit/Loss
E4	-------------------------------
E5	=D5*$B$6-($B$14+($B$21*D5))

The remaining formulas in column E can be created quickly by selecting the range from E5 to E41 and using the Fill Down command.

E6	=D6*$B$6-($B$14+($B$21*D6))
E7	=D7*$B$6-($B$14+($B$21*D7))
E8	=D8*$B$6-($B$14+($B$21*D8))
E9	=D9*$B$6-($B$14+($B$21*D9))
E10	=D10*$B$6-($B$14+($B$21*D10))
E11	=D11*$B$6-($B$14+($B$21*D11))
E12	=D12*$B$6-($B$14+($B$21*D12))
E13	=D13*$B$6-($B$14+($B$21*D13))
E14	=D14*$B$6-($B$14+($B$21*D14))
E15	=D15*$B$6-($B$14+($B$21*D15))
E16	=D16*$B$6-($B$14+($B$21*D16))
E17	=D17*$B$6-($B$14+($B$21*D17))
E18	=D18*$B$6-($B$14+($B$21*D18))
E19	=D19*$B$6-($B$14+($B$21*D19))
E20	=D20*$B$6-($B$14+($B$21*D20))
E21	=D21*$B$6-($B$14+($B$21*D21))
E22	=D22*$B$6-($B$14+($B$21*D22))
E23	=D23*$B$6-($B$14+($B$21*D23))
E24	=D24*$B$6-($B$14+($B$21*D24))
E25	=D25*$B$6-($B$14+($B$21*D25))
E26	=D26*$B$6-($B$14+($B$21*D26))
E27	=D27*$B$6-($B$14+($B$21*D27))

E28	=D28*$B$6-($B$14+($B$21*D28))
E29	=D29*$B$6-($B$14+($B$21*D29))
E30	=D30*$B$6-($B$14+($B$21*D30))
E31	=D31*$B$6-($B$14+($B$21*D31))
E32	=D32*$B$6-($B$14+($B$21*D32))
E33	=D33*$B$6-($B$14+($B$21*D33))
E34	=D34*$B$6-($B$14+($B$21*D34))
E35	=D35*$B$6-($B$14+($B$21*D35))
E36	=D36*$B$6-($B$14+($B$21*D36))
E37	=D37*$B$6-($B$14+($B$21*D37))
E38	=D38*$B$6-($B$14+($B$21*D38))
E39	=D39*$B$6-($B$14+($B$21*D39))
E40	=D40*$B$6-($B$14+($B$21*D40))
E41	=D41*$B$6-($B$14+($B$21*D41))
E42	-----------------------------

Format the ranges from B6 to B21 and from E5 to E41 into dollar and cents with $#,##0.00 ; ($#,##0.00). To use the worksheet, enter your respective fixed and variable costs in the cells provided. In the Quantity Increment cell, enter the quantity that you wish to use as a scale for the break-even analysis. For example, to see how many hundreds of units it will take to break even, enter **100** for a quantity increment. For a more detailed analysis, enter a smaller increment.

You can extend the analysis to cover even more units by simply copying the respective formulas down the column past row 41. However, if you're not breaking even by row 41 of the worksheet, the analysis is telling you that your pricing or manufacturing strategy has a serious flaw!

IRA CALCULATOR

The IRA Calculator worksheet is a straightforward financial tool that is designed to plot the increasing value of an IRA (Individual Retirement Account). Four columns within the worksheet contain a beginning balance in the account, a yearly contribution, an interest rate, and an ending balance. A less complex worksheet would assume a standard interest rate and yearly contribution, but in real life your yearly contribution may vary, and it is virtually impossible to plan for a standard interest rate. Keeping separate columns for these values for each year gives you the ability to insert each year's interest rate and the amount of each IRA contribution.

In column C the beginning balance is entered (starting with 0 in the first row). Column D contains the yearly contribution, which for this example is $1700 the first year, $1850 the second, $1900 the third year, and assumed to be $2000 per year afterwards. Column E contains the interest rate, assumed to be 10.5% the first year, 9.25% the second year, 9.5% the third year, and 9% per year afterwards.

Column F contains the formula that calculates the effect of the accumulating interest and the added yearly investment. The formula calculates on the basis of simple interest by adding the current balance to the yearly contribution, and adding the result multiplied by the yearly interest rate to provide the new balance. Each year's new balance is then carried to the successive balance column. The worksheet is shown in Figure 13-8.

To build the worksheet, enter the following formulas into the cells:

Cell	Entry
B4	Year
B5	1991
B6	=B5+1

To create the following formulas, select the range from B6 to B37 and use the Fill Down command.

B7	=B6+1
B8	=B7+1
B9	=B8+1

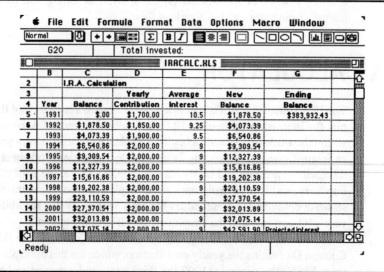

FIGURE 13-8. IRA Calculator worksheet

B10	=B9+1
B11	=B10+1
B12	=B11+1
B13	=B12+1
B14	=B13+1
B15	=B14+1
B16	=B15+1
B17	=B16+1
B18	=B17+1
B19	=B18+1
B20	=B19+1
B21	=B20+1
B22	=B21+1
B23	=B22+1
B24	=B23+1
B25	=B24+1
B26	=B25+1
B27	=B26+1
B28	=B27+1
B29	=B28+1
B30	=B29+1
B31	=B30+1
B32	=B31+1
B33	=B32+1
B34	=B33+1
B35	=B34+1
B36	=B35+1
B37	=B36+1

In column C of the worksheet, enter the following values and formulas:

C2	IRA Calculator
C3	Beginning
C4	Balance
C6	=F5

To create the following formulas, select the range from C6 to C37 and use the Fill Down command.

C7	=F6
C8	=F7
C9	=F8
C10	=F9

C11	=F10
C12	=F11
C13	=F12
C14	=F13
C15	=F14
C16	=F15
C17	=F16
C18	=F17
C19	=F18
C20	=F19
C21	=F20
C22	=F21
C23	=F22
C24	=F23
C25	=F24
C26	=F25
C27	=F26
C28	=F27
C29	=F28
C30	=F29
C31	=F30
C32	=F31
C33	=F32
C34	=F33
C35	=F34
C36	=F35
C37	=F36

In column D of the worksheet, enter the following values and formulas:

D3	Yearly
D4	Contribution
D5	1700
D6	1850
D7	1900
D8	2000

To create the following formulas, select the range from D8 to D37 and use the Fill Down command.

D9	2000
D10	2000
D11	2000

D12	2000
D13	2000
D14	2000
D15	2000
D16	2000
D17	2000
D18	2000
D19	2000
D20	2000
D21	2000
D22	2000
D23	2000
D24	2000
D25	2000
D26	2000
D27	2000
D28	2000
D29	2000
D30	2000
D31	2000
D32	2000
D33	2000
D34	2000
D35	2000
D36	2000
D37	2000

In column E of the worksheet, enter the following values and formulas:

E3	Average
E4	Interest
E5	10.5
E6	9.25
E7	9.5
E8	=$G$19

To create the following formulas, select the range from E8 to E37 and use the Fill Down command.

E9	=$G$19
E10	=$G$19
E11	=$G$19
E12	=$G$19

E13	=$G$19
E14	=$G$19
E15	=$G$19
E16	=$G$19
E17	=$G$19
E18	=$G$19
E19	=$G$19
E20	=$G$19
E21	=$G$19
E22	=$G$19
E23	=$G$19
E24	=$G$19
E25	=$G$19
E26	=$G$19
E27	=$G$19
E28	=$G$19
E29	=$G$19
E30	=$G$19
E31	=$G$19
E32	=$G$19
E33	=$G$19
E34	=$G$19
E35	=$G$19
E36	=$G$19
E37	=$G$19

In column F of the worksheet, enter the following:

F3	New
F4	Balance
F5	=((C5+D5)*E5/100)+C5+D5

Select the range of cells from F5 to F37. Open the Edit menu and choose Fill Down to copy the formula into the successive cells. In column G of the worksheet, enter the following values and formulas:

G3	Ending
G4	Balance
G5	=F37
G16	Projected interest
G17	Rate for
G18	remaining years
G19	9

G20   Total invested:
G21   =SUM(D4:D36)

Using the Number command from the Format menu, format the ranges from C6 to
C37, D5 to D37, and F5 to F37 for dollars and cents. Also format cells G5 and G21
for the same type of display.

Once the formulas have been entered, the worksheet displays the interest accumula-
tion and yearly balances as shown in Figure 13-8. You can change the interest rates
and investment amounts to correspond to your own real and projected investment
rates.

MORTGAGE ANALYSIS AND AMORTIZATION SCHEDULE

The Mortgage worksheet has a straightforward design, using the PMT (payment)
function to calculate the payments on a loan and displaying an amortization schedule
for the term of the loan. Figure 13-9 shows the worksheet.

Cells D5, D6, and D7 of the worksheet contain the principal loan amount, interest
rate, and term of the loan in years. In cell D9, the formula

```
 File  Edit  Formula  Format  Data  Options  Macro  Window
Normal
     D9              =PMT((D6/12),(D7*12),-D5)
                              MORTGAGE.HLS
```

	A	B	C	D	E	F
5		Principal Amount of Loan:		$240,000.00		
6		Interest Rate, in PERCENT:		10.5%		
7		Term of Loan, in Years:		30		
8						
9		MONTHLY MORTGAGE PAYMENT		$2,195.37		
10						
11						
12						
13						
14						
15	YEAR	START BALANCE	END BALANCE	TOTAL PAID	PRINCIPAL	INTERES
16						
17	1	$240,000.00	$238,798.79	$26,344.49	$1,201.21	$25,143.
18	2	$238,798.79	$237,465.20	$26,344.49	$1,333.59	$25,010.
19	3	$237,465.20	$235,984.65	$26,344.49	$1,480.55	$24,863

Ready

FIGURE 13-9.   Worksheet for mortgage calculation and amortization

=PMT((D6/12),(D7*12),-D5)

supplies the rate, number of periods, and present value. The rate and the number of periods are converted to months, and the present value is shown as a negative value, representing cash paid out.

Year one of the amortization schedule begins in Row 17. The starting balance is derived from the amount entered in cell D5. To arrive at the ending balance in column C for the first year, a formula containing the following variation of Excel's PV (Present Value) function is used.

=PV(($D$6/12),(12*($D$7-A17)),-$D$9)

It is now a simple matter to calculate the remaining forms in the row. The total paid (column D of the amortization schedule) is the monthly payment (cell D9) multiplied by 12 to compute a yearly amount. The principal in column E is calculated by subtracting column C of the schedule (the ending balance) from column B (the starting balance). Interest (column F) is then calculated by subtracting the difference between the starting and ending balance from the total paid. As the formulas are duplicated down the worksheet, relative references are adjusted upwards for each successive row location.

To build the worksheet, enter the following formulas in the cells shown. Use the Column Width command on the Format menu to change the width of column A to 5 spaces and the width of columns B, C, D, E, and F to 15 spaces. To enter the year numbers, use the Data Series command. Enter **1** in cell A17, select the range from A17 to A46, choose Series from the Data menu, and select OK in the dialog box to fill the range.

Cell	Entry
A15	YEAR
A16	=====
A17	1
A18	2
A19	3
A20	4
A21	5
A22	6
A23	7
A24	8
A25	9
A26	10
A27	11

A28	12
A29	13
A30	14
A31	15
A32	16
A33	17
A34	18
A35	19
A36	20
A37	21
A38	22
A39	23
A40	24
A41	25
A42	26
A43	27
A44	28
A45	29
A46	30
B3	Mortgage Analysis
B5	Principal amount of loan:
B6	Interest rate, in percent:
B7	Term of loan, in years:
B8	===============
B9	MONTHLY MORTGAGE PAYMENT
B15	STARTING BALANCE
B16	===============
B17	=D5
B18	=C17
C8	===============
C15	ENDING BALANCE
C16	===============
C17	=PV(($D$6/12),(12*($D$7−A17)),−$D$9)
C18	=PV(($D$6/12),(12*($D$7−A18)),−$D$9)
D5	240000
D6	10.5%
D7	30
D8	===============
D9	=PMT((D6/12),(D7*12),−D5)

D15	TOTAL PAID
D16	===============
D17	=$D$9*12
D18	=$D$9*12
E15	PRINCIPAL
E16	===============
E17	=B17-C17
E18	=B18-C18
F15	INTEREST
F16	===============
F17	=D17-(B17-C17)
F18	=D18-(B18-C18)

When you have entered these formulas, select the range of cells from B18 to F46. Open the Edit menu and use the Fill Down command to fill the successive formulas into the selected rows. Select the range from B17 to F46, open the Format menu, and choose #,##0.00 from the Number formats. At this point, your worksheet should resemble the example in Figure 13-9.

Note that the range suggested in this example assumes a 30-year loan. If you enter a period of 15 years but leave the formulas intact for 30 years, you will get an interesting benefit: a nest egg, calculated as an increasing negative balance when the mortgage ends and the amortization schedule shows mortgage payments still being added. To avoid this, just adjust the range when you fill down, as needed, to match the number of years for the mortgage. If you want to get really fancy, you can write a macro that clears the range, gets the number of years from cell D7, selects a new range equivalent to that number of years, and performs a Fill Down command.

PERSONNEL TRACKING DATABASE

This model, which consists of a macro file and a worksheet containing a database, is designed to demonstrate the flexibility offered by Excel's macro language. The macro provides a menu-driven personnel database. Though the worksheet is used to store the data, the user never has to open the worksheet or use any of the database commands. The macro provides numbered menu options for adding records to the database, editing records, deleting records, and printing reports.

The macro contains one Main Menu routine and five subroutines. The Main Menu routine is in column A; the Adder routine, to add records, is in column B; and the

Editor routine, to edit records, is in column C. The Eraser routine in column D erases unwanted records. Column E contains the Printer routine used to print the database. Column F contains the Exits routine, which saves the worksheet containing the database and ends the macro.

In addition to the macro, the system requires a database, which can be placed in a worksheet. The worksheet should be stored with the name Personnel, as this name is used by the macro to open and save the worksheet as necessary. The worksheet field names are placed in row 5, and the first field name must be "social sec." to indicate the Social Security number of the employee. All menu choices offered by the macro for finding and editing an employee's record use the Social Security number as the search criteria.

To build the database, open a new worksheet and enter the following titles in the cells shown. Note that only the "social sec." field in cell A5 is mandatory. If you plan to use this system for your own office, you may want to add additional fields or delete some of the suggested fields to meet your specific needs.

Cell	Entry
A5	social sec.
B5	last name
C5	first name
D5	department
E5	birthdate
F5	hired?
G5	sex
H5	insured?
I5	dependents
J5	address
K5	city
L5	state
M5	ZIP
N5	phone

Use the Column Width command of the Format menu to change the width of column A to 12, columns B and C to 15, columns J and K to 20, column L to 5, column M to 10, and column N to 12. Save the worksheet under the name Personnel. Then open a new macro sheet and enter the following:

Cell	Entry
A1	PERSONNEL SYSTEM
A2	Press Option-Command M!

A3	main_menu
A4	=OPEN("personnel")
A5	=ACTIVATE("personnel")
A6	=SELECT("R5C1:R40C14")
A7	=SET.DATABASE( )
A8	=SELECT(!$A$1)
A9	=FORMULA(INPUT("1 to Add, 2 to Edit, 3 to Delete, 4 to Print, 5 to Exit",1,"MENU"))
A10	=IF(!A1=1,adder( ),GOTO($A$11))
A11	=IF(!A1=2,editor( ),GOTO($A$12))
A12	=IF(!A1=3,eraser( ),GOTO($A$13))
A13	=IF(!A1=4,printer( ),GOTO($A$14))
A14	=IF(!A1=5,exits( ),GOTO($A$15))
A15	=IF(!A1=6,GOTO($A$16),GOTO($A$8))
A16	=SELECT(!A1)
A17	=ALERT("Invalid choice!",3)
A18	=GOTO($A$8)
A19	=RETURN( )
B1	adder
B2	=ALERT("Click on NEW RECORD. Fill in data, press TAB, click on EXIT when done.",2)
B3	=DATA.FORM( )
B4	=RETURN( )
C1	editor
C2	=FORMULA.GOTO(!$A$3)
C3	=FORMULA("social sec.")
C4	=SELECT("R3C1:R4C1")
C5	=SET.CRITERIA( )
C6	=FORMULA.GOTO(!$A$4)
C7	=FORMULA(INPUT("Employee's social security number?", 2,"SOC.SEC."))
C8	=DATA.FIND.NEXT( )
C9	=ALERT("Click FIND NEXT. Tab to desired fields. Click EXIT when done.", 2)
C10	=DATA.FORM( )
C11	=DATA.FIND(FALSE)
C12	=RETURN( )
D1	eraser

D2	=FORMULA.GOTO(!$A$3)
D3	=FORMULA("social sec.")
D4	=SELECT("R3C1:R4C1")
D5	=SET.CRITERIA( )
D6	=FORMULA.GOTO(!$A$4)
D7	=FORMULA(INPUT("Employee's social security number?",2, "SOC.SEC."))
D8	=DATA.FIND.NEXT( )
D9	=IF(ALERT("DELETE this record? Are you sure?",1),GOTO($D$14),GOTO($D$19))
D10	=RETURN( )
D13	yes, delete it!
D14	=DATA.DELETE( )
D15	=DATA.FIND(FALSE)
D16	=RETURN( )
D18	no, don't delete!
D19	=DATA.FIND(FALSE)
D20	=RETURN( )
E1	printer
E2	=FORMULA.GOTO("Database")
E3	=PRINT(1,,,,,FALSE)
E4	=FORMULA.GOTO(!$A$1)
E5	=RETURN( )
F1	exits
F2	=MESSAGE(TRUE,"Saving database... please wait...")
F3	=SAVE( )
F4	=CLOSE( )
F5	=MESSAGE(FALSE)
F6	=HALT( )
F7	=RETURN( )

Now you need to define the names of the main and subroutine macros, so that when the main_menu macro is run, it can locate the other macros. Select cell A3, and use the Define Name command of the Formula menu to name the cell main_menu. Choose Command Macro from the options box, and assign an OPTION-COMMAND key, OPTION-COMMAND-M, by tabbing to or clicking the Option-Command Key box and entering **M**. Finally, press RETURN or select the OK button. Use the Define Name command to assign the other names, as indicated here:

Cell	Definition
B2	Adder
C2	Editor
D2	Eraser
E2	Printer
F2	Exits

When you are finished defining the names, click in cell A1 and then size the macro so that it takes up a small portion of the screen. Do this by clicking the Size box in the lower-right corner of the screen and dragging until the window is the desired size. (Sizing has no effect on how the macro operates, but it improves the appearance of the display.) Save the macro under the name Personnel Macro. Close the personnel worksheet you created earlier if it is still open. (Since the macro contains its own commands to open and close the worksheet, you need not have the worksheet open before using the macro.) Press OPTION-COMMAND-M to start the macro. Try the various menu choices for adding new employees to the database, for editing and deleting employees, and for printing reports.

How the Macro Works

When OPTION-COMMAND-M is pressed, the macro assigned the name main_menu, located in column A of the macro sheet, begins its execution. The first commands open the worksheet containing the personnel database and make that window the active window. A range of cells is selected, and the SET.DATABASE macro function is used to set the database range. The SELECT function makes cell A1 of the worksheet the active cell, and a statement containing the FORMULA and INPUT functions displays a menu and places the response in cell A1.

Depending on the response, one of the IF statements that follow either transfers program control to one of the other macros on the macro sheet or displays an "Invalid choice" error message. If a value of 1 is entered in the cell, control passes to the Adder macro. This macro uses an ALERT function to display instructions for adding records; a DATA.FORM function is used to display the form for adding records to the database. When the user is finished adding records and chooses the Exit button on the form, control passes back to the macro, and the RETURN function passes control to the main_menu macro, where the menu is again displayed.

If a value of 2 is entered in cell A1 in response to the menu, the Editor macro is called. The macro places the field name "social sec." in a blank cell to serve as part of a criteria range. Then the SELECT and SET.CRITERIA functions are used to define a criteria range. Next, the active cell is moved to A4, which is the matching cell in the criteria range. A statement containing the FORMULA and INPUT functions is used to ask for a Social Security number and to enter the response in cell A4. A DATA.FIND.NEXT function finds the appropriate record, and the DATA.FORM function displays the form for editing the record. Once the editing is done, program control passes back to the main_menu macro, where the menu is again displayed.

If a value of 3 is entered in cell A1 in response to the menu, the Eraser macro is called. This macro is similar in design to the Editor macro. It places the field name "social sec." in a blank cell to serve as part of a criteria range. The SELECT and SET.CRITERIA functions are then used to define a criteria range, and the active cell is moved to A4. A statement containing the FORMULA and INPUT functions is used to ask for a Social Security number and to enter the response in cell A4. A DATA.FIND.NEXT function then finds the appropriate record.

At this point, things take a different path than in the Editor macro. A statement containing the IF and ALERT functions displays a dialog box, asking for confirmation that the record should be deleted. If the OK button in the dialog box is selected or if the RETURN key is pressed, the IF statement causes the macro to proceed to cell D14, where a DATA.DELETE function erases the record. If the Cancel button or the ESCAPE key is used, the IF statement causes the macro to proceed to cell D19, where the DATA.FIND(FALSE) function cancels the Find mode, and control returns to the main_menu macro.

If a value of 4 is entered in cell A1 in response to the menu, the Printer macro is called. This straightforward macro uses the PRINT function to begin printing the database. When printing is completed, control returns to the main_menu macro.

A value of 5 in cell A1 causes the Exitmacro to assume control. After displaying a message in the message area, this macro uses the SAVE and CLOSE functions to save and close the personnel database. A MESSAGE(FALSE) function clears the message area, and a HALT statement is used to stop the macro. Without the HALT statement, control would pass right back to the main menu, and the user would never be able to exit normally from the system.

appendix **A**

COMMAND REFERENCE

This appendix describes Excel's worksheet and chart commands. The commands are defined here in the order in which they are displayed on their respective menus. A command followed by an ellipsis in the menu indicates that a dialog box appears after the command is chosen. Possible function-key combinations, where mentioned, require the use of the extended Macintosh keyboard, which has function keys F1 through F12.

FILE MENU COMMANDS

New (COMMAND-N or F11 for new chart; SHIFT-F11 for new worksheet; or COM-MAND-F11 for new macro sheet)   Creates a new worksheet, chart, or macro sheet. If a selection is made in an active worksheet and the File New option is used to create a chart, the chart will be based on the selected worksheet data.

Open (COMMAND-O)   Opens an existing worksheet, chart, macro sheet, or foreign file that can be translated into a worksheet. The name of the existing document can be chosen from a list box that displays Excel files in the current folder. The Open command can be used to open foreign files, which can be text, comma-separated (CSV), SYLK, Lotus (WKS, WK1 or WK3), DIF, dBASE II, III/III PLUS or dBASE IV (DBF2, DBF3, or DBF4), or Excel versions 1.0, 1.5, or 2.2.

Close (COMMAND-W)   Closes the active worksheet, chart, or macro sheet. If the document has been edited, you are asked if you wish to save the changes.

Close All   Closes all documents that are open. Note that this command appears only when you hold down the SHIFT key as you open the File menu.

Links   Opens links between the active document and other documents.

Save (COMMAND-S)   Saves the active file under the existing name. If a name has not yet been specified, you are prompted for a file name. Select the Options button from the resulting dialog box to save files in foreign formats.

Save As   Saves a file under a name you specify. Select the Options button from the resulting dialog box to save files in foreign formats.

Save Workspace   Saves a record of all open files. The resultant file, when opened, opens all files active during the save.

Delete   Deletes files. You must select the file to be deleted in the list box that appears, and you must provide confirmation. Note that this command cannot be undone.

Print Preview   Displays the Print Preview window, which displays an approximation of the worksheet that will be printed.

Page Setup   Specifies settings used to determine the appearance of the printed page.

Print (COMMAND-P)   Prints all worksheet cells containing data, or prints the area defined with the Set Print Area command of the Options menu.

Quit (COMMAND-Q)   Exits Excel and returns the user to the Macintosh desktop (Finder). If active documents have been edited since the last save, you are asked if you want to save first.

EDIT MENU COMMANDS

Undo (COMMAND-Z or F1)   Cancels the effects of the last cell entry or the last command (when possible). The precise name of this command changes to reflect the last action. For example, if the last action was an execution of the Copy command, the Undo command appears on the menu as Undo Copy. Some actions, like deleting files, cannot be undone. In such instances, the command appears as Can't Undo.

Repeat (COMMAND-Y)   Repeats the last command, including any dialog box options you selected. When the last command cannot be repeated, this command appears as Can't Repeat.

Cut (COMMAND-X or F2)   Outlines a selection that will be cut from one location and copied to another when you choose the Paste command. Select a single cell or range of cells and choose Cut. The selection will be outlined with a marquee and stored in memory, ready for the use of the Paste command (see Paste).

Copy (COMMAND-C or F3)   Outlines a selection that will be copied from one location to another when you choose the Paste command. Select a single cell or range of cells and choose Copy. The selection will be outlined with a marquee and stored in memory, ready for the use of the Paste command (see Paste).

Paste (COMMAND-V or F4)   Inserts a selection that was previously defined with the Cut or Copy command. The selection overwrites any existing data in the cells where the new data is pasted. When Paste is used after the Cut command, the range of cells selected to receive the data must be the same size as the cut area.

Clear (COMMAND-B)   With worksheets, clears the active cell or selected cells of formulas, notes, formats, or all three, as specified from the options that appear in the dialog box. With charts, clears the chart's data series, formats, or both (if the chart is the selected object). If the chart is not selected, any selected portion of the formula bar is cleared.

Paste Special   Pastes data or other worksheet properties (such as formats) in special ways. The command combines data contained in the copied cells with the cells in the selection. You can choose to paste all cell properties or only formulas, values, notes, or formats.

Note that Paste Special works differently with charts than it does with worksheets. With charts, the Paste Special command's dialog box displays different options that let you paste values in rows or columns and determine whether the series names and the categories will appear in the first row or in the first column.

Paste Link   Creates a link (or external reference) to data that has been copied to another worksheet.

Delete (COMMAND-K)   Removes a selection from a worksheet. The successive rows or columns following the selection are shifted into the deleted space. A dialog box lets you choose whether successive cells will be shifted up or left to fill the deleted space. If you are deleting entire rows or columns, the dialog box does not appear.

Insert (COMMAND-I)   Inserts cells into a worksheet. The successive rows or columns following the selection are shifted to make room for the deleted space. A dialog box lets you choose whether successive cells will be shifted down or right to make room for the added space. If you are inserting entire rows or columns, the dialog box does not appear.

Fill Right (COMMAND-R)   Copies the cell or cells in the far-left column of a selection into the remaining cells in the selection. All formulas, values, and formats are copied and updated.

Fill Down (COMMAND-D)   Copies the cell or cells in the top row of a selection into the remaining cells in the selection. All formulas, values, and formats are copied and updated.

Fill Workgroup   Applies edits of one worksheet to all other worksheets in a workgroup.

FORMULA MENU COMMANDS

Paste Name   Pastes a name into the formula bar. The command causes a list of all defined names to appear within a list box. The name selected from the list box is pasted into the existing formula.

Paste Function   Pastes a function into the formula bar. The command causes a list of all available functions to appear within a list box. The function selected from the list box is pasted into the existing formula.

Reference (COMMAND-T)   Changes the selected references within the formula bar from relative to absolute, from absolute to mixed, or from mixed to relative.

Define Name (COMMAND-L)   Assigns a name to a selected cell, range of cells, or formula. The names assigned to cells, formulas, and ranges can then be used within other formulas.

Create Names   Creates names for numerous cells at the same time. Text that appears along a row or down a column can be used as names for selected successive rows or columns.

Apply Names   Replaces formula references with names. When the command is chosen, a dialog box displays a list box containing all names that were defined with the Define Name or Create Names command. From the list box choose the desired name that is to apply to the selection.

Note   Creates notes that apply to cells. When the command is chosen, a note can be entered in a dialog box.

Goto (COMMAND-G or F5)   Moves the active cell to a named cell or named reference elsewhere on the active worksheet or on another open worksheet. To move to another cell on the active worksheet, enter the cell reference. To move to the start of a named range, enter the name of the range. To move to a cell or range on another open worksheet, enter the name of the worksheet enclosed in quotation marks, followed by an exclamation point, before entering the reference.

Find (COMMAND-H)   Searches the active worksheet for a specified search string or value. Using the command results in the appearance of a dialog box from which you can search formulas, values, or notes for the specified data. This command searches the entire worksheet unless a range is selected, in which case only the range is searched.

Replace   Searches the active worksheet for a specified search string or value, and replaces the found data with other data. This command performs the search and replace operation on the entire worksheet unless a range is selected, in which case the search and replace operation occurs on the selected range only.

Select Special   Lets you select cells of a specified type such as cells containing text or cells with notes from among a larger selection.

Show Active Cell   Scrolls the worksheet as needed to bring the active cell into view.

Outline   Creates an outline based on existing worksheet data.

Goal Seek   Finds a value that causes a formula to return a desired result.

FORMAT MENU COMMANDS

Number   Provides a list of possible formats that will apply to numeric values. When the command is used, a dialog box lists the standard formats. The format chosen from the list or manually entered at the keyboard will apply to numeric data in the selected cells.

Alignment   Provides a list of possible alignment formats. When the command is used, a dialog box lists choices of General, Left, Center, Right, and Fill. The option selected will apply to the alignment of data in the selected cells. The Left, Center, and Right options align the data at the left, center, or right sides of the cells. The Fill option causes the same character to appear in all spaces of a cell. The General option aligns text left, numbers right, and logical or error values in the center of the cell.

Font   Defines the fonts that will be used for any text displayed in the selected area. When the command is chosen, a dialog box appears. You can select the desired type style, point size, and font colors, and you can specify whether the text will appear as bold, italic, strikeout, underlined, outlined, or shadowed.

Border   Defines a border that can be placed around a cell or a selected range of cells. Borders can be placed on the left, right, top, or bottom of cells, or as an outline around the cell or selected cells. The Border command can also be used to place shading in a cell or cells.

Patterns   Formats cells or worksheet objects with patterns, colors, line styles, or arrowheads.

Cell Protection   Defines a cell or range of cells that will not be locked, or that will have all formulas hidden, when the Protect Document command of the Options menu is used to protect a worksheet. When the Cell Protection command displays a dialog box containing two check boxes, Locked and Hidden, remove the check from the

Locked check box to specify that the selection should remain unlocked when the Protect Document command is used. Put a check in the Hidden box to specify that all formulas in the selection should be hidden when the Protect Document command is used.

Style   Defines and applies styles to a cell.

Row Height   Changes the row height of the selected rows or the row that contains the active cell. Choose the command and when the dialog box appears, enter a value in points for the new row height.

Column Width   Changes the column width of the selected columns or the column containing the active cell. Standard column width is 10 characters. Choose the command and when the dialog box appears, enter a value measured in characters for the new column width.

Justify   Rearranges text in the left column of a range to fill the selected cells. This command is useful for giving large areas of text a neater appearance. Select the range of cells containing the text, and any additional cells that should be filled with the text; then choose the command. The text will be rearranged to fill the selected cells evenly.

Bring to Front   Brings a hidden object to the front.

Send to Back   Places a hidden object behind other objects.

Group/Ungroup   Groups or ungroups selected objects.

Object Placement   Determines how objects are attached to the cells underneath them.

DATA MENU COMMANDS

Form   Opens a form used to add, edit, or delete records within a database. To obtain proper results, a database range must be defined before you use this command. The on-screen form that results when the command is chosen contains entry boxes for each field within the database range. Options are included in the form for selecting the next or prior record, for finding and deleting records, and for restoring entries that have been changed (before leaving the record).

Find (COMMAND-F)   Finds records within a database that match the specified criteria. The first time this command is used, Excel locates the first matching record in the database and enters Find mode. Each time the command is used thereafter, Excel locates the next matching record in the database. If you are in Find mode, the command changes to Exit Find. Choosing the Exit Find command cancels Find mode.

Extract (COMMAND-E)   Finds records that match the specified criteria and copies those records into a selected range (the extract range). The extract range's fields must have the same names as the database range, although all fields need not be included.

Delete   Finds records that match the specified criteria and deletes those records from the database.

Set Database   Defines the database range. First select the cells containing the database (including the field names), and then choose the Set Database command. Excel names the database range "Database" when the command is used.

Set Criteria   Defines the criteria range. First select the cells containing the criteria and the field names, if any, and then choose the Set Criteria command. Excel names the criteria range "Criteria" when the command is used. The criteria rows contain the criteria you use to perform the evaluation for matching records within the database. If the matching criteria are entered underneath a field name, Excel compares the match to that field for each record in the database. If the matching data are not under a field name, the data are computed instead of compared.

Set Extract   Defines a database extract range on a worksheet.

Sort   Sorts the rows or columns of a selection according to the order specified when you select options from within this command's dialog box.

Series   Fills a range of cells with a series of successive numbers or dates. The range can be in the form of rows or columns.

Table   Creates a table based on the input values and formulas entered into a selected range in the worksheet.

Parse   Converts the contents of one column into values in multiple columns. When the command is chosen, a dialog box appears. Use the Guess option to tell Excel to guess the correct method to convert the data, or manually enter brackets on a scale within the dialog box to define the positions in the data conversion.

Consolidate   Consolidates (summarizes) data from multiple worksheets.

OPTIONS MENU COMMANDS

Set Print Area   Defines an area of the worksheet to be printed when the Print command is used. (If the Set Print Area command is never used, all cells containing data are printed.) The Set Print Area command names the selected range "Print_Area."

Set Print Titles   Defines text to appear as titles on every printed page of a worksheet.

Set Page Break   Defines manual page breaks for a worksheet. When the Set Page Break command is chosen, Excel places a page break above and to the left of the active cell. Manual page breaks appear as dotted lines on the worksheet. When the active cell is directly below or to the right of a page break, the command changes to Remove Page Break and can be used to remove the manual page break.

Display   Controls the screen appearance of row and column headings, formulas, gridlines, gridline and heading colors, and optional suppression of zero values.

Freeze Panes   Freezes the top and/or left panes of the active worksheet. Use this command after splitting a worksheet with the split bars. Once panes have been frozen, the command changes to Unfreeze Panes.

Protect Document   Locks a document so that unauthorized changes cannot be made. Documents can be protected with or without a password. Once a document has been protected, the command changes to Unprotect Document. If the document is protected with a password, the same password must be supplied to unprotect the document. If no password is used, the document can be unprotected by choosing Unprotect Document from the Options menu.

Calculation   Provides various options for methods of calculation within a worksheet. When the Calculation command is chosen, a dialog box appears, containing options for automatic or manual calculation, automatic calculation excluding tables, optional iterations, full precision of values or precision as displayed, and whether the 1904 date numbering system (Macintosh standard) should be used.

Calculate Now (COMMAND-= or F9)   Forces recalculation of a worksheet (or the redrawing of a chart) when calculation has been set to manual with the Calculation command. This command recalculates all open documents.

Workspace   Provides settings for various options affecting your use of Excel. When the command is chosen, a dialog box offers options to change styles of cell reference, display or hide the formula bar during editing, display or hide scroll bars, display or hide the status bar when empty, enable or disable command help, select an alternate key to access menus, and control the number of fixed decimal places.

Calculate Document   Forces recalculation of the active document only. Note that this command appears only when you hold down the SHIFT key as you open the Options menu. When you are holding the SHIFT key, the command appears in place of Calculate Now.

Short Menus/Full Menus   Switches between short menus and full menus. When you are using short menus, Excel displays only the most commonly used commands on the pull-down menus. When you are using full menus, all commands are displayed. Note that if a chart is the active document, this option appears in the Chart menu.

MACRO MENU COMMANDS

Run   Runs a macro. When you select the Run command, a dialog box displays the names of all open macros. Once you select the macro, press RETURN or choose the OK button to run the macro.

Record   Records a new macro. When the command is chosen, a dialog box asks for a name to be assigned to the macro and an optional COMMAND-OPTION key to be used to start the macro.

Start Recorder   Starts the recording action of the Macro Recorder. Once started, the command changes to Stop Recorder, and all subsequent actions are recorded within the macro until the Stop Recorder command is chosen.

Set Recorder   Indicates which cells should be used for recording the macro.

Relative Record/Absolute Record   Changes the method of recording cell references within a macro from relative referencing to absolute referencing.

Assign to Object   Assigns a macro that is to run when a worksheet object is selected.

WINDOW MENU COMMANDS

In addition to the Window menu commands listed here, the Window menu also lists the names of all open windows. Any open window can be made the active window by selecting that name from the bottom of the menu.

Help (SHIFT-F1)   Displays the Help menu, from which various help topics may be selected.

New Window   Opens a new window for the existing document.

Show Clipboard   Opens the Macintosh Clipboard.

Show Info   Displays the Info window, which contains the active cell reference and any formulas and notes contained within the cell. When the Info window is active, this command changes to Show Document.

Arrange All   Rearranges all open windows into a neat, tiled pattern of multiple windows.

Workgroup   Selects a group of worksheets, for editing as a group.

Hide   Hides an open window from view. The Hide command differs from using the Close box in that the hidden window disappears from the screen but remains open and accessible to operations.

Unhide   Returns a hidden window to view.

GALLERY MENU
COMMANDS (CHARTS)

Area   Selects an area format for the active chart. When you choose the command, a gallery of area charts is displayed: a simple area chart, a 100% area chart, an area chart with drop lines, an area chart with gridlines, and an area chart with labeled areas. Also provided in the gallery are the Next and Previous option buttons, which can be used to switch to the next and previous types of galleries.

Bar   Selects a bar format for the active chart. When you use the command, a gallery of bar charts is displayed: a simple bar chart, a bar chart for one series with varied patterns, a stacked bar chart, an overlapping bar chart, a 100% stacked bar chart, a simple bar chart with vertical gridlines, and a simple bar chart with value labels. Also provided in the gallery are the Next and Previous option buttons, which can be used to switch to the next and previous types of galleries.

Column   Selects a column format for the active chart. When you choose the command, a gallery of column charts is displayed: a simple column chart, a column chart for one series with varied patterns, a stacked column chart, an overlapping column chart, a 100% stacked column chart, a simple column chart with horizontal gridlines, a column chart with value labels, and a step chart (no spaces between the categories). Also provided in the gallery are the Next and Previous option buttons, which can be used to switch to the next and previous types of galleries.

Line   Selects a line format for the active chart. When you choose the command, a gallery of line charts is displayed: a simple chart with lines and markers; a chart with lines only; a chart with markers only; a chart with lines, markers, and horizontal gridlines; a chart with lines, markers, horizontal, and vertical gridlines; a chart with lines, markers, logarithmic scales, and gridlines; a high-low chart with markers and high-low lines; and a high-low-close chart (for use with stock quotes). Also provided in the gallery are the Next and Previous option buttons, which can be used to switch to the next and previous types of galleries.

Pie   Selects a pie format for the active chart. When you choose the command, a gallery of pie charts is displayed: a simple pie chart, a pie chart with identical wedge patterns and labels for the wedges, a pie chart with the first wedge exploded, a pie chart with all the wedges exploded, a pie chart with labels for the categories, and a pie chart with value labels in percentages. Also provided in the gallery are the Next and Previous option buttons, which can be used to switch to the next and previous types of galleries.

Scatter   Selects a scatter format for the active chart. When you choose the command, a gallery of scatter charts is displayed: a scatter chart with markers, a scatter chart with markers from identical series joined by lines, a scatter chart with markers as well as horizontal and vertical gridlines, a scatter chart with semi-logarithmic gridlines, and a scatter chart with log-log style gridlines. Also provided in the gallery are the Next and Previous option buttons, which can be used to switch to the next and previous types of galleries.

Combination   Selects a combination format for the active chart. When you choose the command, a gallery of combination charts is displayed: a column chart with a line chart as the overlay chart, a column chart with a line chart overlaid and an opposing scale, a double line chart with the lines maintaining independent scales, an area chart with a column chart as the overlay chart, and a bar chart overlaid by a line chart with three data series (for high-low-close stock volumes). Also provided in the gallery are the Next and Previous option buttons, which can be used to switch to the next and previous types of galleries.

3-D Area, 3-D Column, 3-D Line, 3-D Pie   These commands create three-dimensional area, column, line, or pie charts. (See the Area, Column, Line, and Pie commands for descriptions of these types of charts.)

Preferred   Changes the active chart format to a format you select with the Set Preferred command (see Set Preferred).

Set Preferred   Changes the default format that is used by Excel for all new charts. When you select the command, the active chart's format becomes the default format for all new charts.

CHART MENU COMMANDS

Attach Text   Attaches text to a selected portion of a chart. Text can be attached to either axis, to a series or data point, or as a title.

Add Arrow   Adds an arrow to a chart. Once added, the arrow can be moved by selecting it and using the Move and Size commands from the Format menu or by dragging either end with the mouse. When the arrow is selected, the command changes to Delete Arrow, which can then be used to remove an arrow.

Add Legend   Adds a legend to a chart. The chart may need to be resized after the legend is added, because the legend takes up space and makes the chart smaller. Once a legend is added, the command changes to Delete Legend, which can be used to remove the legend.

Axes   Controls whether the category and value axes will be visible. On a main chart or an overlay chart, this command can show or hide the category or the value axis.

Gridlines   Controls the appearance of gridlines within a chart. You can add major or minor gridlines to the category axis or to the value axis.

Add Overlay   Adds an overlay chart. When an overlay chart is added, Excel evenly divides the data series between the main chart and the overlay chart. If the total number of data series is an odd number, the main chart will contain one more data series than the overlay chart. Once you add an overlay, the command changes to Delete Overlay.

Edit Series   Lets you create or edit a data series within a chart.

Select Chart (COMMAND-A)   Selects the entire chart.

Select Plot Area   Selects the plot area, or the area formed by the boundary of both chart axes.

Protect Document   Prevents unauthorized changes to the chart's data series, or its formulas, by protecting it with or without a password.

Color Palette   Selects and customizes colors. Choosing this option reveals a dialog box containing various colors that can be applied to the worksheet. (Of course, your hardware must support color for this option to have any effect.)

Calculate Now (COMMAND-=)   Redraws a chart and recalculates all open worksheets. The command is necessary only when automatic calculation has been turned off.

Short Menus/Full Menus   Switches between displays of short menus and full menus.

FORMAT MENU COMMANDS (CHARTS)

Patterns   Applies a choice of patterns to the selected chart object. First select a chart object, and then select the Patterns command. From the dialog box that appears, you can choose the Invisible, Automatic, Apply to All, and Invert If Negative options, the style of pattern, the colors of the object, the weight of borders, and the types of tick marks, tick labels, and arrowheads (where applicable).

Font   Applies a choice of font styles, sizes, and colors to a selected object containing text. Select the desired object and then use the Font command to display a dialog box from which the desired options can be chosen.

Text   Selects the desired alignment for a text object. Horizontal alignment can be left, right, or centered. Vertical alignment can be top, bottom, or centered. Options are also provided for the display of text in vertical format and for automatic text and automatic size where applicable.

Scale   Changes the characteristics of the scale used for the category or value axis. Select either axis and then choose the Scale command. The Value Axis dialog box lets you choose minimum and maximum scale values, major and minor tick-mark or gridline unit increments, where the category axis will cross, the logarithmic scale, and whether values should be displayed in reverse order. The Category Axis dialog box lets you choose the category number where the value axis will cross, the number of categories between tick labels and tick marks, whether the value axis will cross between categories, and whether categories will be displayed in reverse order.

Legend   Changes the position of the legend on the chart to bottom, corner, top, and vertical alignment.

Main Chart   Changes the type and formats for the main chart. When the command is chosen, a dialog box offers the following options: Area, Bar, Column, Line, Pie, Scatter, Stacked, 100%, Vary by Categories, Drop Lines, High-Low Lines, Over-lapped, % of Overlap, % of Cluster Spacing, and Angle of First Pie Slice. Certain options apply only to certain types of charts; options not available for a particular chart appear dim in the dialog box.

Overlay Chart   Changes the type and formats for the overlay chart. The command operates in the same manner as the Main Chart command (see the previous paragraph), with two additional options. First Series in Overlay Chart determines which data series will be the first to appear in the overlay chart, and Automatic Series Distribution tells Excel to divide the data series between both charts automatically. If an odd number of data series is present, the main chart will be assigned one more data series than the overlay chart.

3-D View   Lets you select the elevation, distortion, rotation, and height for 3-D charts.

Move   Permits movement of selected objects, such as unattached text or arrows. Select the object and then choose the Move command. Use the arrow keys to move the object to the desired location, and then press RETURN. (You can also move objects by selecting and dragging them with the mouse.)

Size   Changes the size of selected objects, such as unattached text or arrows. Select the object and then choose the Size command. Use the arrow keys to change the size of the object, and then press RETURN to complete the change. (You can also resize an object by selecting it with the mouse and dragging the black selection squares.)

INDEX

E

F

The manuscript for this book was prepared and submitted to
Osborne/McGraw-Hill in electronic form. The acquisitions
editor for this project was Roger Stewart, the technical
reviewer was Paul Hoffman, and the project editor was
Madhu Prasher.

Text design by Fred Lass and Lance Ravella,
using Times Roman for text body and Helvetica for display.

Cover art by Bay Graphics Design Associates.
Color separation and cover supplier, Phoenix Color Corporation.
Screens produced with InSet, from InSet Systems, Inc.
Book printed and bound by R.R. Donnelley & Sons Company,
Crawfordsville, Indiana.

▷ *Expand* *Your Skill Even More*

with help from our expert authors. Now that you've gained greater skills with **Excel 3 for the Macintosh Made Easy**, *let us suggest the following related titles that will help you use your computer to full advantage.*

Microsoft® Word Made Easy for the Macintosh™, Version 4, Third Edition
by Paul Hoffman

Discover the power of Microsoft® Word version 4 for the Macintosh™. You'll learn new information on the added features of version 4 throughout the text, including page preview, automatic repagination, and table formatting. You'll also find in-depth discussions of style sheets, outlining, indexing, and more. Practical business-oriented exercises make learning Word hassle-free.

$19.95p ISBN: 0-07-881478-2, 450 pp., 7 3/8 x 9 1/4

PageMaker® 4 for the Macintosh® Made Easy
by Martin S. Matthews

Learn release 4 of Aldus' full-featured desktop publishing software for the Macintosh®. Step-by-step you'll discover the easiest way to create newsletters, catalogs, brochures, financial reports, and much more. Follow hands-on exercises that take you from the beginning of a project to its completion. Learn all the commands, menus, and features of the basic PageMaker software as well as the release 4. You'll also find out how to import graphics and text from other popular software packages.

$19.95p ISBN: 0-07-881650-5, 600 pp., 7 3/8 X 9 1/4

AppleWorks Made Easy, Third Edition
by Carole Boggs Matthews

Here's a new edition of the best selling book that teaches AppleWorks to beginners in a step-by-step format using solid business applications and easy-to-use examples. This in-depth introduction shows you how to use all AppleWorks components—database, spreadsheet, and word processing capabilities—and all the features of athe newest upgrade.

$19.95 ISBN:0-07-881587-8, 528pp., 7 3/8 X 9 1/4
Covers Version 3 for All Apple II Computers

Dr. File Finder's Guide to Shareware (Includes Three 5 1/4" Disks)
by Mike Callahan and Nick Anis Foreword by John C. Dvorak

Nobody knows Shareware like the illustrious Dr. File Finder, known off-line as Mike Callahan. Now, you can learn about dozens of leading Shareware programs, including where and how to get them, and how to access collections found on bulletin board services. Dr. File Finder discusses in detail the very best Shareware available in 17 different software categories. In the true spirit of Shareware, this book/disk package includes three disks full of top programs that you can try out yourself before registering.
$29.95p ISBN: 0-07-881646-7, 750 pp., 7 3/8 X 9 1/4 Dvorak*Osborne/McGraw-Hill

Dvorak's Guide to PC Telecommunications
by John C. Dvorak and Nick Anis

Telecommunications just got SIMPLE—all you need is your computer, a modem, and this exciting book and disk package. Internationally renowned John C. Dvorak, the world's most widely read computer columnist joins forces with programming wiz and author, Nick Anis, to present the most compelling reason for discovering telecommunications. Packaged with this comprehensive guide are two disks jam-packed with reliable, easy-to-use utilities, interactive tutorials, communications software, and special discounts from the major on-line services.
$49.95p ISBN: 0-07-881551-7, 1053 pp., 7 3/8 X 9 1/4, Dvorak*Osborne/McGraw-Hill

Dvorak's Guide to Desktop Telecommunications Special Edition
by John C. Dvorak and Nick Anis Foreword by Peter Norton

The original *Dvorak's Guide to PC Telecommunications* with two program-filled disks became an instant bestseller across the country. In response to popular demand, a special version of this book without disks, *Dvorak's Guide to Desktop Telecommunications*, is being published for readers who want to learn how to go online for research, communications, or entertainment. You'll find a complete rundown on what's available and how to get it, from commerical services like CompuServe to bulletin boards and Shareware.
$34.95p ISBN: 0-07-881668-8, 920 pp., 7 3/8 X 9 1/4 Dvorak*Osborne/McGraw-Hill
Covers Macintosh, Amiga, UNIX & IBM and PC-compatibles

Prodigy® Made Easy
by Pamela Kane

This is **THE** book to help you learn to take full advantage of the popular telecommunications service that takes care of practically all your needs—shopping, weather reports, banking, sports scores, airline tickets, car rentals, games for kids of all ages, and much, much more. This guide begins with the basics and teaches you how to use all the services. You'll also discover tips and shortcuts for using Prodigy more effectively. Jam-packed with illustrations and hands-on examples, this is the first book to reach for after the software is out of the box.
$19.95p, ISBN: 0-07-881708-0, 448 pp., 7 3/8 X 9 1/4

C++: The Complete Reference
by Herbert Schildt

C++ is rapidly winning converts among programmers of all kinds, and Osborne/McGraw-Hill has the book they're looking for: *C++: The Complete Reference* by internationally known C expert Herb Schildt. *C++: The Complete Reference* covers C++ in full detail starting with aspects common to the C and C++ languages. This example-filled book thoroughly discusses those features specific to C++ and includes several chapters on effective C++ software development.
$24.95p ISBN: 0-07-881654-8, 784 pp., 7 3/8 X 9 1/4

The Complete Guide to CompuServe™
(Includes TAPCIS™ on One 5 1/4" Disk to Automate Your CompuServe Connection)

by Brad Schepp and Debra Schepp Foreword by John C. Dvorak Whether you are new to CompuServe or want to broaden your on-line horizons, this book offers complete start-up information, service descriptions, and time-saving tips. The TAPCIS access software gives you all you need to get more value out of every minute of CompuServe time. There has never been a more practical or more comprehensive guide to CompuServe, the on-line telecommunications service with over a half-million subscribers worldwide.
$29.95p ISBN: 0-07-881632-7, 650 pp., 7 3/8 X 9 1/4 Dvorak*Osborne/McGraw-Hill

The SimCity® Planning Commission Handbook
by Johnny L. Wilson

The SimCity® planning simulator may be the most thought-provoking computer game of all, and this book ensures that you'll enjoy all of the game's many dimensions. Each chapter discusses in detail the real-life problems of city planning, and encourages you to explore the consequences of the solutions you choose. Johnny Wilson, the editor of *Computer Gaming World*, also presents prevailing theories of urban design, and challenges you to design a city that works for individuals and industry alike.
$19.95p ISBN: 0-07-881660-2, 200 pp., 7 3/8 X 9 1/4 Silicon Valley

Computer Professional's Dictionary
by Allen Wyatt

For the largest selection of technical terms, concise definitions, and the latest computer jargon, this is the resource to choose. Written with the experienced computer user in mind, over 3,000 terms from "Abbreviated addressing" to "Zmodem" are included covering virtually every aspect of computing. You can quickly locate the meaning or use of a particular word, acronym, or abbreviation. Wyatt gives all programmers, MIS managers, and computer experts a dictionary that truly enlightens.
$19.95, ISBN: 0-07-881705-6, 350 pp. 7 3/8 X 9 1/4

The Computer Virus Handbook
by Richard B. Levin

Foreword by Alfred Glossbrenner What can you do to protect your computer data from being invaded by rogue programs? Rich Levin provides you with a practical guide to minimizing the risk of computer viruses and maximizing the recovery process. You'll learn about antiviral policies for the workplace, including how to evaluate and use antivirus software. Levin discusses eight outstanding antiviral and disk management utility programs and provides you with step-by-step instruction for using each of them.
$24.95p ISBN: 0-07-881647-5, 500 pp., 7 3/8 X 9 1/4

Excel® Made Easy, IBM® PC Version, Second Ed.
by Martin S. Matthews

Even if you've never worked with Excel, spreadsheets, or Windows before, you can easily follow Matthews' detailed instructions for using the newest version of Excel for Windows. After an introduction to Windows and the Excel environment, Matthews discusses the basics before showing you how to share data with other Windows applications, link worksheets, use the macro language—including building automated applications—and handle other advanced features. There's even a handy command reference!
$19.95p, ISBN: 0-07-881723-4, 512 pp., 7 3/8 X 9 1/4

NOVELL® NetWare®: The Complete Reference
by Tom Sheldon

Here's your one-stop, comprehensive guide to NOVELL®'S world-leading networking software. Written by a NetWare® gold-level authorized installer and trainer, this book covers installation, configuration, and day-to-day use of the system. Sheldon also provides a complete Supervisor's Guide to network planning and maintenance. Chapters on networking concepts, hardware, and connections to other networks and mainframes are included.
$39.95p ISBN: 0-07-881594-0, 1000 pp., 7 3/8 x 9 1/4 Covers All Versions Thru 2.15

PCs Made Easy
by James L. Turley

If you are a first-time computer user, no other book meets your needs better than this broad, concise, up-to-date introduction to the use of personal computers. It's designed to help you get maximum information with minimal time invested. Turley explains what PCs are, what they can do, and how to make them do it—without relying on jargon or buzzwords.
$18.95 ISBN: 0-07-881477-4, 319 pp., & 3/8 X 9 1/4
Covers All Personal Computers